From the day Commodore Dewey's battle-ships destroyed the Spanish fleet at Manila to the closing of the Subic Bay naval base in 1992, America and the Philippines have shared a long and tangled history. It has been a century of war and colonialism, earnest reforms and blatant corruption, diplomatic maneuvering and political intrigue, an era colored by dramatic events and striking personalities. In *Bound to Empire*, acclaimed historian H.W. Brands gives us a brilliant account of the American involvement in the Philippines in a sweeping narrative filled with analytical insight.

Ranging from the Spanish-American War to the fall of Ferdinand Marcos and beyond, Brands deftly weaves together the histories of both nations as he assesses America's great experiment with empire. He leaps from the turbulent American scene in the 1890s—the labor unrest, the panic of 1893, the emergence of Progressivism, the growing tension with Spain—to the shores of the newly acquired colony: Dewey's conquest of Manila, the vicious war against the Philippine insurgents, and the founding of American civilian rule. As Brands takes us through the following century, describing the efforts to "civilize" the Filipinos, the shaping of Philippine political practices, the impact of General MacArthur, and World War II and the Cold War, he provides fascinating insight into the forces and institutions that made American rule what it was, and the Republic of the Philippines what it is today. He uncovers the origins of the corruption and nepotism of post-independence

BOUND TO
EMPIRE

BOUND TO EMPIRE

The United States and the Philippines

H. W. BRANDS

New York   Oxford
OXFORD UNIVERSITY PRESS
1992

Oxford University Press

Oxford   New York   Toronto
Delhi   Bombay   Calcutta   Madras   Karachi
Kuala Lumpur   Singapore   Hong Kong   Tokyo
Nairobi   Dar es Salaam   Cape Town
Melbourne   Auckland

and associated companies in
Berlin   Ibadan

Published by Oxford University Press, Inc.,
200 Madison Avenue, New York, New York 10016

Library of Congress Cataloging-in-Publication Data
Brands, H. W.
Bound to empire : the United States and the
Philippines / H. W. Brands.
p. cm.   Includes bibliographical references and index.
ISBN 0-19-507104-2
1. United States—Foreign relations—Philippines.
2. Philippines—Foreign relations—United States.
I. Title.   E183.8.P6B72   1992
327.730599—dc20
91-29230

1 3 5 7 9 8 6 4 2

Printed in the United States of America
on acid-free paper

Preface

Americans have never been comfortable with the idea of empire. Beneficiaries of the first successful anti-imperial revolution of the modern era, Americans have often expressed their outright repugnance for the notion. The charter of American independence denied the right of one people to hold another against the latter's will, and during the initial hundred years of their existence as a sovereign nation Americans applauded the efforts of peoples around the world—Latin Americans, Greeks, Hungarians—to join them on the plateau of self-determination.

Yet much in the American experience belied and undermined the anti-imperial tendency. Only on rare occasions did significant numbers of Americans express compunctions about dispossessing the indigenous inhabitants of North America. In annexing Louisiana, the Floridas, Texas and California, Americans scarcely paused to consider the wishes of the French and Spanish populations involved. Americans would have snatched Canada had Britain not blocked the way, and perhaps Cuba and all of Mexico if not for the divisive influence of slavery. To some extent the slave system itself exhibited features of imperialism, with the object of conquest being not land but labor, and the conquered residing within the metropolis rather than abroad. (Whether America's agrarian South stood in a subordinate semi-imperial relationship to the industrializing North is another question.)

Further, as the institution of slavery abundantly testified, Americans of European descent exhibited the attitudes of racial and cultural superiority that have usually accompanied empire-building, and that certainly did so in the nineteenth century. The sweeping but vague arguments of America's manifest destinarians helped beget the more closely articulated analyses of the Social Darwinists, and together the movements produced a firm belief that expansion of the American system brought benefits to conquered and conquerors both. When to these considerations was added the desire to secure foreign markets for American goods and capital, a desire that increased with advancing industrialization, the temptation to empire grew irresistible.

At the end of the nineteenth century America succumbed. In the war with Spain the United States acquired an overseas empire, of which the most significant part was the Philippine archipelago. Americans took the Philippines for the same reason men have long taken wives (and women, when given a choice in the matter, husbands): they were attractive and available. For a decade economic expansionists had pointed to the islands as a staging area for the penetration of the China market, and navalists eagerly eyed Philippine harbors and fuel resources. The fight with Spain, although triggered by events in the Caribbean, gave these covetous souls an opportunity to grab the Philippines. Grab they did.

The imperialists' coup touched the still-connected anti-imperialist nerve in the American body politic and set off an impassioned debate over the exportability of democracy and other American institutions, over America's role in the world and over the very meaning of the American experiment. The anti-imperialists lost this round: in 1899 the Senate approved a treaty with Spain annexing the Philippines to the United States.

But anti-imperialism did not die. If anything it grew stronger as Filipinos displayed a violent aversion to American rule, waging an anti-imperial war that brought out, to a greater degree than most wars, the worst in both sides. By the time American troops suppressed the resistance, Americans had lost all desire to extend the American writ further, to find another Philippines. One was plenty.

For nearly half a century the Philippines rested at the fulcrum of America's ambivalence toward empire. To which side the balance tipped often depended on who held power in Washington. Republicans usually displayed confidence in the value, to Americans and Filipinos alike, of American possession of the islands, and when the party of Lincoln—the irony was lost on neither Democrats nor Filipinos—controlled the government in Washington the ties binding colony to metropolis generally stayed tight. Democrats, by contrast, commonly looked on the colonial relationship as corruptive of both the United States and the Philippines. Retention of the islands, Democrats believed, contradicted American ideals and prevented the natural development of Filipino society. Periods of Democratic rule normally brought a loosening of imperial bonds, to the point of independence in 1946.

The situation regarding the Philippines, however, was never quite as straightforward as this first approximation suggests. In the United States, special interests disrespected party lines in lobbying for favored treatment. Philippine legislation regularly produced unlikely alliances among conservatives and liberals, Republicans and Democrats. Matters were more complicated still in the Philippines, where everyone claimed the label of nationalist but where the label covered a wide variety of groups and individuals. From the first, American administrators of the islands looked for governing help to the educated and well-to-do among the Filipinos, just as the Spanish had done for three hundred years. The Filipino elites, as *they* had done for three hundred years, demonstrated their mastery of the imperial game, turning the American presence to their own ends. Central among these was the maintenance of their comfortable position.

The collaboration between the American government and the Filipino elites was not without conflict. In principle the United States had committed itself to the introduction of democracy to the Philippines, and during occasional fits of idealism it attempted to put the principle into practice. The Filipino elites usually resisted, fearing a loss of power and preferment. Quarrels among different elite elements spilled over into relations with the Americans. The greatest source of contention, however, lay in the refusal of the Filipino masses to acquiesce in the condominium of the American rulers and the Filipino upper classes. During the late nineteenth century and throughout the twentieth, peasant movements challenged the status quo in the islands. Often the agitation from below forced the elites to the political left, compelling elite leaders to adopt publicly a more nationalistic position than they would have assumed on their own. Equally often the threat of mass unrest caused the elites to look to their American sponsors for political and other support. That the elites spoke the language of Filipino nationalism while relying on the United States, and that American leaders espoused democracy for Filipinos even as Washington reinforced rule by the elites, made for a tangled relationship between the two countries and the two peoples.

Complicating things further during the entire period of direct American control was the presence of an increasingly powerful Japan. Acquisition of the Philippines transformed the United States overnight from an interested observer of Asian affairs into a proprietary player. But because the American government never succeeded in persuading the American people to fund adequately the islands' defense, the Philippines turned out to be a source of American weakness rather than American strength. For forty years American diplomats sought to cover America's exposure with an assortment of treaties and executive agreements, yet ultimately they failed, and the war many had feared for two generations came in December 1941.

America's exposure in the Philippines was, to an obviously greater degree, Filipinos' exposure, as the islands' educated population fully recognized. Sometimes this recognition drove the Filipinos closer to the United States, while at other times it inspired them to look elsewhere for security. During World War II, when American protection broke down entirely, it prompted a significant portion of the Filipino leadership to cooperate with the Japanese occupation forces. At all times it added an extra wrinkle to the already convoluted fabric of Philippine-American relations.

Though the postwar period soon brought a close to the era of formal American control over the Philippines, many of the links connecting the Philippines—and especially the Filipino elites—to the United States survived the termination of direct American rule. The new Philippine government, facing a communist-inspired guerrilla uprising, called for and received American assistance in subduing the rebels. The United States, reading in the rise of Asian communism a challenge to international order and American security, called for and received Philippine assistance in erecting a barrier against further communist expansion. The imperial bond persisted, although in looser and less explicit form than before.

For a while the arrangement worked well enough. During the 1950s the United States extended its anticommunist alliance system from Europe across Asia to the Pacific. The government in Manila vociferously denounced communism and most regimes not so conservative as itself. For its efforts in this regard, and for permitting the United States to retain military bases in the islands, the Philippine government received large payments of American military and economic aid.

Yet the symbiosis, designed to secure stability, eventually generated just the opposite. The American commitment to containing communism outstripped American material and psychological resources, leaving the United States in the morass of Vietnam. In the Philippines, garden-variety corruption gave way to the brutal kleptocracy of Ferdinand Marcos. As had nearly all his predecessors, Marcos portrayed himself as a guarantee against the spread of communism in Asia. But after Vietnam revealed the fallacies of the domino theory, after Marcos became an international embarrassment, and after the Filipino people, including large segments of the upper classes, demonstrated their utter distaste for the dictator, Washington canceled the support it had supplied Marcos for twenty years.

The cancellation, however, applied only to Marcos. During the late 1980s, Washington and Manila again found common ground. Although the communist specter was losing its fear-provoking capacity, the American government continued to desire military base rights. The Philippines enjoyed a more democratic form of government than under Marcos, but the upper classes still exercised inordinate influence and resisted power-sharing claims of the New People's Army and other dissenters. As had happened before, the Filipino elites appeared willing to accept American help in maintaining political stability, and the United States appeared willing to provide it in exchange for services rendered.

But the imperial bond was no longer what it had been. The bases issue got enmeshed in the politics of the approaching 1992 Philippine elections, and the Philippine senate rejected a treaty granting the Americans a ten-year extension of base rights. The Philippine government then offered the Americans three years to wind up their affairs, but even this proved too generous for Philippine nationalists, and at the end of 1991 Manila announced that the Americans must be gone within twelve months. Washington, retrenching financially and watching the Soviet Union self-destruct, acquiesced quietly to the eviction order. Through almost a century of coexistence the governing groups in the United States and the Philippines had supported each other's interests. During that time the two sides had exercised considerable ingenuity adjusting the terms of support to fit changing circumstances. Finally, though, it seemed that the pool of collaborative ingenuity has gone dry.

The present volume is a study in power. In particular, it is an examination of the structure of power that has bound the United States and the Philippines together. There is a wonderful and engrossing tale in the history of the Philippines and of Philippine-American relations. I hope the drama of the tale comes through in the chapters that follow. But telling the tale is not my principal purpose. (Stanley Karnow has accomplished this in a fashion not soon to be repeated.) Instead I concentrate on the essentials of the colonial and postcolonial relationship between the two countries. I focus on those individuals and groups, Americans and Filipinos, who have wielded power, in order to determine what they did with their power and why they did it. I pay greatest attention to the most significant manifestations of power, especially military, political and economic. Cultural relations between the American and Filipino peoples, worthy of examination in their own right, enter the picture here chiefly as they affect power relations.

Two considerations have motivated my approach. The first is a desire to understand how American power has operated in the context of interactions with America's most important colony, during the colonial period and after. How did American power respond to the lesser but not negligible forms of Filipino power? What purposes did American power serve? Was American power a force for good? Whose good? Was American imperialism in the Philippines more benign than other countries' imperialism elsewhere? To what degree has American power in the Philippines in the postcolonial period constituted a kind of neo-imperalism?

The second consideration is a belief that America's relationship with the Philippines can provide a valuable case study in America's international relations generally. The domestic and external forces impelling the United States to acquisition of the Philippines in 1898–99 were the same forces that launched America on a career of globalism. The imperatives of power that shaped American treatment of the Philippines were, mutatis mutandis, the same imperatives that conditioned American responses to the revolutionary developments of the twentieth century throughout Asia and the world. The military, political and economic mechanisms of American power in the Philippines were the same mechanisms by which the United States extended its sway across much of the planet. The compromises and accommodations American leaders made in the Philippines were much like the compromises and accommodations American leaders have made in other countries. The process of power-brokering among different factions in the American polity with respect to the Philippines, and the interplay in this brokering of perceived interests and professed ideals, showed features similar to those that have marked America's overall approach to foreign affairs for two centuries. In sum, to untwist the strands of American relations with the Philippines is to make a fair start toward understanding American relations with humanity at large.

For better and worse, the United States during the last hundred years has had enormous impact on the world, impact greater than that of any other country. Filipinos, also for better and worse, have felt the American impact more directly than almost any other people. Chemists study certain classes of reactions by examining particular instances under heightened temperature and pressure. Historians cannot manipulate their subject matter as chemists do, but they *can* select samples of history that exhibit general tendencies in concentrated form. The nine decades of United States–Philippine relations compose one such sample.

ACKNOWLEDGMENTS

This book never would have reached publication without the assistance of many people and institutions in the United States and the Philippines. To the directors and staffs of the archives and libraries cited in the list of manuscript collections, I offer my thanks for access to documents. To Texas A & M University, I am grateful for research and travel support. I am indebted to Theodore Friend and Gary Hess for reading and commenting on a draft of the book, and especially to Nick Cullather for generously sharing the fruits of his own labors in the Philippines.

Austin   H.W.B.
September 1991

Contents

IV   By Other Means

I

THE CALL

1

Manic Depression
1890s

I. Showing her age

By the beginning of the last decade of the nineteenth century, Americans had tired of centennial observances. The year 1875 had brought commemoration of Lexington and Concord, 1876 of the declaration of independence, 1881 of Yorktown, 1883 of the Treaty of Paris, 1887 of the writing of the Constitution, 1889 of the organization of the government it specified. To be sure, Americans could use reminders of great days past, for the present afforded scant solace. With each passing year America grew more like the Europe Americans and their ancestors had fled. Disparities of wealth increasingly invaded the public consciousness. The census of 1890 reported that the most affluent 1 percent of the nation's population controlled a fortune greater than the combined resources of the remaining 99 percent. Jacob Riis made the same point in the same year, in more eloquent fashion. In *How the Other Half Lives*, Riis depicted the miserable lot of the working poor of the cities, an existence he called "a slavery as real as any that ever disgraced the South." But no ties of paternalism softened the demands of the rapacious capitalist, who controlled both the workplace and the living quarters, usually a stifling room in a squalid slum, of the unfortunate laborer. "Not content with simply robbing the tenant, the owner, in the dual capacity of landlord and employer, reduces him to virtual serfdom by making him become his tenant, on such terms as he sees fit to make, the condition of employment at wages likewise of his own making."[1]

The growth of enormous business enterprises enforced the inequality between worker and capitalist, effectively extinguishing most hopes of rising from the masses. Following the example of John D. Rockefeller and the Standard Oil trust,

corporations consolidated rapidly during the post–Civil War era. Trusts dominated industries in all sectors of American economic life, and when a consumer
bought beef, sugar, whiskey, coal, or kerosene, or a farmer purchased a plow,
reaper, or binder, or a merchant contracted for any number of goods from steel
pipe to stoves, trusts set the prices and took the profits. Whether, in strictly economic terms, the nation's households suffered from the rise of the trusts is a difficult question. Economies of scale tended to offset noncompetitive pricing. But
the loss of individual autonomy the corporatization of the country entailed produced psychological distress that more than overbalanced any pocketbook gain.
America was supposed to be the land of opportunity. Where was opportunity
now? Popular upset with the trusts had developed so far that in 1890 a Republican
senator, John Sherman, introduced into Congress and a Republican president,
Benjamin Harrison, signed into law a measure ostensibly aimed to curb the trusts
and other combinations in restraint of trade. That the Sherman antitrust bill in
practice did almost nothing to hinder the growth of business consolidations, in
fact providing a weapon for use against labor unions, testified to the resilience of
the capitalists and the cleverness of their lawyers.

The congressional session that spawned the Sherman Act also begot the
McKinley tariff, the latest and most successful effort by business interests to curtail foreign competition. With rates averaging nearly 50 percent, the McKinley
tariff—the Ohio congressman's sole legislative claim to prominence but one sufficient to win the support of grateful businessmen and the Republican presidential nomination in 1896—made no pretense at revenue-raising, which would have
required far lower scales. It was, plain and simple, an instrument to boost prices
and profits, a forced transfer payment from consumers to capitalists. As matters
turned out, McKinley and his colleagues overestimated what the traffic would
bear, and largely as a result of their promiscuous presumption the Democrats
recaptured the House of Representatives, retiring McKinley temporarily to Canton.

If sharpening class divisions in the cities made Americans feel that the United
States was growing more like Europe, conditions in the less populated regions
offered little relief. Besides describing the increasingly inegalitarian distribution
of wealth in the country, the 1890 census abandoned the notion of the frontier as
demographically meaningful. The trans-Mississippi West had hardly filled in,
and more land would yet be homesteaded than settlers had claimed to date. But
the West was civilizing by the day. In 1889 and 1890 alone, six new states joined
the previous thirty-eight. Equally telling, the pattern of habitation had become
sufficiently uniform that no connected line could separate the unsettled regions
from the settled. Intellectuals, led by historian Frederick Jackson Turner, would
make much of the passing of the frontier. Yet those individuals struggling to earn
a living in the wheat country of North Dakota, in the high basins of Wyoming,
or in California's central valley needed neither the census director nor academics

to tell them how population pressure drove up land prices and drove out marginal—usually small—operators.

The census meant even less to America's first tenants, who felt the pressure of the country's growing population more directly. Demands from speculators and homesteaders to open Oklahoma to white settlement led Congress in 1889 to withdraw most of the protection it previously had extended over this Indian Territory. The land rush of April of that year summarized all the greedy banality of American treatment of Indians. Within twenty-four hours of the starting-pistol's shot, two million acres once reserved to Indians were seized by fifty thousand whites. During the next four years Washington expropriated and opened to settlement an additional ten million acres.

Farther north the Indians' 1890s commenced with greater brutality. Earlier, after half a decade on the run in the border country along the 49th parallel, Sitting Bull and his followers had surrendered to the American army. The Sioux leader served two years in prison before being released to the Standing Rock reservation in the Dakotas. Known as one who communicated with the spirit world, Sitting Bull became the object of official American suspicion when the millenarian cult of the Ghost Dance spread among the Sioux during the late 1880s. The army arrested him in December 1890, and in the resistance that followed he was killed. Two weeks later the cavalry moved to crush the Ghost Dancers. At the misnamed Battle—it was not a battle at all—of Wounded Knee, soldiers massacred two hundred freezing, starving Sioux.

The end of Indian resistance seemed of a piece with the vanishing of the frontier and with the diminution of the individual's chances to get ahead as an individual. Both signaled the erosion of American exceptionalism, of all that made America different from Europe and allowed Americans to believe they stood outside the normal course of history. Contributing further to this declension were the ever-mounting waves of immigration that yearly washed hundreds of thousands of Old Worlders to American shores. These latest arrivals were distressingly un-American. When immigrants had originated chiefly in the British Isles and Scandinavia and Germany, they blended fairly quickly into the American population. But this group called Italy, Greece, Poland and Russia home. Many had darker skins. Most spoke exotic tongues. Further, to a country that remained overwhelmingly Protestant and traced its origins to a rejection of the excessive influence of Rome in the religious affairs of England, the fact that the new immigrants were predominantly Catholics provoked troubling questions about America's future. The strong admixture of Jews simply made matters worse.

The concern the new immigrants aroused reflected the American obsession with race. The darker the complexion of the recently arrived the less assimilable they seemed to be. Precedent existed for such thinking. In nearly three hundred years American society had failed utterly to assimilate its largest racial minority—

Africans and their descendants. Indeed, during the 1890s the trend was in precisely the opposite direction. The abandonment of the former slaves by the federal government that marked the end of Reconstruction had begun a period during which the southern states sorted out their methods of dealing with their black underclass. As the end of the century approached, most were settling on a variant of what South Africans would call apartheid. In 1890 Mississippi required voters to read and understand—to the satisfaction of a white registrar—selected passages from the state constitution. Other states followed the example, erecting a system of restraints on the activities of blacks that eliminated them from political participation and condemned them to subordinate social and economic status. When the Supreme Court, in the 1896 Plessy case, upheld a Louisiana law mandating segregated railway facilities, what little hope blacks retained of national interest in their plight vanished.

Like most attempts to legislate superiority, the Jim Crow system betrayed a lack of confidence on the part of those doing the legislating. Their relative status no longer assured by the institution of slavery, white southerners erected new barriers to the advancement of blacks. The growing nativist trend similarly demonstrated a failure of faith. For three centuries America had generally embraced immigrants, who supplied transfusions of intellect, culture and energy that invigorated American society. Now the transfusions seemed to promise not invigoration but infection. The themes of racism and nativism twined with the sense of narrowed opportunity and with the broader feeling that America's best days lay in her past. Not everyone shared the sentiment, yet even those who rejected it had to confront its implications. Some would attempt to disprove it by supporting bold new adventures, dramatic demonstrations of the country's continued vigor.

II.   The revolt of the masses

Amid the overall ambience of decline, specific groups had particular grievances. For two decades farmers had confronted falling prices for the produce they sold, and although these were balanced to some extent by lower costs for goods they purchased, deflation increased the burden of debt on a class chronically owing. Farmers also felt the pinch of monopoly most acutely, whether in the form of railroads, commodity brokerages or farm-equipment trusts. While manufacturers battened on profits swollen by the protective tariff, farmers faced the severity of an unprotected and increasingly competitive world market. That hayseed and rube had replaced salt-of-the-earth and backbone-of-the-republic as popular impressions of farmers added wounds to the soul to match the injuries to the wallet.

The pain on the farm elicited attempts to alleviate it. Some sought the solace of the Grange, which began as a secret society before branching out into cooperative marketing and purchasing endeavors. Others favored the Greenback party, the principal exponent of that nostrum of debtors, inflation. But the most important amplifier of farmers' grievances was the Populist party, formed in 1892 of Grangers, Greenbackers and members of the Farmers' Alliance. The Populists nominated James B. Weaver, an Iowa Greenbacker, for president, and ran him on a platform of government ownership of railroads and other utilities, a soak-the-rich income tax, free coinage of silver at 16 to 1 to gold and, in a largely unsuccessful effort to gain the support of urban labor, curbs on immigration and an eight-hour day. Needless to say, the powers-that-were denounced nationalization of the railroads and an income tax as pure socialism. Yet society's respectables saved their special wrath for free silver, which they deemed nothing short of theft. Theft it was, for with silver actually trading at closer to 32 to 1 against gold, minting silver at 16 would amount to a 50 percent devaluation in the currency. Farmers and other debtors would gain as the notes they held depreciated by half, while bankers and their creditor friends would lose commensurately. Of course the creditors had been profiting for years from falling prices, but this the polite classes left unsaid.

Had the farmers succeeded better in reaching out to workers in the cities, their challenge to the status quo might have progressed further. In the event, the workers had their own agenda. Some items were peaceful, especially those advocated by the Knights of Labor, whose Grand Master Workman Terence Powderly spurned strikes and preached the conversion of workers into capitalists by the agency of employee-owned industrial enterprises. Peaceful or not, Powderly's methods were denounced by management as communistic. Meanwhile his more radical comrades-in-toil castigated him as a stooge of the owners and launched a class war in the country's mines, railyards and factories. The direct-actionists began their assault on the citadel of capitalism in the 1870s, when the Molly Maguires waged guerrilla campaigns in the coalfields of western Pennsylvania. Unrest spread to the nation's railroads. One strike on the Baltimore and Ohio line expanded across several states before President Hayes called out federal troops. Amid fighting in several cities some three dozen persons died. In 1886 a bomb exploded at a rally in Haymarket Square in Chicago, called to show solidarity with strikers at the McCormick harvester works. Seven police and four workers were killed in the blast, while seventy individuals were wounded. In the minds of many observers the bombing presaged anarchy and revolution.

The situation deteriorated in the 1890s, which produced the worst labor violence in the nation's history. Hundreds of strikes idled tens of thousands of workers during the first half of the decade, and although most of the stoppages did not lead to bloodshed, many did. In July 1892, steelmen at Andrew Carnegie's Homestead plant put down their tools to protest reductions in pay and demand union recognition. Carnegie, who later would call for tolerance of dissent among Filipinos, extended no such privilege to the hands in his mills and rented an army of Pinkerton agents to break the strike. After pitched battles yielding ten deaths and scores of casualties, the hired guns, supplemented by the local militia, succeeded in quelling the disturbance, although the anti-union forces were compelled to occupy the area for three months to ensure its pacification.

The summer of 1892 also witnessed eruptions of labor unrest in the silver mines of Idaho, where state authorities resorted to martial law to suppress radical agitation. In 1894 a strike shut the Pullman Palace Car Company near Chicago, leading to widespread attacks on persons and property. Eugene Debs, head of the American Railway Union, called a sympathy walkout that eventually blocked rail traffic all across the Middle West. Over the protests of Illinois governor John Peter Altgeld, President Cleveland sent in federal troops to crush the strike and reopen the roads.

Cleveland's display of force succeeded in suppressing the Pullman strike, but it also exacerbated the feeling that America was at war with itself. An Ohio Populist, Jacob Coxey, concluded that if the government could raise an army against the people, the people could mobilize against the government. Coxey mustered an "army" of out-of-workers, and he led his legions to Washington where they tried to petition Congress for unemployment relief and looser money. The expedition failed farcically. The police herded the marchers into camps, ostensibly to safeguard public health, and arrested Coxey for walking on the government's grass. But this anticlimax detractedly only slightly from the message the movement conveyed: that the country had some screws loose and might soon fall to pieces.

III.   The compulsion of depression

Intensifying the distress of the 1890s and exacerbating the various forms of protest was the most serious economic depression the country had ever experienced. In 1893 a large adverse shift in America's balance of payments precipitated a failure of confidence on the part of foreign investors, which in turn triggered a run on the country's gold reserves. The panic that followed brought a collapse of much of the banking system, a shakeout of the corporate sector, a paralyzing contraction of credit, a plummeting in demand and a rapid spread of unemployment. The United States had witnessed economic depressions before but not of this magnitude. Coming as it did in conjunction with the other evil portents of the age, the depression seemed one more indication of American decline.

The panic broke many captains of industry to lower ranks, cashiering some entirely. Those who survived plotted a counterattack. Noting the connection of the collapse to the growing gap between what America purchased abroad and what it sold, business spokesmen advocated a strategy of expanding America's exports as the way to recapture prosperity. To some, Latin America seemed a likely prospect for absorbing the surplus production of the United States. *Banker's Magazine* asserted, "There is no reason why our manufactures should not find an enlarged market in the southern half of this hemisphere." The Atlanta trade journal *Dixie* encouraged exporters to show their products at an industrial fair in Mexico City. The National Association of Manufacturers, formed in 1895 with the express purpose of promoting American wares abroad, sponsored a tour by representatives of American companies to Argentina, Uruguay and Brazil and pressed Washington for assistance in enabling American firms to compete with Britain in Central and South America.[2]

Yet if the markets of Latin America enjoyed the advantage of propinquity, the Far East possessed the allure of magnitude. For a century American merchants had plied the China trade, and although China's failing government had managed to keep the foreign devils at arm's length, confining their activity to Shanghai and other treaty ports, the notion of hundreds of millions of consumers in the hinterland hungering for American products only gained attractiveness with the passing decades. The depression of the 1890s focused the attention of the American business community on China as never before. The economics editor for the *New Orleans Times-Picayune* characterized American trade interests in China as "immense." The *New York Tribune* described America's stake in the China market as "now great" and promising to be "enormous." The *Chicago Inter-Ocean* looked hopefully to a "tenfold" increase in America's business with China. The National Association of Manufacturers waxed enthusiastic over "the great trade" destined to arise in the Orient.[3]

Washington's agents also joined the quest for markets. From the days of Alexander Hamilton the federal government had demonstrated consistent solicitude for the welfare of American business, and American consuls made it *their* business to seek out favorable opportunities for the expansion of American exports. Yet until nearly the end of the nineteenth century this service, while useful, had not been of overriding importance, since the growth of America's domestic demand generally sufficed to clear the country's markets. The depression of the 1890s changed the situation dramatically. Many observers now despaired of the nation's ability ever again to purchase all it could produce. From the state department came the warning: "Every year we shall be confronted with an increasing surplus of manufactured goods for sale in foreign markets if American operatives and artisans are to be kept employed the year round."[4]

While the micro-economic impact—upon individual firms—of the shortfall in demand would by itself have spurred Washington to action, the macro-economic ramifications—upon the country's finances as a whole—made the expansion of exports a priority. As the run on the treasury had demonstrated, the negative tilt in the trade balance threatened America's entire credit structure. In such circumstances it became a matter of high policy to find a fix. Treasury Secretary John Carlisle put the issue bluntly. Americans, Carlisle said, had two alternatives in trying to cover the deficit. They could either "export and sell their commodities in foreign markets" or they could "ship gold." The latter course had touched off the panic. Recovery required the former.[5]

Pursuing Carlisle's recommendation, America's official representatives abroad redoubled their efforts to spur American exports. Like the strategists of the private sector, the public servants found the trading possibilities in the Far East tantalizing. The state department, reviewing business prospects around the world, accounted China "one of the most promising fields for American enterprise, industry, and capital." Charles Denby, the American minister to China, advocated quick action to seize the opportunity the China market afforded the American economy. Identifying a theme others would elaborate, Denby asserted that while America's past resided with the nations across the eastern sea, the country's future lay in the illimitable west. "The Pacific Ocean," Denby predicted, "is destined to bear on its bosom a larger commerce than the Atlantic."[6]

IV.   The ideology of jingoism

If the world across the Pacific promised to relieve the economic suffering of the 1890s, it also held hope for assuaging the social and psychological stresses of the decade. Even while the closing of the frontier heralded the end of the age of American uniqueness, and the revolt on the farms and the war in the factory-yards indicated that the New World was becoming increasingly like the Old, many Americans refused to accept the evidence of decline. Some developed a counter-ideology of continuing American exceptionalism. Belligerently self-assertive, this ideology placed the United States at the apex of historical development and predicted the imminent Americanization of the earth.

Most prominent among ideologists of exception were the Social Darwinists, who revived the traditional doctrine of Manifest Destiny in the guise of social science. The Social Darwinists—mostly Anglo-Saxon types—contended that the success of the Anglo-Saxon race in subduing the lesser peoples of the planet resulted from the greater adaptive value of Anglo-Saxon culture and institutions. The argument was seductive and safely circular. Those groups at the top of the ladder of political and social evolution deserved preeminence by the very fact of their preeminence, while those lower down owed their inferiority to their inferiority. Prescriptively the formula proved even more potent. The mitigation of the disparities between rich and poor, between those who did what they would and those who did what they must, would tamper with nature and jeopardize the future evolution of the species as a whole.

John Fiske cut his intellectual teeth at Harvard, where he thrilled to the philosophy of the English Social Darwinist Herbert Spencer. Fiske afterward wrote, "To have lived when this prodigious truth was advanced, debated, established, was a rare privilege in the centuries. The inspiration of seeing the old mists dissolve and reveal the convergence of all branches of knowledge is something that can hardly be known to the men of a later generation." What Fiske discerned especially in the parting mists was the bright future lying before the United States. In a widely read 1885 essay entitled "Manifest Destiny," Fiske wrote, "The work which the English race began when it colonized North America is destined to go on until every land on the earth's surface that is not already the seat of an old civilization shall become English in its language, in its political habits and traditions, and to a predominant extent in the blood of its people." Fiske held that the success of the Anglo-Saxon race owed partly to its physical fecundity and hardiness and partly to its mastery of modern technology. But in greatest measure past victories had arisen and future triumphs would follow from the governing genius of the race, embodied most clearly in the American constitution. "If the Roman Empire could have possessed that political vitality in all its parts which is secured to the United States by the principles of equal representation and of limited state sovereignty, it might well have defied all the shocks which tribally organized barbarism could ever have directed against it." Fiske predicted with supreme confidence that the United States would, a century hence, embrace "a political aggregate immeasurably surpassing in power and in dimensions any empire that has yet existed."[7]

Josiah Strong was no less convinced than Fiske that the future of humanity rested with the United States. But Strong granted a larger role for Providence as an ally of America. Strong, whose best-selling *Our Country* also appeared in 1885, headed the American Evangelical Alliance, and his tract accomplished the improbable feat of tailoring Darwinism to fit the preconceptions of evangelical Protestantism. Strong asserted that history hung upon certain "great focal points," among which three stood out: the incarnation of Jesus, the German Reformation, and the *"closing years of the nineteenth century"* (Strong's emphasis). The present period, he declared, at once held great dangers and extraordinary promise for Americans, and through Americans for the world. Among the dangers Strong identified immigration, which he labeled an "invasion by an army more than four times as vast as the estimated number of Goths and Vandals that swept over Southern Europe and overwhelmed Rome." A related peril was "Romanism," whose principles were "diametrically opposed" to those of the American republic, whose practitioners received an education "calculated to make them narrow and bigoted" and whose threat to the United States was summarized in the words of the immortal Lafayette—who, having been born a papist, knew whereof he spoke: "If the liberties of the American people are ever destroyed, they will fall by the hands of the Romish clergy." Strong cited other dangers, some more prosaic but nonetheless baleful: intemperance, wealth, city life, socialism and Mormonism.[8]

Yet Strong believed that Americans, by placing their faith in the Protestant

God, could overcome these hazards in glorious fashion. The Anglo-Saxon race, he declared, represented two seminal ideas of world civilization: individual liberty and "pure *spiritual* Christianity." The two were connected. "It was no accident that the great reformation of the sixteenth century originated among a Teutonic, rather than a Latin people. It was the fire of liberty burning in the Saxon heart that flamed up against the absolutism of the pope." With this singular religious and political heritage, the Anglo-Saxon was "divinely commissioned to be, in a peculiar sense, his brother's keeper." Like Fiske, Strong foresaw Anglo-Saxons multiplying rapidly and filling the earth, with the American branch of the family assuming the place of honor. "We are to have not only the larger portion of the Anglo-Saxon race, but we may reasonably expect to develop the highest type of Anglo-Saxon civilization." The benefits of Anglo-Saxonism would spread, as a result not only of the demographic expansion of the race but also of its "instinct" for colonizing. The Anglo-Saxon possessed "unequaled energy" and "indomitable perseverance." "His personal independence made him a pioneer. He excels all others in pushing his way into new countries." And no wonder. "God, with infinite wisdom and skill, is training the Anglo-Saxon race for an hour sure to come in the world's future." In his call to arms—and to alms, ever necessary for the work of the Lord—Strong perorated:

> Men of this generation, from the pyramid top of opportunity on which God has set us, *we look down on forty centuries!* We stretch our hand into the future with power to mold the destinies of unborn millions. . . . It is fully in the hands of the Christians of the United States, during the next ten or fifteen years, to hasten or retard the coming of Christ's kingdom in the world by hundreds, and perhaps thousands, of years. We of this generation and nation occupy the Gibraltar of the ages which commands the world's future.[9]

Not all social theorists of the time took such an optimistic view of the decades ahead. Brooks Adams was distinctly gloomy. Of Adams' 1896 work, *The Law of Civilization and Decay,* Theodore Roosevelt remarked that "few more melancholy books have been written." Like brother Henry, Brooks Adams felt directly the decline of American civilization. While the contemporaries of great-grandfather John and grandfather John Quincy had recognized and rewarded the intellectual and political gifts of the Adams clan, the present generation bestowed the prize of the presidency upon mere Harrisons, Clevelands and McKinleys. Notwithstanding his pessimism, Adams contributed to America's outward thrust of the 1890s by extolling the heroic virtues he claimed had built the great empires of the past. Borrowing from Newtonian mechanics, Adams described the evolution of human society in terms of a "law of force and energy" positing that "the velocity of the social movement of any community is proportionate to its energy and mass" and that "its centralization is proportionate to its velocity." Readers who waded through this theoretical froth got to the firmer ground of Adams' fundamental point: that in the course of cultural development the initially predominant martial character gave way to the economic. This led society into a dead end, since economic traits tended to be derivative and parasitic, in contrast to the originality and vigor of the martial temperament. Adams mourned civilization's decay, and he doubted that the degeneration could be reversed.[10]

Alfred Thayer Mahan agreed with Adams on the merits of the martial character, although Mahan refused to accept Adams' bleak prognosis. The first of a breed that would proliferate in America half a century later—the defense intellectual—Mahan interpreted Social Darwinism in military terms. Like the nuclear-war theologians of the 1950s and after, Mahan dealt in strategic weaponry, which in his day meant capital ships. Yet Mahan cast his net more widely, interpreting naval rivalries as a manifestation of the endless struggle for survival among nations. In his 1890 opus *The Influence of Sea Power upon History*, Mahan wrote that peoples began using the oceans by exploring upon them, progressed to trading across them and ended by fighting over them. As in the past, Mahan predicted, likewise in the future. The lessons of Lepanto and Trafalgar applied to any country that aspired to greatness.

The most obvious of these lessons demonstrated the requirement for a strong fleet. Mahan's work provided the intellectual underpinning for an expansion during the 1890s of the American navy, which only recently ranked twelfth in the world. But Mahan placed equal significance on the infrastructure required to support a country's maritime efforts.

> As a nation, with its unarmed and armed shipping, launches forth from its own shores, the need is soon felt of points upon which the ships can rely for peaceful trading, for refuge and supplies. In the present day, friendly, though foreign, ports are to be found all over the world; and their shelter is enough while peace prevails. It was not always so, nor does peace always endure.

Examining the historical record, Mahan asserted that colonies afforded the surest security to a country with international interests. In 1890, however, he felt compelled to grant that the United States would not likely soon acquire colonies. Failing this, Washington must make other arrangements for the safety of its overseas commerce. The acquisition of rights to coaling and repair stations was "one of the first duties" of a responsible federal government.[11]

Intellectuals like Mahan required the assistance of practicing politicians to convert such schemes into policy. In 1887, when Theodore Roosevelt first met Mahan at the Naval War College, Roosevelt was not practicing, having retired from New York politics to mourn his deceased wife and the moribund reform wing of the Republican party in the state. But Roosevelt intended to resume practice at a suitable opportunity. And having written on the naval war of 1812 he shared Mahan's interest in sea power. When Mahan's book appeared in 1890, Roosevelt lauded it in the highest terms. "Captain Mahan has written distinctively the best and most important, and also by far the most interesting, book on naval history which has been produced on either side of the water for many a long year," Roosevelt asserted in a review in the *Atlantic Monthly*. Roosevelt was especially taken with Mahan's elucidation of "the practical importance of the study of naval history in the past to those who wish to estimate and use aright the navies of the present." Glossing the text somewhat, Roosevelt credited Mahan with pointing out the deficiencies in America's naval posture: the need for a large merchant marine, for adequate fortifications and repair facilities along the nation's coasts and especially for a fighting fleet. Speaking more clearly in his own voice, Roosevelt declared,

> Our ships should be the best of their kind—this is the first desideratum; but in addition there should be plenty of them. We need a large navy, composed not merely of cruisers, but containing also a full proportion of powerful battleships, able to meet those of any other nation. It is not economy—it is niggardly and foolish short-sightedness—to cramp our naval expenditures, while squandering money right and left on everything else, from pensions to public buildings.[12]

Roosevelt was not a profound thinker, but he was alert to the intellectual currents of his day, and this alertness—together with his lack of profundity, rare in any age—made him in significant respects a spokesman for his era. Of equal importance, the political posts Roosevelt successively held placed him in positions to act upon his convictions. Roosevelt shared the optimism of Fiske and Strong, and he took Mahan's analysis as a challenge to American patriotism. While rejecting Adams' dismalism, he deemed Adams' work a spur to action. "If our population decreases; if we lose the virile, manly qualities, and sink into a nation of mere hucksters, putting gain above national honor, and subordinating everything to mere ease of life; then we shall indeed reach a condition worse than that of the ancient civilizations in the years of their decay." Needless to say, T.R. did not intend to concede to history a monopoly on manliness.[13]

Roosevelt deemed a day without a demonstration of strength—personal or national (he tended to equate the two)—a day lost forever. A friend from college remarked that Roosevelt "wants to be killing something all the time." This individual continued, "He would like above all things to go to war with some one." Roosevelt considered it a point of pride to cultivate a thin skin in matters touching the country's affairs. "I am not hostile to any European power in the abstract," he explained at a time of transatlantic tension. "I am simply an American first and last, and therefore hostile to any power which wrongs us."

Roosevelt interpreted wrongs broadly. After the outbreak of the Spanish-American War in 1898 he heard that the pope had expressed displeasure with members of the American clergy for not trying to stop the fighting against Catholic Spain. Roosevelt flashed indignant at the mere thought. "I would resent as an impertinence any European, whether Pope, Kaiser, Czar or President, daring to be angry with an American because of his action or nonaction as regards any question between America and an outside nation." He added, for good measure, "If any man, clerical or lay, Bishop, Archbishop, priest, or civilian, was in any way guilty of treasonable practices with Spain during our war, he should be shot or hung."[14]

Although Roosevelt believed that the British could act as thick-headedly as other Europeans, he subscribed with enthusiasm to the notion of Anglo-Saxon cultural superiority. Roosevelt was not a racist in quite the same sense as many of his contemporaries, for while he often used the term "race" loosely he usually referred to the acquired attributes of a people rather than their inherited characteristics. He admired the Japanese for their military and political successes as much as he disdained the Chinese for their weakness. "What wonderful people the Japanese are," he wrote at the time of the Russo-Japanese War. "They are quite as remarkable industrially as in warfare. . . . I believe that Japan will take its place as a great civilized power of a formidable type." But Japanese success, Roosevelt judged, owed to Japan's emulation of the great nations of the West, especially Britain and the United States. He considered it peculiarly the mission of Anglo-Saxons to carry culture to the barbarians. "It is to the interest of civilization," he wrote in the period of the Boer War, "that the English speaking race should be dominant in South Africa"—exactly as it was to civilization's gain that the United States "should be dominant in the Western Hemisphere."

While many leaders throughout history have desired the fruits of war for their countries, Roosevelt valued war for its own sake. Such a taste not even he would announce too openly, although he came close on more than one occasion. In 1889, when Berlin was making difficulties, he told a friend, "Frankly I don't know that I should be sorry to see a bit of a spar with Germany. The burning of New York and a few other sea coast cities would be a good object lesson in the need of an adequate system of coast defenses, and I think it would have a good effect on our large German population to force them to an ostentatiously patriotic display of anger against Germany." Two years later he condemned the Harrison administration for not declaring war on Chile. His close associate John Hay remarked of Roosevelt, then civil service commissioner, "For two nickels he would declare war himself—shut up the Civil Service Commission and wage it sole." In 1896, as strain with Spain over Cuba increased, Roosevelt commented, "If it wasn't wrong I should say that personally I would rather welcome a foreign war." A short while later he added, "I should welcome almost any war, for I think this country needs one." Reviewing one of Mahan's later books, Roosevelt declared, "There is no place in the world for nations who have become enervated by soft and easy life, or who have lost their fibre of vigorous hardiness and manliness." In a widely remarked lecture before the Naval War College he asserted, "All the great masterful races have been fighting races." If a race lost "the hard fighting virtues," then "no matter how skilled in commerce and finance, in sci-

ence or art, it has lost its proud right to stand as the equal of the best." He concluded, "No triumph of peace is quite so great as the supreme triumphs of war."[15]

Anglo-Saxonists like Roosevelt, Fiske and Strong took heart from the spread
of Anglo-Saxon institutions consequent to the expansion during the 1880s and
1890s of the British empire, though they naturally thought America could do a
better job of the spreading. Not alone was Britannia expanding: in this period
nearly all the colonial powers were scrambling for Africa, Southeast and East Asia
and whatever else had not been locked away. The example reinforced expan-
sionist tendencies in the United States, at two levels. At the idealistic level, the
European cult of the imperial mission encouraged those Americans who would
regenerate the world. If Britain, France, Germany and the others had a mission
to civilize humanity, all the more did America. At the practical level, the rush
for colonies indicated that if the United States did not join the race soon, there
would be no prizes left. On this point navalists like Mahan and commercialists
like Charles Denby joined hands with the Anglo-Saxonists. Coaling stations,
export markets, benighted souls and backward societies all were going fast.

V.   The diplomacy of distraction

The ideology of American superiority catalyzed the general unrest of the decade
into a combustible form of belligerent nationalism. America swaggered through
the 1890s, daring the world to cross it. In 1891 a civil war in Chile found Washington backing the government of President José Balmaceda against Congres-
sionalist rebels. The Congressionalists viewed Harrison's secretary of state James
G. Blaine with particular distrust, for ten years earlier, as Garfield's chief diplomat, Blaine had taken Peru's part against Chile in the War of the Pacific. In the
1891 case, however, "Jingo Jim" was, if anything, more conciliatory than Harrison. When the American legation in Santiago granted asylum to eighty refugees
from the fighting and the by-now victorious Congressionalists responded by surrounding the American compound, Harrison dispatched an indignant message to
the new government. Shortly thereafter the commander of the U.S.S. *Baltimore*
unwisely authorized shore leave in Valparaiso for more than a hundred sailors
who drank their pay and triggered an ugly riot. Two tars were killed and seven-
teen wounded, while the local police looked on. Harrison adopted the novel position that while God might watch over children and the insane, Chile must take
care of inebriated Americans. As an American officer put it, the Americans "went
ashore, many of them, for the purpose of getting drunk, which they did on Chilean rum paid for with good United States money. When in this condition they
were more entitled to protection than if they had been sober."

Harrison also insisted on treating the attack on men in American uniform as
an attack on the United States itself. He demanded satisfaction. The Chilean

government, still smarting from Washington's support for the losers in the civil war, replied by publicly calling Harrison a liar. Harrison added an apology and reparations to his demand. Otherwise, he intimated, the United States would certainly sever diplomatic ties and might declare war. The president went so far as to send the American Congress a message inviting a declaration of belligerency. At the last minute Chile gave way. Warned by European envoys to expect no help in the event of hostilities, the government in Santiago apologized and offered an indemnity. Washington accepted.[16]

American assertiveness took a territorial turn twelve months later. At the beginning of 1893, American expatriates in Hawaii fomented a revolution against the government of Queen Liliuokalani, overthrowing the monarchy and calling for annexation to the United States. The American minister in the islands, John Stevens, thought the coup a grand idea and guaranteed its success by ordering the landing of a squadron of marines from the conveniently close U.S.S. *Boston*. Expansionists in America cheered the energy of the men on the spot and began pinning Old Glory halfway across their maps of the Pacific. But the revolutionists had timed their action badly, for the White House was now occupied by Grover Cleveland. The Democratic president was not opposed to expansion per se. During his earlier administration he had declared Hawaii an "outpost of American commerce and the stepping-stone to the growing trade of the Pacific." Yet Cleveland, who had made his name in politics as a reformer, objected to the means by which the annexationists had operated. The United States, he said, did not go around overthrowing foreign governments. He criticized the "false pretexts" under which Stevens had called the American marines ashore, and he asserted that the United States could not annex the islands "without justly incurring the imputation of acquiring them by unjustifiable methods." He rejected the request for annexation.[17]

The annexationists would have their day once Cleveland left office. In the meantime the Democratic administration had to deal with the perception that it was weak on international affairs. Had he been able to point to victories on domestic matters, Cleveland could have ignored criticism of his foreign policy. Americans have never demanded much of their leaders regarding matters abroad while life flows smoothly at home. But as the depression deepened, as workers fought Pinkertons and farmers turned socialist, as Roosevelt ranted and other Republicans joined him, and as members of his own party began defecting, evidenced by the Democrats' loss of both houses of Congress in 1894, Cleveland began searching for issues to take Americans' minds off their troubles. He found one in an obscure location.

For half a century Britain and Venezuela had engaged in a desultory dispute over the location of the boundary between the latter country and the British colony of Guiana. For most of that time no one had much cared where the frontier lay, since it ran through jungle of which both sides had plenty. Then prospectors struck gold, changing the nature of the debate entirely. Venezuela suspended diplomatic ties with Britain in 1887 and called for international arbitration. Britain refused. Washington expressed mild interest in the subject, but it lay essentially quiescent until 1895.

In June of that year Cleveland shifted his attorney general, Richard Olney, to the state department following the untimely death of Secretary Walter Gresham. Olney provided the perfect reinforcement to Cleveland's sense of propriety, having responded to a daughter's indiscretion by banishing her from his home, never to see her again, although they lived in the same city for thirty years. Olney also knew how to count votes, and he seized the Venezuela issue at once. He dictated a memorandum to the British government insisting that London accept arbitration. Giving the lion's tail an added twist, he reaffirmed the Monroe Doctrine in breathtaking fashion. "Today the United States is practically sovereign on this continent," Olney wrote, "and its fiat is law upon the subjects to which it confines its interposition." Why did America enjoy such eminence?, he asked rhetorically.

> It is not because of the pure friendship or good will felt for it. It is not simply by reason of its high character as a civilized state, nor because wisdom and justice and equity are the invariable characteristics of the dealings of the United States. It is because, in addition to all other grounds, its infinite resources combined with its isolated position render it master of the situation and practically invulnerable as against any or all other powers.

Theodore Roosevelt could hardly have puffed the American chest out farther than this.[18]

The British, who had never acknowledged the legitimacy of even the narrowest interpretation of the Monroe Doctrine, had no intention of accepting Olney's sweeping extension. Lord Salisbury, the prime and foreign minister, did not consider the American note worthy of a prompt reply. He conspicuously spent the next four months on other matters. When he got around to responding he denied that the Monroe Doctrine had any standing in international law. Even if it did, he said, "the disputed frontier of Venezuela has nothing to do with any of the questions dealt with by President Monroe."[19]

Cleveland bristled at Salisbury's flippancy, and in a public message to Congress the president insisted that the Monroe Doctrine assuredly *was* international law and that it *did* apply to the present controversy. Because Britain refused to arbitrate the matter, the United States would nominate a commission to investigate. Should Britain refuse to accept the commission's report and persist in flouting decency and justice, the United States would consider such action "a willful aggression upon its rights and interests" and would be obliged "to resist by every means in its power."[20]

These were fighting words. The jingoes thrilled. Congress voted $100,000 to fund the boundary commission. The Irish National Alliance promised 100,000 troops for an invasion of Canada. Senator Henry Cabot Lodge, a Roosevelt crony who had urged a firm line from the beginning, wrote with satisfaction, "I first alone in the wilderness cried out about Venezuela last June and was called a Jingo for my pains. Jingoes are plenty enough now." Roosevelt said, "Let war come if it must. I don't care whether our sea coast cities are bombarded or not; we would take Canada." Roosevelt added hopefully, "If there is a muss I shall try to have a hand in it myself! They'll have to employ a lot of men just as green as I am even for the conquest of Canada." The British ambassador in Washington, observing the scene, wrote home that the American capital was in an "extraordinary state of excitement" and that the whole country appeared to be in "a condition of mind which can only be described as hysterical."[21]

American hysteria alone might not have caused Salisbury to reconsider. But at the same time Britain faced an incipient war in southern Africa, where British colonials and the German kaiser were doing their best to foment trouble, and friction with Russia over difficulties in Turkey and the Far East. Under the circumstances London needed no more enemies. Cleveland similarly thought again when the war scare disrupted financial markets in the United States and threatened to provoke another run on the nation's gold reserves. The British agreed in principle to arbitration, and the Americans consented to discuss what would be arbitrated. The talks moved slowly, which was all to the good. By the time an international commission awarded Britain most of the disputed territory, American passions had found another outlet.

2

Dewey . . . or Don't We?
1898–1899

I.   Coup de Maine

John Seeley, the nineteenth-century historian of British imperialism, claimed that Britain acquired its empire in "a fit of absence of mind." Seeley was wrong about Britain, and Americans who ascribed a similar accidental quality to their country's colony-gathering were equally in error. Empires do not happen by accident. America, like Britain, gained an empire because Americans wanted one and went out and got it.

This is not to say that *all* Americans wanted an empire, or that America got precisely the empire American imperialists sought. Plenty of Americans objected, and the anti-imperialists' objections limited the reach and graspingness of the empire-builders. The fight between the two groups, conducted in the popular press, in journals of opinion, in Congress and on the hustings, set the pattern for a debate that would continue until the present. Each side professed adherence to high ideals and to general principles of democracy, of service to humanity and of America's mission to the world. Yet the arguments that really told, then as later, were those that appealed to interests—to the interests of the listeners and readers and voters as individuals, as groups and as a nation. Different individuals and groups possessed competing individual and group interests and offered contradictory interpretations of the national interest. Hence the debate.

In 1895, in the midst of the war scare with Britain over Venezuela, when America remained mired in depression and chaos threatened on all fronts, nationalists in Cuba launched another in a long series of freedom fights against their Spanish rulers. Spain displayed particular ineptitude suppressing the revolt, and although Madrid committed more than 100,000 troops to the conflict the Spanish succeeded only in brutalizing the populace and swelling insurgent ranks. The

Cubans claimed few victories on the battlefield, but in the arena of world, or at least American, opinion they accomplished much more. Cuban publicists tapped into the American press, recounting and exaggerating Spanish abuses, including the infamous *reconcentrado* policy, which uprooted peasants and placed them in disease-ridden camps and converted the countryside into a free-fire zone. The new American president, William McKinley, publicly denounced the reconcentrado policy as "extermination."[1]

Although McKinley was neither a jingo nor an enthusiast of expansion, his party contained many of both, and with the penny papers outbidding each other in atrocity stories and fire-eaters in Congress demanding American intervention, a rebellion in Republican ranks seemed a genuine possibility. McKinley often showed more shrewdness than character, and in this instance he calmed the uprising by joining it. In June 1897 he informed Spain of America's conviction that human rights for the Cuban people took precedence over the prerogatives of Spanish sovereignty, and he demanded that the Spanish government terminate its reconcentrado policy and implement permanent reforms in the island.

Spain naturally refused, with a haughtiness guaranteed to goad. The Spanish minister in Washington subsequently penned a nasty letter about McKinley that leaked. At the beginning of 1898 the American navy department sent the U.S.S. *Maine* to Havana, ostensibly to protect American nationals, implicitly to pressure the Spanish. When the ship exploded under mysterious circumstances, killing hundreds of American sailors, an international collision became unavoidable. This time the jingoes, Mahanites and expansionists would not let opportunity pass. At their urging Congress appropriated $50 million for war preparations and directed the president to intervene on behalf of the insurgents. McKinley issued an ultimatum effectively demanding Cuban independence. Spain sneered and broke relations. McKinley and Congress replied in kind. In the fourth week of April, Washington and Madrid exchanged war declarations.

By this time the pro-war faction had done its work well enough that a majority of the country almost certainly favored the idea. Spain seemed the clear villain in this morality play, and after a decade of discouragement at home Americans were more than willing to seek success abroad. The fact that success would probably come quickly and easily made the conflict the more appealing. The country needed a victory, not a challenge, and heroes, not necessarily heroism.

But the war America actually fought was different from the one most Americans believed they were getting into. Although Cuba was the cause of the war, Spain was the enemy. Spain held territories around the globe. With the war declaration these territories—which included the Philippines—became potential prizes. From the time tension with Spain over Cuba had begun ratcheting, the navy department had prepared contingency plans. One of June 1896 specified that in the event of hostilities American ships in the Far East should proceed to Manila, there to engage and if possible destroy the Spanish fleet and capture the

Philippine capital. Such action would serve the triple objective of preventing the Spanish vessels from joining the fight in the American theater, of depriving Spain of the revenue of the islands and of gaining a bargaining chip, at least, for subsequent peace negotiations.[2]

War plans mean nothing without the political and logistical support to put them into effect, as Americans and Filipinos would learn to their dismay four decades later. No one understood this fact better than Theodore Roosevelt, who upon McKinley's inauguration assumed the crucial post of assistant navy secretary. For the first time Roosevelt was in a position to act on his grand ideas, and as with everything he attempted, from eliminating vice in New York to exterminating the big game of Africa, he set to his task with unparalleled zeal. He exercised to the limit, and beyond, the authority Congress granted the navy to purchase ships and supplies. He personally oversaw matters of transfer and promotion, ensuring that the most energetic commanders received the most important assignments. Looking back more than a decade later, William Howard Taft—by then no Roosevelt partisan—conceded, regarding the war with Spain, "If it had not been for Theodore Roosevelt we would never have been in a position to declare war, for it was he and only he who got from Congress sufficient ammunition to back any bluff we might make with actual play."[3]

As war approached in the first months of 1898 Roosevelt paid particular heed to the situation in the Pacific. Three years earlier Japan had emerged as the region's principal power by militarily thrashing China. The major European countries with ambitions in the Far East, especially Germany, had thus far prevented Japan from taking full advantage of its victory. But the Japanese were growing restive, and when Berlin parlayed the killing of two German missionaries into control of the port of Kiaochow, a scramble for China, like the recent and continuing scramble for Africa, appeared imminent. Roosevelt and other American expansionists confronted the bleak prospect of seeing the door to China and the China market slam before Americans fairly got a foot in.

After lunch on February 25 Navy Secretary John Long, exhausted by the hubbub surrounding the destruction of the *Maine*, went home to rest. In Long's absence Roosevelt became acting secretary, and he actively used his temporary powers. "The very devil seemed to possess him yesterday afternoon," Long remarked in his diary upon his return. Examining the telegrams Roosevelt had sent, Long discovered instructions to the commanders of the European and South Atlantic squadrons, directing them where to rendezvous if war came. Roosevelt told American captains around the world to lay in large fuel supplies. Most portentously he confirmed the earlier plan for attacking the Philippines. In a cable to Commodore George Dewey, whose fighting temper Roosevelt admired and whose assignment to the Asiatic squadron he had engineered, Roosevelt wrote,

Order the squadron except *Monocacy* to Hong Kong. Keep full of coal. In the event of declaration of war with Spain, your duty will be to see that the Spanish squadron does not leave the Asiatic coast, and then offensive operations in the Philippine Islands.[4]

Long might have rescinded this directive, but he did not. An attack on the Philippines remained as common-sensical as it had been from the day the navy's planners first broached the subject. But war-planners' common sense is not always common knowledge, and the navy certainly did not advertise what it was about. As a result America went to war against Spain in April 1898 with a strategy of which most Americans knew nothing. Generals and admirals have rated surprise at anywhere from one-third of victory up. The expansionists, by achieving surprise in their contest with their American opponents, nearly won the political battle before Dewey fired his first shot.

Spanish officials found Dewey's appearance in Manila less startling. After receiving Roosevelt's cable Dewey had requested the American consul in the Philippines, O. F. Williams, to snoop around and acquire what information he could regarding Manila's defenses and the Spanish fleet's readiness for war. Williams responded with clumsy diligence, and between his investigations and the overall Spanish-American tension he became non grata. The Spanish governor suggested he depart, saying his life was in danger from mobs. Williams left, but not before passing along intelligence Dewey characterized as "highly valuable."[5]

At noon on April 25 Dewey received a message from Navy Secretary Long:

War has commenced between the United States and Spain. Proceed at once to Philippine Islands. Commence operations particularly against the Spanish fleet. You must capture vessels or destroy. Use utmost endeavor.

Dewey had just repositioned his squadron from Hong Kong to Mirs Bay, an anchorage some thirty miles distant, where he ran his crews through target practice and battle drills. He waited briefly for Williams and the latest news from the Philippines. On April 27 he led two columns of vessels into the South China Sea, bound for Manila.[6]

En route Dewey passed Luzon's Subic Bay, which he described as a magnificent future site for a naval base. He arrived at the entrance to Manila Bay on the afternoon of April 30. Several hours later the American ships skirted south of Corregidor, the island guarding approach to the capital. Shore batteries opened fire, which Dewey's *Boston* and *McCulloch* returned. Neither side did much damage. By dawn the American vessels had penetrated twenty miles nearly to Manila, where they came under bombardment from guns in the city and in Cavite to the southeast. At this point Dewey's six warships attacked the anchored Spanish fleet. Describing the engagement for Washington's benefit, Dewey wrote,

The squadron maintained a continuous and precise fire at ranges varying from 5,000 to 2,000 yards, countermarching in a line approximately parallel to that of the Spanish fleet. The enemy's fire was vigorous, but generally ineffective.

The battle lasted six hours. By noon the Spanish ships were in flames and their guns silent. When the cannons of Fort Santiago at the mouth of the Pasig River, and of Intramuros, the old walled town, continued to fire, Dewey sent word to the governor that unless they ceased he would shell the city. By one o'clock all fighting ended. Three Spanish warships had been sunk, seven had burned. Spanish casualties numbered in the hundreds. Dewey lost no ships, and of the men under his command none were killed and but seven wounded, these slightly. "The squadron is in as good condition now as before the battle," Dewey reported.[7]

II.   Islands or canned goods?

McKinley later remarked disingenuously that had Dewey taken his good-as-new squadron and steamed back to Hong Kong, he would have saved his country a great deal of trouble. In the context of the hour such action was nearly unthinkable, not least because it contradicted standing American strategy. Anyone could see that the war with Spain, like most wars, was a limited conflict and would end in a negotiated settlement. As the navy plan of 1896 had envisaged, the Philippines provided Washington a bit of barter. To abandon the islands without compelling cause would be foolish. Whether American diplomats cashed their bargaining chip at the peace talks or pocketed it, the disposition of the Philippines was a matter that could await the war's end.

Although McKinley avoided committing himself one way or the other, time favored retention. In demonstration of America's disinterestedness, Congress had attached to the war resolution an amendment proposed by Colorado Senator Henry Teller forbidding annexation of Cuba. Political considerations, in particular the suspicions of anti-imperialist Democrats, forced the expansionists to swallow the amendment. But the Teller measure said nothing about the Philippines, and by declaring Cuba out of bounds it increased demand for other spoils of victory. Dewey's triumph in Manila, followed by successes in the Caribbean, reinforced the expansionists' case and added to their weight in the Republican party. It would have required a stronger man than McKinley to face them down, even had he been so inclined. In fact the president himself was growing increasingly enamored of expansionism. By July he was expressing support for "the general principle of holding on to what we get."[8]

McKinley later defended his decision for annexation, which he claimed to have arrived at reluctantly, as the best course available. He rejected returning the Philippines to the Spanish, whose record in Cuba as well in the Philippines showed them unfit to govern other peoples. Nor could he in conscience hand the Philippines over to a third country. Spain might be the worst of the European colonial powers, but none was any good. With the Far East balanced on a knife's edge of suspicion among the imperialists, to favor one would alienate the rest and might start a war. Relinquishing the islands to a commercial rival would be "bad business." The Filipinos were unprepared for independence. Lacking economic and social preconditions for self-government and especially self-defense, they would not last long in the shark-infested waters of the western Pacific. Only annexation of the islands by America remained. "There was nothing left to do," McKinley said, "but take them all, and educate the Filipinos, and uplift and civilize them."[9]

McKinley's argument did not entirely lack justification, though he left much unsaid. Returning the Philippines to Spain or transferring the islands to Germany or France or Britain or Japan would indeed have been ignoble, unprofitable and dangerous. McKinley was probably correct in thinking Philippine independence would be fleeting. Considering what the imperialists had done to the rest of the region and were preparing to do in China, the life expectancy of an independent Philippines was not great.

Had McKinley been as concerned for the welfare of the Filipinos as he professed to be, he might have considered an American protectorate over the islands. Yet a protectorate held little attraction for Americans, since it would have burdened the United States with the defense of the Philippines while affording few of the advantages of sovereignty. Although Washington did establish a protectorate over Cuba, in the Cuban case most Americans could see a direct connection between events in the Caribbean and American security, and they did not object overmuch to paying for Cuba's defense. Americans demonstrated no comparable perspective regarding the Philippines. As matters turned out, American taxpayers refused to provide adequately for the protection of the archipelago even when the American flag flew over it. They would have done still less for a self-governing Philippines.

McKinley could have tried to arrange an international agreement for the neutralization of the Philippines. Such a scheme might have worked awhile. Belgium had been neutralized for most of a century. But as the Belgian example would soon demonstrate, neutralization succeeded only as long as the powers chose to let it succeed, and it collapsed the moment one of them decided to ignore the scrap of paper containing the guarantees. In any case the United States in the 1890s likely lacked the political flexibility and sophistication to make neutralization work. American voters would ask what was in it for them, and the government would be hard pressed to provide a simple, satisfying answer. Moreover, a neutralization plan would have involved foreign entanglements—prima facie evidence, in American eyes, of its folly.

From the perspective of American interests, as interpreted by McKinley, this left annexation. For a time the president toyed with partitioning the archipelago, thinking the United States might take Luzon and otherwise dispose of the rest of the islands. After the fighting against Spain ended in August he sent American peace commissioners to Paris with orders to demand only Luzon. But he gradually recognized that partition would require choosing one of the rejected options for the remaining islands, with unacceptable consequences in America and abroad. At the end of October he wrote to the head of the American commission, regarding American sentiment on the subject:

> There is a very general feeling that the United States, whatever it might prefer as to the Philippines, is in a situation where it cannot let go. The interdependency of the several islands, their close relations with Luzon, the very grave problem of what will become of the part we do not take, are receiving the thoughtful consideration of the people, and it is my judgment that the well-considered opinion of the majority would be that duty requires we should take the archipelago.[10]

The Spanish initially objected to giving up the islands, but they were in no position to make objection stick. After some haggling they capitulated, salving their sores with twenty million American dollars. On December 10 the two sides affixed signatures to a treaty formally ending the war and delivering title of the Philippines to the United States.

III.   The battle of Capitol Hill

On rare occasions the American Senate lives up to its claim to be the most deliberative body in the world. It did following the war with Mexico, when Webster, Clay and Calhoun fashioned the compromises that allowed the Union to last another ten years before dissolving into fratricide. It did again a century later, following another war, when it debated whether the country had matured sufficiently to survive peacetime alliances. And it did halfway between, following the Spanish-American War, when it debated the treaty of Paris and considered the consequences of acquiring a foreign empire.

Deliberativeness need not imply high-mindedness. It certainly did not in the case of the Philippines. The debate over the Paris treaty turned far less on matters of idealism than on bare-knuckled self-interest. Indeed, speakers appealed to some of the basest instincts of listeners, and when the vote-casting took place few casters gave much thought to the welfare of any persons without political leverage in the United States. Notable among the excluded—not for the last time— were the Filipinos.

The fight over the treaty started before the Senate formally considered it, and the contest spilled well beyond Washington. The Philippine issue and the broader question of American imperialism roused violent feelings for and against throughout the United States. Opponents decried annexation as placing America on a par with the predatory imperialists of Europe. Charles Eliot Norton, formerly a businessman with connections in the Far East but more recently a Harvard professor and editor of or contributor to most of America's principal reviews, feared that the acquisition of empire would bring upon the United States "the misery and the burdens that war and standing armies have brought upon the nations of the Old World." Trying to fathom the ill-considered enthusiasm come over America, Norton wrote, "All the evil spirits of the Old World which we trusted were exorcised in the New, have taken possession of her, and under their influence she has gone mad." Norton asserted that in embracing empire America was forsaking her identity. "She has lost her unique position as a potential leader in the progress of civilization, and has taken up her place simply as one of the grasping and selfish nations of the present day."[11]

E. L. Godkin, a friend of Norton, had an equally dreary opinion of American empire. The dyspeptic editor of the *Nation* saw no end of troubles in the Philippines and beyond. Earlier Godkin had objected to the profligate extension of American jurisdiction, declaring, "We do not want any more States until we can civilize Kansas." Now he listed the arguments against overseas expansion:

> The sudden departure from our traditions; the absence from our system of any machinery for governing dependencies; the admission of alien, inferior, and mongrel races to our nationality; the opening of fresh fields to carpetbaggers, speculators, and corruptionists; the un-Americanism of governing a large body of people against their will, and by persons not responsible to them; the entrance on a policy of conquest and annexation while our own continent was still unreclaimed, our population unassimilated, and many of our most serious political problems still unsolved; and finally the danger of the endorsement of a gross fraud for the first time by a Christian nation.

Dewey's victory at Manila, Godkin said, had made McKinley "drunk with glory and flattery." Empire would be the country's undoing. "I can not help thinking this triumph over Spain seals the fate of the American republic."[12]

Carl Schurz, like Godkin a first-generation immigrant who adopted America but not all its excitements, agreed that acquisition of an overseas empire heralded the demise of American democracy. Schurz had arrived in the United States from Prussia in the wake of the failed revolt of 1848. He had joined the Republican party and served in the Union army during the Civil War. With many of the older anti-imperialists, who likewise had suffered through secession and civil war, Schurz felt particular dismay that America would lightly abandon what it had purchased at great price. "The character and future of the Republic and the welfare of its people now living and yet to be born are in unprecedented jeopardy," he wrote. The expansionists had thrown over the values of Jefferson and Lincoln. Ambition and greed ruled. Militarism would follow. War against the Filipinos was nearly unavoidable. "The Filipinos fought against Spain for their freedom and independence, and unless they abandon their recently proclaimed purpose for their freedom and independence, they will fight against us."[13]

Andrew Carnegie also opposed annexation on grounds it would lead to war. But the conflict the steelmaker-philanthropist feared most was one between the United States and the Europeans. Although the imperialists were at war's brink around the world, Carnegie wrote, nowhere was tension so great as in the Far East. "It is in that region the thunderbolt is expected. It is there the storm is to burst." Carnegie pointed out that the British had allowed Dewey the use of Hong Kong in launching his attack on Manila, and he contended that American possession of the Philippines still rested on British good will—"rather a humiliating position, I should say, for the Republic." Should the British undergo a change of heart, the United States would be dangerously exposed.

Carnegie joined Schurz and the others in predicting the decay of American civilization consequent to annexation. To defend their new empire Americans would have to adopt the tools and techniques of imperialism: "brutal physical strength, fighting men with material forces, warships and artillery." Expansionists claimed to desire the uplifting of the Filipinos. Carnegie did not deny the Filipinos' need, but he rejected the possibility of accomplishment. "Has the influence of the superior race upon the inferior ever proved beneficial to either? I know of no case in which it has been or is." Just the opposite was likely to occur. Annexing the Philippines would require military occupation, which would antagonize the Filipinos and corrupt America's youth. "Soldiers in foreign camps, so far from being missionaries for good, require missionaries themselves more than the natives."[14]

Opponents of annexation in Congress elaborated these objections and introduced others. Democratic representative Jehu Baker of Illinois defended American values and institutions against the importation of foreign counterfeits. "The English system," Baker said, "rests upon monarchy, inequality, aristocracy and rank. The American system rests upon democracy and equality, and severely excludes legalized aristocracy and rank." An imperialist policy, he asserted, would tragically diminish or abolish the difference.

> This would be one of the most lamentable self-degradations in the history of mankind. . . . The attempt to suddenly sweep us into a colonial policy similar to that of Great Britain—so suddenly that we have scarce time to note where the leap will carry us—is, in my opinion, the most audacious and reckless performance of jingoism that this or any other country has ever witnessed.[15]

Jerry Simpson, Kansas Populist, similarly detected the odious mark of jingoism on the Paris treaty. Simpson spied a sinister design in the administration's whole handling of the war and the peace. He predicted that McKinley's supporters would play upon the surge of militarism in America to strengthen the army, which the party of big business would then use to suppress domestic dissent. "That is what they want it for, along with a scheme for colonial empire, and to place on the throne in this country William McKinley, President of the United States, Emperor of the West Indian Islands and of the Philippines." Simpson warned his colleagues in the House against the beguilement of empire. "Empire!" he shouted. "Do gentlemen understand the meaning of the word 'empire' as applied to a republic? It means that we are taking the first step toward the strong centralized power that will finally result in this Republic being turned into an empire."[16]

Other opponents of annexation appealed to the pocketbooks of their constituents. Republican congressman Henry Johnson of Indiana expressed a concern that would characterize debate over the Philippines for forty years and would figure centrally in the eventual decision to have done with governing the islands. Annexation, Johnson said, would bring the Philippines within the American tariff wall. "Annexation of these islands, under the Constitution, will make impossible a tariff against their sugar, tobacco, hemp and other products raised by cheap tropical labor." He predicted "immense injury to the American farmer and laborer" from Philippine imports, and he asserted that "no American will make money there except the possessors of great wealth, who will reap enormous gains from the profits which they will realize from the sale of these products in the free markets of the United States." Persons injured by cheap imports would suffer a second time by having to subsidize the American empire. "They, in common with all of our people, will have to bear the burden of a heavy increase in taxation in support of the Army and Navy of this country, which must be greatly enlarged in order to protect and defend these islands and the great corporations which are doing business there."[17]

In the Senate, Hernando Money also addressed the trade issue. The Mississippi Democrat assured his colleagues he did not lack patriotic fervor, saying he had felt "in every ruddy drop that visited my heart a tingling of joyous pride when the great exploits of our sailors and soldiers astonished the world." He had experienced a "thrill of exultation" and a "glow of enthusiasm" when the American flag "waved in supremacy" over the Philippines. But he cautioned senators not to get carried away. He denied the argument that American trade with Asia required possession of the islands. "Are conquests and subjugation necessary to the spread of American products? Have we depended heretofore upon those aids so much vaunted in this debate?" Of course not. "The commerce of the United States, fortunately for this great Republic, has been founded more wisely upon the superior skill of its artisans. . . . That which carries American commerce abroad is not the protection of this Government; it is not that the flag of the fighting Navy of the United States is found on every sea and in every port; it is the skill of the American workingman."[18]

Democrat John Daniel of Virginia resurrected an argument that fifty years earlier had helped frustrate expansionists' plans to seize all of Mexico. Did the people of the United States, he asked in a voice of cloying intimacy, comprehend the implications of clasping the Filipinos to their bosom? "Today we are the United States of America. Tomorrow, if a treaty now pending in the Senate is ratified, we will be the United States of America and Asia." The joining involved more than a mere political coalition. "It is a marriage of nations. This twain will become one flesh. They become bone of our bone and flesh of our flesh. Henceforth and forever, according to the terminology of this treaty, the Filipinos and Americans are one."

Daniel understood the power of the specter of miscegenation, and he exploited it to the full. He described the Philippines as a racial "witch's caldron," and he intoned:

> Black spirits and white,
> Red spirits and gray,
> Mingle, mingle, mingle,
> You that mingle may.

He retailed the most scurrilous and preposterous stories about the Filipinos. "The travelers who have been there tell us and have written in the books that they are not only of all hues and colors, but there are spotted people there and, what I have never heard of in any other country, there are striped people there with zebra signs upon them." Daniel did not vouch for the veracity of these tales, but he considered them worth repeating. The Senate and the American public must know what they were getting into by selling their birthright for "this Asiatic mess of pottage."[19]

Despite their skills at demagoguery, the opponents of annexation labored under a distinct disadvantage: the perils they predicted lay beyond the horizon of the present, a frontier often nearly impenetrable by political argumentation in America. The supporters of annexation, in contrast, could capitalize on the momentum of current events. After a decade riven by political turbulence, economic hardship and social upheaval, Americans imbibed the tonic of foreign success with gusto. The war with Spain unified the country as it had not been unified for years, since before the election of Lincoln. To the members of the war party went the laurels of rapid and relatively painless victory. They had taken the initiative and risks of calling for war. They had predicted a glorious triumph. They had achieved it. Who listened to the mugwumps now?

The annexationists also enjoyed the nine-tenths advantage of the status quo. The anti-imperialists contended that acquisition of the Philippines constituted a break with American tradition. They were right, although the annexationists partially deflected the assertion by pointing to the long career of American territorial expansion. But at the moment of the debate over the Paris treaty American forces occupied Manila and its neighborhood, and the American flag flew above the walls of Intramuros and Fort Santiago. The current status quo favored continued occupation.

Proponents of annexation exploited this fact, reminding readers and listeners that abandoning the Philippines would require striking the American flag, raised at the cost of American blood and treasure. "We have hoisted our flag," Roosevelt declared, "and it is not fashioned of the stuff which can be quickly hauled down." Henry Cabot Lodge asserted that the United States occupied Manila "rightfully by all laws of war and by all international law." The Massachusetts Republican added, "We hold it, as we have a right to hold it, under the agreement with Spain." To hand it back would be an "act of infamy."[20]

The expansionists liked to stress Spanish dereliction in governing the Philippines, American innocence in acquiring the islands and the inevitability of the entire affair. Falling short of frankness, Lodge told a correspondent, "I, of course, did not dream of the Philippines, which I think no one thought of, until the first of May." Lodge went on to say, "When a great change comes in the attitude and policy of a nation, although it may have been preparing for a century, it always comes suddenly at the last and always goes farther than even those who foresaw it anticipate." Lodge continued, "It makes little difference today what any of us thought about the war six months ago." The war with Spain was "not only righteous but inevitable." Inevitable as well was an expanded role for the United States. "We are going to hold possessions over the seas, be they more or less."[21]

Lodge was a key figure in the contest over annexation, frustrating opponents of the treaty with the considerable parliamentary skills he would display in his long career in the Senate. Lodge had worked closely with Roosevelt during the war in an effort to assure McKinley's support for taking the islands. The anti-imperialist Edward Atkinson later described Lodge's relationship to Roosevelt: "Lodge is the Mephistopheles whispering poison in his ear all the time." After the first month of fighting Lodge wrote Roosevelt expressing pleasure at the course of battle, but cautioning, "The one point where haste is needed is the Philippines." Lodge feared that Spain might capitulate before the United States got all it wanted and deserved. Roosevelt agreed, replying from the front in Cuba, "You must prevent any talk of peace until we get Porto Rico and the Philippines." At the end of May Lodge reported signs that McKinley was seeing the situation in the proper light. "I think I can say to you, in confidence but in absolute certainty," he told Roosevelt, "that the administration is grasping the whole policy at last. . . . Unless I am utterly and profoundly mistaken the administration is now fully committed to the large policy that we both desire."[22]

Lodge found the outcome of the war gratifying, and he enjoyed the discomfiture of the treaty's foes. He described the anti-imperialists as "very comic," and when a petition drive opposing the treaty netted only 2,000 signatures in six weeks he commented, "I should hardly have thought it possible that the result should have been so trivial from so much exertion." The struggle for the treaty pitted Republicans against Democrats, as well as expansionists against anti-imperialists. Lodge, writing Roosevelt from Washington, was pleased to predict a double victory. "The drift of public opinion in favor of an imperial policy seems to be absolutely overwhelming, and the Democrats here seem to be going to pieces over it." To which Roosevelt responded that it served them right. Roosevelt judged opponents of the treaty, including renegade Republican George Hoar, to be "little better than traitors," and he charged the Democrats with displaying "a lamentable indifference to the true interests of the nation."[23]

During the Senate debate on the Paris treaty Lodge adduced arguments dismissing the alternatives to annexation and described American possession as both honorable and just. He took particular pains to counter the contention that the existence of a Filipino insurgent army somehow disqualified the United States from governing the islands. He reminded his colleagues that the insurgents had laid down arms prior to the commencement of the Spanish-American War and had retaken the field only with Dewey's arrival. "The insurgent force," Lodge declared, "as an effective force, and the insurgent rebellion, as an effective rebellion, existed solely because of the victory of Admiral Dewey." Lodge denied that the United States had usurped any Filipino claim to sovereignty. "There was no sovereignty there whatever except the sovereignty of Spain, and we succeeded to the sovereignty." As to charges of American mistreatment of Filipinos, these were figments of fevered Democratic imaginations. "There has never been an act of oppression against the Filipinos by any American soldiers or by the American forces of any kind in the Philippine Islands. Those patriots have never been oppressed by any American in the active service of this country, or by any American act. Their oppression exists solely in speeches in the United States Senate." Lodge went so far as to suggest that the American contingent had acted perhaps *too* generously toward the Filipinos. "They have been treated with the utmost consideration and the utmost kindness, and, after the fashion of Orientals, they have mistaken kindness for timidity."[24]

Lodge did not indulge in public displays of enthusiasm. He took seriously his serious reputation as America's scholar-in-politics, and when a challenger, Woodrow Wilson, later arose, Lodge became his mortal—literally, as it happened—foe. But Lodge did not need to wax particularly eloquent on the Philippine question, for Indiana's new senator, Albert Beveridge, spouted sufficient purple for the entire Republican party. Beveridge burst onto the senatorial scene with a performance noteworthy both for its shameless excess, even by the standards of the day, and as a summary of the annexationists' case. Declaring the islands "ours forever," Beveridge informed his auditors that they lived in an age of imperialism. A prize like the Philippines would not come again. "This island empire is the last land left in all the oceans." Beyond the Philippines lay the "illimitable markets" of China. As in former days, America's destiny followed the westering sun.

> Our largest trade henceforth must be with Asia. The Pacific is our ocean. More and more Europe will manufacture the most it needs, secure from its colonies the most it consumes. Where shall we turn for consumers of our surplus? Geography answers the question. China is our natural customer. She is nearer to us than to England, Germany, or Russia, the commercial powers of the present and the future. . . . The Philippines gives us a base at the door of all the East.

Describing China's current trade as but a shadow of what it would surely become, Lodge pointed out that China currently possessed not even five hundred miles of railroad. In two generations she would need, and would possess, twenty thousand miles.

> Who can estimate her commerce then? That statesman commits a crime against American trade—against the American grower of cotton and wheat and tobacco, the American manufacturer of machinery and clothing—who fails to put America where she may command that trade. Germany's Chinese trade is increasing like magic. She has established ship lines and secured a tangible foothold on China's very soil. Russia's Chinese trade is growing beyond belief. She is spending the revenues of the Empire to finish her railroad into Pekin itself, and she is in physical possession of the imperial province of Manchuria. Japan's China trade is multiplying in volume and value. She is bending her energy to her merchant marine, and is located along China's very coast; but Manila is nearer China than Yokohama is. The Philippines command the commercial situation of the entire East.

The natural beauty and bounty of the islands sent Beveridge into a rhapsody.

> I have cruised more than 2,000 miles through the archipelago, every moment a surprise at its loveliness and wealth. I have ridden hundreds of miles on the islands, every foot of the way a revelation of vegetable and mineral riches. No land in America surpasses in fertility the plains and valleys of Luzon. Rice and coffee, sugar and coconuts, hemp and tobacco, and many products of the temperate as well as the tropic zone grow in various sections of the archipelago. . . . The wood of the Philippines can supply the furniture of the world for a century to come. At Cebu the best informed man in the island told me that 40 miles of Cebu's mountain chain are practically mountains of coal. . . . I have a nugget of pure gold picked up in its present form on the banks of a Philippine creek. I have gold dust washed out by crude processes of careless natives from the sands of a Philippine stream.

Naming the Philippines the "Gibraltar of the Pacific," Beveridge stated that the islands would safeguard America's west coast against any possible foe.

The essential question, Beveridge concluded, was infinitely deeper than party politics or constitutional power. "It is elemental. It is racial. God has not been preparing the English-speaking and Teutonic peoples for a thousand years for nothing but vain and idle self-contemplation and self-admiration." By no means. "He has made us the master organizers of the world to establish system where chaos reigns. He has given us the spirit of progress to overwhelm the forces of reaction throughout the earth." The reward would match the challenge. "It holds for us all the profit, all the glory, all the happiness possible to man."[25]

IV.   To fight another day

Beveridge's wine-dark prose did not demolish the opposition to the Paris treaty, although his phrases made colorful copy for editors and publicists. Instead the anti-imperialists were done in by their friends, of whom the principal culprit was William Jennings Bryan. The once and future presidential candidate opposed retention of the Philippines, preferring that the islands be granted independence. But Bryan had his eye on the campaign of 1900, and he hoped to clear the deck of issues other than free silver and the trusts. With this objective—and also for the reason he admitted to, that rejection of the treaty would leave the United States technically at war with Spain, whereas approval of the pact would free Americans to deal with the Philippine question on its separate merits—Bryan urged his followers to vote for ratification.[26]

The erstwhile allies of the peerless leader felt they had been blindsided. Opponents of annexation offered amendments designed to kill the treaty. Senator George Vest of Missouri proposed a resolution declaring that the American government had no power to acquire territory without pledging that such territory ultimately be granted statehood. Arthur Gorman of Maryland attempted to alter the treaty to specify simply the termination of Spanish sovereignty over the Philippines without including cession to the United States. Augustus Bacon of Georgia wanted to extend the Teller amendment to the Philippines. Samuel McEnery recommended a disclaimer that the American government did not desire the permanent attachment of the islands to the United States.

After several weeks of maneuvering the treaty came to a straight yes-or-no decision. The ratifiers won by a margin of 57 to 27, one more than the necessary two-thirds. Only two Republicans—Hoar, whose support for Filipino nationalism was reinforced by petitions from dozens of towns in the islands calling for independence, and Edward Everett Hale—voted against ratification, while ten Democrats, four Populists and a handful of others of Bryanesque views voted in favor. Almost certainly the treaty would have failed had Bryan stood his anti-imperialist ground.

Bryan's position embittered and alienated many of the anti-imperialists. Hoar told a friend that Bryan was "the most thoroughly guilty man in the United States of the wrong of this whole Philippine business." When Hoar's friend asked if he really meant to say Bryan was more culpable than McKinley, Hoar replied that he did indeed, since Bryan sinned through cynicism while McKinley merely erred through ignorance.[27]

If Bryan's strategy did not please the opponents of annexation, neither did it gain him significant numbers of votes in the 1900 election. By the autumn of 1900 the United States was in the thick of a war against Filipino nationalists, which made the Philippines an issue in the campaign whether Bryan wished it or not. The Democrats stated in their platform, "We condemn and denounce the Philippine policy of the present administration," and they called for an end to the fighting and for independence for the Filipinos. Yet Bryan, already reluctant to divert attention from the domestic matters he deemed more pressing, had to tread lightly on the war lest he appear disrespectful of the American soldiers killed and wounded in the conflict.

Consequently the Republicans found it easy to portray Bryan as woolly on foreign affairs—not a difficult task in any event. In the keynote address at the GOP convention Lodge contrasted the Democrats' uninformed altruism to the hard-headed realism of the Republicans. "We make no hypocritical pretense of being in the Philippines solely on account of others," Lodge said. "While we regard the welfare of these people as a sacred trust, we regard the welfare of the American people first." Speaking directly to the prejudices of his audience, Lodge added, "We believe in trade expansion."[28]

Circumstances at home provided Bryan no greater opening. McKinley's administration witnessed—Republicans predictably said caused—the return of prosperity, which essentially spiked Bryan's silver and antitrust guns. Bryan lost the election, with little evidence indicating a significant role for the Philippines one way or the other.[29]

Yet if the Philippines did not decide the election of 1900, the outcome of the great debate of 1898–99 settled larger issues. In taking the islands Americans gave notice of a broad redefinition of American interests. Americans might have charted their future in narrower continental terms. They might have strengthened the Monroe Doctrine and aimed for strictly hemispheric hegemony. Instead they opted for a global destiny. An Asian power from the moment the Senate ratified the treaty of Paris, the United States before long found itself embroiled in the affairs of most of the planet.

Did Americans understand what they were getting into? Not entirely. No one guessing the future ever does. But for all the demagoguery and political positioning, the debaters succeeded in raising the central questions involved in creating an American empire. And while possession of the Philippines brought troubles unimagined, or at least unacknowledged, by the two-thirds of the Senate voting for annexation, the vote and the overall mood of the times indicated that the country was fairly well pleased with its imperial prospects.

II

FRETFUL
COEXISTENCE

3

The Water Cure and Other
Remedies for Philippine Nationalism
1899–1901

I.   Rizal to Bonifacio to Aguinaldo

If Philippine nationalism had a father, it was José Rizal. If a date of birth, 1887. If a birth certificate, *Noli Me Tangere*. Rizal was a poet and a doctor, son of a well-to-do sugar planter who had assimilated, to the limited degree the Spanish allowed, into the Spanish community of government officials, soldiers and friars that dominated Philippine political life. Rizal early displayed an aptitude for literature and a preference for the Tagalog language. At eight he was composing verses in the vernacular:

> Our tongue was like those of others;
> Having alphabet and letters of its own.
> But these, like a small lake craft exposed
> To the monsoon's fury, were wrecked
> Long ago in the night of time.

At eleven he enrolled in Manila at the best school in the islands, where he shared lodging with the bastard sons of Spanish priests. Over the objections of his mother, who predicted with fair accuracy that "if he goes on to learn more, it will lead to him being beheaded," Rizal continued his education at the Dominican University of Santo Tomás. Later he traveled to Madrid, where he studied medicine. In Madrid he also learned what it meant to be an *indio*, even a relatively privileged one, in Spain's empire. The experience inspired a novel expressing the ambivalence he felt.[1]

Rizal completed *Noli Me Tangere*—the title came from the words of the resurrected Jesus to Mary Magdalene—in Berlin, where he was working at an oph-

thalmic clinic after further study in Paris and Heidelberg. He had the book privately printed, personally distributing a few copies to friends but shipping the
bulk of the run of 2000 volumes to contacts in Spain and the Philippines. The
book scored an immediate success in Manila, and when booksellers exhausted
their supplies it circulated on a black market at prices five times the original. The
novel's significance consisted in the fact that its characters, especially the villains,
were instantly recognizable to readers. A friend, offering congratulations, wrote,

> Who does not know Fray Damaso? Ah, I have known him closely, and although, in
> your brilliant personification of him in the novel, he wears the garb of a dirty Fran-
> ciscan, always coarse, always tyrannical, always corrupt, I have met him and studied
> him in real life in the Philippines, at times in the white habit of the Augustinian,
> sometimes as a Franciscan, as you have presented him, and sometimes in the bare
> feet and tunic of a Recollect.

If the numerous Fray Damosos in the Philippines did not admit to recognizing
themselves in Rizal's book, they found the portrait sufficiently close to reality to
warrant making an example of its author. The Augustinian who headed the governor-general's censorship committee denounced Rizal for purveying "foreign
teachings and doctrines" calculated "to inspire among the submissive and loyal
sons of Spain in these far-off isles a profound and abiding hatred of the Mother
Country." The pernicious book was banned.

Rizal had appeared in Manila shortly after his book, but the uproar it provoked
persuaded him to leave again. He returned to Europe, this time via the Pacific
and the United States. America did not impress him. Arriving on a ship full of
Chinese emigrants, barred from entrance to the United States by the 1882 Chinese exclusion act, he had difficulty convincing officials in San Francisco that the
law did not apply to him. He traveled across the continent by train and enjoyed
the scenery but not the service. "The steward of the Pullman car, an American,"
he wrote, "is somewhat of a thief."[2]

Exile in Europe afforded time to pen a sequel to *Noli Me Tangere*. When his
friends smuggled *El Filibusterismo* into the Philippines, Rizal became more notorious than ever. Yet incendiary though *El Filibusterismo* was, it was less than a
militant call to arms, for it portrayed a revolution gone sour and demonstrated the
author's mixed emotions regarding the condition of his compatriots. Rizal judged
impossible continued submission to Spain and especially to the despotism of the
friars. But in revolution he saw only evil in another guise. The distinction was lost
on the authorities in Manila, and when Rizal returned in 1892 he was quickly
arrested and dispatched to internal exile at Dapitan on Mindanao.

Rizal's arrest added impetus to the Philippine nationalist movement, for the
reason that the poet made a better symbol than an organizer. As a member of the
educated class of *ilustrados*, Rizal was caught between the Spanish rulers and the
Filipino peasantry, unable to identify fully with either. The Spanish would not

accept him as an equal, but the existence they allowed was not sufficiently intolerable to drive him to revolution. While life was not good, it could have been worse.

With Rizal removed, the initiative in the nationalist movement passed into hands less hesitant. On July 6, 1892, Andrés Bonifacio, a former peddler of lower-class origins, founded a secret society known as the *Kataastaasan Kagalanggalang Katipunan ng mga Anak ng Bayan* ("The Highest and Most Honorable Society of the Sons of the Country"), or Katipunan. Although the immediate origins of the Katipunan lay in frustration at the diffidence of elitist reformers like Rizal, Bonifacio and his co-conspirators built upon a tradition of popular agitation that stretched far back into the nineteenth century—and would continue throughout the twentieth.

As early as the 1840s the peasant leader Apolinario de la Cruz had organized a short-lived rebellion in Tayabas province. Apolinario came to revolution circuitously. Born about 1814 to parents of the upper peasantry, in his teens he set his heart on a religious calling. To his frustration he ran up against proscriptions on indios taking monastic orders. He responded by gathering a following of similarly dissatisfied individuals, which prompted the local curate, sensing a challenge to the status quo, to cry heresy. A raid by government authorities in October 1840 produced evidence that gave rise to charges of sedition and set off a sequence of events that included a brief rebellion, culminating in Apolinario's arrest and execution. As a message to would-be imitators, the Spanish cut Apolinario's corpse into several pieces and placed his severed head in a cage along one of the main roads in the province.[3]

Apolinario was not so easily foiled. Thirty years later he reportedly appeared, in company with a fellow martyr of 1841 and the Virgin Mary, to a group of peasants feeling particularly oppressed. Januario Labios, the son-in-law of one of Apolinario's followers, raised the banner of revolt. Claiming privileged communication with Providence, Labios prophesied a deluge that would tear away houses and farms and most of the established order. By taking certain precautions—by deepening streambeds and reinforcing their dwellings with posts in the shape of crosses—and by praying and making a pilgrimage to a certain holy mountain, the elect might be spared. When large numbers of peasants from Tayabas and neighboring provinces embarked on the pilgrimage, the government once again became alarmed. The army dispersed the pilgrims and destroyed groves of trees sacred to the cult. Labios disappeared, from the mountain and from history.[4]

Sensitive to this tradition of popular unrest, the Spanish interpreted the mere fact of Bonifacio's organizing the Katipunan as a threat. Bonifacio, knowing they would, adopted elaborate precautions to prevent detection. Each member of the Katipunan pledged to recruit two new members, the three together forming a cell. But the two recruits would not know each other, only the recruiter, thereby minimizing the damage an informant might do. Eventually, impatient with the slow growth this method produced, Bonifacio and the Katipunan leadership loosened the procedure, leading to a rapid increase in membership—and to their discovery.

Three questions ritually asked of initiates demonstrated the aims of the Katipunan. What was the condition of the Philippines in early times? What is the condition today? What will the condition be in the future? The correct answers described a golden age before the arrival of Magellan, a degraded and corrupt present and a return to independence and happiness upon the expulsion of the Spanish. Following the administration of a blood oath, the initiate received a short lecture and a reminder:

> We, the sons of the People, established this association in order to redeem the Mother Country from slavery. As such it is imperative that we should be united, that we should look up to each other as more than mere brothers, to help each other in any emergency, and always consider that all of us are of the same color and race. This is our real origin: that we are not of different races—we are not only relatives, but also true sons of one mother.[5]

Even in exile Rizal remained the most visible of Filipino nationalists, and Bonifacio and the Katipunan acknowledged the poet's symbolic primacy. But they grew increasingly restive at the failure of the ilustrados to take tangible action against the Spanish. The open break came in May 1896 when a Kapitunan delegation covertly visited Rizal in Dapitan and requested that he assume leadership of an insurrection. Rizal declined, saying the time was not ripe for launching an armed struggle. The elite would not join an insurrection, he argued, and without the support of the wealthy and educated the revolt would fail.

While Bonifacio and the Katipunan leadership assessed this rebuff, the government forced their hand. In July 1896 the police in Manila discovered a Katipunan network. Mass arrests followed, prompting Bonifacio to call an emergency meeting. Although some members advocated retreat, Bonifacio insisted on pressing forward. His views carried the meeting, and in August the revolt began.[6]

Almost from the first, atrocities marked the fighting on both sides. The *insurrectos*, whose numbers mounted to tens of thousands concentrated in Cavite province but spread over most of Luzon, settled scores with some of the friars and government officials they managed to lay hands on. The government, taking its cue from a recently appointed governor-general who declared that "for the traitors no punishment seems to me adequate and commensurate with the magnitude of the crime they committed against their king and country," employed torture and terror in an effort to quell the uprising.[7]

Ironically, in light of his opposition to the revolt, Rizal soon became one of its victims. Shortly before the fighting commenced the government had decided to let Rizal travel to Spain, aboard a Spanish ship. He was arrested along the way and returned to Manila, where he was arraigned for treason. During a long and elaborate trial the government attempted to neutralize Rizal's nationalist influence, with partial success. In December 1896 he issued a statement demonstrating his continued conviction that violence would lead to nothing but misery for the people of the Philippines. "Reforms," he wrote, "if they are to bear fruit, must come from above, for reforms that come from below are upheavals both violent and transitory." He continued, in a stinging rebuke to Bonifacio:

> I cannot do less than condemn, as I do condemn, this ridiculous and barbarous uprising, plotted behind my back, which both dishonors us Filipinos and discredits those who might have taken our part. I abominate the crimes for which it is responsible and I will have no part in it. With all my heart I am sorry for those who have rashly allowed themselves to be deceived. Let them return to their homes, and may God pardon those who have acted in bad faith.

If Rizal in living contributed little to the revolution, in dying—before a firing squad at the end of December—he provided a martyr and an icon. The effect owed principally to the circulation of "Ultimo Adios," a last testament smuggled from death row, in which Rizal declared his final solidarity with the forces striving for Philippine independence.

> Farewell, my adored country, region beloved of the sun,
> Pearl of the Orient Sea, our lost Eden.
> Departing in happiness, to you I give the sad, withered remains of my life;
> And had it been a life more brilliant, more fine, more fulfilled,
> Even so it is to you I would have given it, willingly to you.
>
> Others are giving you their lives on fields of battle,
> Fighting joyfully, without hesitation or thought for the consequence.
> How it takes place is not important. Cypress, laurel, or lily,
> Scaffold or battlefield, in combat or in cruel martyrdom,
> It is the same when what is asked of you is for your country and your home.[8]

With double irony, Bonifacio, who more than any other had sparked the uprising, also became a victim—not of the Spanish, but of his fellow insurrectos. Following early victories against government troops, the rebels began to scent victory. As they did they commenced jostling for position in the race for power that would surely follow. A political showdown occurred in March 1897 at Tejeros in Cavite province. An unruly meeting elected the brilliant young military commander, Emilio Aguinaldo, to the presidency of the provisional government. Bonifacio received only the interior ministry. As if this were not sufficient affront to the instigator of the revolution, one Aguinaldo partisan challenged Bonifacio's qualifications for even the interior post. Incensed, Bonifacio demanded a retraction. When the challenger refused, Bonifacio pulled a pistol. A shootout was averted, but Bonifacio announced, "I, as chairman of this assembly, and as President of the Supreme Council of the Katipunan, as all of you do not deny, declare this assembly dissolved, and I annul all that has been approved and resolved." He stalked out, followed by his supporters.

The rift soon became unspannable. Aguinaldo, controlling the army and now claiming the presidency, rightly suspected Bonifacio of fomenting a mutiny against the revolution, or at least against Aguinaldo. Bonifacio indeed called upon the people of the Philippines to follow him rather than Aguinaldo. At one point Bonifacio commandeered the services of a rebel contingent sent to relieve beleaguered forces led by Aguinaldo's brother, who was killed when the relief never arrived. The outraged Aguinaldo ordered Bonifacio's arrest. A court-martial found Bonifacio guilty of plotting to overthrow the revolutionary government. The court prescribed the death penalty, but Aguinaldo commuted the sentence to banishment, on grounds, as the commutation order put it, that the Philippine government "never wishes to shed blood uselessly." Yet under pressure from associates, who contended that so long as Bonifacio lived he would jeopardize the integrity of the revolution, Aguinaldo rescinded the order. On May 10, 1897, the sentence was carried out.[9]

Not surprisingly the split among the rebels did not bode well for their cause. Neither did the arrival of a new Spanish commander, Fernando Primo de Rivera, with twenty-five thousand additional troops. During the summer of 1897 Primo de Rivera applied an effective combination of military pressure and political promises against the insurgents. Reversing the no-quarter policy of his predecessor, he enticed the rebels to surrender their arms by pledging to curb the powers of the friars, to allow Filipinos representation in the Spanish Cortes, to grant freedom of speech and association and to let the leaders of the revolt go unchallenged into exile. At the same time he stepped up patrols and raids on rebel positions.

Not trusting Primo de Rivera and not knowing whether Madrid would back him even if he were sincere, Aguinaldo and his council of war hesitated to accept the offer. But with ammunition and morale running low, they finally decided they had no alternative. In December 1897 Aguinaldo agreed to Primo de Rivera's terms in a meeting at Biak-na-Bato. With forty of his associates he came down from the mountains and set sail for Hong Kong.[10]

II. The commodore and the general

The Spanish had two good reasons for the generosity of their settlement with Aguinaldo. The first was that they had no intention of honoring their commitments to the rebels, as they demonstrated not long after Aguinaldo left the islands. The second was that they were facing the growing likelihood of war with the United States. The Biak-na-Bato agreement preceded the explosion of the *Maine* by two months. Two months after the blast, hostilities between the two countries commenced.

Because America went to war in the name of opposing Spanish oppression, albeit in Cuba, and because Americans possessed a long history of anti-imperialism, Filipino nationalists expected sympathy for their cause. Initially they received it, or so they thought. Following Dewey's destruction of the Spanish fleet the American commander cabled Washington that he could capture the city of Manila with forces on hand, but seizure and retention of the rest of the archipelago would require reinforcements. While the war department prepared to dispatch the needed troops, American officials contacted Aguinaldo in Singapore, where he had stopped on his way to Europe after several weeks in Hong Kong. The American consul in Singapore, E. Spencer Pratt, pointed out the advantages of joint American-Filipino action against the Spanish. Pratt remarked that since Madrid had failed to comply with its part of the Biak-na-Bato accord, honor no longer bound Aguinaldo in the matter. Pratt went on to say, in Aguinaldo's recollection of their conversation, that the United States would grant the Philippines greater freedom and material benefits than Spain had ever promised. Aguinaldo asked for details, indicating he would appreciate a written response. Pratt requested time to consult Dewey. The next day the consul summoned Aguinaldo. As the latter recorded in his diary,

> Pratt said Dewey replied that the United States would at least recognize the independence of the Philippines under the protection of the U.S. Navy. The consul added that there was no necessity for entering into a formal written agreement because the word of the Commodore and the U.S. Consul were in fact equivalent to the most solemn pledge, that their verbal promises and assurances would be honored to the letter and were not to be classed with Spanish promises or Spanish ideas of a man's word of honor. The Consul concluded by declaring, "The Government of the United States is a very honest, just and powerful government."[11]

Aguinaldo chose to accept Pratt's oral assurances—a decision that proved a serious blunder. Witnesses later confirmed that the consul had indeed promised American support for Philippine independence. H. W. Bray, an Englishman in Singapore who acted as interpreter in the Pratt-Aguinaldo meetings, wrote to Senator Hoar in Washington after the American government began moving toward annexation, declaring, "As the man who introduced General Aguinaldo to the American Government through the Consul at Singapore, I frankly state that the conditions under which Aguinaldo promised to cooperate with Dewey were Independence under a protectorate. I am prepared to swear to this."[12]

Whether the culprit in the case was Pratt or Dewey remains unclear. Dewey denied making any commitments to Aguinaldo, whom he attempted to tarnish with faint praise. "Aguinaldo had been at one time a copyist in the Cavite arsenal under the Spanish regime," Dewey wrote. "He was not yet thirty, a soft-spoken, unimpressive little man." The admiral went on to describe his reasons for dealing with the insurgent general.

> Obviously, as our purpose was to weaken the Spaniards in every legitimate way, thus hastening the conclusion of hostilities in a war which was made to free Cuba from

Spanish oppression, operations by the insurgents against Spanish oppression in the
Philippines under certain restrictions would be welcome.

Dewey went on to assert categorically that he had promised nothing regarding
the future. "From my observation of Aguinaldo and his advisers I decided that it
would be unwise to co-operate with him or his adherents in an official manner,"
Dewey declared. "In short, my policy was to avoid any entangling alliance with
the insurgents, while I appreciated that, pending the arrival of our troops, they
might be of service."[13]

Whatever the controversy over who pledged what to whom says about the
integrity of those involved, it had little substantive effect on the course of the
events that immediately followed. Aguinaldo should have realized that neither
Dewey's nor Pratt's promises would bind the American government in Washington. Perhaps he did. In any event the rebel general was in no position to dictate
terms to the Americans. With the Spanish fleet on the bottom of Manila Bay and
the capital city at the Americans' mercy, to have held out for better conditions
might have left Aguinaldo adrift, figuratively and literally, on the China Sea. Recognizing his weakness, he made a fast trip to Hong Kong for consultation with
the other exiles and then accepted passage on the American cutter *McCulloch*,
which arrived off Manila on May 19.

At once Aguinaldo reassembled the insurgent forces. Five days after landing
he announced that "the great and powerful North American nation has demonstrated its disinterested protection to deliver us from servitude and preserve
the liberty of this Archipelago." He resumed leadership of the revolution as president of the provisional government and commander-in-chief. His troops proceeded to capture much of the region of Cavite, whence they advanced on
Manila, taking more than two thousand Spanish prisoners.[14]

Dewey kept his distance. On May 26 Navy Secretary Long cabled to warn him
to "exercise discretion most fully in all matters." Long added, "It is desirable, as
far as possible, and consistent for your success and safety, not to have political
alliances with the insurgents or any faction in the islands that would incur liability
to maintain their cause in the future." Dewey replied that he had given Aguinaldo no pledges.

> Consistently I have refrained from assisting him in any way with the force under my
> command, and on several occasions I have declined requests that I should do so. . . .
> My relations with him are cordial, but I am not in his confidence. The United States
> has not been bound in any way to assist the insurgents by any act or promises.

As something of an aside, Dewey commented, "In my opinion, these people are
far superior in their intelligence and more capable of self-government than the
natives of Cuba, and I am familiar with both races."[15]

The first body of American troops, numbering just over two thousand, arrived
at Cavite at the end of June. Two larger units, leaving San Francisco about the

same time, did not reach the Philippines until the latter part of July. Through the first week of August American forces invested Manila, which already was surrounded by Aguinaldo's soldiers. On August 9 Dewey and the commander of the American ground troops, General Wesley Merritt, requested the surrender of the Manila garrison. The Spanish refused as a matter of honor.

Sensing that the Americans were preparing to attack the city and claim possession for themselves alone, Aguinaldo ordered his troops onto the walls. The Spanish by now recognized the hopelessness of their position, and they decided that surrendering to the Americans entailed less humiliation than capitulating to the colonials. The result was a curious affair in which Spanish soldiers fought to keep the Filipinos out of the city while they allowed the Americans to enter, more or less unchallenged. On August 13 the Spanish commander delivered his sword to General Merritt. That Washington and Madrid had agreed to a ceasefire the day before—a fact of which all in the Philippines remained ignorant due to Dewey's cutting of the submarine cable—added to the singularity of the situation.

Merritt, inquiring of the war department regarding a possible joint occupation of Manila with Aguinaldo's forces, received an unequivocal reply. "There must be no joint occupation with the insurgents. . . . The insurgents and all others must recognize the military occupation and authority of the United States."[16]

III.   Rekindling the revolution

Needless to say, the outcome of the half-battle for Manila displeased Aguinaldo and his followers. In June the leaders of the revolution had declared the independence of the Philippines and called upon the Filipino people to assert their "modest but dignified place in the concert of the free nations." During the next two months, while the revolutionary army fought the Spanish and gained control of much of central Luzon, the revolution's political arm erected the machinery of government at both the national and local levels. Because the Americans' refusal to allow Filipino forces to enter Manila prevented the seating of the government there, Aguinaldo and his advisers decided at the beginning of September to locate their government at Malolos, thirty miles to the northwest.[17]

The first order of business at Malolos was drafting a constitution for the Philippine republic. Debate over the charter consumed two months and produced a document specifying as centerpiece of government a unicameral parliament to which the republic's president was responsible. Provinces enjoyed considerable autonomy under the plan, while a bill of rights protected individuals. The debate over the constitution might have continued longer, especially on the question of whether Roman Catholicism should be identified as the state religion—it was not, largely as a result of hard feelings toward the friars—but the Malolos delegates wished to get the government of the republic into operation before the conclusion of peace negotiations between the United States and Spain.

Although they beat the deadline, the Filipino leaders then had to deal with the fact that the Paris treaty, as it related to the Philippines, simply transferred title from one set of imperialists to another. The Filipinos recognized that the American Senate had yet to accept the treaty, and from the rising voices of the antiimperialist movement in America they guessed, accurately, that ratification was no sure thing. Placing their primary hopes on Bryan, whom an official of the Malolos government went so far as to call "one of the heroes of the world," and on the opponents of annexation in the Senate, they also lobbied the McKinley administration to reconsider the treaty. Felipe Agoncillo, Malolos' chief diplomatic agent, had spoken to McKinley at the beginning of October. McKinley put the envoy off, telling him to go to Paris where the treaty was being negotiated. He obliged, arguing on arrival in France that Spain lacked legal standing to convey the Philippines to the United States since the Philippines belonged solely to the Filipinos. Both parties to the talks ignored him.[18]

From Paris Agoncillo returned to Washington. He unsuccessfully sought interviews with officials of the McKinley administration. Personally shunned, he filed a memorandum with the state department that succinctly recounted recent events and outlined the Filipinos' case for independence and recognition by the United States.

1. American precept and example have influenced my people to desire an independent government.

2. Suffering, as did the Americans, from alien rule, they rose and drove out foreign masters.

3. They established, and for seven months have maintained, a form of government resembling the American, in that it is based on the right of the people to rule.

4. According to doctrines laid down by distinguished American Secretaries of State, this government is entitled to recognition by the American Republic.

5. The expelled government of Spain, having, at the time of the signing of the Treaty of Peace, been in possession of but one port, and the remainder of the Philippines, except Manila, having been in the possession of the Philippine Republic, and all attributes of sovereignty having passed from Spain, that country could give no title to the United States for the Philippine Islands.

6. Spain having no title to give, her claim cannot be rendered better by the ratification of the Treaty of Peace.

7. From the foregoing, it would seem to follow that the present recognition of the first Republic of Asia by the greatest Republic of America would be consonant with right, justice, and precedent.[19]

This and subsequent representations had no favorable effect, and as the Senate moved to vote on the treaty armed conflict between American and Filipino forces grew increasingly likely. In December American troops arrived before the city of Iloilo, intending occupation. They discovered that Filipino forces had already taken control and were disinclined to relinquish it. An uneasy standoff ensued. The situation was reproduced in other parts of the country, leading Aguinaldo in January to warn Filipino patriots not to be "seduced by promises and vain words" of any persons who would steal their birthright. All revolutionary soldiers, he reminded his followers, had "taken an oath to carry on the struggle and fight to the death for our country."[20]

Aguinaldo went on to denounce the "violent and aggressive" actions of the United States, "which has arrogated to itself the title of 'champion of oppressed nations.'" He delivered a warning:

> My government is ready to open hostilities if the American troops attempt to take forcible possession of such portion of the territory as comes under its jurisdiction. I denounce these acts before the world, in order that the conscience of mankind may pronounce its infallible verdict as to who are the true oppressors of nations and the tormentors of human kind. Upon their heads be all the blood which may be shed.

With neither side willing to back down, fighting was inevitable. It commenced outside Manila on February 4. Within hours Aguinaldo issued a declaration of war, asserting, "I have done everything possible to avoid armed conflict, in the hope of securing our independence through peaceful means and without entailing the costliest sacrifices." He continued, "But all my attempts have proved vain in the face of the unmeasured pride of the American Government and of its representatives in these Islands, who have insisted on considering me a rebel because I defend the sacred interests of my country."[21]

The outbreak of fighting in the Philippines shortly preceded the Senate's vote on the Paris treaty. Suspicious observers then and skeptical historians since have questioned the coincidence, which may have helped the cause of ratification. When a decision turns on two votes, every factor can be important. But no direct evidence has surfaced indicating an effort by the McKinley administration to precipitate hostilities in the interest of ratification. Indeed, even the most ardent expansionists would have considered such a scheme risky and as likely to backfire, by demonstrating the high costs of annexation, as not. In any case, domestic political considerations in the United States, especially Bryan's defection, had greater influence on the vote than developments in the islands—setting a pattern that would characterize American relations with the Philippines throughout the era of American control.

The Philippine-American War divided into two phases. The first, conventional phase lasted from February 1899 until November of that year. During this period Aguinaldo commanded a regular army and engaged the Americans in set-piece battles, although with decreasing success as American reinforcements continued to arrive. In the middle of November 1899 Aguinaldo abandoned conventional tactics and dispersed his troops, inaugurating the second phase of the war.

From late 1899 until May 1902, when the last of the insurgents laid down arms, the Filipinos adopted a guerrilla strategy, requiring the Americans to fight a counterinsurgency conflict.

The commander of American forces in the Philippines, General Elwell Otis, was the Philippine war's answer to George McClellan, without the latter's good looks. Despite the sweeping powers he wielded as both field commander and military governor, Otis jealously husbanded his resources for a repeatedly postponed decisive thrust. To colonels enamored of Teddy Roosevelt's brash daring, Otis appeared mired in paperwork and concern for his lines of communication. With less originality than scorn they played on his first name to produce the junior-mess epithet "Nervous Nelly."

Like McClellan, Otis eventually realized he could put off action no longer. He ordered an assault on the rebel capital of Malolos. Following a week of fighting on the approaches to the town the attacking force under General Arthur MacArthur awoke on the last day of March to find the place deserted. Otis, disappointed at this failure to capture the insurgent army, prepared a larger operation against the stronghold of Calumpit, where the insurgent general Antonio Luna had gathered a large body of troops. Calumpit eventually fell to the Americans, but Luna managed to extricate his forces, partly because of Otis's meddling with the orders of his subordinates.

In reporting the victory, Otis informed Washington that it was a stroke of fortune he had not crushed the insurgency at one blow. Now the Filipino people would have more time to become disenchanted with the oppressiveness of rule by the revolutionary government. The loss of illusions would make the Americans' task of pacifying the population easier.[22]

Although Otis in this case was trying to excuse his failure, his argument contained a certain truth. General Luna, frustrated at the Americans' advantage in firepower and at what he deemed a lack of discipline among his own soldiers, undertook a disciplinary campaign. He fired officers, throwing several in jail. He demanded greater numbers of conscripts and ordered the death penalty for a wide assortment of infractions, some quite minor, leading the irreverent (and foolhardy) in his ranks to call him "General Article One." He browbeat the peasantry and cowed cabinet officials. When certain of the latter, surveying the deteriorating military situation, suggested a negotiated settlement with the Americans, Luna flew into a rage. He struck the foreign secretary and arrested him for treason.

Aguinaldo, perceiving the damage Luna was doing to the revolutionary movement and perhaps crediting rumors that Luna wished to displace him, summoned the general to a meeting at Cabanatuan. Luna, who apparently expected a request to head a new cabinet, agreed to the conference. Under circumstances that remain unclear and for which responsibility was never definitively established, Luna met a violent death there.[23]

Squabbling at the top, although not to the point of assassination, also marked the American leadership during this period. At the beginning of March a special commission appointed by McKinley and headed by Jacob Gould Schurman, president of Cornell University, arrived in Manila. The commission had the task, as their charge put it, of examining "the existing social and political state of the various populations" and "the legislative needs of the various groups of inhabitants," and of determining "the measures which should be instituted for the maintenance of order, peace and the public welfare." Schurman had accepted the appointment with reservations. In an interview with McKinley he said frankly, "I am opposed to your Philippine policy. I never wanted the Philippine Islands." McKinley, with the guilelessness that caused opponents repeatedly to underestimate him, replied, "Oh, that need not trouble you. I didn't want the Philippine Islands either, and in the protocol to the treaty I left myself free not to take them. But in the end there was no alternative."[24]

McKinley had appointed the commission in January as part of an effort to head off an open break between the United States and the Filipino nationalists. Because the tension was increasing rapidly, Secretary of State John Hay urged the commission members to proceed to Manila with "all possible dispatch." Yet the commission, which in addition to Schurman included Charles Denby, formerly minister to China, and Dean Worcester, an ornithologist from the University of Michigan whose collecting expeditions had acquainted him with the islands, as well as Otis and Dewey, arrived too late to prevent the rupture. When the civilian members got to Manila Otis claimed that the onset of fighting had annulled the commission's authority. The general particularly objected to the commission's interviewing Filipinos—which was precisely what Schurman, Denby and Worcester had come to do—as subversive of his military mission and reckless with the lives of his soldiers. Otis tried to persuade the war department to effect the commission's recall. This failed, but Otis and Dewey boycotted the commission's meetings.[25]

Shortly after the civilians' arrival the commission issued a proclamation pledging to the people of the Philippines "the most ample liberty of self-government" consistent with the "maintenance of a wise, just, stable, effective, and economical administration of public affairs" and compatible with the "sovereign and international rights and obligations of the United States." The commission spelled out what this meant: limited autonomy under American guidance, civil liberties and fair and efficient administration. What the offer amounted to, although no one knew this at the time, was a promise to allow the Philippines about as much independence as Cuba would enjoy during the next several decades.[26]

Schurman deemed the announcement a success. "The Proclamation has produced a good effect by its spirit and contents," he wrote Secretary Hay. It was "especially efficacious in removing doubts and establishing certainty in regard to the United States attitude." Schurman judged the American position in the islands "much improved" over the previous months. Still, he was not willing to predict an imminent end to hostilities. "The insurgents, fed on silly lies, with leaders ambitious of power and money, may continue fighting until the rainy season stops everything." He added that the rebels' "incapacity to recognize facts, including their defeats," was "our greatest danger."[27]

The revolutionary government would not touch Schurman's offer. Apolinario Mabini, the president of the cabinet, offered an acid rejoinder. Noting that American professions of equality afforded little protection to people of color in the United States, Mabini asserted to his compatriots that "even if the Constitution of the United States be declared law in the Philippines, and the North American Congress grants us all, absolutely all, the rights and liberties of American citizens and the autonomy of the States recognized by the said Constitution, which is the greatest good which we may expect from annexation, race hatred will curtail these prerogatives." Filipinos, Mabini declared, must not fall victim to false promises nor allow soft words to weaken their resolve.

> Open your eyes, my beloved countrymen, while there is yet time. Fight without truce or rest, without vacillation or dismay, without measuring the time or duration. . . . Let us fight while there is in us an atom of strength; let us acquit ourselves as gallant men, now that to the present generation is reserved the battle and the sacrifices. It matters not if we die in the midst or at the end of the painful journey; the generations to come, while praying over our tombs, will reward us with tears of love and gratitude, not of bitter reproach.[28]

Notwithstanding the heroic rhetoric, the revolutionary government in April 1899 proposed a ceasefire. Otis, rightly sensing weakness, refused to grant a breathing space and rejected the proposal. In June Aguinaldo relocated the government, which had been meeting in San Isidro after the evacuation of Malolos, to Tarlac.

When American units engaged the revolutionaries during this period, the former usually prevailed easily. Yet victory in single battles brought the United States hardly closer to ultimate triumph. In August Otis summarized the problem.

> Little difficulty attends the act of taking possession of and temporarily holding any section of the country. A column of 3,000 men could march through and successfully contend with any force which the insurgents could place in its route, but they would close behind it and again prey upon the inhabitants, persecuting without mercy those who had manifested any friendly feeling toward the American troops.[29]

Although the rainy season of 1899 slowed fighting somewhat, when the rains ended the opposing troops again hit the roads and trails and each other. October brought the fiercest battles of the war. Otis launched a three-pronged effort to capture Tarlac and destroy Aguinaldo's army. American soldiers took the town on October 12, forcing the revolutionary government to move once more, to Bay-ambang. Days later the Americans captured the new capital. But in each case Aguinaldo managed to skip away just ahead of the invaders.

IV. The dirty war

By this time Aguinaldo could see that a conventional approach to the war would only fail. For several weeks various of his advisers had advocated scattering the troops and adopting a guerrilla strategy. By avoiding major clashes with the bet-ter-armed Americans, they argued, and by concentrating on operations designed to harass and demoralize the invaders, the revolution stood a better chance of success. Aguinaldo and his general staff earlier had rejected this advice as defeat-ist. Antonio Luna had done so with particular violence, which had contributed to his demise. Now there seemed no other course. In November Aguinaldo ordered his army to break into small units and take to the countryside. He per-sonally led one of the larger groups, a contingent of twelve hundred, into the mountains of the north.

The adoption of a guerrilla strategy coincided with increasing contention among the insurgents. As had been the case since Bonifacio and the Katipunan broke with Rizal, class differences plagued the nationalist movement. While Philippine independence appealed in the abstract to nearly all Filipinos, members of the elite wondered what a thorough-going revolution would do to their privi-leged position in the political, economic and social scheme of the islands. To the concerns of the ilustrados were added ethnic suspicions, especially among non-Tagalogs who feared that in an independent Philippines the Tagalog-speakers, predominant in the Manila area, would try to monopolize power. Finally, more than a few revolutionaries detected dictatorial tendencies in Aguinaldo.

The Americans did their best to widen the rifts within the nationalist move-ment. From the beginning the Schurman commission established close ties with defectors from the Malolos government and others who found American rule more appealing than that of Aguinaldo and his backers. Schurman reported with satisfaction that the commission's April proclamation brought "leading Filipinos" to visit daily. The commission encouraged the defectors by reiterating and elab-orating the April offer of the largest measure of local self-government consistent with peace and order.[30]

The insurgents' military reverses of the autumn of 1899 weakened the attrac-tiveness of their cause and exacerbated the split between accommodationists and irreconcilables. Prominent in the camp of the former was Trinidad Pardo de Tav-era, an ilustrado who like Rizal combined medical and literary attainments and who had held a cabinet post in the Aguinaldo government. Pardo de Tavera's nationalism owed as much to his disgust at the backwardness of Spanish rule as to any positive sense of solidarity with his Filipino brothers and sisters. Convinced that modernization held the key to the future of the Philippines, he found it relatively easy to accept the rule of the United States, the most modern country in the world. Reform, not independence, was the issue he cared most about. "My wishes," he wrote, "have nothing to do with the question of whether the sovereign power shall reside in foreign hands, as now, or in our own, as we aspire. I want to prepare the people so that they can not be oppressed by Government, so that they can not be exploited by the authorities, and in order that they may not look upon office as the only thing worth striving for and possessing." Pardo de Tavera believed the United States could teach Filipinos important lessons in this area. He thought he could help.[31]

To encourage the accommodationists the Schurman commission recommended that the American military government in the islands give way to a civilian administration. In a report delivered to McKinley in January 1900 Schurman and his associates said,

> The general substitution throughout the archipelago of civil for military government (though, of course, with the retention of a strong military arm) would do more than any other single occurrence to reconcile the Filipinos to American sovereignty, which would then stand revealed, not merely as an irresistible power, but as an instrument for the preservation and development of the rights and liberties of the Filipinos and the promotion of their happiness and prosperity. To secure the confidence and affection of the Filipinos it is necessary not only to study their interests, but to consult their wishes, to sympathize with their ideals and prejudices even, and (so far as the public safety permits) to let them in all local affairs govern themselves in their own way.

McKinley accepted this recommendation, and shortly after receiving the Schurman report the president appointed a second commission, headed by William Howard Taft, to establish a civilian administration for the islands.[32]

While the Americans were attempting to capitalize on divisions among the Filipinos, the Filipinos were hoping to do the same regarding the Americans. Fully cognizant of the debate the Philippine question had raised in the United States, Aguinaldo played for time, thinking that what he could not win on the battlefield in the islands he might gain in the arena of American politics. Aguinaldo assured his followers that much of the world already supported the insurgent cause, and he said he detected a trend in the same direction in the United States. "In America there is a great party that insists on the United States government recognizing Filipino independence," Aguinaldo declared. "They will compel their country to fulfill the promises made to us in all solemnity and faith. . . . The great Democratic party of the United States will win the next fall election. . . . Imperialism will fail in its mad attempts to subjugate us by force of arms."[33]

Aguinaldo may have been serious, in which case his foresight proved as poor as Bryan's. He may simply have been trying to maintain morale. In any event fighting continued. The insurgents' turn to a guerrilla strategy contributed to growing brutality on both sides. One writer on the conflict commented, unsympathetically toward Aguinaldo but with descriptive accuracy,

> If war in certain of its aspects is a temporary reversion to barbarism, guerrilla warfare is a temporary reversion to savagery. The man who orders it assumes a grave responsibility before the people whose fate is in his hands, for serious as is the material destruction which this method of warfare entails, the destruction to the orderly habits of mind and thought which, at bottom, are civilization, is even more serious. Robbery and brigandage, murder and arson follow in its wake. Guerrilla warfare means a policy of destruction, a policy of terror.

As commonly occurs in such circumstances, the ordinary people of the Philippines probably wanted most of all to be let alone. Yet the insurgents knew they could win only by making the islands ungovernable for the Americans, which led them to adopt policies designed to polarize the populace. Aguinaldo resuscitated the Katipunan as an agency of enforcement of proper revolutionary behavior and an instrument of punishment of collaboration. At first the Katipunan followed orders to turn suspected collaborators over to military officers for trial, but later the organization, and especially its progeny the Magdudukuts ("Secret Avengers"), dispensed with such niceties in favor of swifter retribution. Aguinaldo encouraged the Magdudukuts, declaring it the policy of the revolution to "exterminate all traitors."[34]

Guerrilla armies, ever on the move and usually short of supplies, do not often develop reputations for benign treatment of prisoners. While Aguinaldo's army committed no greater crimes in this regard than many others in similar straits, captured Americans fared poorly. Sometimes they were actively maltreated. Almost always they nearly starved. Evidence that the insurgents preferred to kill wounded enemies rather than be burdened with their care disposed Americans likewise to refuse to give quarter. Even had American commanders been inclined to toleration, which as the war lengthened they were not, controlling companies in the bush was impossible. The better to blend in with the population, Aguinaldo's forces doffed their uniforms, making it the more difficult to tell the friendlies from the unfriendlies. All "gugus"—or, often, "niggers"—soon came to look alike.

Defeating the guerrillas required gathering information about their movements. Potential informants, who eventually included nearly everyone as the opposing troops marched back and forth across the countryside, found themselves in the unfortunate position of risking punishment by the Americans for keeping quiet and assassination by the insurgents for talking. The most notorious technique adopted by the Americans for eliciting information was the "water cure." The victim had a large volume of water forced down his throat, to the point of severely distending his stomach and abdomen. Then his interrogators stood or knelt or jumped up and down on his swollen belly, until he decided to talk, which he usually did, or died, which also happened.

Not surprisingly, in light of the controversy surrounding the American presence in the Philippines in the first place, charges of American abuses circulated freely in the United States. Predictably the American government denied the charges or explained them away. Secretary of War Elihu Root described the circumstances confronting American troops:

> The war on the part of the Filipinos has been conducted with the barbarous cruelty common among uncivilized races, and with general disregard of the rules of civilized warfare. They deliberately adopted the policy of killing all natives, however peaceful, who were friendly to our Government, and in literally thousands of instances these poor creatures, dependent upon our soldiers for protection, have been assassinated.
>
> The Filipino troops have frequently fired upon our men from under protection of flags of truce, tortured to death American prisoners who have fallen into their hands, buried alive both Americans and friendly natives, and horribly mutilated the bodies of the American dead.

Root did not deny that some American troops had reacted inappropriately to this provocation. In the heat of the moment, he said, it was unavoidable that "soldiers fighting against such an enemy, and with their own eyes witnessing such deeds, should occasionally be regardless of their orders and retaliate by unjustifiable severities. . . . Such things happen in every war, even between two civilized nations, and they will always happen while war lasts." But they were no more the norm of American conduct in the Philippines, Root averred, than violent crime was the rule of life in the United States. On the whole the war in the Philippines was being conducted with "scrupulous regard for the rules of civilized warfare, with careful and genuine consideration for the prisoner and the noncombatant, with self-restraint, and with humanity never surpassed, if ever equaled, in any conflict, worthy only of praise, and reflecting credit upon the American people."[35]

Root denied too much. Indeed Americans were often provoked, but American troops hardly acted with "humanity never surpassed." American commanders rightfully rejected allegations that they actively sanctioned brutality. Yet by indicating a greater interest in results than in methods they let pass much that would not have borne careful scrutiny. To some degree they soothed their consciences with the knowledge that Americans often left administration of the water cure and other forms of interrogation and punishment to Filipino collaborators, especially the infamous Macabebe Scouts. All the same, evidence indicating American participation in torture is irrefutable.[36]

Part of Root's own testimony hinted at the sources of American toleration of atrocities beyond the quota characteristic of wars generally. By stressing that the tactics adopted by the Filipinos were symptomatic of "the barbarous cruelty common among uncivilized races," Root reminded his American listeners of a point most of them, even those who opposed annexation, accepted: that the conflict in the Philippines matched civilized Americans against uncivilized Filipinos. Almost no one claimed openly that the presumed civilization gap justified the various excesses American troops committed, but many considered it sufficient explanation. In fact some went so far as to blame the Filipinos for Americans' misconduct. Questioning Commissioner Taft on the issue of American brutality, Senator Thomas Patterson put the matter bluntly: "When a war is conducted by a superior race against those whom they consider inferior in the scale of civilization, is it not the experience of the world that the superior race will almost involuntarily practice inhuman conduct?" Taft replied, "There is much greater danger in such a case than in dealing with whites. There is no doubt about that."[37]

Although Root and other American officials could claim that the water cure lacked official approval, they could not deny responsibility for the policy of reconcentration. General J. Franklin Bell inaugurated the policy in Batangas province, and just as it had for the Spanish in Cuba, reconcentration in the Philippines represented a logical solution to the problem of sorting insurgent soldiers from noncombatants. In the Philippine version the inhabitants of a region were gathered into fenced, guarded compounds. Anyone found beyond camp after curfew was considered a guerrilla and liable to summary execution.

However logical, the reconcentration policy was almost guaranteed to alienate the Filipino populace. It did. The innocent were uprooted with the guilty— assuming, which most Filipinos did not, that the guerrillas were guilty of something. When disease hit the camps, as inevitably occurred in that tropical climate; it carried off children and the old in disproportionate numbers. The survivors grew hostile, many permanently, against the Americans.

Reconcentration also inflamed anti-imperialist opinion in the United States. Dozens of papers decried the policy. Numerous editors likened Bell to Spain's architect of reconcentration, Valeriano ("Butcher") Weyler. Others threw back at McKinley his comment that reconcentration was "not civilized warfare." A Baltimore journal could not decide whether it was more ironic or tragic that "we have actually come to do the thing we went to war to banish." A Detroit commentator wondered what the long-term consequences of reconcentration would be. "Is the policy of force to win us the respect and affection of a people who are saying almost unanimously that they do not like us and our ways and that they wish to be left to themselves?"[38]

While editors and politicians in the United States debated the propriety of American actions, American officers and troops in the Philippines continued their muddy, bloody chase of Aguinaldo. Since the summer of 1899 the capture of the insurgent leader had been the focus of American military efforts. But Aguinaldo always remained just out of reach. Manifestoes appeared over his signature.

"Open your eyes, my beloved compatriots, while there is time," one broadside implored in May 1900. "Fight without respite or rest, without hesitation or faltering." Yet so elusive was the rebel general that some Americans concluded that the messages were fakes and Aguinaldo was dead.[39]

One American who thought otherwise was Frederick Funston, the most controversial American officer to emerge from this contentious war. Funston, a man whose relish for battle was surpassed only by his obsession with glory, was to the Philippine war what Teddy Roosevelt was to the war in Cuba, except that Funston actually made a military difference. The Kansas native had led the 1898 charge into Malolos, only to find it deserted. At the more serious and contested battle of Calumpit, Funston had daringly seized a vital railroad bridge before the retreating insurgents could destroy it. For his heroism he was decorated and promoted.

But tales of atrocities also attached to Funston, including one to the effect that he had ordered the execution of Filipino prisoners. Funston denied it, although in a manner indicating he considered the charge almost frivolous. As he explained to an American reporter,

> I am afraid that some people at home will lie awake nights worrying about the ethics of this war, thinking that our enemy is fighting for the right of self-government. The word independent, which these people roll over their tongues so glibly, is to them a word, and not much more. It means with them simply a license to raise hell, and if they get control they would raise a fine crop of it. They are, as a rule, an illiterate, semi-savage people, who are waging war, not against tyranny, but against Anglo-Saxon order and decency.

Press correspondents quickly recognized that Funston provided good copy. To his delight they followed him everywhere. He expounded on the American objective in the Philippines: to "rawhide these bullet-headed Asians until they yell for mercy." He praised his Kansas troops, who "go for the enemy as if they were chasing jackrabbits." He philosophized on the islands' inhabitants: "A Filipino is chronically tired. He is born tired; he stays tired and he dies tired. If you hire him he will labor a few days, and then he goes out of the work business for about a week, while he attends a fiesta or two. It doesn't matter how much you pay him. A Filipino will work as hard for fifty cents a week as he will for fifty cents a day." Funston described Aguinaldo as "a cold-blooded murderer and a would-be dictator."[40]

Funston reckoned that capturing Aguinaldo would provide a brilliant finish to the war for both the United States and Funston. He laid a plan that, while beyond the bounds of the Hague convention, was nonetheless clever and, as it proved, effective. In the spring of 1901 American intelligence units intercepted a message from Aguinaldo to his brother, asking for reinforcements. Under duress the messenger revealed where the Filipino general was hiding. Funston arranged an ambush. He dressed a squadron of Macabebes in insurgent uniforms and cast them as the requested reinforcements. He portrayed himself and four other Americans as prisoners. To add verisimilitude he forwarded to Aguinaldo's base forged documents confirming the dispatch of the relief column. The ruse allowed the group to traverse fifty miles of hostile territory nearly to Aguinaldo's camp without raising suspicion.

A slight problem developed when Aguinaldo directed the "reinforcements" to leave the American prisoners some distance from the camp. The Macabebes feigned doing so, while Funston and the Americans simply fell behind the main body of the commandos. The Macabebes entered the camp unmolested, then opened fire on Aguinaldo's guard. Funston and the Americans rushed the site and grabbed Aguinaldo. Before the insurgents had time to regroup, the Americans and Macabebes spirited Aguinaldo away to the coast, where a waiting American warship picked them up.[41]

Funston assumed correctly that Aguinaldo's capture would be a personal coup. The press lionized him. The president personally congratulated him. The war department made him the youngest regular brigadier general in the army.

Although Funston erred in thinking his feat would end the insurgency, the loss of Aguinaldo signaled the beginning of the end for the rebels. On April 1, 1901, at the Malacañang palace in Manila the guerrilla commander swore an oath accepting the authority of the United States over the Philippines and pledging his allegiance to the American government. Three weeks later he publicly called on his followers to lay down arms. "Let the stream of blood cease to flow; let there be an end to tears and desolation," Aguinaldo said. "The lesson which the war holds out and the significance of which I realized only recently, leads me to the firm conviction that the complete termination of hostilities and a lasting peace are not only desirable but also absolutely essential for the well-being of the Philippines."[42]

4

Progressivism from Above
1901–1907

I. The search for order

If Aguinaldo believed peace was essential to the well-being of Filipinos, Washington thought Filipino well-being essential, or at least strongly conducive, to peace. The latter conviction motivated a proclamation by the Schurman commission that the United States intended to govern the Philippines with the interests and welfare of the Filipino people in mind. It also informed McKinley's appointment of the Taft commission to organize a civil government for the islands.

Until the beginning of 1901 the McKinley administration ruled the Philippines by executive fiat. While the war continued the president decreed laws and regulations for the islands, acting in his capacity as commander-in-chief of the armed forces. But with the termination of meaningful resistance impending, Congress insisted on affirming its prerogatives. Even as Funston chased Aguinaldo through the forests of northern Luzon the legislature approved a measure calling on McKinley to establish a permanent government for the Philippines. In addition the Spooner amendment—to the same military appropriations bill of March 1901 that included the Platt amendment for Cuba—required the president to report regularly on conditions in the Philippines, and it reserved to Congress the right to alter or repeal actions taken by the president or in his name.

The Spooner amendment did not long apply to McKinley, who fell to an anarchist's bullet and died in September. McKinley's death brought Theodore Roosevelt to the presidency, depriving the country of the opportunity to witness how one of the most unconfinable personalities in American history would have dealt with the nation's most confining office. Republican regulars were appalled. The bosses had made Roosevelt the vice-presidential nominee in Philadelphia the summer before to balance the ticket and get the raving progressive out of New York and into a quiet institution where he wouldn't hurt anyone. But now the "wild man," to use Mark Hanna's phrase, was on the loose, and there would be the devil to pay.

With Roosevelt's swearing-in, progressivism, heretofore rooted in local and state politics, blossomed at the federal level. The progressives constituted an unruly army and pursued a variety of sometimes loosely related objectives. But their agenda coalesced around the notion of rationalizing society, of applying the principles of scientific thought to the social problems of the day. Progressives tended to view poverty, unemployment, corruption in government, consumer fraud, abuse of the environment, and nearly everything else wrong with America as due to the country's failure to mobilize adequately its intellectual resources. They looked to education and expertise to remedy America's ills. Taking the method of science as their model, they proposed to make of America their great experiment.

That imperialism and progressivism arose simultaneously in the United States was not coincidental. Each embodied the notion that the world could be significantly bettered by the energy and wisdom of a peculiarly favored group of people—in the progressive case, the educated upper-middle and professional classes; in the imperialist case, Anglo-Saxon Americans. To a considerable degree, American imperialism of the early twentieth century, especially during the Republican ascendancy of Roosevelt and Taft, was progressivism writ large.

In such circumstances it was scarcely surprising that the Philippines, the primary proving ground for imperialism, also became a laboratory for progressivism. In the United States progressives had to contend with backsliders, trimmers and the otherwise unregenerate. In the Philippines the progressives had to deal with similarly benighted folk—but there such people could not vote. American progressivism, like most schemes for earthly salvation, included a strong elitist and authoritarian strain. The progressives were certain they knew best what the rest of society required, and they aimed to act on their knowledge. Democratic sensibilities in the United States forced a masking of the inclination to authoritarianism, so that a scheme for social control like prohibition of alcohol was spoken of in terms of moral uplift. In the Philippines no comparable delicacy was necessary. Americans would remake Filipino society, whether the Filipinos liked it or not.

II.   A big man for a big job

The society the Americans intended to remake could hardly have differed more from the model the progressives aimed for. Racially, the mostly Malay Filipinos rated in the average American mind well below the dark-skinned European immigrants whose growing numbers in America caused old-stock types such dismay. Linguistically, the four-score languages and dialects of the islands made the babble of Ellis Island sound almost monoglot. Religiously, many Americans judged it a toss-up whether the large majority of Filipino Catholics (including the schismatic Aglipayans) or the small minorities of Muslims, Buddhists, Shintoists and pagans were farther from the progressively Protestant God. Socially, economically and politically, the hybrid system of traditional *barangay* and Spanish *repartimiento* often appeared to combine the worst features of Asian feudalism and popish autocracy.

The presence of the elite ilustrados offered some hope, if only because the ilustrados had shown themselves adaptable to necessity. They had acquired Spanish ways under the Spanish, and they might acquire American ways under the Americans. (That many of the ilustrados had come by their Spanish ways at least partly through heredity complicated the issue, since race-mixing was not on the progressive agenda. The larger admixture of Chinese blood among the upper class complicated the situation still further.) But the ilustrados' numbers were small relative to the population as a whole. The vast majority of the nearly seven million Filipinos lived on or near the land, cultivating small plots of their own or working the larger holdings of the gentry. Their style of life had not changed much in centuries. They dwelt in bamboo and nipa huts with little furniture and slept on the floor. They ate chiefly rice, with vegetables and fruit, poultry, pork and fish added. Even assuming the cooperation of the ilustrados, this larger portion of the Filipino people presented the Americans an enormous challenge.

At first glance, William Howard Taft did not appear quite the person to meet the challenge. In later years an observer described Taft as "a large, good-natured body, entirely surrounded by people who know exactly what they want." Whether Taft knew what *he* wanted and whether he could achieve it were less clear. In fact he did and usually could, although his girth disguised his gifts. A college-mate voiced a common misconception when he remarked that Taft "stood high, but that was because he was a plodder and not because he was particularly bright." The opposite was more nearly correct, as Taft's father recognized. Referring to his son's high school teacher, Taft senior commented that the man "hit your case when he said that you had the best head of any of my boys and if you were not too lazy you would have great success."[1]

Fate linked the destinies of Taft and Roosevelt, to the lasting distress of each, and linked both to the early history of United States–Philippine relations. The two men could not have differed more. Roosevelt bullied life, rattling china and overpowering opponents. Taft was content to accept what life cast his way. Roosevelt possessed the ultimate executive temperament, thriving in the White House and by main force inventing the modern presidency. Taft had the character of a judge and the goal of a seat on the Supreme Court. This he eventually achieved, but not before the presidency nearly ruined his career.

Taft's executive detour began in January 1900, when a cable from President McKinley requesting an interview interrupted his labors on the federal circuit court for Tennessee, Kentucky, Michigan and his home state of Ohio. Taft had no idea what the president had in mind. Afterward he recalled his surprise at being asked by McKinley to chair a new commission for the Philippines. "He might as well have told me that he wanted me to take a flying machine," Taft said.[2]

Roosevelt would have leaped at the offer. In fact, at just the time McKinley appointed Taft, Roosevelt told Henry Cabot Lodge that being the first civilian governor of the Philippines was a job "I should really like to do." Aware he was being considered for the vice presidency, Roosevelt remarked that between the two he preferred the Philippine position.[3]

Taft had to think the matter over. He hesitated to relinquish his judicial post. "Perhaps it is the comfort and dignity and power without worry I like," he wrote. The Philippine assignment entailed undoubted discomfort: after accepting Taft often found the tropical heat of the islands unbearable. The new position would certainly produce a greater crop of worries than the judge was accustomed to. But War Secretary Root urged Taft to think of his country. "You have had an easy time of it holding office since you were twenty-one," Root declared. "Now your country needs you. This is a task worthy any man. This is the parting of the ways. You may go on holding the job you have in a humdrum, mediocre way. But here is something that will test you, something in the way of effort and struggle, and the question is, will you take the harder or the easier task?" McKinley dealt the deciding blow to Taft's reluctance when he assured him that accepting would not harm his judicial career and strongly hinted at appointment to the Supreme Court when a seat became available.[4]

Taft arrived in Manila in June 1900, accompanied by fellow commissioners Dean Worcester, of Michigan and the Schurman panel and the only member of the Taft board with personal experience in the islands; Henry Ide, a Vermont jurist who had served as chief justice of American Samoa; Luke Wright, a Tennessee lawyer and veteran of the Confederate army; and Bernard Moses, a history professor from the University of California. Arthur MacArthur, Otis's successor as military governor, was not particularly pleased at the commission's coming. Worcester described the scene:

Although the thermometer was in the nineties, a certain frigidity pervaded the atmosphere on our arrival, which General MacArthur, the military governor, seemed to regard in the light of an intrusion. He had been directed to provide suitable office quarters for us. To our amazement we found desks for five commissioners and five private secretaries placed in one little room in the Ayuntamiento [the American headquarters]. While it was possible to get through the room without scrambling over them, it would have been equally possible to circle it, walking on them, without stepping on the floor. In the course of our first long official interview with the General, he informed us that we were "an injection into an otherwise normal situation." ... It was General MacArthur's honestly held and frankly expressed opinion that what the Filipinos needed was "military government pinned to their backs for ten years with bayonets."

MacArthur later changed his opinion, becoming an advocate of devolution to civil government, but at first he made it difficult for the commissioners even to meet Filipinos. He also held them to the letter of their appointment, which stated they would receive legislative authority on September 1. He refused to grant them any power until then.[5]

Among the first orders of business was getting to know the territory. This in itself was a strenuous undertaking. Taft's reports contained regular descriptions of the diverse ailments he and his fellow commissioners were exposed to, from diarrhea to malaria and tuberculosis. Journeys about the archipelago required sea travel in sometimes uncertain weather, adding mal de mer to the maux de terre. Official visitations demanded enduring the hospitality and unfamiliar cuisine of locals who hoped to impress the representatives of Washington.

Despite the strain the commissioners found their travels rewarding. Worcester explained:

> Having escaped the perils of the deep, and the much graver perils of the dinner table, we returned to Manila, wearier, wiser, and sadder men than we had started, for we had learned much of the superstitions, the ignorance and the obsessions which prevailed among the Filipinos, and we knew that many of the men who from love of country had accepted office under us had done so at the peril of their lives. We had all had an excellent opportunity to come to know the Filipinos. Their dignity of bearing, their courtesy, their friendly hospitality, their love of imposing functions, and of fiestas and display, their childishness and irresponsibility in many matters, their passion for gambling, for litigation and for political intrigue, even the loves and hatreds of some of them, had been spread before us like an open book.[6]

When September and authority came the commission set to work with a will. In its first year it passed 449 measures. While the guerrilla war persisted the commissioners gave priority to legislation calculated to undermine support for the insurgents. They took their cue from testimony given to the Schurman commission by Felipe Calderón, a Manila lawyer and landowner who had helped draft the Malolos constitution but subsequently turned away from the revolution. Calderón offered an analysis of the uprising and a suggestion for ending it. Filipinos fell into three classes, he said: "the rich and intelligent element, the poorer element of the country—the element that is willing to devote itself to work—and an element that may be called intermediate, made up of clerks and writers." Calderón asserted that the third class was responsible for the rebellion. These agitators would not willingly accept peace under any circumstances, since chaos and war afforded them entree to power they would not enjoy in settled circumstances.

The United States should ignore them for the present. Instead the Americans should concentrate their efforts on the first and second groups, who sought peace "because they are weary of the state of anarchy which exists." These two groups remained suspicious of the Americans, despite Washington's fine words. They had accepted Spain's pledges of reform and been disillusioned. "The common people now lack confidence in the Americans because there have in the past been enacted laws which have never been carried out. The Spaniards made them promises which have never been fulfilled." Filipinos wanted substance to back America's sentiments. "The most important thing is to show them actual deeds." Calderón went on to say that it was difficult "to dominate the Philippine people by force." Easier, he claimed, "to dominate them by leading them on by attraction."[7]

Accepting Calderón's counsel, the Taft commission directed its efforts at Calderón's first and second groups—the ilustrados and the silent majority of peasants—in an effort to neutralize the third group of radicals and revolutionary intelligentsia. To the first class the commission offered a piece of the action: political participation and a measure of responsibility. To the second group it held out a piece of bread: a higher standard of living, with some political power eventually.

As an initial measure to coopt the ilustrados, the Taft commission established governments at the local and provincial levels. Building on a foundation laid by the Schurman panel, which had organized municipalities in certain pacified provinces, Taft and his fellows in January 1901 promulgated a comprehensive municipal code. Shortly thereafter they passed an analogous act for provincial governments. The Taft municipal code, like the ad hoc arrangement of the Schurman period, borrowed from the pueblo system instituted during the last years of Spanish rule. Many of the old pueblo boundaries delineated those of the new towns. The office of el presidente became that of the town president. The president was elected by secret ballot, as were the municipal vice president and members of the town council. The president and council appointed various municipal officials and disbursed funds allotted by the higher levels of government and whatever revenues they raised on their own. The Taft provincial code likewise accepted most Spanish geographic boundaries, although it diverged from Spanish precedent in other respects. A board of three members governed each province. Of these three the provincial governor was elected indirectly by the council members of the towns in the province. The other two members, the treasurer and the supervisor, were appointed by the American commission.[8]

The aim of all this was to involve Filipinos of what the Americans considered the better sort in the management of Filipino affairs. To a considerable extent the scheme worked. Before long the ilustrados broadly supported the American administration. Organizing under the banner of the Partido Federal, more than one hundred prominent ilustrados called for an end to anti-American activities in the islands, acceptance of American sovereignty, extension and elaboration of local and provincial self-government, and the Philippines' ultimate annexation to America as a state.

The Filipinos who joined the Partido Federal did so for various reasons. Felipe Buencamino, the original moving spirit of the party, decided Aguinaldo was more interested in Aguinaldo than in the good of the Filipinos. Buencamino hoped the Federalistas would form a barrier to Aguinaldo's ambitions. In petitioning Taft for permission to form the party, Buencamino and his associates said they were attempting to prevent the Philippines from being handed over to "robbers, assassins and abductors of the honest and peaceable people." Pedro Paterno, another prominent Federalista, was not sure the Philippines ought to go the whole way to statehood. He preferred something on the order of autonomy under an American protectorate. But at the moment Paterno believed the Philippines needed peace more than anything else, and he backed the Partido Federal as the likeliest instrument to that end. Pardo de Tavera, whom Taft described as "the most consistent Americanista in the islands" and who was elected president of the party at its founding conference, contended that the political and cultural incoherence of the Philippines rendered the islands unfit for independence and therefore that attachment to the United States afforded the greatest hope for social progress.[9]

Naturally the lure of office attracted many. The Partido Federal soon came to comprise nearly 300 local committees and more than 150,000 members. The Taft commission drew almost exclusively from this conservative cadre in filling numerous appointive posts reserved for Filipinos. On account of their traditional standing in the Filipino community and of American-dictated restrictions on the franchise, Federalists locked up nearly all the elective positions as well, including most of the provincial governorships.[10]

For the first several years of the American era the arrangement served both sides well. "The spread of the Federal party is wonderful," Taft told Root. Taft described the Partido Federal as the "strongest instrumentality" for bringing peace, and he asserted that "it ought to be favored and encouraged as much as possible." It was. The Federalistas got the plums of office, and in exchange they helped dissolve the insurgency and dissipate demands for independence.[11]

Yet problems arose. One, which would come into the open in 1907, resulted from the refusal of important factions in the islands, including members of Calderón's third group of revolutionary agitators, to accept the American-ilustrado condominium of political power. The insurgency finally ran out of steam in April 1902, when General Miguel Malvar, the last of the major rebel leaders, surrendered. But the collapse of the rebellion did not mark the end of the nationalist movement, nor did it signal popular acceptance of the ilustrados' local political hegemony.

The cooption scheme suffered other deficiencies. While the Taft commission could deliver offices to Filipinos, it had less luck transferring American progressive notions of how officeholders should conduct themselves. Coming from a cultural tradition in which personal loyalties mattered more than concern for an abstract public interest—from a tradition, in fact, not unlike that which allowed the progressives' betes noires in the United States, the urban political bosses, to win the support of recent immigrants to America—Filipino officials tended to look after their own first. Much like the American bosses, they deemed politics a bargain in which votes were exchanged for services rendered and in which a certain amount of what the progressives called graft was simply a perquisite of power.

Taft could not claim that the Americans in the islands were setting the best personal example. Rectitude generally marked the actions of those at the top of the American hierarchy, but further down standards slipped considerably. To Taft's dismay the government of the Philippines did not attract the upstanding sort of Americans he had hoped for. In March 1903 he described the problem to Root. "We are beginning to reap a new crop of defalcations," Taft wrote, "due to the temptations to dishonesty that beset young Americans removed from the restraints of home life, without their families and with a disposition to gamble or drink or lead a lewd life." Taft remarked half-seriously that the Philippines appeared to be playing the role for America Australia had played for Britain. "The number of sweet-scented Americans that we have in the Islands, thugs, toughs, drunkards, vagrants, and thieves indicates that you must be becoming more moral in the states by reason of the loss of these gentry."[12]

III.   Education for life

The institutional example of the American government of the Philippines was hardly better. Trading offices for acquiescence in American rule, as the Taft government was doing, was not what the progressives had set out to accomplish in the islands. In fact the practice contradicted the essential values of progressivism, partaking more of the workings of the urban political machines. Yet in the interests of an ostensibly higher good, in this case pacification of the Filipinos and adherence of the archipelago to the United States, the American government was willing to compromise its principles. It would not be the last time.

Even while they contributed to the delinquency of Filipinos, the American rulers sought to mitigate the effects of their contribution by the favored progressive device of education. Just as progressives in the United States hoped to instill middle-class values in recent immigrants to America, so American progressives in the Philippines aimed to bring traditional American mores to the islands.

At times it appeared a monumental task. Commissioner Schurman had despaired that the Filipinos would ever be able to stand on their own. "Filipinos in general are incapable of self-government," Schurman wrote. "The masses are ignorant and the few capable are without experience, except of Spanish misgovernment." Edwin Kemmerer, an adviser on economic matters, remarked,

> The average Filipino is proverbial for his lack of foresight and thrift. He is a creature of the present; his wants do not extend far into the future and even if they did he does not possess the capacity of sacrificing the trifling pleasure of the moment in order to satisfy them. The influence of this lack of foresight, of this inability to feel future wants, upon his honesty, his industry, in fact upon his entire character as a man, and his efficiency as a laborer, are well known.

Taft developed a similar view. As he told an audience on a visit to America,

> In the Philippine Islands ninety per cent of the inhabitants are still in a hopeless condition of ignorance, and utterly unable intelligently to wield political control. They are subject, like the waves of the sea, to the influence of the moment, and any educated Filipino can carry them in one direction or another, as the opportunity and occasion shall permit.

Commissioner Luke Wright asserted of the Filipinos that "the great mass of them care but little under what form of government they live, and the educated and intelligent among them as a rule recognize their utter inability to maintain an independent government of their own." Henry Hill Bandholtz, head of the Philippine Constabulary, attributed the problem to a basic deficiency of common sense. Bandholtz commented in wonder and frustration that "while a native will sell you a mango for ten cents, it is frequently impossible to induce him to sell you two dozen for two pesos and two pesetas. . . . If you propose to buy all, he will frequently refuse point blank, stating that that would leave him without any to sell to other people." Bandholtz saw little reason for hope. "As long as we have intellects of this class to deal with," he declared, "there is no use."[13]

To some extent the Americans' disparagement of the Filipinos was designed, consciously or otherwise, to excuse the failings of the American government and magnify its successes. And to a considerable degree the criticism reflected the racist and ethnocentric bias characteristic of contemporary American society, a bias nearly all Americans brought to the islands. Either way the gap between Filipino practices and American expectations justified, in American thinking, a major effort of cultural intervention. Education would provide the vehicle.

Taft's notion of education embraced the progressive ideal of readying persons broadly for life in a democratic society. "The problem the United States has entered upon in these Islands," Taft said, "is to prepare a whole people for self-government, and that problem includes not only the teaching of that people how to read, write and figure in arithmetic, but also to teach that people that if they would have prosperity they must labor and to teach them how to labor." On another occasion Taft put the connection between education and government more succinctly: "We must have a self-governing people before we can turn this government over to them."[14]

While Taft set the tone of educational policy, he left the details of implementation to individuals with greater expertise in the subject. To head his education program Taft selected Fred Atkinson, a secondary-school principal from Massachusetts recommended by Charles Eliot, the reforming president of Harvard University. Atkinson impressed Taft with what the commissioner called Atkinson's "thorough preparation in the modern educational methods" and with his belief that Filipino education must first be utilitarian. Atkinson explained his thinking:

> We must beware the possibility of overdoing the matter of higher education and unfitting the Filipino for practical work. We should heed the lesson taught us in our reconstruction period when we started to educate the negro. The education of the masses here must be an agricultural and industrial one, after the pattern of our Tuskegee Institute at home.

Taft also appreciated the pragmatic administrative approach Atkinson brought to his post. Atkinson knew what he wanted to achieve, but he recognized that any definitive selection of methods must await results of the first trials in mass education in the islands. Though American objectives might set the goals, Philippine realities must indicate the path to those goals. "The field is so new in the Philippines that experience in the United States can hardly seem to furnish much of a guide for what must be done here. It will be largely original work."[15]

This work encompassed the establishment of primary schools in nearly every Filipino barrio, intermediate schools in the principal barrios, or *poblaciónes*, of the municipalities, and secondary schools in every province. An agricultural institute was founded on the island of Negros, while Manila received several institutions of higher education, including a normal school, an arts and trades school, a nautical school, a nursing school and the University of the Philippines. Staffing many of the schools were members of an initial group of six hundred eager Americans, who arrived in August 1901 aboard the transport *Thomas* and who lived in Philippine memory afterward as the "Thomasites."

If in politics the Americans followed Spanish examples in the Philippines, in educational matters they largely ignored precedent. Under Spain's rule public schools had existed, established by royal fiat in 1863. But the public schools were chronically underfunded, and the instruction provided was, in the accurate words of Joseph Ralston Hayden, later vice governor of the islands, "so slight and so archaic as to be inadequate as a preparation for life in a modern society." Consequently education remained largely the work of the Roman Catholic church. Catholic education in the Philippines compared favorably with church-sponsored efforts in Spain and in Spain's other colonies. A 1903 estimate put the literacy rate among individuals over nine years of age at 44 percent. Even so, dissatisfaction with the educational system had figured significantly in the activities of the Malolos government, and the republicans enacted a number of measures designed to

strengthen education from bottom to top, specifying hours of instruction, curric-
ula, qualifications for teachers and the like.[16]

But a revolutionary war was not the most propitious time for educational
reform, and in any event the Americans possessed their own ideas regarding education. The Americans intended especially to diminish the role of the Catholic
church, which to most American progressives seemed an institution based on
superstition and devoted to anachronism. Yet just as considerations of political
expedience were watering down America's devotion to democracy in the Philippines, so the pressures of the moment militated against a complete separation
of church and state. In hearings before the Taft commission a variety of witnesses
expressed sufficient distress at the thought of entirely secular schools that the
commission feared a popular boycott.

The commissioners compromised on the issue. Bernard Moses and Henry Ide
favored a total ban on publicly supported religious education, as did education
chief Fred Atkinson and most spokesmen for the ilustrados, who, having dises-
tablished the Catholic church in the Malolos constitution, had no desire to see it
reenter government through the back door of the schools. But the rest of the
commissioners—Taft, Worcester and Wright—preferred a measure outlawing
religious instruction on public-school premises during school hours while opening
buildings three days a week to after-school classes conducted by priests and other
teachers of religion. Taft summarized the reasoning of the commission's majority
when he explained, "It was of the highest importance that the Filipino people
should understand that the Commission did not come here to change the religion
of anybody." If the commission could make the Filipino people realize this, "then
it would be worth all the inconvenience or occasional friction between over-zeal-
ous priests and tactless teachers, which might possibly occur."[17]

A second issue, of even greater importance, involved the language of instruction. Because no single language served as the mother tongue for a majority of
the Filipino population, with each of eight languages claiming significant numbers of speakers and dozens more serving smaller populations, none offered itself
as the obvious national idiom. The Spanish government had used Spanish as the
language of government and schools, and the ilustrados, educated in the Spanish
system and comfortable in the Spanish language, generally preferred to retain it.
But beyond the fact that Spanish had little currency outside the ilustrado class,
the adoption of Spanish would have created daunting political problems in the
United States. Washington would have been hard pressed to defend a decision
in favor of Spanish to Americans recently encouraged to see Spain as the epitome
of decadence. Though accepting Spanish as a language did not necessarily imply
adopting Spain's cultural and political values, the experience of German-speakers
in the United States during World War I would demonstrate the capacity of
demagogues to create a connection in the public mind between use of a language
and loyalty to the country of its origin. Besides, from the purely logistical stand-

point of staffing the new schools, there were not enough educated Filipinos to accomplish the task. The teachers would have to come from America, where it was far easier to find anglophones than speakers of Spanish.

The ideology of imperialism also figured in the decision for English. Most progressives, certainly the majority of those attracted to service in the Philippines, accepted the idea of Anglo-Saxon superiority. Americans would civilize and uplift the Filipinos by bringing them American culture, language included. English was spreading throughout the world as various populations recognized its worth, and Filipinos would benefit from joining the favored group. Education superintendent David Barrows, successor to Atkinson, explained:

> English is the lingua franca of the Far East. It is spoken in the ports from Hakodate to Australia. It is the common language of business and social intercourse between the different nations from America westward to the Levant. It is without rival the most useful language which a man can know. It will be more used within the next ten years, and to the Filipino the possession of English is the gateway into that busy and fervid life of commerce, of modern science, of diplomacy and politics in which he aspires to shine.[18]

Atkinson, Barrows and other American officials believed English would foster a spirit of democracy. Notwithstanding the overthrow of Spanish rule, Americans still detected the shadow of tradition across the land. In particular they decried what they called "caciquism." Taft defined the phenomenon as "the subjection of the ordinary uneducated Filipino to a boss or master who lives in the neighborhood, and who by reason of his wealth and education is regarded as entitled to control by the ignorant." James LeRoy, a Taft commission staffer, depicted the arrangement in greater detail:

> Imagine a rural community, secure in the political dominion of one selectman, or of one or two families of selectmen, and at the social wink and nod of the unofficial manor house. But picture that sort of local leadership set up in a community where only two, four, or twelve families out of a population of ten thousand or more live in stone houses with wood floors, and the rest in cane shacks, dependent on those above them for employment or a piece of land to till, or the money advances inevitably needed each year to till it. Finally, transfer your manor to the tropics, where fertility of soil and enervation of climate breed laziness and inertia, above and below in society, and you have some idea of what caciquism is in Philippine village life.[19]

Just as progressives in America sought to break the rule of political bosses over the unlettered masses, so American progressives in the Philippines sought to overthrow the caciques. English would serve as an important tool in the process, for it would deprive the caciques of influence independent of that derived from the Americans. Taft and other American officials did not intend a social revolution in the Philippines. Their reliance on the ilustrados and the Partido Federal indicated clearly their contentment with a political system controlled by an elite. But just as did progressives in the United States, they insisted that this be an enlightened elite, which by their definition meant one that embraced American values—and America's language. By emphasizing English, American officials would help transfer the loyalties of the peasants from the reactionary caciques to the more forward-looking elite associated with the American government. And because resentment against the caciques had fueled peasant unrest for decades, the switch to English would serve the objective of social stabilization, particularly necessary in the chaotic—often criminally so—aftermath of the war. Barrows predicted,

> If we can give the Filipino husbandman a knowledge of the English language, and even the most elemental acquaintance with English writings, we will free him from that degraded dependence upon the man of influence of his own race which made possible not merely insurrection but that fairly unparalleled epidemic of crime which we have seen in the islands during the past few years.[20]

For these reasons the commission specified English as the language of instruction in all schools. In choosing such a course the commission members interpreted in their own fashion the directions they had received from McKinley, which stated explicitly that education should be conducted "in the first instance in every part of the islands in the language of the people." Fortunately for loose construction the directions also asserted that "in view of the great number of languages spoken by the different tribes, it is especially important to the prosperity of the islands that a common medium of communication be established, and it is equally obvious that this medium should be the English language." The commission decided to stress the latter injunction, and in a short time English replaced the various vernaculars in schools throughout the country.[21]

IV.   God and country

The virile Protestantism that gave wide circulation to the ideas of Josiah Strong and provided much of the impetus to American imperialism predictably emerged as a powerful influence in the Philippines. When McKinley told a group of Methodists that his decision to annex the Philippines reflected his felt obligation to "Christianize" the Filipinos—90 percent of whom were Catholics—he gave away the American religious agenda in the islands. Simply on grounds of concern for the eternal well-being of Filipino souls, most Americans would have agreed that the Filipinos needed Christianizing, the Catholic Filipinos most of all. Because Catholicism seemed to summarize the backward, anti-progressive traditionalism of the islands' people, Protestant proselytizing also dovetailed with the progressives' plans for social, political and cultural reform.[22]

Protestant spokespersons had early taken a forward position in the debate over the annexation of the Philippines. Two weeks after Dewey's victory at Manila

Bay the Presbyterian general assembly announced that "God has given into our hands, that is, into the hands of American Christians, the Philippine Islands." The Presbyterians went on to say that "by the very guns of our battleships" God had "summoned us to go up and possess the land." Not all Protestants heard the same message over the roar of battle, and one skeptic reminded his listeners that the kingdom of heaven was scheduled to arrive "as a mustard seed and not as a thirteen-inch shell." But on the whole the Protestant establishment supported annexation, and when it became accomplished fact clerics and laity prepared to do their part in the service of gospel and flag.[23]

Persons who see justice on both sides of contentious issues rarely become missionaries. Those Protestant missionaries who migrated to the Philippines seldom questioned American motives or policy. If not all subscribed entirely to the view expressed by one Baptist that "the purpose and attitude of our country is absolutely altruistic," few quarreled with the overall thrust of his remarks. The missionaries had little sympathy with the notion that Aguinaldo and the insurgents were freedom fighters. On the contrary, the missionaries usually considered the motives of the rebels sinfully selfish. The secretary of the Presbyterian missionary board characterized Aguinaldo as an "Oriental despot." Once in power, he said, Aguinaldo would inaugurate a rule as bloody as the Turkish sultan's.[24]

While many Americans still shied from the term "imperialism" as descriptive of what the United States was about in the Philippines, the missionaries often had fewer compunctions. The Reverend Wallace Radcliffe asserted forthrightly,

> Imperialism is in the air; but it has new definitions and better inventions. It is republicanism "writ large." It is imperialism, not for domination but for civilization; not for absolutism but for self-government. American imperialism is enthusiastic, optimistic and beneficial republicanism. Imperialism expresses itself by expansion. I believe in imperialism because I believe in foreign missions. Our Foreign Mission Board can teach Congress how to deal with remote dependencies. . . . The peal of the trumpet rings out over the Pacific. The Church must go where America goes.

Another enthusiast asked rhetorically, "Has it ever occurred to you that Jesus was the most imperial of the imperialists?" The *Foreign Missionary Journal* denounced anti-imperialism as "the invention of the devil to oppose foreign missions."[25]

The Protestant missionaries approved a firm policy of regeneration on the part of American officials, and they opposed what they considered equivocation in the face of local resistance. They objected vigorously to the Taft commission's compromise on the issue of religious instruction in the schools. Immediately upon annexation a Protestant clergyman predicted that the Catholics would make "desperate efforts to hold the schools in their power and try to perpetuate the old system." When the Taft commission allowed priests to use public-school facilities for religious instruction, Protestants feared that the Catholics' subversive attempts were succeeding. A Baptist missionary accused the government of surrendering to the "Romanist party." From Pangasinan province a Methodist teacher reported that the Catholics had infested the schools, forcing students to attend mass and warning them to close their ears to the Protestants. The missionaries were especially sensitive on the issue of the schools, for they considered American-sponsored education their primary weapon in the struggle against the Philippines' papist legacy. As one Baptist put the matter, "Every public school can be counted an evangelical force in a Roman Catholic country."[26]

While differing on details with Taft and the administration in Manila, the missionaries shared the larger objectives of the American government of the islands. They desired to break the hold of what they considered ignorance and superstition on the Filipino people and to replace these traditionalist relics with the values of modern education, hard work and progress. They sought to diminish the attachment of the peasants to the caciques and the priests and to reorient them toward the American government and the American and Filipino classes associated with the United States. The situation under the Americans mirrored that under the Spanish: the secular and religious arms of the ruling power were cooperating in the pacification of the Philippines and the connection of the colony to the metropolis. The missionaries did not usually forget their ultimate heavenly objective, but in the meantime they were happy enough to collaborate with Caesar. In common with more than a few other Americans interested in the islands, the missionaries understood an important possible side effect of success in their endeavors to transfer American standards to the Philippines. As one missionary predicted, regarding America's Filipino charges, "By the time they are really ready for independence, they will not want it. . . . They will then realize what an honor it is to be a part of the greatest nation in the world."[27]

V.   The sweet taste of power

The missionaries experienced little success proselytizing the Filipinos, and even ninety years later the vast majority in the islands remained firmly wedded to Catholicism. Nor did the missionaries or the secular reformers have much luck inculcating in Filipinos the political and social standards of American progressivism. The next several decades would demonstrate the Filipinos' considerable resistance to the importation of American value systems. One of the particular frustrations of the American experience in the Philippines was the unwillingness of Filipinos to accept American notions of efficiency and honesty in government. To a significant degree the Americans had themselves to blame, as their cozy arrangement with the Partido Federal demonstrated. Yet this hardly lessened the irony of the fact that while Americans came to the Philippines espousing the principles of the Civil Service League, they left the place looking worse than Tammany Hall.

Had selflessness exhausted the Americans' program, they would have been sorely discouraged. On the other hand, had selflessness constituted the entire, or even the primary, impetus behind acquisition of the Philippines, the United States never would have bothered. The desire to do well by the Filipinos was not a trivial consideration for Americans. If nothing else it provided ethical cover for baser motives. But it was precisely these baser motives that paid the political freight—that determined the timing and circumstances of going in, staying and eventually getting out.

That American interest in the Philippines transcended the eleemosynary was revealed in the first instance by Americans' insistence that the government of the islands cover its costs. The Schurman commission asserted that though Philippine finances should be managed "not for the advantage of the sovereign power but for the benefit of the people and the development of the country," the islands "should be made self-supporting." The Schurman board considered this rule important enough to warrant underlining: the panel declared that self-sufficiency "should be the principal aim of the United States in the financial administration of the Philippines."

Schurman foresaw little difficulty achieving this goal. In light of the islands' natural wealth, "the archipelago will be easily capable of maintaining itself." Philippine wealth would appreciate with improvements in transportation and developments in opportunities for investment. Consequently the economic burden of administration would fall only lightly on the Filipino people.[28]

The Taft commission accepted the Schurman recommendations and attempted to implement them. The Americans inherited from the Spanish a tax code based on the *cédula*, originally a head tax levied on the indios in recognition of Spain's sovereignty. In the last year before the revolution disrupted tax collections, the cédula and its variants, including a poll tax on Chinese in the islands and lump-sum tribute payments from tribal groups who resisted individual capitation, accounted for nearly three-fifths of government revenues. Most of the balance came from fees associated with two government monopolies, one of lotteries and the other of the opium trade.

To the progressives' way of thinking the system needed overhaul. Needless to say, an America working toward prohibition found it embarrassing to rely for revenue on government opium sales, despite opium's being legal in the United States at the time of annexation. The traffic was phased out, and with it the revenues it generated. The lottery for similar reasons was canceled. As for the cédula, although its rate increased with income, the increase was insufficient to make it a meaningfully graduated tax. In a country of gross disparities of wealth it weighed far more heavily on the poor than on the rich.

But revising the cédula, for example along lines that in the United States were leading to a federal income tax, threatened to alienate the elite the Americans were counting on to support American rule in the islands. In various hearings on the tax code the ilustrados stated their objections vigorously. Their arguments mixed the sophistical with the straightforward. Changes, they said, would disrupt society, would injure the innocent, would stifle economic development. At bottom the ilustrados simply disliked the idea of paying more.

As a result the American commission retreated from its reforming ideas, in some instances falling back beyond the original position. The code adopted scrapped even the mildly graduated scales of the cédula, levying instead a flat one peso per person. It abandoned a proposed tax on corporations, a measure progressives in America were advocating for the United States. It set aside an inheritance tax, also a device favored by progressives at home.[29]

If political convenience tempered the progressive impulse in matters relating to Philippine internal taxes, the pulling and hauling increased exponentially when tariffs between the Philippines and America came under consideration. The Republican party had been and would remain the party of high duties. From well before the McKinley tariff of 1890 to after the Hawley-Smoot tariff of 1930 the GOP looked out for the interests of American business, leaving consumers and foreigners to fend for themselves. Progressive Republicans like Roosevelt managed to chain the dogs of protection for a time, but the leash occasionally loosened. Taft was as progressive as Roosevelt in certain matters, and when he ran for president in 1908 the former Philippine governor promised tariff reform. Following election and inauguration he called a special session of Congress to consider the matter. Yet while the Payne-Aldrich tariff that emerged, and which Taft dutifully defended as the Republicans' best ever, decreased duties averaged across the board, it raised the tax on several hundred of the most competitive items.

How the Republicans' tariff tricks affected the Philippines depended on the islands' political status vis-à-vis the United States. Were they foreign territories and hence subject to import taxes? Or had annexation made them part of the United States, landing them inside the tariff wall? These questions, which also involved Puerto Rico, were part of a larger constellation of issues involving rights of individuals as well as of property. Basic to all was the question of the degree to which American law, in particular the American constitution, applied to the island possessions. As the phrase of the day went, Did the constitution follow the flag?

The Supreme Court settled the matter, after a fashion, in 1901, in a decision in what collectively were called the insular cases. The court declared that while certain fundamental rights, such as those guaranteed by the first ten amendments to the constitution, automatically applied to the Philippines and Puerto Rico, the rest of the constitution did not necessarily do so, and would only if Congress positively decreed to such effect. Elihu Root summarized the court's ruling with the remark that "the constitution follows the flag, but it does not catch up with it." Taft, noting the narrow five-to-four vote on the insular cases, commented wryly,

> I do not know who it is that said so, but it amused me very much when I heard it, that the position of the court was in this wise: that four of the judges said the Constitution did follow the flag, that four of them said it did not ... and one said, "It sometimes follows the flag and sometimes does not, and I will tell you when it does and when it does not."

The insular decision, which seemed to many observers to reflect the political mood of the times, also provoked the best-known remark by Finley Peter Dunne's cynical Mr. Dooley: "No matter whether the Constitution follows the flag or not, th' Supreme Court follows th' illiction returns."[30]

The insular decision placed the Philippines neither inside nor outside the American tariff wall. General rates passed by Congress did not apply to goods entering America from the Philippines, but Congress might mandate special schedules for the islands. In pursuit of one such schedule Taft traveled to Washington at the end of 1901. Promoting a bill reorganizing the Philippine government, Taft also lobbied for a large reduction—at least 50 percent, preferably 75—in the rates of the current tariff on imports from the Philippines. A reduction of this magnitude, Taft thought, was needed to make Philippine products competitive in America, thereby promoting Philippine prosperity. Yet Taft respected the political clout of those groups that would be competing against imports from the islands, and he cast his argument in different terms. He explained his request for a reduction to the Senate Philippines committee:

> We asked for that action chiefly for a sentimental reason. The immediate effect and the effect for some years upon the traffic between the United States and the islands of a reduction of 50 per cent, or 75 per cent, I think, is not likely to be very large. Trade of that sort is established gradually, but if we go back to the Filipino people with the statement that Congress has recognized the relation of the United States to these islands as differing from that of Cuba, for instance, which is not "territory belonging to the United States," to use the expression of the Supreme Court, we shall be in a position to point them not only to the Government bill, which we hope may pass, but also to this discrimination in their favor, which will be a great aid to us in fulfilling the statements we have made that the American people are friendly to them and are anxious to show that friendliness by something substantial.

Some of the committee members chose to take Taft's comments with a grain of salt—or, more appropriately in this case, sugar. Senator Charles Culberson of Texas reminded Taft of an earlier statement by the commission that a 50 percent reduction in the tariff on sugar and other commodities would cause Philippine exports to America to grow by "leaps and bounds." Did the commissioner still hold that view? Taft replied that "leaps and bounds" was a "rhetorical expression." He asserted again that the proposed reduction in the tariff would not greatly magnify trade, and in any event Philippine production would hardly shatter prices in America. "I do not think the amount of sugar raised there now will very materially affect the market here." He conceded that tobacco growers in the Philippines would benefit "to some extent," but again not so much as to disrupt domestic sales in the United States.[31]

While Taft sought to reassure American sugar and tobacco producers, he appealed to other, broader, business interests. He explained that a small immediate investment, in the form of tariff preference, would yield substantial dividends in the future. "Fair and proper treatment to the Philippines now," he predicted, "will eventually result in their being our most valuable possessions. The Eastern trade offers a great chance for our surplus manufactured goods and produce, as well as employment for American banks, capital, vessels, etc." Taft hoped for eventual free trade with the islands, and although this seemed out of the question for the time being, he allowed himself to speculate:

> If we ultimately take the Philippines in behind the tariff wall . . . and give them the benefit for their peculiar products of the markets of the United States, it will have a tendency to develop that whole country, of inviting the capital of the United States into the islands, and of creating a trade between the islands and this country which can not but be beneficial to both. . . . Is it wild to suppose that the people of the islands will understand the benefit that they derive from such association with the United States and will prefer to maintain some sort of bond so that they may be within the tariff wall and enjoy the markets, rather than separate themselves and become independent and lose the valuable business which our guardianship of them and our obligation to look after them has brought to them?[32]

Taft's argument for free trade as a device to encourage Filipino loyalty to the United States would bear fruit later, but in this case his efforts fell short. The bill Congress passed and Roosevelt signed into law in March 1902 called for a reduction of only 25 percent in the rates that applied to the Philippines—half what Taft considered minimally acceptable and one-third what he really wanted.

Taft got less than he desired from Congress on another economic issue as well. For decades the Philippine economy had suffered from dislocations in its money supply, especially in the balance between gold and silver. The Philippine currency was small compared with those of its neighbors and trading partners, and for decades relative values of gold and silver had fluctuated wildly, reacting to shifting patterns of trade and to such political upheavals as the Sepoy Mutiny in India, the Boer War in South Africa and the Boxer rebellion in China—not to mention the Philippine revolt against Spain and the war against the United States. The resulting chaos had benefited speculators but rendered impossible stable growth of the Philippine economy. Taft requested Congress to take action on the issue, so that Filipino businessmen might make informed investment decisions. The legislators initially declined. Lawmakers from the western silver states opposed a gold standard for the Philippines, as setting a bad precedent for America and diminishing the value of silver stocks. The silverites also pointed out the futility of gold for the Philippines, given the proximity of the islands to China, which used silver. Eastern gold bugs, having held the line against Populists and Democrats in the United States, resisted silver for the Philippines.

Eventually and grudgingly, and with an eye to increasing the value of America's Philippine investment, Congress allowed a bimetallic currency for the islands. But the delay and difficulty Taft experienced achieving it, like his failure to persuade the legislators to roll back the tariff significantly and the compromises he made on tax reform, demonstrated once again the limits perceived political necessity placed upon the progressive inclinations of American administrators in the islands. The United States professed to rule the Philippines in the interests of Filipinos. It did—in the interest of some Filipinos, the members of the upper class Washington needed to help govern the country. Yet even in the case of the ilustrados, and as a general principle, the United States ran the Philippines in the interests of Americans, specifically Americans informed and energetic enough to seize the appropriate levers of power in Washington. Any connection between these interests and those of the Filipino people at large—or, for that matter, of the American people at large—was basically coincidental.

VI.   Rising sun, seen through half-open door

Behind the debates over the tariff, money and tax reform lay a growing American concern about the shifting balance of power in the Far East. Since the 1890s observant Americans had watched Japan with interest tending to suspicion. Few would have admitted it, but what triggered American attention was the fact that Japan was attempting much the same thing in Asia and the Pacific as the United States, and with better reason. Many of the arguments of American propagandists of expansion applied, a fortiori, to Japan. The Meiji restoration had introduced the Japanese to western ideas, including the Malthusian notion that populations inevitably outstrip resources. Malthus enjoyed a vogue among Japan's intellectuals in the late nineteenth century, causing Japanese leaders to look abroad to relieve the pressure. One group encouraged peaceful emigration to such countries as the United States, Hawaii, China, Korea and the Philippines. An apostle of emigration—Japan's answer to John Fiske—predicted that within a generation "there will be established new Japans wherever the waves of the Pacific washed, the lights of the southern polestar reached, or the warm Black Currents enveloped. . . . Certainly our future history will be a history of the establishment of new Japans everywhere in the world." Another group urged a more forceful—Nippo-Rooseveltian, as it were—approach. This school did not exclude the emigrationists. In fact the publicist just cited declared, as tension with China grew in the mid-1890s, "I am not advocating plundering of other lands.

But I insist on war with China in order to transform Japan, hitherto a contracting nation, into an expansive nation." The war with China came, and success followed, lending prestige and credibility to the militarists. Heady with victory, they spoke of taking Manchuria, Korea and Taiwan, perhaps even planting the flag in the Philippines.[33]

At this time American eyes had yet to look possessively upon the Philippines, but Japanese and Americans bumped in another Pacific locale: Hawaii. Cleveland's decision against annexation after the 1893 coup left Hawaii in a state of limbo, a state some in America considered an invitation to intrigue or pressure from Japan. Japanese in Hawaii numbered more than 20,000, a figure far beyond that of Americans and sufficient for the Japanese government to feel politically required to demonstrate care for their protection. It did so by sending Japanese warships for periodic visits. This *Maine*-like tactic alarmed the Americans in Hawaii and their continental supporters, who conjured a specter of the yellow peril and agitated to curtail Japanese influence. Tension peaked in 1897 when officials in Honolulu turned back three ships carrying more than a thousand would-be immigrants from Japan. Tokyo took offense and sent a forceful note to the Hawaiian government, delivered via cruiser. The protest backfired. In cranking American fears still further Japan's action clinched the case of America's Hawaii-annexationists. By joint resolution Congress approved acquisition in 1898.

The annexation of Hawaii put that archipelago beyond Japan's reach, as the treaty of Paris did for the Philippines the following year. But by transforming the United States into a full-fledged Asian-Pacific power, the developments of the late 1890s placed America and Japan even more in each other's paths. They also put both in the way of the European imperialists. At the turn of the century the world's chancelleries worried overtime about China. Creeping senescence was paralyzing the sick man of the east, and the principal question appeared to be whether the vultures would let the carcass quit quivering before they dined. Yet the very weakness of the Qing dynasty afforded a certain protection. With Europe increasingly armed and the powers preparing for the war many expected imminently, not British nor French nor Germans nor Russians wished to make the move that would trip the juggernaut.

America's interest consisted in keeping the vultures aloft and the juggernaut still. What remained of America's anti-imperialist tradition, remobilized by the fight over the Philippines, would probably not have allowed an American government to seize a sphere for the United States from a disintegrating China, if circumstances came to that. Besides, by maintaining China whole and open to foreign trade, the United States would maintain the access to markets that formed the raison d'être of its Asian policy. To this end the McKinley administration issued a pair of statements, commonly labeled the Open Door notes, calling for the continued territorial integrity of China and for equal commercial opportunity therein.

America's open-door policy soon achieved shibboleth status in America's approach to Asian affairs. This development was somewhat surprising, since the idea actually originated with the British and relied for enforcement on potential violators' fears of each other rather than on unlikely American sanctions. On the other hand, perhaps it was not so surprising, since in both respects the open door followed the early example of that hoariest of American dogmas, the Monroe Doctrine.

Shibboleth or not, the open door had both its spirit and its letter violated almost from the beginning. Russia transgressed in a major way first. Taking advantage of China's debilitation, the Russians sent troops into the northeastern province of Manchuria and gave every indication of converting it into an exclusive sphere of influence, perhaps an outright colony. Secretary of State John Hay registered a protest with the Kremlin, to no avail. Slightly more efficacious was the Anglo-Japanese alliance of 1902, which led Moscow to pledge withdrawal. But Russian actions belied the pledge, and in May 1903 Admiral Robley Evans, commander of the American Asiatic squadron, warned the navy department,

> The condition of affairs in China I regard as growing more and more serious. The extraordinary activity of the Russians in the accumulation of munitions at Port Arthur, their evident disinclination to evacuate Manchuria and the daily increasing uneasiness and antagonistic feeling among them as well as the aggressions and unfriendly activity of the French [Russia's allies] in the southern provinces of China, calls for deep and careful consideration of those in authority in regard to the protection of American interests in China.

Russia's moves, Evans continued, had aroused hostility among the Chinese toward foreigners generally. Recently locals had assaulted a crew of American engineers surveying a railway route north of Canton. Predicting a violent outbreak at any time, Evans reported that he was holding a contingent of marines in readiness at Subic Bay in the Philippines.[34]

Concern at Russia's darkening of the open door caused Washington to welcome, at least at first, Japan's success at arms in the Russo-Japanese War of 1904–5. Elihu Root, no longer war secretary but still a close adviser to the president, applauded Japan's initiative in launching a surprise attack on the Russian fleet, even while negotiations to resolve disputes between the two countries continued. "Was not the way the Japs began the fight bully?," Root wrote. "Some people in the United States might well learn the lesson that mere bigness does not take the place of perfect preparation and readiness for instant action." Although Americans would later complain at Japan's penchant for shooting first and declaring after, Roosevelt agreed with Root. The president expressed the highest respect for the Japanese as "a wonderful and civilized people" who were "entitled to stand on an absolute equality with all the other peoples of the civilized world."[35]

Yet when the Japanese kept winning, raising the possibility of a Russian collapse in the Far East, Roosevelt and other American officials began to worry. American strategy in Asia rested on a balance of power in the area. Only such a balance rendered at all conceivable an open-door policy. First Russia had challenged the balance, and now Japan was doing so. "If the Japanese win out," Roosevelt predicted, "not only the Slav, but all of us will have to reckon with a great new force in eastern Asia. The victory will make Japan by itself a formidable power in the Orient, because all the other powers having interests there will have divided interests, divided cares, double burdens, whereas Japan will have but one care, one interest, one burden."[36]

To preserve what remained of the power balance Roosevelt invited the belligerents to America to negotiate an end to the fighting. Czar Nicholas accepted the invitation, partly because he faced an incipient revolution to add to his military reverses. The Japanese accepted too, recognizing the advantages in quitting while they were ahead in a contest with a country that might eventually bring to bear resources beyond anything they could summon. The negotiations at Portsmouth, New Hampshire, ended the war and won Roosevelt a Nobel peace prize.

They also contributed to growing ill feeling in Japan toward the United States. Japan's negotiators left for Portsmouth carrying popular expectations of a settlement that would match their country's recent successes on land and sea. They returned with considerably less. Although Nicholas agreed to withdraw from Manchuria and other sensitive areas and to recognize Japan's preeminence in Korea, he refused to pay the war indemnity the Japanese people had been led to prepare for. The failure on the last issue, a failure Tokyo's negotiators were happy to blame on American pressure, set off a wave of anti-American rioting in Tokyo. Not for the last time Japanese perceived the United States frustrating their country's legitimate aspirations.

Events of the next several months aggravated the problem. In 1906 the school board of San Francisco ordered the segregation of Japanese students from pupils of European descent. Despite the small number of children involved, less than one hundred, and although the segregation policy already applied to Chinese and Koreans, Japan interpreted the action as an insult and filed a complaint with the state department. Roosevelt lacked authority to overrule San Francisco in the matter, but he brought the board to Washington for a lecture on foreign affairs. The lecture left the schoolmasters unmoved. They responded more positively, however, to a presidential promise to seek restrictions on Japanese immigration. Eventually an informal arrangement was achieved by which San Francisco lifted its segregation order in exchange for Japan's pledge to curtail emigration to America. All saved face, yet the affair added to Japan's resentment of the United States.

In another area Japan could hardly complain. The Russo-Japanese War, following the Sino-Japanese War of the previous decade, removed the principal military barrier to Japan's primacy in Korea. At the same time Japan's demonstrated aggressiveness made the American position in the Philippines seem insecure. For the moment Washington did not fear a Japanese assault on the islands, but one could never tell the future. To gain a clearer view, Roosevelt in the summer of 1905 ordered Taft, now war secretary, to Tokyo to confer with Japanese prime minister Taro Katsura. The two men struck a bargain. Japan swore off the Philippines, and the United States conceded Japan's preeminence in Korea. The settlement was specified in an "agreed memorandum" of a conversation between Taft and Katsura. The pertinent paragraphs summarized the American and Japanese positions. They also indicated the delicacy of doing deals with Japan.

> TAFT: Certain pro-Russian influences in the United States are spreading the theory that Japanese victory [in the Russo-Japanese War] would be a certain prelude to her aggression in the direction of the Philippine Islands. But Japan's only real interest in the Philippines would be to have them governed by a strong and friendly power such as the United States. Japan did not desire to have the islands governed either by natives, unfit for the task, or by some unfriendly power.
>
> KATSURA: This is absolutely correct. Japan had no aggressive designs whatever on the Philippines and the insinuation of a "Yellow Peril" was only a malicious and clumsy slander circulated to damage Japan. . . . As to the Korean question, Korea was the direct cause of the war with Russia, so a complete solution was a logical consequence. If left to herself after the war, Korea would certainly drift back to her former habit of entering into agreement with other powers and thus would be renewed the international complications which existed before the war. Therefore, Japan felt compelled to take some definite step to end the possibility of Korea lapsing into her former condition. This would mean another war.
>
> TAFT: The observations of the prime minister seem wholly reasonable. The personal view of the secretary of war was that Japan should establish a suzerainty over Korea.

When Roosevelt approved Taft's position—"Your conversation with Count Katsura absolutely correct in every respect," the president cabled—Japan secured its free hand in Korea while America gained a measure of assurance regarding the Philippines.[37]

Yet American officials understood that Japan would honor the Taft-Katsura accord only while it served Japanese interests. Manila remained edgy. Harry Bandholtz noted that while many Filipinos had initially applauded the victory of their fellow Asians, the Japanese, over the European Russians, second thoughts about what this portended for the Philippines had since set in. If Bandholtz projected some of his own feelings onto the Filipinos, he did not miss the mark completely when he wrote that "several months ago . . . the sentiment was in favor of Japan, but the thinking Filipinos realize now that all their future hopes are centered in America."[38]

In Washington, Roosevelt saw that should Japan move threateningly in the direction of the Philippines the United States would have a difficult time. The president wrote to Taft,

> The Philippines form our heel of Achilles. They are all that makes the present situation with Japan dangerous. . . . Personally I should be glad to see the islands made independent, with perhaps some kind of international guarantee for the preservation of order, or with some warning on our part that if they did not keep order we would have to interfere again; this among other reasons because I would rather see this nation fight all her life than to see her give them up to Japan or any other nation under duress.

In words that, like Bandholtz's, included a certain self-revelation, Roosevelt remarked, "In the excitement of the Spanish War people wanted to take the islands. They had an idea they would be a valuable possession. Now they think they are of no value." He added, "I am bound to say that in the physical sense I don't see where they are of any value to us or where they are likely to be of any value." American governance brought benefits to the Filipinos, he thought, and provided a workout for the American character. But few in the United States judged this sufficient compensation for the expense of ensuring the Philippines' security. "It is very difficult to awaken any public interest in providing any adequate defense of the islands," Roosevelt lamented.[39]

The American public might have expressed greater interest in defending the Philippines had the American military come to an agreement on how the task should be accomplished. From birth in the eighteenth century the army and navy had bickered over priorities and resources. Appearances indicated that they packed the squabble into the mess kits and footlockers of the soldiers and sailors they sent to the Philippines in 1898. Dewey lobbied for the construction of a major naval base at Olongapo on Subic Bay, and by 1904 the admirals gained approval to begin construction. The army protested the selection of the site, which was surrounded by hills, as overly vulnerable and refused to guarantee its defense. General Leonard Wood surveyed the position and declared that holding it would require 125,000 troops, far more than the army could spare. The navy responded that what Wood and the other generals really disliked about Olongapo was its distance from the comforts of Manila. When the army proposed a station on Manila Bay as an alternative to Subic the admirals nodded knowingly. The bickering continued, sapping American support for Philippine security and rendering the islands less secure than they already were.[40]

5

Politics from Below
1907–1912

I.   Nationalism by other means

By 1907 the essential framework for American-Philippine relations—the tacit agreement between American officials and the Filipino upper class, whereby the former declined to press for full democratization and otherwise compromised their progressive principles, in exchange for the political collaboration of the latter—was in place. During the next several years the arrangement came under challenge. The exhaustion of military resistance to American rule had not marked an end to the independence movement. It simply signaled a change in tactics. Convinced they could not defeat the Americans in the field, Filipino nationalists switched to weapons of politics. In doing so they reignited the struggle within Filipino society that earlier had produced the split between Rizal and Bonifacio and the falling out between Aguinaldo's partisans and defectors from Malolos like Pardo de Tavera. The contest now shaped up as a clash between the Partido Federal and a variety of radical challengers to the status quo.

Anticipating this threat from the left, the Federalistas made the first move. At its conception the party had nominally embraced the idea of statehood as the ultimate destiny for the Philippines. But this gesture was more a political maneuver than an indicator of any deep-seated conviction. While the war continued, the Americans treated advocacy of independence as sedition. Convinced the war must end, the conservatives needed an alternative to independence that would preserve the self-respect of the Filipino people, themselves included. Statehood, with its implication of equality with the Americans, served the purpose.

The cessation of fighting brought the removal of the ban on independence advocacy and afforded the Federalistas a broader range of options. At the same time, the turn to politics of those who most recently had put down their guns forced the party to reconsider its platform. In addition, statehood was losing attractiveness on its own merits. In 1904 the American commission appointed a group of Federalistas to a delegation to a world's fair in St. Louis. Members of the group found America's reality, especially its system of racial segregation and its exclusion of nearly all Asians, disturbingly less than its promise. The majority of the Federalistas decided that even were statehood possible—and after this experience many doubted that the Americans would ever let a land of Asians become a state—they did not want it. The party knocked the statehood plank out of its platform at its 1905 convention, substituting a call for eventual independence. Eighteen months later, recognizing that the change in policy had left it bearing a misleading name, the party rechristened itself the Partido Nacional Progresista, with an agenda calling for incremental devolution of authority until the Filipinos exercised complete sovereignty.[1]

The change of course by the Federalistas, now Progresistas, reflected an understanding on the part of the conservatives that nationalism held an irresistible appeal for the Filipino people. As it would elsewhere in Asia during the next half-century, nationalism in the Philippines promised to carry all before it. To argue for anything less than complete self-determination became tantamount to conceding the racial and cultural inferiority of Filipinos. The question, at least in public, no longer turned on *whether* the Philippines should gain independence, but *when*. Differences of opinion on the latter issue provoked a proliferation of parties, some of which—the Inmediatistas and the Urgentistas—wrote their timetables into their names.

The most important of the new parties was the Partido Nacionalista, which, after a few false starts on the wrong side of the American commission, organized early in 1907 as the fusion of several smaller groups. Without excluding the possibility of some security arrangement with the United States, the Nacionalista platform insisted on "the attainment of the immediate independence of the Philippine Islands to constitute it into a free and sovereign nation under a democratic government."[2]

In 1907 Filipinos participated for the first time in elections for a national assembly. In terms of Philippine politics the campaign essentially reduced to an effort by the Progresistas to tighten their slipping grip on political power, against attempts by the Nacionalistas to pry them loose. The Progresista party labored under the contradiction of having to solicit Filipinos' votes while effectively telling the Filipinos they were not yet fit to rule themselves. In the absence of more galvanizing issues the Progresistas stressed sound administration. As one poster put the matter,

> The National Progresista Party asks for your support on election day because it stands for good roads, clean government, adjustment of tariff, wider public education, adequate commercial laws, enforcement of sanitary laws, fostering of commercial

interests, abolition of prison labour competition, legislative support to boost Manila, more substantial recognition of police and fire departments, retirement and pensions for insular civil service.

This was hardly a script to thrill the throngs. Yet worse followed. In a dig at the radical fringe, the Progresistas announced, "We do not want electrically urgent or immediate independence, but will willingly wait until Uncle Sam sees fit to grant it."

The Nacionalistas had a far easier time, telling Filipinos what they wanted to hear: that they were ready to rule themselves *now*. Nor did it damage Nacionalista chances, during a period of postwar economic stagnation and consequent dissatisfaction with the status quo, that the Nacionalistas could run against Manila—against both the Americans and their Progresista apologists. On occasion the rhetoric got brutal. The *Manila Times* carried a speech of one Nacionalista orator—which the speaker later denied giving—portraying the Philippines' fate in violent terms.

> The mother of all Filipinos of colour is already prostituted in her veins because she is continually undermined by her enemy, which, even though great and powerful, has never been satisfied with the drinking of the blood of the poorest. In order to save the Philippines from this position, in order that she may be able to struggle against her great and powerful enemy that is possessed of war and cannons of steel and crafty men, it is necessary that all Filipinos of colour unite; it is necessary to form a solid and compact mass that will know how to protect with clenched fists.
>
> The Union among Filipinos, the union of all the sons of a common country, will cause an agitation in the nerves of its enemies. Even though America is great, she cannot prevail against a united Philippines. We should elect a leader who will guide us and will know how to conduct us in the decisive struggle against the nation which declares itself a liberator but is nothing more than a wretch, that is only anxious to drink the blood of its victims.[3]

Not surprisingly, some American officials considered such language unconducive to public tranquillity. Governor-General James Smith, successor to Taft, who had replaced Elihu Root in the war department, felt obligated to try to calm the atmosphere. Smith issued a warning against inflammatory speechmaking. On the other hand, Harry Bandholtz saw little reason for alarm. "Of course, there are always a few 'locos' howling for change," Bandholtz said. "But the thinking Filipinos realize now that all their future hopes are centered in America."[4]

Whatever else it accomplished, the haranguing got out the vote. In the July 1907 polling 94 percent of registered voters—who, admittedly, constituted a small portion of the population—marked ballots. The Nacionalistas scored a thumping victory, receiving 34,000 of 98,000 votes, against 24,000 for the Progresistas and the balance for candidates affiliated with neither party. Translated to seats in the assembly, the figures gave 59 of 80 to the Nacionalistas and 16 to the Progresistas.

Curiously, even the American community in Manila supported the Nacionalistas. Whether this resulted from the considerable personal popularity of the two local Nacionalista candidates or, as some alleged, from a silent deal between Nacionalista office-seekers and a group of American businessmen who expected favors in return, was beyond the capacity of contemporary (or subsequent) political analysis to determine. The Progresista charge that the Americans voted Nacionalista in hopes that the assembly would prove a radical failure, thereby discrediting the ultimate cause of Filipino self-government, was sour grapes.[5]

II.   Faceoff

While the Filipinos were rearranging their part of the political landscape of the islands, the American leadership also was shifting. Taft had departed at the end of 1903, worn down by the stresses of life in the tropics, which he exacerbated with a strict regimen of plenty of food and little exercise. Unaccountably he calculated that a body required more fuel at low latitudes. "In this climate," Taft claimed to a friend, "one's vital forces are drawn upon by work so much that one's appetite is very strong." He added, "One's desire to sleep is also very great." From whatever causes, Taft suffered a series of debilitating ailments: malaria, then dengue fever, and finally a rectal abscess that even after surgery made lying painful, sitting worse and walking entirely out of the question. After three years in the islands he was ready to go home.[6]

Luke Wright, who had served as acting governor during Taft's incapacity, followed him into the governor's office. Although Wright enjoyed the respect of the community of American administrators, military officers and businessmen in Manila, he got on less well with the Filipinos. In part Wright's troubles owed to his lack of political heft. Wright did not possess the ties to the Republican establishment in Washington that made Taft a man to contend with, and observant Filipinos recognized his limitations in this regard. In part Wright's difficulties resulted from his southern background, which created undispelled suspicions that he, even more than most Americans, deemed Asians inferior. In greatest part Wright's problems reflected the fact that the Filipinos as a group were simply becoming more fractious. Radical nationalists now formed a coherent force on the left, and they pulled the center of gravity of Filipino politics in their direction. Even conservatives found it advisable to place a certain distance between themselves and the Americans. Wright handled the situation poorly, and before long his relations with Filipino leaders broke down completely. Pardo de Tavera boycotted the governor's receptions. He and Benito Legarda blocked Wright's efforts to reform the tax system. Both men complained over Wright's head to Taft, who as secretary of war was Wright's boss.[7]

Following a personal visit to the islands, Taft, with Roosevelt's concurrence, decided to replace Wright. Henry Ide briefly filled the Manila post until the arrival of James Smith. An attorney from California, Smith had served as a brigadier general during the Philippine-American war and later as governor of Negros. A Roman Catholic and a conciliator by nature, Smith seemed to both Taft and Roosevelt a man who might mend the fraying alliance with the Federalista-Progresistas. This estimate proved correct, although the alliance lost some relevance as the Nacionalistas eclipsed the Progresistas. Smith presided over the election and inauguration of the first Philippine assembly, but otherwise he left few tracks in the spongy turf of the islands' politics.

W. Cameron Forbes was another matter. First as secretary of commerce and then as governor-general, Forbes developed a reputation as the Philippines' great roadbuilder, the man who pulled the country out of the mud. In Forbes' view roads represented a great deal more than transportation, capturing the very essence of government. After one of his numerous excursions around the islands Forbes remarked in his journal,

> The difference between American and native administration is nowhere more evident than on the roads. In the center of towns, where the municipal presidentes are supposed to maintain the roads, and where they are most used, there were puddles and holes, no ditches, and generally a mess. We had to slow up and still got jolted towards the sky. Upon reaching the outskirts of town, the fair, white-crowned, and ditched road would begin, with its deposits of road material all in neatly made bamboo enclosures, and jolting and jarring ceased, and the world flew or flowed by.

Forbes disdained the Spanish legacy in the islands, which he saw especially evident in Spain's transportation system. Describing the layout of the roads, Forbes wrote, "Under the Spanish rule nobody cared apparently whether the lines were correct or not. Under ours they must be exact." Forbes derived satisfaction from the appreciation common folk showed for his efforts. On a trip through Cebu people waved banners at his approach. "One had the inscription 'Forbes significa grandes obras,' which means 'Forbes means large public works'—which is the kind of thing I like to have them think."[8]

Forbes held the view, as Taft had before him, that economic development of the Philippines must precede political independence. Forbes was convinced that without a solid economic underpinning self-rule would quickly degenerate into misrule, either dictatorship or anarchy. The United States should not publicly deny the possibility of independence, but American officials ought to hold out independence as a reward for good behavior on the part of the Filipinos. "I am adopting the policy of telling them that if they really want it to get busy and get those things without which it is impossible," Forbes told Taft. Although Forbes privately questioned that the Filipinos would ever be able to look after themselves, he did not broadcast his doubts. He explained to Taft, "I don't write or speak in favor of independence, as I don't believe in it. . . . I believe in the desire for it, and I never discourage that." Forbes said he hoped to turn this desire into "a motive force for progress and material development." Looking to the future, the governor continued,

> I really expect when the time comes that they have thirty million people, and the rate of wages has reached, say, two pesos per day, and exports and imports, say, five times as much per capita as they are today, the Islands will then for the first time be strong enough to maintain a separate government.
> But whether the individuals will be strong enough to maintain order and dispense justice is another question. Each advance should be made tentatively under such circumstances that the step could be withdrawn if the ice seemed to be too thin.[9]

Forbes had decided opinions, often but not always negative, about Filipino politicians. One Manila legislator, Dominador Gómez, embodied most of what Forbes considered wrong with Filipino politics. "Gómez seems to win by means of his tremendous and grandiloquent flow of language, which bewilders and captivates the imagination of his hearers. He has not a moral fiber in his body, would betray his dearest friend for a dollar, and is really the most fantastic scoundrel of whose record I have any knowledge." Recent elections had returned a number of provincial officials from whom Forbes did not expect much. Three in particular he described as "very weak specimens." Forbes distrusted the early ally of the American regime, Pardo de Tavera. Following a visit with the latter Forbes remarked, "Pardo de Tavera is back. He says he will mix no more in politics; that he is my warmest friend and adherent, and pledges unconditional loyalty to the administration. We will see." Forbes judged more generously those officials he appointed himself. One appointee he deemed "distinctly a success." Another he characterized as "extremely brilliant and diligent."[10]

Forbes cared little for the opinion of many Filipinos, perhaps most. But the esteem of a certain few he valued. Chief among these was Sergio Osmeña, the speaker of the assembly and the outstanding figure in Filipino politics during the first two decades of American rule. A native of Cebu, Osmeña had made a reputation for himself in provincial affairs, earning Forbes' particular respect for supervising road improvements and generally demonstrating a flair for executive efficiency. Osmeña joined the Nacionalista party at its founding, and with the Nacionalistas' victory in 1907 he assumed a leadership role on the national level. Possessing an incisive mind, he proved himself a master of parliamentary detail as well as of the coalition-building necessary to success in legislative politics. He understood the uses of patronage, which he utilized to promote his program. He also recognized the advantages of cultivating Forbes, who as governor could effectively veto any measures the assembly sent up. On one occasion Osmeña gave a fire-eating speech in favor of independence, concluding by ramming through the assembly a motion directing the Philippine resident commissioner in Washington to petition Congress for self-rule. He then walked into Forbes' office and disarmingly told the governor not to take his speech or motion too seriously. An election was approaching, he said, and his supporters needed an issue to campaign on.[11]

At a personal level Osmeña's efforts succeeded, so well that Forbes thought himself responsible for the friendly feeling between the two. After one disagreement the governor remarked in his journal, "I found I had roughed Osmeña a bit hard . . . and had to smooth him down, which I did with a firkin of butter and a mason's trowel."[12]

But personal diplomacy had limits, and after an initial period of cooperation the assembly, led by Osmeña, and the commission, under Forbes, found themselves frequently at odds. With the government still breaking new political ground, each side sought to establish precedent in its favor.

The interests of the two were not incompatible. Despite the nationalistic rhetoric of the majority party in the assembly, the delegates were hardly a group of flaming radicals. Most were young. Of the eighty delegates, nine had not seen their thirtieth birthday, fifty-six were forty years or younger and only ten were over fifty. They were privileged, largely scions of the ilustrado class. Many had gone to school in Europe. A majority—fifty of eighty—were lawyers. Over a quarter had held office during the Spanish period. Nearly three-quarters had occupied positions of military or civilian responsibility in the Malolos republic. Seventy-three had previously served in some capacity under the Americans. This last statistic alone testified to the moderation, if not outright conservatism, of the cohort.[13]

The members of the Philippine assembly probably to a man considered themselves nationalists, even the non-Nacionalistas. Nationalists they were, in the sense that they placed the interests of the Philippines ahead of those of the United States or any other foreign power. They favored independence, sooner or later. But despite the fact that necessity required aspirants to leadership to call for independence in the imminent future, many were willing to accept American rule for the time being. They had carved a comfortable niche for themselves and were reluctant to relinquish it. Theirs was the class that had learned to play by Spain's rules while Spain ruled, and when the Spanish galleon of empire sank they jumped ship to join the Americans. Later, when the Americans would leave them defenseless in the face of Japan's attack, many would figure a way to get along with the Japanese. A privileged minority in a country for centuries dominated by outsiders, they learned to collaborate.

But collaboration was not capitulation, and they consistently pursued their own self-interest—which they often identified, as elites do, with the interests of the country as a whole. This identification with the masses, largely though not entirely spurious, afforded the Filipino elite extra leverage in dealing with the Americans. Despite occasional fits of candor by Henry Cabot Lodge and others, Washington never officially retreated from the notion that American rule in the

Philippines was justifiable only as long as it benefited the Filipinos. Yet Americans did not usually think to ask *which* Filipinos their governance was supposed to benefit. To the degree, therefore, that members of the upper class could pass themselves off as spokesmen for the Filipino people, they could enlist the support of America's collective conscience, such as it was, for their own aims.

Elite leaders particularly sought to capture control of the law-making process in Manila. As in America's bicameral legislature, Philippine bills had to gain the approval of both houses—the elected assembly and the appointed commission, in the Philippine case—to take effect. This meant that each could stymie the other. Nothing in the organic law of the islands differentiated the ordinary statute-writing authority of the assembly from that of the commission, but within a short time the assembly began agitating to apply to the Philippines the American practice whereby the more representative half of the legislature initiated money bills. The commission rejected the idea.

Frustrated, the leaders of the assembly launched a direct assault on the commission. They designed and succeeded in persuading their colleagues to pass a measure that would have abolished the commission and replaced it with an elected senate. Electors to the senate would come almost exclusively from the upper class, having to own property worth ten thousand pesos, to pay one thousand pesos in taxes annually or to hold public office. Forbes and the commission, who did not desire to participate in their own political liquidation, vetoed the measure.

Considering the foregone nature of the commission's reaction to this bill, the assembly's approval amounted primarily to an effort by Osmeña and the Nacionalistas to embarrass the Americans. At the same time, the maneuver provided cover for an indirect effort at undermining American control. During the Spanish era the ilustrados had blunted the power of the colonial government by entrenching themselves in the provinces and towns and making it impossible for Spain to govern without their assistance. They employed the same strategy under the Americans, with considerable success. But they wanted more. Through a civil service bureau the American administration tried to prevent gross corruption and abuses of patronage. Filipino office-holders objected to this oversight as demeaning and restrictive. The assembly proposed a bill that would have gutted the bureau. Although the Americans were willing, in the interests of elite cooperation, to tolerate a certain erosion of progressive standards, they felt they had to draw the line somewhere. The commission vetoed the bill.

The commission also stood against a proposal to reorganize the judicial system. The Americans had followed the Spanish example of trial by judges—justices of the peace in minor disputes, circuit judges for more serious matters. The assembly, wrapping itself in the American constitution, called for trial by jury. Rhetoric aside, the ilustrados believed they would have greater control over juries, chosen from lists drawn up by the elite-controlled municipal councils, than over American-appointed judges. The commission threw out the plan.[14]

Within a few years of the assembly's origin the struggle between assembly and commission had deteriorated into political warfare. It was not uncommon for Forbes and the commission to set aside several assembly measures in a row. A comment by the governor-general near the end of the 1909 legislative session was typical. "The Assembly is sending up a lot of very foolish legislation, and I expect we shall have to refuse to concur in about eight or ten consecutive laws," Forbes wrote. "I don't know how they'll take this, but I shall try to engineer it so either the refusals will be handed down in the last few days, or that they will come little by little and interspersed with laws we can approve."[15]

A visit by Secretary of War Jacob Dickinson did nothing to resolve the deadlock. Although Filipinos found Dickinson a fresh breath compared with Forbes, they saw little of substance in his tour to occasion hope. In one of the kinder commentaries *La Voz de Mindanao* asked editorially, regarding the secretary's presence, "Will it be favorable or adverse? Here is a difficult question to answer." The mouthpiece of the Nacionalista party, *El Ideal*, wondered more pointedly, "Will the farce continue?"[16]

Hoping to squeeze concessions from Forbes and the commission, Osmeña and the assembly took the budget hostage. Proclaiming their right to initiate appropriation bills, the Nacionalistas announced they would not consider money measures arising in the commission. Forbes responded by ignoring the assembly's budget. The funding process froze. Rescue arrived only when the American Congress, exercising its residual power to act as a deus-ex-machina in such instances, amended the Philippine organic act to allow the governor to extend the previous year's budget without assembly concurrence.

IV.   Pride and prejudice

Beyond the political issues involved, the impasse in the Philippine government reflected continuing social tension between the American and Filipino communities. With some exceptions the Manila Americans, as the group of United States nationals in the capital called themselves, made little effort to disguise the fact that they considered Filipinos beneath them. They hoped for good relations with the natives, but such relations required recognition by the Filipinos of their proper place. That the Americans annually made a great celebration of the occupation of Manila indicated both their priorities and their insensitivity to feelings of the country's indigenous population.

During the summer of 1907, as occupation day approached, a group of Filipinos held a rally on the Luneta, a favorite meeting ground in Manila, to congratulate themselves on the recent Nacionalista victory at the polls. Soon thousands joined the gathering. Amid increasingly excited speechmaking someone hauled down an American flag and ran up the staff in its place the banner of Bonifacio's Katipunan.

The American community reacted with outrage. American-controlled newspapers in Manila demanded punishment of the demonstrators, while a circular, signed by eighty prominent members of the American community, issued a summons: "PATRIOTIC MEETING to discuss whether the sovereignty of the Islands to be represented by other than the American flag. ALL AMERICANS INVITED." A few days later three thousand Americans packed the Manila opera house to hear a succession of incensed speakers vent their emotions. Captain Thomas Leonard declaimed,

> The hillsides and valleys of these islands were dotted not long ago with the graves of American soldiers. The Burial Corps has done its work. . . . But those graves, my friends, are not forgotten, nor the cause for which they who so lately occupied them fought. . . .
> We have extended the right hand of amity and good fellowship to the Filipinos. . . . I am glad we have done so, and I have a firm belief that we shall continue to do so—*whether they want us to or not.* [Applause and cries of "That's right!"]
> When the American flag is pulled down it will only be by the unanimous consent of the people of the United States. [More applause.] You will all have more gray hairs in your head than you've got now when they give this consent. [Great applause and laughter.]

Shortly after this meeting the commission, acting unilaterally because the assembly had not convened, banned the display of the Katipunan flag.[17]

The Americans could defend their actions in this case on grounds of patriotism, but racism composed the continuing subtext in nearly all phases of expatriate life. While much of the racism was paternalistic and relatively genteel, too often it was simply mean-spirited and despicable. Episcopal Bishop Charles Brent, an acknowledged beacon to the American community, congratulated the clan on their fine work in bringing the Filipinos to life. "What the Americans have done," Brent said, "is to get the Filipinos out of bed. They are now instructing them how to dress themselves." The editor of the *Cablenews-American* declared that Filipinos had to be "led by the hand" to the higher ground of modern life. "Only by occidental civilization and leadership can they be lifted from the slough of ignorance and sloth, in which they have wallowed for centuries." The *Manila Times* commented on elections to local municipal offices by decrying the accession to power of "men with whom we decline to even brush elbows in the streets." The *Cablenews-American*, reflecting on the same balloting, asserted that "the natives have befouled their own nest."

The Filipino press responded predictably to statements of this sort. One paper, *El Renacimiento,* charted radical opinion until a libel suit brought by Commissioner Worcester forced its closing. The radicals then shifted to *La Vanguardia*, whence they mocked the Americans for their arrogance. An editorial sketched the haughty imperialist with venomous sarcasm:

> Destiny, the supreme dictator of the world, has surrounded him with a luminous aureole of prestige and glory. Privileges are for him, prerogatives for him also. And the people are compelled to recognize those distinctions of his.
>
> He is white, he is a dominator, he is rich, he is strong, he has war machines, he is wise and he is feared by the world. The people are colored, dominated, poor, weak, they have scarcely a bolo to kill their animals, ignorant and scorned by everybody.
>
> Does not this difference of conditions really give the former a relative superiority? The master goes to the club, the opera, the races. The people hide themselves in a suspicious shack and sit beside a table with a green cloth, they go to the cock-pit, which is not at all a decent place, and if they want to see theatrical performances they go to the humble *moro-moro* comedies. Therefore, the master thinks he has a right to do what he pleases with the people when they trouble him. Has one of the latter obstructed his passage on the sidewalk? Push him. Has one brushed his neat suit in the street-car? Push him. . . .
>
> It is all reduced to pushes, if not to clubbings and kicks. After all, what consideration can a dirty and ignorant *tao*, whose intimacy with the spurred and crested "biped" has reduced him to the ranks of its most intimate friend, merit from decent persons? What treatment can a semi-savage, who eats rice with his fingers and talks a language which is not a language but a string of ill-sounding monosyllables which vex one's ears, expect? Why should one show any consideration for persons who belong to the lowest social scale, who have a flat nose, thick lips and simian aspect, with tattooing and breach-clouts, who eat raw meat, the last representatives of an inferior and primitive caste destined to disappear before the impulse of civilization?[18]

IV.   Payne and suffering

"It is all reduced to pushes," *La Vanguardia*'s editor asserted, and despite whatever benevolence the Thomasites, missionaries and other Americans brought to their work, pushes indeed formed the essence of American imperialism in the islands. Racism formed a barrier to good relations during the entire period of American rule and to a lesser degree afterward. But even had the Americans been thoroughly unprejudiced, the question of power—which the Americans possessed and the Filipinos wanted—would have separated the two communities. "The Philippines for the Filipinos," the catch-phrase of American policy, sounded reassuring. Yet because Americans reserved definition to themselves, the slogan meant little for the Filipinos.

The problem of definition became painfully clear in the summer of 1909 when the American Congress debated changes in American tariff legislation. The beginning of Taft's presidential administration, which was promising tariff reform, coincided with the tenth anniversary of the treaty of Paris. A clause of the treaty placed Spain on the same footing as the United States in respect of commerce with the Philippines. Whatever tariff applied to American imports to the islands applied also to Spanish imports. This provision inhibited tariff reform in the Philippines, for any move toward free trade in American goods would have opened the door to Spanish traffic as well, doubly damaging Filipino producers and twice trimming the revenues available to the Philippine government.

Spain's most-favored-nation status expired in 1909, conveniently coincident with Taft's special congressional session on tariff revision. The president, as he had done while commissioner, advocated reduction of tariffs on Philippine goods. In particular he promoted reciprocal free trade between the United States and the Philippines. Sugar and tobacco interests in America opposed the idea, although without particular vigor, since production in the Philippines was not great enough to destabilize prices or market shares. After some bargaining the sugar and tobacco men accepted a proposal by Representative Sereno Payne of New York that placed sugar and tobacco on the free list but subjected the sweets and smokes to relatively high quotas, above current levels of Philippine exports. Rice producers put up a stiffer fight, succeeding in keeping rice off the free list entirely. With these provisions the Payne bill became law in August 1909.[19]

It did so over the protests of Filipino leaders. Shortly after Payne introduced his bill into the American Congress, Manuel Quezon, an up-and-coming Nacionalista, countered with a resolution in the Philippine assembly denouncing free trade with the United States. Quezon defended his resolution on grounds that Filipinos were not getting a square deal, that the Payne quotas applied only to products shipped from the Philippines to America, and not vice versa, and that free entry of American goods would deprive the Philippine treasury of needed revenues, requiring the government to raise taxes or curtail services. The Payne measure, he contended, would do serious damage to the Philippine economy and Filipino society.

Quezon also argued that free trade would have a pernicious effect on the Philippines' political future:

> Free trade between the United States and the Philippines would attract powerful American companies to the Philippines and would make American capital the absolute owner of our market. . . . That the coming of large American companies would bring as a result the monopoly of the wealth of the country by them is a fact that is beyond all doubt; they would first take possession of our market, through lack of competition, and then of our agriculture.

The Philippines would be woven so tightly into the American net that there would be no getting out.

> We believe that, as a consequence of free trade, more American interests would be created in the Philippines, and that the bonds of union would be far stronger. . . . It is unquestionable that the large American interests here established and those

stronger bonds of union would constitute a greater impediment than that which now exists for the obtainment of our independence. It is simply natural, simply logical, to suppose that American capital would consider itself better protected, better supported under the Government of the United States, than under an independent Filipino Government, and, therefore, that it would prefer to remain under the protection of the star-spangled banner, than under a Filipino banner.

Quezon's argument carried the day in the assembly. With even the opposition Progresistas backing the resolution, Quezon's measure passed unanimously.[20]

Forbes considered the vote prima facie evidence of the assembly's wrongheadedness. Believing economic growth to be the principal goal of the American government of the Philippines, Forbes endorsed all actions tending to encourage trade and investment. He disapproved measures working in the opposite direction. He vetoed Quezon's resolution and applauded when the American Congress accepted the Payne bill over Filipino objections. Forbes credited the Taft administration with a signal success.

> This is a real achievement, and one which should put Mr. Taft's name high in rank as a matter of history. He has turned the trick necessary to bring the Filipinos from poverty to prosperity, to make of these struggling, half-starved, half-clothed millions a great, strong, robust, well-fed, well-nurtured, and well-developed people. He has fought the fight of justice, of right, against big odds, at the risk of personal popularity and career, and has won. . . . Great is Taft, and I am glad to throw a wreath of laurel as he goes swinging grandly by.

Regarding the Filipinos who opposed the Payne bill, Forbes thought they convicted themselves of ignorance, as they would soon discover. "Those fool Assemblymen who voted unanimously against free trade will have a chance to see practically what asses they have made of themselves in the eyes of the world." Whether they would admit their mistake was another question. In the meantime Forbes noted with satisfaction that the commodity markets were registering their support for the Payne law. "Sugar jumped up like mad today, and orders for many millions of cigars are crowding in."[21]

For all his contempt for the financial acumen of the assembly, Forbes in fact did not disagree with the analysis underlying Filipino objections to free trade. Where he differed was in the evaluation he made of an intimate Philippine-American economic connection. Quezon and the Nacionalistas feared the influx of American capital consequent to the inception of free trade. Forbes welcomed it. Only American capital, Forbes held, would provide the wherewithal necessary to Philippine development. Forbes concurred completely with the view expressed earlier by Vice Governor Henry Ide regarding the Philippines: "The people have not the money with which to employ the necessary labor, to purchase the essential animals and agricultural machinery for developing their lands, and carrying on the industry that lies at the basis of all prosperity of these islands." Ide asserted that "the extreme need of capital for these purposes is entirely manifest." Capital, Forbes and Ide believed, could not be coerced. It had to be attracted. It would be attracted only to places offering security and an opportunity for reasonable returns. "Capital," Forbes wrote, "demands a stable government. Capital is not interested in the color or design of the flag; it wants just and equitable laws, sound and uniform policy on the part of the government, just and fair treatment in the courts."[22]

In his concern for the security of American capital, Forbes placed himself squarely in the mainstream of official American thinking. The Taft years in Washington—the Forbes years in Manila—marked the heyday of American dollar diplomacy. The Republicans consciously determined to employ American investment in the struggle against global chaos. Theodore Roosevelt had brandished his big stick—the threat and use of American military force—to promote American interests, especially in Latin America. Taft and Secretary of State Philander Knox, a former corporate lawyer, pursued a more subtle policy. By the strategic placement of American capital, they would so tie foreign countries to the United States as to render military action superfluous. Once bound to the American market, these countries would remain safely within the American sphere of political influence. Quezon knew whereof he spoke.

The Republicans' motives were essentially selfish. The United States would benefit from increased influence in the targeted countries, and the administration's supporters on Wall Street would gain profits from the capital invested. Yet the Republicans also believed that what served American interests served important interests of individuals in the affected countries, including the Philippines. "The security of foreign capital," Forbes explained, "is merely an incident in the general security of property rights to the Filipino." And property rights for Filipinos, along with foreign investment, were a prerequisite to the growth of the Philippine economy, without which other rights could never develop.

For these reasons Forbes looked upon the Payne tariff as a boon. American investment would be encouraged and protected, as would Filipino investment. "Both are now permanently secured," he declared.[23]

Essential free trade between the United States and the Philippines, which was rendered freer still in 1913 when Congress dropped the sugar and tobacco quotas, fulfilled most of the expectations of those concerned. "The vivifying effect to the Islands resulting from the Payne Bill is something little short of marvellous," Forbes wrote in 1910. The foreign commerce of the Philippines leaped sharply between 1908 and 1910 and commenced a long and almost monotonously steady growth, quadrupling in dollar terms from 1908 to 1926. At the same time the economic dependence of the islands on the United States increased greatly. In 1908 exports to America accounted for 32 percent of total Philippine exports. By 1926 the United States claimed 73 percent. Growth on the import side was larger still. In 1908 imports from America made up 17 percent of total imports. In 1926 the figure was 60 percent. For better—in Forbes' view—or worse—in Quezon's and the Nacionalistas'—the islands grew firmly attached to the American economic system.[24]

A related development that followed shortly upon passage of the Payne bill heightened the concern of Filipinos regarding American economic penetration. In 1901, under pressure from anti-imperialists and progressive distrusters of big business, Congress had written into the Spooner amendment a prohibition on the sale of public land in the Philippines and on awarding franchises upon such land to private firms. The Cooper, or Organic, Act of 1902 had relaxed this restriction somewhat: now individuals could purchase 40 acres and corporations up to 2,500 acres of public land. The Cooper Act also began the process of privatizing the large domain owned by the Catholic religious orders, the so-called friar lands. Remembering that opposition to the friars had fueled the rebellion against Spain, and desiring to remove this source of popular unrest, as well as to bring the Catholic orders to heel, the American government sought to dispossess the friars as quickly as reasonable. The Cooper measure authorized the American commission to buy the friar lands and issue bonds to finance the purchase.

Republican reverence for the rights of property prevented anything that hinted at expropriation, and for the friar lands actually to change ownership required the consent of the friars. To facilitate the transaction Taft traveled to Rome in 1902. An audience with Pope Leo XIII proved friendly enough. "The old boy is quite bubbling with humor," Taft remarked afterward. "He was as lively as a cricket." Leo agreed in principle to the sale of the friar lands, but price proved a sticking point. Taft thought $5 million a fair figure, although he considered going as high as $8 million. The Vatican initially insisted on $10.7 million. Eventually the margin narrowed, and in November 1903 the two sides struck a deal that called for the transfer of just under 400,000 acres for slightly more than $7.5 million.[25]

Lest a transfer of Filipino resentment to the new American owners accompany the transfer of ownership, the commission sought to sell the friar lands to the tenants thereon or to any other likely purchasers. During the next several years a substantial start was made toward this goal, and in the process a sizable class of small landowners was created. But marketing proceeded more slowly than Taft hoped, and the burden of administering the program—surveying the land, appraising tracts, financing purchases and collecting debts—grew increasingly onerous and expensive. To ease the task and speed sales Washington in 1908 repealed the Cooper restrictions on the size of purchases by individuals. The matter became moot anyway the following year when Attorney General George Wickersham ruled that the Cooper restrictions regulating the sale of land in the Philippines owned by the government of the United States did not apply to the friar properties, which belonged to the government of the Philippines—a distinction only lawyers could appreciate.

Wickersham's ruling came in the context of efforts by agents of parties unknown, but suspected to include the huge American Sugar Refining Company, to buy more than 50,000 acres of uncultivated and unoccupied land, formerly part of a friar estate on the island of Mindoro. Taft, now president, heartily approved the sale. "I saw an opportunity to help the Government to $300,000," he remarked later, "and to increase the agricultural investment in a backward island by double that sum."

The Mindoro purchase triggered reports of other imminent transactions, and it prompted a new round of objection from Filipino nationalists. Quezon complained to War Secretary Dickinson, "It is the firm belief of the Filipinos that the ownership of large tracts of land by foreigners constitutes a menace to the independence both political and economical of the Archipelago." Osmeña connected the question of land sales to other irritants involving control of the Philippine economy. Like Quezon he linked the lot to the issue of Philippine independence:

> All the Filipinos believe the development of the now unproductive natural resources of the land to be necessary and understand the need for the aid of capital from without; but at the same time they cry out against the policy of selling large tracts of land to corporations, against the granting of perpetual franchises to railway companies, against the great privileges granted to public-service companies, and against the preponderance of commercial communities and interests.
>
> This apparent inconsistence has its origin in the firm belief that the future of the people is threatened by the invasion of that capital, which, once invested here, will when the time comes be opposed to any change of sovereignty, because it will not consider itself to be sufficiently safe and protected, except under its own.

Osmeña went on to assert that if the Americans really valued the economic development of the Philippines they would grant independence, for then Filipino distrust of foreign capital would turn to approbation.

> If this government were the image and creature of the people, these fears would not be entertained, and the present cries of protest would be converted into shouts of praise and benediction, because the people would have complete faith and entire certainty that their interests and their future in the hands of such a government would be under the protection of such guarantees as to permit the development of native capital together with the foreign.[26]

IV.   The politics of indirection

Filipino concerns about capitalist encroachment echoed in America. The maneuverings of the sugar trust prompted a Colorado congressman, John Martin, to demand an investigation of the Mindoro purchase. Martin denounced the deal as contrary to ethics, sound administration and common sense. He did not have to mention that a policy allowing development of the Philippine cane-sugar industry on an international-commercial scale would damage the interests of the beet-sugar growers in his state. The House agreed to the investigation, which lasted until the spring of 1911. Depressingly for Martin and the price of beets, the probe failed to uncover willful disregard of the law, and although a minority of the investigating committee challenged the wisdom of the land sales, the majority upheld the policy.

The controversy over the friar lands also helped revive the anti-imperialist movement in the United States, re-raising the issue of the ultimate destiny of the Philippines. The end of the Philippine war had extinguished most of the obvious opposition to American control of the islands, although a few hardy souls kept the flame burning. Edward Atkinson told Andrew Carnegie in 1902 that the Philippine question "reminds me of the old abolitionist times," and he predicted a resurgence of public consciousness on the issue. The surge was slow in coming. To some degree the anti-imperialists should have blamed themselves for the lack of popular interest. Writing the Republicans off as a lost cause, the antis staked their hopes on the Democratic party. Erving Winslow, secretary of the Anti-Imperialist League, explained the strategy: "If the Democrats are so committed to our cause that they have to carry it along, we shall win the battle."[27]

Had Winslow said the antis would win the war, he would have been right. But battles were a different matter, especially in the era of Republican control of the executive branch. While McKinley's victory in 1900 had signaled a setback for the cause of Philippine independence, the election of the arch-imperialist Roosevelt in 1904 represented a disaster. Nor did Taft's elevation from the war department to the White House in 1908 afford relief. Americans in the Philippines had rooted for Taft from a distance. Harry Bandholtz commented to a friend, "We feel he is the only one who understands the Philippine situation and is deeply interested in it." Taft's victory seemed a confirmation of Republican policies to date and a guarantee of their continuance.[28]

Yet the anti-imperialist movement struggled along. Moorfield Storey attempted to rally the troops during the dark days after Taft's election with a brave postmortem:

> It may be said that the strongest opponent of our views has been chosen President; and this is true. But he was not chosen for this reason. . . . We know that all over the country men regret that we ever took the Philippines and are anxious to be rid of them. No longer a probable blessing, they are regarded as a source of trouble and expense—an actual curse.[29]

Storey overstated the case, as the antis habitually did. While he was probably correct in describing widespread regret over the decision to annex, his characterization of the islands as a curse reflected the perceptions of a minority. As with most issues of foreign policy most of the time, most Americans didn't care much about the Philippines one way or the other. If the islands remained quiet, the majority of voters were willing to let the Republicans have their way there.

The Filipinos recognized this fact, which was one of the reasons they made noise about the Payne Act and the sale of friar lands. They monitored carefully the course of the debate in the United States between imperialists and antis. *El Renacimiento* in 1907 gave top-head coverage to a confrontation between William Jennings Bryan, who demanded early independence for the islands, and Albert Beveridge, who advocated holding what America had. The Filipinos scanned the American political horizon for signs of the groundswell of anti-imperialism Atkinson and others predicted. The investigation of the Mindoro land sale provided hope. So did the congressional elections of 1910, in which anti-imperialist Democrats used the friar lands issue against the Taft administration and (largely for other reasons) gained control of the House of Representatives.[30]

When the Democrats organized the lower chamber in 1911 William Jones of Virginia took charge of the committee on insular affairs. Jones had no patience with arguments that retention of the Philippines served either American or Filipino interests, and he gave a sympathetic hearing to Quezon, now resident commissioner in Washington. At Quezon's urging—indeed with drafting help from Quezon, who informed a friend in Manila that "the Jones bill has been written with my cooperation"—Jones introduced a measure calling for creation of an elected upper house of the Philippine legislature, to replace the Philippine commission, and for independence within a decade. Under the terms of this first Jones bill the United States would retain for twenty years the right to station soldiers in the islands.[31]

Quezon could be very devious, and as with most things Quezon had a hand in, the Jones bill disguised as much as it revealed. Quezon realized that with the Republicans still in control of the Senate and Taft planted in the White House, the Jones bill stood no chance of becoming law. But in Quezon's calculations this deficiency marred the measure only a little. The resident commissioner had his eye on 1912, a year of elections in both the United States and the Philippines. Quezon understood American politics well enough to see that the question of Philippine independence would not select or disqualify a candidate for the presidency. Even so, with the Democrats gaining strength while the Republicans showed signs of the split that would soon fracture the party, it did not hurt to solidify the identification of the Democrats with Philippine independence. If the Democrats won, as appeared increasingly likely, Filipinos would be in a position to cash in.

Quezon also had an audience in the Philippines. He and Osmeña and other Nacionalista leaders occupied their usual precarious position. As always they confronted the collaborators' dilemma. To exercise any power and accomplish anything constructive for class and country required cultivating, or at least not alienating, the Americans. Yet to maintain credibility with Filipinos necessitated keeping a certain distance from the colonial overlords. Balancing the two demands was delicate business—but it was just what Quezon excelled at.

Quezon knew that the Jones bill would never survive the scrutiny of the Republican Senate. Therefore he could load it up with whatever provisions would play well in Manila. In reality he was as ambivalent about independence as most privileged Filipinos, and even while publicly promoting the Jones measure, he proposed to the Bureau of Insular Affairs, the branch of the war department responsible for the Philippines, an alternative postponing independence for at least a quarter-century. Needless to say, had word of his heresy leaked out he would have disavowed it at once.[32]

As expected the Jones bill expired in the Senate. Quezon was not in the least disheartened. With the American election approaching he looked forward with confidence to the end of both the Taft administration in Washington and the Forbes regime in Manila. Writing to Pardo de Tavera he predicted, "The present administration will surely fall, and naturally there will be a complete change of personnel on the Commission."[33]

6

Filipinization
1913–1920

I.   The Wilsonian imperative

The election of 1912 offered voters two and a half alternatives regarding the future of the Philippines, with the Democrats marking out a position distinctly different from that of the Republicans. The latter stood pat on the policies of the Taft era; the Republican platform declared indignantly that "our duty toward the Filipino people is a national obligation which should remain entirely free from partisan politics." The Democrats attacked this attitude frontally:

> We reaffirm the position thrice announced by the Democracy in National Convention assembled, against a policy of imperialism and colonial exploitation in the Philippines or elsewhere. We condemn the experiment in imperialism as an inexcusable blunder which has involved us in enormous expense, brought us weakness instead of strength, and laid our nation open to the charge of abandonment of the fundamental doctrine of self-government. We favor the immediate declaration of the Nation's purpose to recognize the independence of the Philippine Islands as soon as a stable government can be established, such independence to be guaranteed by us until the neutralization of the islands can be secured by treaty with other powers. In recognizing the independence of the Philippines, our Government should retain such lands as may be necessary for coaling stations and naval bases.[1]

The Progressives presented the half alternative. Roosevelt's coalition of renegade Republicans, disaffected Democrats and odd others embraced views on the Philippines ranging from ours forever to independence yesterday. Failing to find a plank wide enough for all to stand on, the Progressives as a party ignored the issue. The candidate was ambivalent. As his earlier "Achilles' heel" comment indicated, Roosevelt would have been content to see the Philippines turned loose if the islands' independence, particularly from Japan, could be assured. Yet he believed this would shortchange the Filipinos. The best fate for them, he wrote, would be to remain under America's tutelage "for the next century." Unfortunately Americans did not appear likely to bear up that long. Roosevelt doubted that "our people will patiently submit, as in my judgment they ought to, to doing an onerous duty for which they will get no thanks and no material reward." The Rough Rider was not about to cut and run, but neither did he seem likely to endorse the policies of the now-despised (by Roosevelt) Taft. Precisely what he would do he was not saying.[2]

Had the election narrowed to Taft and Wilson, voters might have made their preference on the Philippine question felt, although finding an archipelagic mandate amid the other issues would have proved as problematic as in 1900. But even had voters paid close attention to the fate of the Philippines in studying their ballots, the entry of a third party, one that took no clear stand, obscured the issue more than usual.

All the same, by choosing between the two leading candidates, Woodrow Wilson and Roosevelt, on the basis of their positions on the fundamental question of individual liberty versus governmental power, voters indirectly charted the future of the Philippines. While both Wilson and Roosevelt campaigned as progressives, their competing visions of the progressive society reflected divergent philosophies. What the Democrats called the New Freedom promised to roll back the economic and social consolidation that had accompanied the industrialization of America. Distrustful of power, Wilson pledged to restore autonomy to the individual by cutting big business down to size. He would return America to its pre-industrial roots, giving the common people greater control over their destinies. Anti-imperialism generally, and devolution in the Philippines in particular, fit neatly into the Wilsonian scheme.

Roosevelt's only complaint about power was that as president he had not had enough. Roosevelt accepted, indeed embraced, consolidation. He considered it both inevitable and beneficial, provided it did not get out of hand. Under the banner of his New Nationalism, Roosevelt aimed to harness the economies of scale to the public welfare. For all his reputation as a trust-buster, Roosevelt had no desire to dismantle corporate America. In Roosevelt's thinking antitrust legislation was principally a device to gain the attention of the Morgans and Rockefellers, who in their own way stood as greatly in need of civilizing as the wildest aborigine. But once they acknowledged that the people, as represented by the president and Congress, set the boundaries of acceptable conduct, they might go about their business of making themselves and America rich. Voters seeking a return to America's pre-imperial roots found little encouragement here.

Consequently, although the Philippine question hardly decided the presidential contest, the polling had significant implications for the islands' future. Observers in Manila certainly thought so. "Everybody over here is deeply concerned in the outcome of the approaching election," Harry Bandholtz wrote at the beginning of November 1912. The American community predictably cheered for their patron and hero Taft. Wilson they looked upon with undisguised suspicion, on account not only of the Democrats' platform but of the continuing influence in the Democratic party of that semi-scourge of imperialism, Bryan, reported to be in line for appointment as secretary of state. Most preferred Roosevelt to Wilson but without enthusiasm. They held the spoiling of Taft's chances for reelection against Roosevelt, and they found his growing fuzziness on the imperialist issue disconcerting.[3]

Filipinos, on the other hand, set their hopes on Wilson, and when the Democratic candidate won they rejoiced. Ten thousand marched through the streets of Manila. Twice that number crowded the Luneta to listen to Osmeña, Quezon and Aguinaldo memorialize the great event. La Vanguardia hailed Wilson as the new Moses who would "preside over our triumphal entrance into the Promised Land after redeeming us from the long captivity to which the imperial Pharoahs reduced us."[4]

Perhaps it was a Freudian slip, but what the editor of La Vanguardia overlooked was that Moses never made it into Israel. Yet the allusion was correct in another sense, for if Wilson parted the waters, the Filipinos had almost the biblical forty years to go before they reached their land of milk and honey, such as it was. The delay resulted not from any lack of good will on the part of Wilson, who in fact went beyond the requirements of political necessity in making the cause of the Filipinos his own. Accepting the nomination in August 1912, Wilson declared, "We are not the owners of the Philippine Islands. We hold them in trust for the people who live in them. They are theirs, for the uses of their life. We are not even their partners. It is our duty, as trustees, to make whatever arrangement of government will be most suitable to their freedom and development."[5]

Wilson as president intended to make his impact felt upon American Philippine policy. A man of Wilson's gravity trod lightly nowhere. As in his dealings with Mexico, Germany and Russia, Wilson considered relations with the Philippines an arena for the application of a rigorous code of moral conduct. The United States had pledged to govern in the interests of the Filipino people and to bring democracy to the islands. The pledge must be fulfilled. Taft, of course, would not have disagreed, but where Taft thought the Filipinos must first demonstrate their capacity for self-government, Wilson was prepared to let them learn by doing.

Unluckily for the cause of Philippine independence, first one thing and then another distracted the new president. Elected chiefly for his stand on domestic issues, Wilson naturally placed priority there. Tariff reform, revision of the banking system and strengthening antitrust legislation preoccupied Wilson during his first months in office. Such energy as remained for foreign affairs was absorbed by the revolution in Mexico, into which Wilson injected the United States, first diplomatically, then militarily. By the time the president tired of chastening Carranza and chasing Villa, Europe had entangled itself in a suicidal war and was doing its best to enmesh America. At this point, a change of American course regarding the Philippines seemed inopportune.

II. Home rules

If Wilson declined to push for early Philippine independence, he did undertake significant changes in the governance of the islands. Because the Philippines had known only Republican administrations, the guard-changing in Washington sent shivers through the American community in Manila. The American officials had worshipped Taft, or at least they did in retrospect when confronted by the alternative, Wilson. They entertained the conceit, common among placemen long in office, that they were above politics, and they believed they had made themselves indispensable as America's cadre of Philippine experts. The housecleaning the Democrats inaugurated came as a shock.

Actually the new administration granted Forbes and his close associates a longer stay of replacement than they had any right to expect—not because of Forbes' stern warnings against untimely action but because of the president's other worries. Wilson allowed the governor to retain his post until September 1913, yet even then Forbes vacated Malacañang muttering against the president's "very vicious injection of party politics into a situation hitherto kept clear of it."[6]

As Forbes' successor, Wilson sent out Francis Burton Harrison. Born in Virginia, educated at Yale, a progressive who nonetheless did not disdain to cooperate with party bosses when circumstances demanded, Harrison had risen to prominence in New York's political environment by a path much like that which had carried Wilson to the governor's mansion in New Jersey. The parallels did not extend to private life. Where Wilson remained the righteous Presbyterian, Harrison adopted a more relaxed attitude on matters of morality. His "marital adventures," as a chronicler of the American community in the Philippines described them, fascinated and scandalized Manila, whose hostesses loved feigning confusion over precisely how many of Harrison's "succession of wives" actually lived at Malacañang. The consensus put the figure at three, although inexpert observers tended to miscount two of the wives, who were sisters.[7]

Harrison owed his appointment largely to the machinations of Quezon. Following inauguration, Wilson had sounded out the resident commissioner on the subject of the governorship. As Quezon later recalled the meeting, Wilson first asked whether he ought to keep Forbes on. Quezon, careful as ever in dealing with Americans, replied, in effect, that Wilson had no choice.

> Mr. President, if it is your intention to disregard the Democratic platform and merely carry on the policies of the Republican Administration, then you can find no better man for the job than Governor-General Forbes. If, on the contrary, you intend to

take immediate steps, as in my opinion you should take, to make good on the now historic commitment of your party to grant independence to the Philippines as soon as possible, then Governor Forbes can neither be the spokesman for nor the executor of your policies in the Philippines.

Wilson hinted that he might accept suggestions for a replacement.

Quezon always made a point of acquainting himself with influential individuals in Washington, and he knew Harrison as the ranking Democrat on the House ways and means committee and an enthusiast of tariff reform. Harrison had expressed interest in the Philippines for some time and sympathy toward the aspirations of the Filipino people. Yet Quezon caught him by surprise during a conversation in which Harrison was trying to gain the commissioner's support for a friend's appointment to the governorship, when Quezon asked whether Harrison himself would accept the job. Harrison thought the matter over briefly and decided he would.

Quezon then got Senator Jones to back Harrison. Jones lined up Secretary of State Bryan. Bryan proposed Harrison to Wilson. The Senate waived hearings out of congressional courtesy. Within the month Harrison boarded a Pacific Mail liner at San Francisco, bound for Manila.[8]

Quezon congratulated himself on good work. He wrote a friend that Harrison was "the best selection that could have been made." Quezon described Harrison as a "thorough filipinista," and he predicted that the new governor would "redeem the commitments" of the Democratic party toward the Philippines.[9]

Forbes departed Malacañang in a grump, convinced the work of the previous fourteen years was already being undone. He especially resented Quezon's role in the appointment of his successor. Remarking in a letter to the secretary of war his "alarm" at the influence of the resident commissioner, Forbes said, "There could not be anything more dangerous to the peace and welfare of the Islands than to have Quezon think he can run the Governor-General and make and unmake him."[10]

Harrison's arrival statement deepened Forbes' depression. Speaking explicitly for the president, Harrison announced,

> We regard ourselves as trustees acting not for the advantage of the United States but for the benefit of the people of the Philippine Islands. Every step we take will be taken with a view to the ultimate independence of the Islands, and as a preparation for that independence. And we hope to move towards that end as rapidly as the safety and permanent interests of the Islands will permit. After each step taken, experience will guide us to the next.

As representative of the party of American anti-imperialism, Harrison could hardly have asserted less, and neither Forbes nor the Manila Americans would have objected had Harrison stopped here, although they might have winced at the word "rapidly." But what Harrison said next confirmed the retentionists' worst fears of Democratic irresponsibility.

The administration will take one step at once and will give to the native citizens of the Islands a majority in the Appointive Commission; and thus in the Upper as well as in the Lower House of the Legislature a majority representation will be secured to them.[11]

At a stroke, the Wilson administration was handing over domestic self-government to the Filipinos. This fell short of independence, to be sure. The United States retained responsibility for the security of the islands. The Philippines would still lack a foreign policy. Moreover, what Washington gave, Washington could withdraw. Even so, with Filipinos adding a majority in the commission to their monopoly of the assembly and with the governor-general, whose powers had been defined on the assumption of American control of the commission, lacking a personal veto, the Filipinos now essentially would manage most of their own affairs.

As a complementary measure Harrison made clear that he intended to take seriously the staffing policy first enunciated by McKinley but honored since the arrival of Taft more in the breach than in the observance: that whenever possible Filipinos should fill administrative posts. Over the years, between the narrow interpretation the Republican governors placed on McKinley's mandate and the bureausclerosis that afflicts any large organization, American nationals entrenched themselves in the great majority of government positions in the islands. To Harrison this seemed a disgraceful repudiation of the principle that the United States should be tutoring Filipinos in the arts of self-government. Indeed, to one who knew the ways of Tammany Hall from firsthand experience, it appeared distressingly like feeding at the public trough. Since the Filipinos were paying the Americans' salaries, Harrison thought Filipino grievances on this score doubly legitimate.

The new governor began uprooting at once. "The bureaus here are top heavy with Americans," he wrote to War Secretary Lindley Garrison, "and the Filipinos really have very little share in the management of their own government. If they are ever to be tested to their political capacity, I conceive it to be my duty to give them a chance to fill whatever vacancies may occur in offices for which they are palpably fitted." Harrison did his best to ensure that vacancies occurred. He immediately asked for and received resignations from several department directors and assistant directors. When the chief and number two at the bureau of printing took a complaint over his head to Washington he fired them. He dismissed the head of the Manila police force and the city's prosecuting attorney. The crashing big trees brought down smaller ones. In placing Filipinos in positions of authority, Harrison provoked resignations from many individuals who refused to serve under native supervisors. By the end of his first year in office Harrison had succeeded in trimming the American contingent in the government nearly 20 percent and raising Filipino representation by a comparable amount.[12]

The Filipinos applauded. *La Vanguardia* hailed the "magical effect" of Harrison's coming and acclaimed it the "dawn of a new era." But the Manila Americans resisted. Because Harrison had no experience in the Philippines before his appointment as governor, the Americans considered him incapable of judging their work, and they attributed his personnel decisions to a partisan vendetta. The *Cablenews-American* reported replacements in tones varying from sarcasm to outrage. One headline announced, "Three More Stalwart Upbuilders of Philippine Prosperity Fall Before Onward March of Reconstruction," while another shrilled, "Hoggsette and Wilson Surrender Their Scalps to Governor General Harrison." Dean Worcester, the former commissioner, decried the Harrison-Wilson policy as delivering the Philippines over to a group of graspers "wholly unfit" for exercising power. Addressing a group of Manila merchants, Worcester said, "The Filipino politicians are like the horse-leech's daughters crying, 'Give! Give!'" At some point, Worcester predicted, they would have to be slapped down.

Other critics adopted the device of predicting a failure of business confidence, which would have dire effects on the Philippine economy. Before Harrison had hardly landed, the *Manila Times* asserted, "The business community, irrespective of nationality, is suffering acutely from the unwholesome fear felt and expressed by employees of the government that their possessions were neither secure nor permanent under the present administration." The *Philippines Free Press* declared, "In business nearly everyone is marking time. Everywhere retrenchment is the word." The *Weekly Times* observed the completion of Harrison's initial year with a scathing indictment, summarized in a sentence: "All that Mr. Harrison did was destructive—and a child might have done as well."[13]

Worcester proved the most effective in carrying the anti-Filipinization case to the American people. Taking to print in an effort to explain what he deemed the wrecking of the Philippine government, Worcester described the supporters of the Democrats' policy as falling into three groups. The first comprised "honest and sincere officials of the United States government with a rank and file composed of good citizens." Though true of heart, these persons "have no first hand knowledge of conditions in the Philippines and have been deceived by plausible misrepresentations into believing that nothing of real importance has been happening to the civil service." In the second group Worcester placed individuals who recognized the seriousness of the changes Harrison had effected but who believed "that the changes made have been in the interest of economy and efficiency; that many of the numerous Americans eliminated were unworthy to hold their positions; that others could well be, and have been, replaced by efficient Filipinos at smaller salaries." To these individuals Filipinization appeared both good politics and good economics. Worcester reserved special scorn for the third and largest category of Filipinizers:

> In it we find the politicians who have wrought the havoc. They know only too well what has been done, having themselves done it deliberately. Some of them have

been controlled by the belief that the Philippines have become a source of great danger and expense to the United States and have been anxious to get rid of them at any
cost, regardless of the interests of their inhabitants. Others have sought to snatch
whatever temporary popularity might be gained by posing as friends of the Filipinos
and to utilize it for their own political advancement. Finally there are the theorists
to whom hard facts are as the dust beneath their feet. They tell us that all men are
born free and equal but overlook the equally obvious consideration that they do not
long remain so, and that the early generalization of freedom and equality among
adult Filipinos involves active interference from without.[14]

The Democrats managed to shrug off much of the complaining. Harrison
described those he replaced as either "exceedingly disloyal to me or else violently
opposed to the policies of President Wilson." The governor added, "The Government was fearfully overmanned, anyway, and is more efficient for the reduction." Secretary Garrison remarked, "Those who are displaced always make a lot
of noise and get their friends interested in condemning those in authority." Garrison noted that especially in a closed community like that of the Americans in
Manila, persons not taken into the confidence of the government often reacted
emotionally. "They retaliate by unfounded condemnation and general damn-
ing."[15]

Yet there was something to the objections of Worcester and the others. Efficiency in government services declined, as predicted. In certain areas—mail
delivery, for example, which slowed—the consequences were merely irritating.
In others the results were graver. Since the advent of the Americans the Philippine government had vigorously attacked the problem of rinderpest, the deadly
cattle disease. The counter-rinderpest measures, which included quarantines and
related restrictions on the movement of cattle and the actions of owners, often
generated resistance on the part of those who would benefit in the long run once
the disease was eliminated. The rinderpest campaign was one of those painful
things governments not answerable to the governed can do better than popularly
chosen administrations. By the end of the Forbes period victory was in sight. But
once Filipinos gained control of the law-making process the legislature succumbed to pressure from the pained to relent on enforcement. Before long the
disease reversed its remission and began to spread, threatening the cattle industry
country-wide. Worcester smugly but not inaccurately described the situation as
"a practical result of Filipinization in the complete demonstration of the opposition of the populace to measures necessary for their own economic salvation,
and of the unwillingness and inability of provincial and municipal officers to
enforce such measures."[16]

In another area Filipinization contributed to the kind of graft the country later
became famous for. Harrison, no less than Forbes, recognized that meaningful
independence for the Philippines required economic development. But where
Forbes had relied chiefly on private enterprise to foster development, declaring
that "the Government can not make prosperity, the Government can not create

wealth, it can only assist," Harrison had greater confidence in the public sector. To encourage the growth of the Philippine economy as well as to give Filipinos direct experience managing their affairs, Harrison recommended the establishment of a government bank. The legislature complied, and in 1916 the Philippine National Bank opened its windows for business.[17]

Although initially headed by H. Parker Willis, on loan from the American Federal Reserve system, the Philippine bank adopted a more expansive policy than America's Fed would have countenanced. Willis soon wearied of being outvoted by the bank's board of directors and resigned. Eventually the bank's presidency passed to Venancio Concepción, previously a general in the revolutionary army and a man who once had saved Osmeña's life. Concepción cared little for banking as a science. He considered it a livelihood—for himself and family and friends. Under Concepción the bank embarked on a lively course of lending to real estate speculators, who had a variety of quick-rich schemes; to the sugar, hemp and coconut oil industries, which were riding a wartime boom; and to numerous individuals and firms possessing more connections than collateral. When one of the bank's American directors, Archibald Harrison, the brother of the governor-general, investigated reports of irregularities in lending practices and discovered that many of the reports were true, Concepción engineered a vote in the legislature cutting off funds for the investigation. Archibald Harrison, incensed, quit and went home to America.

Concepción's balloon remained aloft while the war kept prices high, but roaring inflation, fueled by the practice of recycling pesos supposedly consigned to the incinerator, and increasing discrepancies on the bank's books eventually caught up with him. The collapse of overextended borrowers left the bank holding worthless notes. One complicated transaction involving reserve funds resulted in the unexplained disappearance of 80 million pesos. In 1920 Concepción decided to call it a career and stepped down.[18]

III. Jones again, victorious

To the skeptically inclined the fiasco of the Philippine bank and other troubles incident to Filipinization provided irrefutable evidence of the unreadiness of the islands for independence. Even Harrison had to concede that the bank had acted in an "extravagant and foolish manner." For the most part, though, Harrison and the proponents of home rule considered the difficulties simply inefficiencies endemic to democracy. The United States had survived the Grant administration, Democrats reminded their Republican antagonists. Likewise the Philippines would overcome this rough start.[19]

As a result, while the Democrats controlled the White House and Congress, movement toward Philippine independence continued, albeit slowly. In the first years of the Wilson administration impatient observers in the Philippines expressed the view that the change from the Republicans was more a matter of style than of substance. *La Democracia*, a journal of moderate opinion, wrote of Harrison that "at bottom the pledges and declarations of the first Democratic governor of the Philippines, reiterating the message of President Wilson, do not differ much from the sugar-coated statements of his Republican predecessors."[20]

Harrison, however, was not the source of such delay as existed on the subject of Philippine independence. If anything the governor was more of an independista than the independistas themselves. Quezon in Washington continued to work for congressional legislation committing the United States to Philippine independence, but the resident commissioner, as before, harbored reservations about the Philippines' readiness for complete self-responsibility. The world remained a dangerous place. With Japan more voracious than ever, having swallowed Korea and, more ominously from the Philippine perspective, Taiwan, the ability of Filipinos to defend themselves was open to considerable doubt.

Personal calculations also entered the accounting. Washington's delivery of home rule to the Filipinos had led to the primacy—indeed supremacy—of the Nacionalista party. The status quo had the advantage for Quezon, Osmeña and other Nacionalista leaders of affording power without responsibility. While the Americans remained in the islands they provided convenient scapegoats when things went wrong. Consequently the Nacionalistas held to the course of promoting independence rhetorically without pushing hard in practice.

In 1914 a leftist faction led by Teodoro Sandiko, a well-known veteran of the revolution closely associated with Aguinaldo, broke away from the Nacionalistas. Sandiko's group formed a third party—after the Nacionalistas and Progresistas—called the Partido Democrata Nacional, although members were more commonly known as Terceristas. Their paper *Consolidación* published, significantly, in Tagalog and waged a campaign of criticism against both the ruling Nacionalistas, whom the Terceristas dubbed "Mazarins," and the "American imperialists."[21]

Responding to this pressure, Quezon worked the corridors of Washington, aiming for a new Philippines government act that would neutralize the Terceristas without disrupting the status quo in the near or middle future. After consulting with Frank McIntyre, chief of the Bureau of Insular Affairs, Quezon proposed an arrangement formalizing and extending Philippine home rule and calling for a census to be held in 1925 and every ten years thereafter, to determine the literacy level of the Filipino people. When 60 percent of adult males could read and write English, or 75 percent any language, a referendum on independence would be held. Should the vote favor independence, a constitutional convention would follow, leading to a transfer of sovereignty.

Obviously this involved procedure would prevent independence for a long time. Quezon himself estimated that at least a generation would elapse before independence arrived. McIntyre, taken aback by the conservatism of this program, asked Quezon what support it might elicit in the Philippines. Would Osmeña approve? Quezon said he thought so. How about Harrison? Had Quezon presented the plan to the governor? "My God, no!" replied Quezon, displaying, or at least affecting, shock. "I think he believes in independence. He thinks he can turn us loose in about four years."[22]

McIntyre reported his conversations with Quezon to Secretary Garrison and to Wilson. The president read with interest of Quezon's diffidence regarding early independence. After discussing the matter with the resident commissioner personally, Wilson announced his support for legislation pledging the United States to eventual independence without specifying a timetable.

In August 1914 Congressman Jones of the insular affairs committee submitted a resolution redefining the relationship between the United States and the Philippines. The body of the bill contained a variety of reforms increasing Filipino participation in government but no provision for independence. The bill's preamble, however, contained a commitment to independence, as well as an endorsement of the Wilson administration's Filipinization policy:

> Whereas it was never the intention of the people of the United States in the incipiency of the War with Spain to make it a war of conquest or for territorial aggrandizement; and
>
> Whereas it is, as it has always been, the purpose of the people of the United States to withdraw their sovereignty over the Philippine Islands and recognize their independence as soon as a stable government can be established therein; and
>
> Whereas for the speedy accomplishment of such purpose it is desirable to place in the hands of the people of the Philippines as large a control of their domestic affairs as can be given them without, in the meantime, impairing the exercise of the rights of sovereignty by the people of the United States, in order that, by the use and exercise of popular franchise and governmental powers, they may be the better prepared to fully assume the responsibilities and enjoy all the privileges of complete independence;
>
> Therefore. . . .

The House approved the Jones bill in October, with Democrats providing most of the 212 ayes and Republicans nearly all the 60 nays. But despite Wilson's personal backing—the president declared the resolution a "great measure of constructive justice"—the bill bogged down in the Senate, vanishing with the Sixty-third Congress in March 1915.[23]

The administration tried again when the new Congress met the following December. Expecting trouble from Republican retentionists, the proponents of independence were ambushed by Democratic Senator James Clarke of Arkansas, who offered an amendment mandating independence for the Philippines in not more than four years. Clarke muddled the issue not only by his amendment, which put the Democratic party on the independence spot, but by his apparent unconcern at what might befall the Philippines after independence. Though the

Clarke amendment provided for efforts to neutralize the islands for a period
beyond devolution, the senator himself thought a takeover by Japan might not
be a bad thing. The *Boston Globe* reported a conversation with Clarke:

> Japan, he said, had accomplished much for Korea, and because of racial similarities
> would do much in the Philippines. Inasmuch as the United States had made it unde-
> sirable for the Japanese to get a footing in this hemisphere, he thought the United
> States should be willing to keep out of the Asiatic countries. The manner in which
> Japan could get possession of the Philippines, he said, was a matter for the Philippines
> to settle after they became independent.[24]

The Wilson administration disliked the Clarke amendment, with Lindley
Garrison deeming it a dereliction of duty while Wilson considered it merely
unwise. Yet the president, already on record as favoring Philippine independence, refused to make it an issue, and when the Senate split evenly on a modified
version of the Clarke proposal—without the neutralization clause—Vice President Thomas Marshall cast the tie-breaking vote in favor.

The House, however, deleted the Clarke amendment in approving the Jones
bill. This raised the possibility that although the administration and a majority of
Congress had gone on record in favor of independence, with the Senate placing
the date at no more than four years in the future, the Jones bill might again die.
Francis Harrison and others in Manila found the uncertainty distressing. "The
responsibility and strain of the work in the Philippines has been greatly increased
during these past two years by the pendency of this legislation in Congress," the
governor remarked. As the measure went to reconciliation Harrison reported that
the Filipinos were "profoundly discouraged over what they believe to be the failure of the Jones bill."[25]

The Filipino leaders held their breath. While they most desired a timetable-
less Jones bill, they could hardly lobby against a provision setting a date for independence. Moreover, the Nacionalistas had invested too much politically in the
Jones measure to lightly let it fail. Jones alone would be best, but Jones and Clarke
would be better than neither. Osmeña told Harrison that the Jones legislation
involved equally "the fundamental principles of your great constitution" and "the
future and all the vital interests of a Christian and civilized people of more than
ten million souls." To Quezon, Osmeña predicted that failure of the Jones bill
would be "very detrimental to all concerned." Quezon, anticipating a continuation of the fight, declared that "a more thorough campaign of education" of the
American people was "definitely needed." In a perceptive comment containing
implications for American policy toward the Philippines during the entire period
of contact between the two countries, Quezon told Harrison, "I have not the
slightest doubt but that the American people in general are favorable to Philippine independence. The trouble is that the people at large are not interested
enough in this subject to write to their congressmen, and the only voice that is

being heard is the voice of those who are interested in retention, who are, naturally, actively working to defeat the bill."[26]

Fortunately for Harrison, Osmeña, Quezon and other proponents of the Jones bill, the Senate's representatives to the reconciliation conference dropped their insistence on a timetable. The measure, less Clarke, survived.

The Jones Act, which Wilson signed on August 29, 1916, set the pattern for the government of the Philippines that obtained until the creation of the commonwealth in 1936. It replaced the commission and assembly with a senate and house of representatives, both elected by the people of the Philippines. The governor-general, still appointed by the president, possessed a reversible veto, but items passed over his veto remained subject to rejection by the president. The Jones Act also extended the principle of the Payne tariff, mandating free trade between the United States and the Philippines.

The significance of the Jones Act lay in two factors chiefly. First, it rendered permanent, by enshrining in law rather than executive fiat, Filipino control of both houses of the legislature. Second, the preamble of the act solidified the American commitment to Philippine independence, which heretofore had been limited to presidential statements and recommendations of ad hoc committees.

IV.   Safe for . . . ?

Wilson's refusal to take a forthright position on the Clarke amendment to the Jones bill betrayed the distraction the president felt now more than ever. The revolution in Mexico had led the administration into a vain quest to force the Mexican people to behave according to Wilsonian standards. Only by a whisker of Pancho Villa's mustache did the United States avoid war, at precisely the time Congress was wrestling with the Jones measure. The conflict in Europe had grown into stalemated carnage. Despite Wilson's efforts to keep America above the fray, the contest inexorably drew the United States closer. The sinking of the *Lusitania* triggered American outrage at German lawlessness. The administration's decision to allow loans to the belligerents contributed to a further pro-Allied tilt, since most American funds flowed to Britain and France. When Germany announced unrestricted submarine warfare at the beginning of 1917, Wilson's hand was forced.

Between the German announcement and America's declaration of war, another development raised ominous questions for the Philippines. British intelligence intercepted and delivered to the United States the so-called Zimmermann telegram, which besides calling for a German-Mexican alliance revealed German efforts to persuade Japan, at the moment an Allied power, to jump to the German camp. The idea had attractions for Tokyo, since if the United States entered the war Japan would find itself fighting on the same side as the three countries that most threatened its aspirations in Asia: Britain, Russia and the United States. The American naval attaché in Tokyo reported sympathy for a reversal of course. "None of the Japanese really like England," the attaché wrote. "They nearly all hate America, and most admire Germany."[27]

From the American perspective a war against Japan, simultaneous with a war against Germany, raised logistical nightmares, especially relating to the Philippines. In 1908 a joint army-navy planning board had decided to concentrate America's military attention on Manila, directing the services to fortify Corregidor at Manila Bay's mouth and relegating Subic Bay to secondary status. The choice reeked of politics. Roosevelt acidly inquired how Subic, after years of being described as essential, suddenly lost its value. But the choice also reflected a decision by the navy not to base its Pacific fleet as far west as the Philippines. The admirals opted for Pearl Harbor instead.[28]

The decision for Pearl Harbor followed in significant part from fear that the fleet would be overly exposed to Japan if stationed in the Philippines. While the decision safeguarded the fleet, it increased the Philippines' vulnerability. In 1910 the Naval War College drafted a contingency plan for war against the Japanese. Plan Orange identified three possible precipitants of hostilities: Japan's desire for special rights in Manchuria, the still-tense immigration issue and Tokyo's hankering after insular possessions in the Pacific. The potential casi belli were interrelated. Japan might use an affront on the immigration question, for instance, as a pretext for military action in Manchuria or against the Philippines. The navy's planners predicted that in the event of a Japanese southward thrust the United States could not successfully defend the Philippines. Absent the basing of the Pacific fleet in the islands, American vessels were too far away to counter Japan's ships. Shore defenses could not stand up to a major assault from the sea.[29]

Something similar to one of the predicted precipitants occurred in 1913 when the California legislature passed a measure excluding Japanese—along with other Asians—from owning land in the state. Japan erupted in demonstrations, causing American officers to gird for war. The war department sent orders to the American commander in the Philippines, General J. Franklin Bell: "Have full Corregidor garrison well in hand and enough on island to prevent any surprise." Under cover of maneuvers American forces in the Philippines went on alert. Such steps succeeded principally in raising the level of tension. In Tokyo newspapers screamed, "America Prepares for War!" Secretary of State Bryan, not entirely cognizant of what the country's generals and admirals were up to, tried to calm the Japanese by saying that changes in American force positioning in the Philippines had been scheduled long before.[30]

Like previous crises this one blew over, but not before adding to transpacific distrust. The opening of the Panama Canal in 1914 promised some relief for American planners. By trimming the transit time between Pacific and Atlantic the canal allowed increased strategic flexibility. Yet the canal required defending, which diminished the gains it produced. Europe's simultaneous collapse into war added another plot twist to the war-gamers' scenarios.

The discovery of the Zimmermann telegram increased American fears the more. The Philippines, alarmingly vulnerable to Japanese attack already, would be nearly defenseless should the United States get involved in a two-ocean conflict. Preparing for the worst, the navy ordered "immediate steps" to close Subic Bay and mine the entrance to the harbor. Should the Japanese gain a foothold there, the United States might never root them out.[31]

In the event the worst did not occur—this time. Japan chose to stick with the Allies. The war brought to the Philippines not military disaster but economic prosperity, as the belligerents purchased the products of the islands in record quantities. Yet the boom turned out to be a mixed blessing, contributing as it did to the maladministration and corruption already evident in the country.

In another sense also the war proved a setback for the Philippines. Despite Wilson's stirring rhetoric about self-determination and securing the world for democracy, the conflict had much the opposite effect in the Far East. The Japanese made out like bandits. After the opening of hostilities in Europe Tokyo grabbed Germany's holdings in the Pacific, including islands lying athwart American resupply routes from Hawaii to the Philippines. The Japanese pressured China to accept the "twenty-one demands," which would have granted Japan a protectorate over China. The Chinese refused, calling on the United States for help. Washington warned Tokyo against the use of force in China. Japan retreated—temporarily.

With the American entry into the European war the Japanese resumed pressure on China, to the extent of hinting to the United States that if America did not recognize Japan's preeminent status in China the Japanese government might reconsider Zimmermann's offer. This time it was the Wilson administration that blinked. Secretary of State Robert Lansing met with Viscount Kikujiro Ishii and agreed to recognize Japan's "special interests" in China. Although Japan simultaneously declared its support for the principles of the open door in China, the declaration was contradicted by the Lansing-Ishii accord and amounted to a device for saving the face of the Wilson administration.[32]

Japan emerged from the war stronger and more confident than ever, a development that augured ill for the Philippines.

7

Republicanization
1921–1926

I. Assessing the damage

The war and its aftermath, especially the Senate's rejection of the Versailles treaty and the League of Nations, had yet another crucial effect on the Philippines. With the Democrats discredited, the Republicans regained the White House, which combined with their pre-existing majorities in Congress to return them to control of America's Philippine policy. Washington no longer exercised day-to-day direction of affairs in the islands. Not even diehard retentionists seriously considered repealing the Jones Act. But because the Jones measure left the date of independence indeterminate and because the president wielded ultimate veto power over Philippine legislation, there existed substantial scope for the Republicans to reverse the actions of the Democrats.

The Republicans certainly thought the Democrats' actions required reversing, all the more after Wilson announced just before leaving office that the moment had come to move on to independence for the islands. The new president, Warren Harding, had no such intention. Although Harding cared little one way or the other about the Philippines, loyalists from the Taft era immediately set to educating him on the subject. Cameron Forbes could not wait for Harding's inauguration to press the need for reform, calling on the president-elect in January to denounce the Harrison regime and recommend that a commission of investigation be dispatched to the islands. When Harding responded more slowly than Forbes thought necessary, Forbes nudged him again.[1]

Harding obliged by appointing a commission consisting of Forbes and General Leonard Wood, the latter serving as chairman. The commission had the ostensible assignment of ascertaining the fitness of the Philippines for immediate independence, but because the answer was a preordained no, especially with the likes of Forbes doing the investigating, its real purpose was to justify a shift to a more conservative policy. To its credit the commission spared no effort examining the situation on the ground. As Forbes and Wood reported to Washington after an exhausting five months in the islands, they and their staff visited 449 municipalities in 47 of the 48 provinces, traversing 15,000 miles by steamship, railroad, automobile, horse and foot. They held public hearings and private interviews. They spoke with individuals from all parts of the islands and from a wide variety of occupations and social conditions. "Our duty," Forbes told a gathering in one village, "is not to decide but to learn the needs of the people."[2]

Forbes and Wood learned, if such is the right word, what they expected to learn: that the Philippines were not ready for independence. "The desire for independence is general, but not universal," Forbes wrote to War Secretary John Weeks as the commission's work neared its end.

> It is tempered, as we have advised you, by a very strong feeling on the part of many that the time is not ripe for it. The position of the people, while demanding independence—and sometimes absolute and immediate independence—has been very generally that they believe in the fairness, wisdom and disinterestedness of the United States and will abide cheerfully by whatever decision is made. And if we find they are not ready for independence now, they propose to buckle to and make themselves ready for it later.[3]

Forbes conceded the delicacy of the commission's task in offering recommendations. Numerous individuals who had confidentially expressed satisfaction with the status quo refused to do so openly for fear of incurring popular displeasure. Not all had been cowed, though. One young woman gained Forbes' respect by responding vigorously to testimony by the local municipal president, who advocated unfettered independence at once. "I think the president must be crazy," she said. "I think anybody who has any sense at all knows perfectly well that we are wholly unable to protect ourselves. We have not a place where we can make a gun in the Islands and no training necessary to defend ourselves. We would be just as helpless as a child in the hands of enemies. Even the common people know this."[4]

But such individuals merely proved the rule of overt insistence on independence. Although Forbes averred that the relations of the commission with Filipinos on the whole had been "delightful," he warned that an undercurrent of tension between Americans and Filipinos existed, and if the commission spoke carelessly trouble could easily ensue. "The situation is very critical and might blow up at any time, leaving you with an insurrection on your hands," he told Weeks. Forbes went on to describe his and Woods' efforts to guide popular opinion in a favorable direction. "We have been trying very carefully and gradually to get people thinking about the need of a protectorate." He could not say with confidence how successful they had been, and he cautioned the administration to refrain from raising the independence issue until matters cleared.[5]

During the next several weeks Forbes reflected on the problem. Attempting to identify the source of Filipino touchiness on the independence issue, he decided it was a manifestation of "racial pride." He explained to the secretary of war, "The Filipino is intensely proud of his people and is quite ambitious. Filipinos are constantly talking about taking their place in the sisterhood of nations." Still, Forbes was convinced the Filipinos would settle for considerably less than true independence:

> Like most Orientals they seem to be more interested in the form than in the substance. They would at the present time be very glad to accept a thing that would be a little different from what they have now which they could call independence, but it could be hedged around with so many conditions lodged in the hands of representatives of the United States that their actual powers would be limited rather than augmented in the change.

Forbes advocated that whatever formula the administration selected, beneath the "velvet glove" there must be "the strong hand."[6]

The Wood-Forbes report, delivered to the president at the end of 1921, encapsulated Forbes' recommendations. At the same time it served the partisan purpose of criticizing the Wilson administration's handling of Philippine affairs. Briefly recounting the recent history of government in the islands, the report focused on three periods. The first comprised the years from 1907 to 1913, when "under the strong, conservative influence of the commission with American majority, the legislation passed was constructive and good, with marked emphasis placed upon the improvement of education and construction of permanent improvements." The second period lasted from 1913 until 1916. During this phase "the restraining influence was withdrawn with the appearance of a Filipino majority on the commission. . . . There were marked tendencies to inject politics into administration and to interfere with administrative efficiency." The third, most recent phase had produced an even more dismal record. "With an elected House and Senate, the legislation in this period became increasingly radical in its paternalism and government interference with business." The story of the Philippine National Bank, to cite an egregious case, was "one of the most unfortunate and darkest pages in Philippine history." Of particular concern to Forbes—he of the "obras grandes"—was the sad condition of the country's infrastructure. "The roads are falling into disrepair, some are impassable and the system of maintenance is carried on spasmodically."

Filipinization had not entirely undone the good work that had gone before. "We find the people happy, peaceful, and in the main prosperous, and keenly appreciative of the benefits of American rule." They would remain so under steady American guidance. Concluding, the Wood-Forbes report asserted that

the United States would shirk its obligations to the Filipinos if it let understandable but premature aspirations for independence dictate American policy:

> We find that the people are not organized economically nor from the standpoint of
> national defense to maintain an independent government. . . .
>   The experience of the past eight years, during which they have had practical
> autonomy, has not been such as to justify the people of the United States relinquish-
> ing supervision of the Government of the Philippine Islands, withdrawing their army
> and navy, and leaving the islands a prey to any powerful nation coveting their rich
> soil and potential commercial advantages. . . .
>   It would be a betrayal of the Philippine people, a misfortune to the American peo-
> ple, a distinct step backward in the path of progress, and a discreditable neglect of
> our national duty were we to withdraw from the islands and terminate our relation-
> ship there without giving the Filipinos the best chance possible to have an orderly
> and permanently stable government.[7]

II. From Moroland to Manila

To no one's surprise Harding accepted the Wood-Forbes report, including its
recommendation that Washington refrain from further steps toward independence "until the people have had time to absorb and thoroughly master the powers already in their hands." Somewhat less expectedly the Republican president
appointed Leonard Wood governor-general to succeed Harrison.

Wood's career was nearly one of the great stories of the middle age of American history. Born a bit too late to fight in the Civil War, Wood found his New
Hampshire upbringing and Harvard education confining, so he took his medical
degree and headed west to become a civilian contract surgeon with the army,
then pacifying Apaches in Arizona. The military life entered Wood's blood while
he and the cavalry chased Geronimo around the rimrock country, and he took a
commission with the regular army. When the Spanish-American War broke out
he and friend Theodore Roosevelt organized the Rough Riders, which he commanded with sufficient valor to receive promotion to major general. After the war
ended and Roosevelt went on to bigger things in Republican politics in America,
Wood remained in Cuba as military governor.

By the end of 1902 Cuba had reverted to local civilian control, although under
an American protectorate, and Wood, the quintessential man of action, needed
a new field in which to vent his energies. Roosevelt, now president, obliged his
old comrade by naming him governor of Moro province in the Philippines. The
Moros—the Spanish name for the Muslim inhabitants of Mindanao and nearby
islands—and their "pagan" neighbors never failed to fascinate American observers. Few writers among the scores to portray the early years of the American
occupation could resist penning a chapter or two on the proud and unruly inhabitants of the southern portion of the archipelago. Despite the fact that the Mus-

lims constituted less than 5 percent of the population of the Philippines, politicians and commentators, not to mention ethnologists and anthropologists, never
ceased pondering *The Moro Problem*, as one typical title of 1913 put it, or wondering "What Next for the Moro?" as a writer in the American journal *Foreign
Affairs* asked in 1928.[8]

Wood's biographer, writing at about the time of the latter piece, described the
territory Wood approached in 1903:

> It was a wild country and a wilder people. . . . Mindanao, with its thirty-six thousand
> square miles of mountains and lakes and cultivated valleys, coral reefs and mangrove
> swamps, rivers flowing through a trackless jungle, forests, dark and terrifying, and
> grassy plateaus, bright under the sun, was about the size of Great Britain's green and
> refractory neighbor [Ireland], but it possessed only some fifty miles of rutted roads,
> no railroads, and only four or five towns of any consequence. . . .
>
> The Filipinos were in the majority, but the Moros held the whip hand. They were
> in the main Malays who had come long before the Spaniards, as conquerors and mis-
> sionaries, in successive waves from the Malay Peninsula, Java, Borneo, and Sumatra.
> They lived in scattered villages around the fortified *cotta* and the *datto* they recog-
> nized as their chief. . . .
>
> The religious conceptions and ethical standards of the Koran which the Arab mis-
> sionaries had brought had taken hold of their imaginations and their habits of life
> sufficiently to make them resent bitterly the efforts of the Spaniards to convert them
> to Christianity; but in the course of the centuries they had drifted away from the
> religious teachings and neglected the laws, retaining only congenial precepts which
> related to plurality of wives, the control of concubines, the institution of slavery, and
> the slaughter of infidels.
>
> They were as a people ignorant, so far as formal education went. Here and there
> a Moro could read and write Arabic, and knew something of the Koran, but they
> were few. Many had, however, a practical education forced upon them by their envi-
> ronment. They were extraordinary shipbuilders and navigators; skilled in handicrafts;
> patient workers in brass and magnificent swordsmiths and armorers. They were cour-
> teous, moreover; they were cleanly; they were great talkers. They had a keen sport-
> ing instinct, a delightful sense of humor; honor, dignity, pride, self-respect, courage.
>
> But they knew nothing of economics beyond barter, nothing of government
> beyond autocracy, nothing of hygiene or sanitation beyond the Koran's primitive
> injunctions. They thought civilization was nonsense and, with more courage than
> most Occidentals who might be inclined to agree with them, expressed their opinion.
> The *kris* [a wavy-bladed dagger] was their god and Mohammed was his prophet.

What the Catholics of Ireland and the Gurkhas of Nepal would have been to
the British empire, had those two peoples been rolled into one, the Moros seemed
to American imperialists. Their religion was wrongheaded but not unrecogniz-
able. Their culture was rudimentary but not without charm. Their stubbornness
and independence of mind rendered them fractious and nearly impossible as subjects—the Spanish had given up trying to conquer them centuries before—but
their bravery and skill at arms made them the worthiest of opponents. For this
reason, going out to govern the Moros possessed an appeal for Americans lacking

in the more settled regions of the Philippines. "You have the opportunity to
become a second Rajali Brooke," Dean Worcester said in 1914 to Frank Carpenter, chief of the department of Mindanao and Sulu. "Honestly, don't you
think it would really be worth while to break away from peanut politics and make
a good stiff fight to get for the backward peoples under your control the things
that they really need?"[9]

The Americans' mission to Moroland brought a satisfaction attempts to uplift
the rest of the islands often lacked. Not that getting America's message across
was easy. Frank McCoy, an assistant to Wood, wrote home about the problems
of dealing with the natives of the region:

> It is hard to explain our presence to a Moro. Try to take his point of view. "Here are
> these big, strong Americanos with lots of soldiers and money to burn. They have
> driven the Spaniards out. What do they want? They don't rob us of our money, or
> anything else, nor raid for women or slaves. The Spaniards used to capture us and
> baptize us. These Americans have not interfered with our religion or customs, bar-
> ring the bad ones. What do they want?"

Most of the real-life Moros were not so puzzled as McCoy's, and they hardly
thought the only customs the Americans aimed to abolish were the bad ones. It
was true enough that the new imperialists decided not to disturb such cultural
idiosyncracies as polygamy—after all, it was no secret that Mormons in parts of
Utah still married multiply—but when the Americans drew the line at piracy and
open slavery, they resisted.[10]

As a consequence opposition to American rule continued in the southern
islands long after the insurrection in Luzon had sputtered out. Wood regularly
led military expeditions, some quite sanguinary, against different groups of
Moros, believing they must learn to accept American authority. After one expedition he wrote in his diary,

> There is only one way to deal with these people, and that is to be absolutely just and
> absolutely firm. When a crime is committed the offender must be surrendered or
> punishment must promptly be applied.
>   The Moros of this section are as a class a treacherous unreliable lot of slave hunters
> and land pirates. Our conciliatory and good-natured policy with them resulted in the
> establishment among them of the firm conviction that we were both cowardly and
> weak, and out of this conviction grew an absolute contempt for our authority.
>   Firmness and the prompt application of disciplinary measures will maintain order,
> prevent loss of life and property and permit good government and prosperity among
> these people. Dilatory tactics, indecision and lack of firmness will result in a carnival
> of crime and an absolute contempt for all authority in this region.[11]

Despite his firmness Wood never succeeded in mastering the Moros. Neither
did anyone else. They continued in a state of semi-rebellion against American
rule until 1916, when the Jones Act dumped the problem on the Philippine legislature. The Filipinos had hardly better luck, then or afterward.

Meanwhile Wood moved on. From 1906 until 1910 he commanded the American troops in the Philippines. In 1910 Taft summoned him to Washington to become army chief of staff. His continued connections to Roosevelt caused him trouble with the Wilson administration, and when America went to war in 1917 the president bypassed Wood for the less-senior John Pershing as leader of the American expeditionary force. Wilson's slight increased Wood's stature among Republicans, and when the GOP convened in 1920 to pick a candidate for president Wood ran among the leaders. But the convention deadlocked, the party bosses repaired to the legendary smoke-filled room of Chicago's Blackstone hotel, and Warren Harding emerged holding the brass ring.

Harding's nomination did not come free. Following the Republican candidate's victory in November he recognized the necessity to do something for, and with, Wood. Although the former chief of staff most wanted to be secretary of war, Harding's managers had set this plum aside for the presumably more deserving John Weeks of Massachusetts. Harding instead asked Wood to join Forbes on the Philippine investigative commission and following its report to stay on as governor-general.

Even by the abysmal standards of the Harding administration the selection of Wood as Philippine governor was uninspired. If ever a good man found himself in the wrong job, Wood did in Manila. He acted as though he were still in Mindanao and the leaders of the Philippine legislature were a gang of Moros. Of tact he knew nothing. Firmness would conquer all. In the midst of one of the recurrent crises that marked his tenure in Malacañang he wrote Weeks that troubles would work themselves out if Washington held fast. "The main thing is the continuance of a perfectly patient, courteous, firm tone on the part of the Government here and the Government at home." With Forbes and others from the Taft period Wood thought Harrison had gone far beyond the directives of Congress and prudence in allowing control of Philippine affairs to pass into the hands of the Filipinos. "We have a very difficult situation here and much to do," he wrote as he took up his new post. Woods determined to restore the balance of political power in the Philippines and resolved to relinquish no measure of power he could retain to himself. Cameron Forbes had once described his own attitude to power: "My position is this: that when there are implied powers I am willing to use them." Leonard Wood demonstrated himself no less insistent on the prerogatives of his office.[12]

In certain respects the problem Wood faced paralleled that of British imperial officials in the American colonies after the Seven Years' War. London in the 1760s and Washington in the 1920s both sought to enforce imperial law against colonists grown accustomed to laxity from the metropolis and a considerable degree of autonomy. Each found the task thankless and difficult. The efforts of each provoked a rebellion, one violent, the other peaceful but hardly less acrimonious. Each rebellion eventually resulted in the rending of the imperial bond.

III.   Osmeña versus Quezon . . .

Just as a shrewder ministry than Grenville's could have lessened the pain of reorganizing the British empire after 1763, so a more agile politician than Wood might have managed the reassertion of Washington's control of the Philippines after 1920. Conditions in the islands lent themselves to outside manipulation, for a rift developed between the leading figures of the dominant Nacionalista party: Osmeña and Quezon.

The potential for a rupture had existed for more than a decade, ever since the ambitious Quezon's successes in Washington had begun calling into question the primacy of Osmeña. "I am looking forward with great interest to your triumphant return to the islands," Harrison wrote Quezon at the time of the Jones Act. Osmeña's interest was no less than Harrison's, but he was not exactly looking forward to Quezon's return. The two men could hardly have been less alike. Teodoro Kalaw, a colleague and admirer of both, once attempted to describe the differences between them. Kalaw's account, which succeeds as well as any in capturing the diverse characters of the two, bears repeating at some length. Of Quezon he wrote,

> When I first knew Quezon, I did not consider him destined for greatness. Brilliant he was, yes, and highly intelligent, "a born leader," "a magnetic personality," "a forceful speaker." But I had seen many other brilliant personalities fade out or grow lusterless with time. . . . I believed in other more lasting qualities than just brilliance and magnetism. I believed in serious study rather than intuitive insight; I believed in deliberation rather than impulse; I believed in solid facts rather than flashy witticisms.
>
> Quezon broke all my rules. I felt I could not rely on his statements because a change in circumstances could eventually make him contradict them. What kind of a leader was this, I said to myself, who had a good word for every side of every question? Who could be quoted as being for independence, *against* independence, for a dominion status, *against* a commonwealth, for free trade, *against* free trade, and so on down the list? This was not leadership, I said; it was either clowning or opportunism.

Gradually Kalaw discerned that whatever his inconsistencies Quezon could not be convicted of insincerity.

> The fact is, whenever Quezon considers matters, he seldom if ever bothers himself with details. He glances rapidly through papers and memoranda, makes a clean-cut decision then and there, gives out his dictum with assurance and authority, picks out with almost miraculous psychological accuracy the proper man to carry it out, and then forgets about the whole case.
>
> Scientists and researchers despair at the uncanniness with which his hand can flip through the accumulated work of years and put his finger on the unguarded slip of a second. Needless to say, Quezon is laughingly very proud of this gift. Time and again he tells his technicians, "The trouble with you bookworms is that you neglect your conclusions in your diligence for figures."

The careful Osmeña stood in striking contrast to the plunging Quezon. Kalaw warmed more easily to the former. " 'This man,' I said to myself, 'has looked well into himself and knows what he wants. He will be true to it, as the lodestar is to the North Pole. I can follow him because he is sincere.'" Unlike Quezon, who relied on intuition, Osmeña possessed "the scholar's love for completeness" and took pride in the thoroughness with which he studied matters before arriving at decisions. Quezon, given to reversals of course, found it easy to embrace those with whom he recently had differed.

Osmeña, on the other hand, and as everybody well knew, recognized his friends. But better than that, he remembered his enemies. It is not that he has been incapable of taking them in with him and making use of their services. More unexaggeratedly than Quezon, he has given reward where reward was due. But once a friend had defaulted, he could no more hope to belong to the inner circle. For Osmeña, like the sentimentalist that he really was, could not easily forgive and forget, not because of the consequent *mal* effects of disloyalty but due to the personal pain of loss. Biographers have poignantly described the depths of Lincoln's sorrow at the secession of the South from the Union. Sometimes I think Osmeña's feelings at the discovery of a new gap in his followers' ranks has the same quality.

Kalaw recognized the supreme importance of the personal touch in Filipino politics. Here he thought the divergence in styles between Quezon and Osmeña most marked.

Quezon would be guilty of more serious blunders in his political career were it not for that golden gift God gave him when he was born: his insight into men's minds and hearts. It can be said that his judgment of men is well-nigh perfect. He uses this knowledge with the ease and familiarity of a concert pianist practicing his scales. He switches hitherto unknown men from their obscure positions into jobs of national importance and smiles with satisfaction when he sees them make names for themselves. He receives some upstart of a socialist with the deference due an ambassador and chuckles to himself when he reads in the papers the next day the amazing statement that the laboring class has given him its utmost confidence and support. Not infrequently he has given some well-known puffed-up name a public scolding worthy of a fish-wife, only to have than same cream-puff crawl back to him with double his former protestations of loyalty—and financial contributions. Manila, after another incident of this sort, lapses into the old refrain: "Only Quezon can get away with that."

But if Quezon knows his people well, Osmeña goes him one better, for Osmeña knows his Quezon with, shall we say, infinite understanding. Osmeña has very often stood at one side, smiling quietly at Quezon's railings and stormings, at his abusive and colorful language, even when directed against Osmeña himself. More than anyone else, I doubt if even second to Quezon's own wife, Osmeña knows this tumultuous and emotional intellect for the simple, almost primitive, instinct that it fundamentally is. Quezon may often have been puzzled by Osmeña's taciturn attitudes, but Osmeña has always taken all of Quezon's attitudinizing at its real face value.[13]

For most of the period before the passage of the Jones Act, Quezon deferred to Osmeña as leader of the Nacionalista party. Yet Quezon's position as resident commissioner in Washington inevitably gave him stature of a kind Osmeña could not match. When the Wilson administration chose to loosen the reins and commit the United States to independence for the Philippines, Quezon credibly claimed much of the credit.

Recognizing that Manila now became the center of action, Quezon returned to the islands, creating a stir on his arrival, and ran for the newly created senate. His victory and subsequent elevation to the upper chamber's presidency placed him directly in competition with Osmeña, who remained speaker of the lower house. Despite protestations of loyalty to Osmeña and the Nacionalista party, Quezon indicated his belief that as presiding officer of the senate he outranked the leader of the house. Various issues cast the differences between the two men into increasing relief, but Osmeña's continued control of the party machinery enabled him to keep Quezon at bay. In 1919, for example, Quezon and Osmeña took opposing positions on a question regarding a government subsidy to a private corporation. Although the majority of involved party members agreed with Quezon on the merits of the issue, when Osmeña threatened to resign over the matter Quezon's followers defected to the speaker.[14]

The arrival of the Wood-Forbes commission in 1921 placed both Quezon and Osmeña on best behavior, as they sought to demonstrate their country's capacity for self-government. Their display of harmony had little effect on the commission's report, and the dispute broke into the open once more at the end of 1921. A legislative measure reorganizing the judiciary provided the occasion for battle. Under Quezon's direction the senate passed a bill transferring certain powers from the Philippine supreme court to the legislature. When Osmeña resisted the move, saying he was content to rest the powers in question with the justices, who would safeguard the interests even of unpopular minorities, Quezon charged the speaker with a lack of confidence in the Filipino people. Reminding his listeners that Washington controlled appointments to the supreme court, Quezon declared, "If you love to be ruled by men appointed by a foreign sovereign power, you tie yourselves to slavery."

Efforts to resolve this issue and the larger question of who would head the Nacionalistas occupied party officials through a succession of conventions. Osmeña contended that as spokesman of the Nacionalistas in the more-popularly elected body he represented the will of the rank and file. In a climactic session in December 1921 the speaker demanded recognition of his preeminence. "Virtually I am de facto leader of the ruling party in the government at present. I have been tacitly considered as such. I want it now to be defined and put squarely to the people. Under the present condition, I am held responsible and even blamed for anything that happens or may happen in the government." Quezon responded by denouncing Osmeña as power-hungry and tyrannical. The speaker denied the allegations, but with his usual finesse he deflated the charges by saying he would surrender his prerogatives to a committee of the house.

This failed to satisfy Quezon, although it forced the senate president to make a similar gesture of abnegation. He persisted in hammering on the issue of what he deemed Osmeña's excessive power.

> I will always stand by my theory of collective leadership even if I have to leave the Nacionalista Party. The time has come for the establishment in the Islands of political parties which should fight for principles, not necessarily for the control of the government. I do not care if those who are supporting the theory of collective leadership are never returned to power, but I am sure that if the question is put squarely to the people in the coming elections, the voters of the old generation and the young men of today will support them.

With these words, and with the further statement, which instantly gained fame, that "my loyalty to my party ends where my loyalty to my country begins," Quezon led a walkout. In February 1922 the break became official. The senate president and his followers announced the formation of the Partido Nacionalista-Colectivista.[15]

Teodoro Kalaw, who viewed the contest for power from within the Nacionalista movement, assessed the breach in his diary; at the same time he illuminated a decade of Filipino politics:

> March 1, 1922—Quezon has finally won victory for his party. All our efforts and those of the Speaker proved useless to stop the secession. The split has been worked on for years, and planned behind the back of Osmeña. Technically, it is a bloodless coup d'etat. Quezon took advantage of the Speaker's position to undermine him and pull him down.
>
> When the Jones Law was implemented by Governor-General Harrison, it was agreed to have a Filipino leader in the administration who would unobtrusively win away political powers from the Governor-General for the benefit of the Filipinos. Osmeña fulfilled this assignment. For all practical purposes, he was the Governor-General. The most important matters of state weighed upon his shoulders. Thus Osmeña became so burdened with the study of important matters of government that he was forced to abandon the details of political party administration, a field which was immediately taken over and cultivated by Quezon.
>
> The circumstances, besides, of Quezon's being in the Senate and of his speaking English well, gave him the opportunity to deal the final blow with the aid mainly of the English-speaking younger generation. Quezon took advantage of this advantage.[16]

IV.   . . . versus Wood

As Kalaw's comments indicated, Quezon's challenge to Osmeña succeeded partly because of the former's mastery of the American political idiom. Osmeña never warmed to Americans the way Quezon did. Osmena particularly distrusted

American business interests, which he considered, not without reason, to be behind much ill that befell the Philippines. During discussions leading to the Jones Act he warned Quezon and Harrison against the designs of American businessmen who would try to subvert Philippine independence. When markets for Philippine commodities fell after World War I he blamed an "artificial situation" fostered by American corporate interests. These interests, he alleged, were also out to discredit the Philippine National Bank—admittedly no great task. Osmeña's suspicions of Americans engendered a reciprocal coolness on their part. At the end of the next war this coolness would prove his political undoing.[17]

Quezon, on the other hand, appears genuinely to have liked Americans. They certainly liked him. Quezon was a difficult man not to like. His combination of deference and self-assurance particularly appealed to citizens of a country trying to practice a democratic form of imperialism. Quezon's political success, achieved entirely during the period of American rule, owed in considerable measure to his ability to inspire in American leaders friendliness and confidence. More precisely, Quezon's success resulted from his ability to use this friendliness and confidence for his own purposes.

Not all Americans succumbed to the Quezon charm. Forbes thought Quezon too slippery for America's good. Leonard Wood liked him even less. The split in the ruling party threw Filipino politics into disarray, and where earlier the Nacionalistas had dominated the field, now three parties—Nacionalistas, Colectivistas and the formerly inconsequential Democratas—vied on a fairly equal basis. The elections of 1922 handed the Colectivistas a majority in the senate and a plurality in the house. Nacionalistas and Democratas balanced almost evenly, with the former claiming a two-seat edge over the latter in the senate while falling three seats shy in the house. The most significant outcome of the election involved Osmeña, who abandoned his position as speaker of the house to run for the senate. He gained election to the upper body, but when the Colectivistas garnered a majority there he found himself in Quezon's shadow.

The full implications of this latest installment of the Quezon-Osmeña struggle did not become immediately apparent, for another battle, between the legislature and the executive, took precedence. The inflexible and unimaginative Wood made a target Quezon could not resist. In attacking the American governor Quezon confirmed his nationalist bona fides and forced the Nacionalistas, who could hardly rally to Wood's defense, to fall in behind. Quezon's success in the matter caused Wood's aide Frank McCoy to characterize Quezon and Osmeña as the "upper and lower millstones" of the governor's existence. Wood himself remarked to Secretary Weeks, after a meeting with Quezon and Quezon's lieutenant in the house, Speaker Manuel Roxas, "They haven't at heart the best interests of their people and their progress or welfare, but they are keen to have a more unrestrained control of the government." On another occasion Wood described a meeting with Quezon and Roxas, during which he had asked the two to channel the Colectivistas' and others' dissatisfaction in a constructive direction. They indicated they would not. Wood attributed the refusal to cowardice congenital in Filipino leaders. "They are all of them unwilling to draw up and agree to any definitive proposition, and admitted that if they agreed to anything that was conservative and rational, some more radical individual would take advantage of it and charge them with having weakened in the cause of independence."[18]

Wood initially kept his complaints to himself and Weeks, realizing open criticism would strengthen his opponents. A silent foe did not suit Quezon. Shortly after Wood's arrival the senate president explained his strategy to the departed though still interested and sympathetic Francis Harrison. "My attitude toward Wood is that of watchful waiting. It is my purpose to cooperate with him and, for that matter, with anyone that may be appointed governor, as long—but no longer—as he adopts the policy of giving the people of the Philippines the opportunity to exercise the rights that have been granted them and act in consonance with the best interests of my country." Quezon had expected the Wood appointment to be short-term, knowing that the general had received an offer to head the University of Pennsylvania. Wood, however, opted in favor of Manila, and by the summer of 1923 Quezon had had enough of watchful waiting.[19]

While any number of pretexts would have served to bring the conflict with Wood to a head, the one Quezon chose turned on a case of alleged corruption involving an American official named Ray Conley, the chief of the gambling squad of the Manila secret service. The city's mayor, Ramón Fernandez, after receiving reports that Conley was taking bribes, ordered an investigation. The probe provided sufficient evidence of wrong-doing for the mayor to suspend Conley. Philippine interior secretary José Laurel, reviewing the case, confirmed the suspension. But Wood suspected a frameup by influential Filipinos resentful of Conley's refusal to wink at their illegal activities. The governor also deemed the case a test by the Filipinos of his staunchness as representative of the president of the United States. He ordered a second investigation, which cleared Conley. Wood reinstated him.

Wood did not think much of Conley personally. As he conceded to Frank McCoy, "We are pulling the whole Government into a political row over a man who, aside from the principle of justice, is not worth the trouble." Wood admitted to McCoy that Conley had lied about certain matters related to the investigation. Nonetheless the governor determined to take a stand. "Justice we must sustain," he told McCoy, "no matter whom it hits."[20]

At this point Laurel and Fernandez resigned in protest. Quezon denounced the governor for overreaching and for interfering in matters falling within the compass of the legislature, to which alone, Quezon claimed, the secretary of the interior answered. After a heated debate between Quezon and Wood at Malacañang regarding the relative spheres of the legislative and executive branches and their relation to the Conley case, Gordon Johnston, one of Wood's assistants from Rough Rider and Moro days, burst out, "Mr. Quezon, are you talking about Conley or are you talking about parliamentary government?"

"I don't give a God-damn about Conley," Quezon retorted.

"I thought not," Johnston countered. "Then you are just wasting the general's time and your own. You know as well as I that the general can't change the form of government of the Philippines. We are all operating under the Jones Law. If you want to change that law, the place for you to go is the Congress of the United States."[21]

Wood tried to downplay the dispute, advising Weeks, "Please pay no attention to sensational rumors that may creep into the press from time to time. Some of our brethren here feel that they have to shout in order to let the world know they are still with us." But the crisis escalated three days later when the advisory council of state and the cabinet, led by Quezon, quit en masse.[22]

The Filipino leaders justified their resignations on grounds of high ethics. Laurel declared, "I cannot have under my department a man like Conley whom I consider dishonest." Quezon took refuge in the Jones Act, asserting that the resigners were "defending the spirit of the law enacted for these Islands by the representatives of the American people." In a letter to Wood the group elaborated their complaints:

> We have observed for some time now that it is your policy and desire, as Governor-General, to intervene in, and control, even to the smallest detail, the affairs of our government, both national and local, in utter disregard of the authority and responsibility of the Department heads and other officials concerned. This policy recently culminated in an unfortunate incident which shocked public opinion in this country, when you, by undue interference in the powers and jurisdiction of the Secretary of the Interior and the Mayor of the City of Manila, reinstated a member of the secret service force of the City who had been legally suspended from office.

Wood, expecting the letter, dressed for the occasion in full armor as commanding general of American troops in the Philippines. He informed the resigners that he considered their action a challenge to the authority of the United States government. Word leaked that he had ordered the army to prepare for hostilities should the contest turn violent. This prompted Quezon to write a second letter expressing his concern that "the Government feels there is imminent danger of a disturbance of public order, or that there is an attempt to start a rebellion." Quezon declared, "I desire most emphatically to affirm that the people of the Philippine Islands are loyal to the United States Government, and that they are not contemplating any revolt against the sovereignty of the United States. . . . It is not true that the action of the members of the Council of State and the Secretaries of Department in resigning is a challenge to the authority of the United States in the Philippine Islands." Quezon did say, however, that he and his colleagues intended to take their complaints to Washington and had so informed President Harding.[23]

Subsequent developments postponed the Washington trip a few months. In the meantime Quezon attempted to embarrass Wood further. Quezon elevated a senator to a vacant post as resident commissioner, thereby providing justification for an election campaign, to replace the senator, that would highlight the dispute with Wood. Quezon orchestrated the nomination of Fernandez, the former Manila mayor. The campaign produced what Wood described as a "sharp, ugly fight with a great deal of personal abuse, charge and countercharge." The fight polarized the Manila community, arraying Americans against Filipinos and forcing to the surface the always latent, at best, race issue. Hoping to calm the situation, Weeks suggested that Wood take a vacation, perhaps a tour of Japan. Wood declined. The deadlock continued.[24]

Politics provided the forum and much of the impetus behind the continuing cabinet crisis of the Wood years, but questions of economics underlay the struggle. Recalling events of the period, Quezon later told Teodoro Kalaw, "When all these can be written down calmly, it will be shown that in the fight with General Wood, I defended not only our political autonomy but also our economic heritage. General Wood wanted to hand over to American capitalists the Philippine National Bank, the Manila Railroad, and our sugar centrals."[25]

Though Wood might have phrased the matter differently, he would not have disputed the essential thrust of Quezon's argument. In the Republican tradition of Taft and Forbes, Wood looked to American private investment to foster the development of the Philippines. Filipinos still lacked the capital to do the job themselves, and in light of the corruption and inefficiency of the years of Filipinization it appeared evident, to Wood at any rate, that they lacked the character and ability as well. Wood took as an essential part of his task the restoration of the discipline of the market to the Philippine economy. Referring to the big centrifugal sugar mills, he told Weeks, "There is one thing certain, that we must get the centrals out of government management." In another letter Wood delineated an instance demonstrating how well-connected individuals had used the political system to benefit themselves, to the detriment of the country as a whole.

> While the heavy government investments in sugar in Negros tended to help build up the sugar industry and thereby help conditions in the Islands, these investments have mostly aided a few of the old sugar-growing families and have been made to the disadvantage of the planters and small farmers in other parts of the Islands, and resulted in the curtailment of public works, public education, public health, and other activities incident to the tying up of these large sums.

Wood conceded that problems created in a decade could not be remedied in a day. But he thought the application of "conservative and sound business methods," by which he meant the techniques of American private enterprise, would put the Philippine economy right again.[26]

Wood was less explicit than Forbes had been in drawing the connection between American economic penetration of the islands and American political control. Wood promoted privatization primarily on grounds of efficiency. But privatization, under circumstances then obtaining in the Philippines, implied Americanization, and the result would be the same. Quezon and the Filipino leaders recognized this, which was why they objected. That privatization also diminished the personal political and economic power of upper-class Filipinos reinforced their opposition.

Wood was nothing if not tenacious, and despite Filipino complaints he pressed ahead. He lectured audiences of all sizes on the blessings of private enterprise. As he explained to Weeks,

> I never miss the opportunity to tell the people that they cannot increase their revenues to the point necessary to maintain the sort of government that they wish to maintain unless capital can be encouraged to come the Islands. I think we are making some headway but it is an uphill fight, due to the little politicians, the men who are the real enemies of the country, constantly creating misunderstandings and misleading the people.

At times Wood sounded like a one-man chamber of commerce. He advocated agricultural diversification, promoting rubber especially. "The cultivation of rubber is peculiarly adapted to Philippine methods and conditions," he explained to Bureau of Insular Affairs chief McIntyre. Rubber, Wood said, might "soon become one of the leading products of the islands." He added, "There is a growing interest in it which I am doing all I properly can to encourage." Wood lobbied for the development of Manila as a crossroads of the southwestern Pacific. The Philippine capital, he argued, had "distinct advantages" in this regard, among them the communications facilities provided as an adjunct to the American military presence, a sound currency, an active and growing "English speaking and American thinking" work force, a free press, and of course an incomparable harbor. Blessed with such advantages, Wood said, Manila could grow into a "distributing center for the Orient." America would provide the guidance. The Filipinos need only supply cooperation.[27]

V.   Petitioning the crown

But Filipino leaders were not about to cooperate with Wood, to build another Hong Kong or for any other purpose. Refusing to have anything to do with the governor, they prepared to carry their fight to America. Harding's death in the summer of 1923 forced a delay, but in December Speaker Roxas arrived in Washington with a message for Congress. Consciously written in the style and cadence of the American declaration of independence, the Filipino statement included a bill of particulars against Wood:

> He has set to naught all understanding that the Filipino people have had with the American government, and has ignored the assurances given them by the late President. . . .

He has surrounded himself with a secret Cabinet composed of military and other extra-legal advisers, which have encroached upon the legitimate functions of the Filipino officials in the government.

He has broken asunder the bonds of harmony that had united Americans and Filipinos after the bloody struggle of 1899, a harmony that reached its highest expression during the first years of autonomous government.

He has placed himself over and above the laws enacted by the Philippine Legislature, laws that have never been declared null and void by the courts or by the Congress of the United States.

He has claimed for himself an unlimited executive responsibility that neither existing laws nor practices already established have recognized. . . .

He has abused the veto power. . . .

He has disregarded the rights of the Senate. . . .

He has destroyed our budgetary system. . . .

He has endeavored to defeat the economic policies duly laid down by the Philippine Legislature. . . .

He has sought to establish a colonial despotism here worse than that which has cursed our country for the last ten generations.

There was more along these lines, the upshot being that Wood had "deviated from the policy of the American government to give the Filipino people an ever increasing self-government, a policy announced by every President beginning with President McKinley, and ratified by the Congress of the United States and the Jones Law." The petition concluded, "The time for Philippine independence has come. It can be postponed no longer. Filipino welfare calls for it; Filipino ideals long for it; and the good name and pledged faith of America require it."[28]

From Manila, Wood sought by silence to dismiss the indictment. A friendly reporter asked why he did not respond to these "abominable lies." Wood answered, "Every time a jackass brays, must I get up and explain what he means?" Wood asserted that the petitioners were demagoguing the independence issue. "The question of independence is like the desire of the Christian to go to Heaven," he said. "They all want to go there, but not now. That is the real situation here. You don't see a lot of good and enthusiastic church people rushing out and buying coffins to go to Heaven. You don't see any parades here or any manifestations of independence."[29]

The Roxas mission hit a wall in Washington. Calvin Coolidge responded to the Filipino petition as favorably as George III did to Thomas Jefferson's draft. The president denied that the United States had ever had self-interested designs upon the Philippines. "A great responsibility came unsought to the American people," he told Roxas. "The fortunes of war brought American power to your islands, playing the part of an unexpected and welcome deliverer." Coolidge affirmed his complete confidence in Wood. "If the Filipino people cannot cooperate in the support and encouragement of as good an administration as has been afforded under Governor-General Wood, their failure will be rather a testimony of unpreparedness for the full obligations of citizenship than an evidence of patriotic eagerness to advance their country." The president asserted that the petition did not represent a consensus of Filipino opinion. Should the United States accede to the wishes of the petitioners, it would fail in its moral obligations.[30]

Coolidge's claim that sovereignty over the Philippines came unsought to America was ludicrous, but on one point he spoke the truth. The Roxas mission did not represent a consensus of Filipino opinion, even the opinion of Filipinos active politically. The opposition Democratas, although asked to send a delegate, boycotted.

In April 1924, however, a second, larger group including both Nacionalista Consolidados, an anti-Wood coalition patched together by Quezon and Osmeña, and Democratas set off for America. Quezon and Osmeña, the leaders of the delegation, timed their trip to coincide with the Republican national convention, which they rightly guessed would nominate the next president. Speaking before the GOP platform committee at Cleveland's city hall, Osmeña asserted that American policy toward the Philippines was "now beyond the stage of speculation and controversy." From the era of McKinley, Osmeña said, the United States had pledged itself to Philippine independence. The Jones Act had gone so far as to specify a time: when the islands achieved a stable government. "This stable government has already been organized," Osmeña declared, "and therefore the pledge of independence should now be redeemed without further delay. . . . The Philippine question should be solved once and for all—and solved in the only way compatible with the honor of America and the just and legitimate aspirations of the Filipino people."[31]

Osmeña and Quezon had no more luck than Roxas, and the overwhelming margin by which American voters returned Coolidge to the White House signaled defeat for Filipino hopes of imminent progress toward independence. The stalemate with Wood continued unabated. Only an act of providence, it appeared, would unseize the situation. Although they chose not to admit as much in public, the Filipino leaders recognized that more than obstructionism on the part of the Coolidge administration was involved in Washington's keeping Wood on. Amzi Kelly, a Manila attorney and an associate of Quezon, delineated the understanding of informed Filipinos regarding the Wood affair.

> Washington evidently realizes that the present governor is out of step and out of harmony with the people in the Philippines and is, I think, looking for a place in America for him. In this regard and with this particular man, Leonard Wood, who is now old and greatly beloved for his past achievements and honorable record, even the President must proceed in his removal with extreme caution so as not to give offense and wound the feelings of a magnificent American.[32]

Understanding of Washington's predicament did not translate into sympathy for Wood. The Filipinos maintained their drumfire of criticism—which simply confirmed, in Wood's mind and that of his supporters, the correctness of the governor-general's position. "The G-G has been through a hell of a time for the past year," Frank McCoy commiserated, "and has stood gaff without a sign of weakness." McCoy added that Wood's fortitude was "a fine Anglo-Saxon performance as against the meannesses of Orientals."[33]

Remarks like McCoy's indicated the depths to which Philippine-American relations had sunk. In 1926 Teodoro Kalaw, then executive secretary of the Philippine independence commission, described the position of the Philippines in American politics as "worse than at any other time with regards to the possibility of independence." Kalaw noted a survey of American editorial opinion revealing that 80 of 87 newspapers examined opposed Philippine independence, with the opponents clustered among America's larger papers. The return of the Republicans had reversed the accomplishments of the Wilson administration. Kalaw wrote, "The elements whose designs over the Philippines predominate are the capitalists, and these place as a condition sine qua non of their investments the permanent retention of our country." Kalaw thought that under present circumstances Filipinos might be fortunate simply to preserve what aspects of autonomy they already exercised.[34]

8

The Bottom Line
1927–1934

I. Deus ex deus

Providence eventually relieved the impasse between the Filipino leadership and the office of the governor-general. Likely no other agent could have accomplished the feat. "The talk of a deadlock is all nonsense," Wood told Frank McCoy. "The only deadlock that there is is between my determination to have the law obeyed and the agitators' determination not to obey it, and the deadlock which comes between loyalty and disloyalty." The Filipinos were equally adamant. Having publicly denounced Wood as a tyrant, they could retreat only with considerable loss of face, personally and politically. But on a visit to the United States in 1927 Wood had a doctor check for recurrence of a benign tumor removed from his skull two decades earlier. Concerned at what he saw, the doctor called for another operation. Hemorrhaging occurred during surgery. Wood died without waking.[1]

Wood's untimely death proved timely for both sides in the dispute in Manila. Each party had proved its point. Neither was benefiting from the ongoing paralysis. Coolidge could now appoint a conciliator without appearing to back down, while the Filipinos could resume cooperation as a gesture of posthumous, and inexpensive, grace—which grace Quezon demonstrated personally by a letter of sympathy to Wood's widow.[2]

Washington wisely took the opportunity to name a successor who, although differing little with Wood on questions of American prerogatives, could not have been more dissimilar temperamentally. As had Wood, Henry Stimson had taken a professional degree at Harvard, but where Wood left Cambridge to pursue Geronimo across the mesas of Arizona, Stimson, after service with Elihu Root's law firm in New York, accepted Roosevelt's summons to chase Morgans and Harrimans through the canyons of Wall Street. While prosecuting railroads for antitrust violations, Stimson made an enemy of the American Sugar Refining Company, which had benefited enormously from the rebates the railroads paid it. Stimson learned much about the sugar industry that would prove useful in the Philippines, as well as a valuable lesson in the politics of big business. Expecting a lengthy court fight, Stimson was surprised when the sugar trust capitulated early. "Damn it, Stimson," the company's chief counsel said, "we think you're wrong on the law and wrong on the facts, but we can't stand the publicity."[3]

Like many another crusading prosecutor, Stimson tried his hand at elective politics. His 1910 bid for the governorship of New York failed, and he settled for heading up Taft's war department, where he learned more about the Philippines. Wilson's victory retired Stimson from public service until the American entry into World War I prompted his enlistment as an artillery officer. Subsequent practice in corporate law made his fortune as well as his reputation for finding common ground between contending parties. In 1926 Coolidge tapped him to settle a dispute between Chile and Peru. The following year he helped negotiate a halt to a Nicaraguan civil war.

Stimson kept touch with Philippine affairs, going so far in 1926 as to attempt to bridge the Wood-Filipino gap. After long discussions with Wood, Quezon and Osmeña, Stimson produced an outline of an approach to responsible cabinet government. But Wood could not bring himself to accept legislative constraints on his power, and the scheme collapsed.

Partly from loyalty to the Coolidge administration and partly from philosophical agreement with the broad objectives the Republicans had pursued in the islands from the first, Stimson publicly defended the American position in the Philippines. In an article in the *Saturday Evening Post* he lauded Wood's "unfailing patience" and "titanic energy" in confronting a difficult and thankless task. In the face of daunting obstacles Wood had accomplished much:

> The damage done by the reckless experiment of the Harrison administration has been practically repaired. The currency has been restored to par. The bank has been saved from insolvency. The government is living within its income. Taxation, which is very moderate, is being satisfactorily paid. Sanitation has been restored and, while eternal vigilance is necessary, that vigilance at present is being maintained. . . . There is in general throughout the Islands a very evident condition of ease and contentment.[4]

Neither Taft nor Forbes could have stated the retentionist case more persuasively, but such were Stimson's personal gifts that when Wood died Quezon and Osmeña rushed to Washington to urge Stimson's appointment as successor. The two Filipino leaders corresponded with and talked to Stimson, reassuring themselves of his good wishes toward the Philippines. Osmeña commented on "satisfactory conferences" with Stimson. Stimson reciprocated Quezon's expressed desire that Philippine-American relations once more be distinguished by "frankness and friendliness."

Despite their approval of Stimson, the Filipino politicians wished to avoid the appearance of supplication. Quezon reminded Harrison that though Stimson was "a well bred man" he was still "an imperialist and a friend of Wood." Quezon adopted an oblique approach in a letter to insular affairs chief McIntyre. After asserting that he and Osmeña backed Stimson, Quezon added, "I communicate this to you without directly saying that I take any responsibility in the matter; but should the administration consider the appointment of Stimson, you already know how we feel. . . . Please destroy this letter and return it to me." McIntyre, as anxious as Quezon to repair the political process in Manila, lent his own support to Stimson—and returned Quezon's letter, shredded. Coolidge accepted the recommendations, and Stimson headed for the Philippines.[5]

The brief Stimson era began in March 1928 with the new governor's inauguration. Immediately he revived the council of state, in suspended animation since Quezon and the other Filipino leaders walked out in 1923. Stimson made clear that the council would fill merely an advisory capacity, yet the fact that he took trouble to solicit Filipino opinions and considered them seriously sufficed for the moment to bring the Filipinos back aboard. "You will have the cordial cooperation of the Legislature," Quezon assured the governor.[6]

Of greater importance for the success of his administration, Stimson demonstrated that he considered Filipinos his equals. Wood had proved considerably less than satisfactory in this regard. At the onset of the cabinet crisis Wood told Secretary of Justice José Abad Santos, "Mr. Secretary, this question is one between Americans and Filipinos. Naturally I have to be with the Americans." To which Abad Santos, until then loyal to the governor, replied, "I have sided with you in this case even at the risk of being held suspect by my friends. But since you make the racial question the issue, I find myself obliged also to be with my kind."[7]

Stimson transformed the matter at once. On arrival in Manila he discovered that the church of his first choice barred Filipinos. He immediately joined another, which did not. At the inaugural ball he and Mrs. Stimson danced a game, if less than expert, version of the local *rigodón*. Several weeks later Mrs. Stimson donned Filipina attire for a party hosted by the Philippine legislature. Stimson listened carefully even to those Filipino views he disagreed with, and he won the respect of nearly all persons he had contact with. To a certain extent Stimson's open-mindedness flowed from his basic approach to life. It reflected deliberation as well. As Stimson afterward explained to Coolidge,

> When I assumed office I was warned that the nature of the oriental was such that it would be dangerous for me to confer with them without the presence of American witnesses. I rejected this advice, feeling that it was better to trust and be betrayed than to make mutual confidence impossible. So far as I am aware, I was not betrayed

in a single instance; and the character of our conferences became such that I was frequently made the recipient of confidences by the Filipino leaders which proved of priceless value to my administration.

Stimson added that he took pains never to catch his Filipino associates unaware, apprising them in advance of decisions favorable and unfavorable. He also gave them credit whenever possible for actions that reflected well on them, and in every instance he stressed their participation in setting policy. "These precautions may seem trivial," he told Coolidge, "but in such a situation as exists in the Philippines I am satisfied that they are vital, and unless they are constantly borne in mind, misunderstandings and suspicions are inevitable."[8]

Quezon, for one, valued the consideration. "I am praying for the success of your administration," the senate president wrote the new governor. In later years Quezon said he had respected no American representative in the Philippines as much as he did Stimson. Quezon wrote,

> He never left me in doubt as to what he had in mind whenever he expressed his ideas on any subject. There was never any mental reservation whenever he talked to me, and he therefore made me feel that he gave me his entire confidence exactly as he would have done it if I had been an American sitting at his council table as the senior member of his official family.

The respect for Stimson extended to Quezon's household. As a mark of affection Quezon's wife habitually referred to the governor as "mi viejo."[9]

The improvement in personal relations mattered the more since substantively Stimson had little to offer beyond what Wood had conceded. To be sure, the new governor, while reaffirming the fundamental importance of the Jones Act, added that the 1916 measure "certainly does not contemplate that I should substitute my own personal judgment for the official judgment of the various executive officers." Likewise he declared that his power of supervision "should ordinarily not be invoked to interfere with the conduct of government by my subordinates, unless they have been guilty of some misconduct or negligence deserving of grave reprehension or even removal from office." Coming from Wood, this last statement might have provoked another walkout, since Wood tended to presume misconduct and negligence in Filipino officials. But Stimson operated on the presumption of innocence and competence, sometimes stretching the definition in the interest of amicability.[10]

In other respects Stimson was a throwback to the Taft-Forbes days. Privately he looked askance at independence in the foreseeable future. Publicly he refused to discuss the issue. Saying nothing, he told an American associate, was the best way to "shut up the whole business and get the minds of the people upon something which they could do and obtain rather than upon something which was entirely beyond their legal and physical powers." He adopted the familiar Republican position that economic development must precede political autonomy. "It is the simple truth," he declared in his first speech to the Filipinos, ". . . that individual freedom and the practice of self-government are found to be most prevalent and firmly held in those communities and nations which have a highly developed system of industry and commerce as a foundation." He wondered that Filipino leaders should wish to sever their country's connections with "the foremost industrial nation in the world—the nation where not only has mechanical invention made the greatest advances, but where the organization and methods of industry and the relations of capital and labor are more enlightened than in any other country under the sun." Filipinos could only benefit from continued association. "Is it not the part of wisdom and of prudence for this people to absorb to the uttermost the lessons and benefits which can be derived from the teachings of such a successful practitioner?"[11]

In pursuit of his goal of Philippine development Stimson, like Taft, Forbes and Wood, sought to make the islands attractive to foreign investment. He appreciated the force of Filipino objections against foreign control of the Philippine economy. "The existence of this native sentiment has not been generally recognized in the United States," he reported to the president after twelve months in Manila, "but the events of my own year's experience brought it to my attention as one of the deepest and most controlling currents of public opinion in the Islands and one which it would be folly to disregard or attempt to defy." This said, Stimson proceeded to seek liberalization of Philippine corporate law to grant foreign investors greater security and freedom. He succeeded in a number of instances. Yet he trod carefully, and in winning approval of less restrictive measures he allowed the inclusion of provisions circumscribing the activities of holding companies, especially as they related to ownership of land. His solicitousness of Filipino opinion on the land issue extended so far that he actively discouraged one American company, a rubber producer, from purchasing large parcels of real estate lest the move alarm Filipino nationalists.[12]

II.   Crash

As had Taft before him, Stimson proved too valuable to the Republican party to leave in Manila. In January 1929 Stimson accepted appointment as Herbert Hoover's secretary of state. Short though it was, Stimson's tenure as governor marked both the islands and the man. While the question of the Philippines' future remained as vexatious as ever, civility had returned to relations between leaders of the two countries. Stimson was just what Quezon needed. After Wood, Stimson provided a vehicle for Quezon to get back to doing what he did best: charming Americans. Increasingly, as Quezon went, so went the Philippines. For Stimson the year in the Philippines afforded a reminder of America's stake in the

Pacific often lacking in the Eurocentric eastern establishment that dominated American foreign policy. Stimson's perception of this stake would play a significant role in his reactions to the Far Eastern crises that occupied much of his time as Hoover's secretary of state and later as Franklin Roosevelt's secretary of war.

The Hoover administration's first crisis, though, occurred on the home front, in what to a Republican administration should have been the friendly confines of lower Manhattan. The stock market crash of 1929 was Hoover's great piece of bad luck, and it could not have happened to an otherwise luckier fellow. After college Hoover had run off to Asia where he commenced a brilliant career as the sort of capitalist Quezon and Osmeña worried about, and where he witnessed at first hand the Boxer rebellion in China that prompted the second of John Hay's Open Door notes. Mining was Hoover's field. He displayed a gift for converting most anything he dug out of the ground to gold. After making his pile he turned to public service, ferrying stranded Americans home from warring Europe in 1914 and afterward shipping relief supplies in the opposite direction. Democrats and Republicans wooed him. The latter won him. He served as secretary of commerce under Harding and Coolidge, and when Coolidge did not choose to run in 1928 Hoover accepted the party's nomination. The future, Hoover's and America's both, seemed assured following his election. The conquest of poverty appeared imminent. Then Wall Street laid its egg.

Hoover's career, until Black Thursday, had been a triumph of the individual, of the self-made man, or so Hoover and America's other Algerites chose to interpret it. To a considerable degree Americans during the age of Hoover—the 1920s—attempted to apply the same individualist model to their country's relations with the world. After the defeat of the Versailles treaty the United States did not so much turn its back on the international community as adopt an every-country-for-itself approach. America never crawled into a cave. It hosted the Washington conference on Asia. It sponsored the Dawes and Young plans for the reordering of the European economy. It intervened repeatedly in Central America and the Caribbean. Yet with few exceptions the emphasis always lay on American unilateralism and self-reliance—Hooverism applied to foreign relations.

The domestic and international strands of Hooverism came together in Washington's response to the 1929 crash. As the world sank into the slough of economic despond the Republican Congress passed and the Republican president signed the Hawley-Smoot tariff, which put import duties at record levels. Economists by the hundreds predicted that such an action would trigger a trade war. For once the profession proved correct. The violence spread from commerce to finance as the European powers agitated to scale back debt and reparation payments. Unsatisfied with Washington's response and unable to earn the dollars that might have made repayment possible, the Europeans defaulted. The United

States, now lacking even the cares of the creditor, stood more unencumbered than ever. Millions of Americans could not have been happier at the unencumbering—and wished the country could trim its ties to thankless dependencies like the Philippines as well.

III.   The Manchurian antidote

For the United States a unilateral response to the world depression was misguided but not suicidal. More self-sufficient than most nations, America could at least conceive of riding out the worst of the slump autarkically. Japan enjoyed no such luxury. The international collapse shook the Japanese economy to bedrock, ravaging the farming and fishing sectors and devastating export industries. Perennially short of resources, Japan had to sell in order to buy, and as foreign markets vanished, with the help of the Hawleys and Smoots of the world, Japan confronted the grim specter of national disaster. A Japanese did not have to be a raving xenophobe to think the next war had already begun.

Raving xenophobes did exist in Japan, as in most countries at most times. But where they usually inhabit the fringes of respectability, the events of the early 1930s propelled Japan's ravers toward the center of power. The trade war discredited liberal internationalists and strengthened the militant nationalists who advocating cutting the Gordian knot of Japanese insufficiency with the sword of empire. To the militarists foreign conquest offered a solution to several problems at once: how to expand markets for Japanese products, how to guarantee sources of raw materials, how to restore national self-confidence at a moment of soul-searching, and how to consolidate political power at home. Manchuria, China's Rhineland and the cockpit of Northeast Asia—and lately the object of a dispute between the Nationalist government of China and the Communists of the Soviet Union—offered an additional incentive to would-be conquerors from Japan: security for Japan's position in Korea. Consequently in September 1931 Japanese officers engineered an incident, an explosion, on the South Manchurian Railway that they expanded into a pretext for the occupation of Mukden and eventually for the seizure of the entire province.

Eight years later the Germans would apply the Manchurian treatment to Poland and start a second world war in the process. In 1931 the memories of the first war were too fresh. During the 1920s the powers had done all they could to prevent a repetition of that ghastly conflict. In 1921 Washington issued invitations to a conference for the purpose of capping naval arms. Although many observers expected the meeting to embrace peace in the abstract without accomplishing anything tangible, Secretary of State Charles Evans Hughes greeted the guests with a breathtakingly detailed proposal that included the scrapping of more than sixty major ships by the United States, Britain and Japan and a ten-year moratorium on the construction of new vessels. Once the spluttering subsided, the powers decided that Hughes' plan might not be such a bad idea. None relished the thought of an arms race, but each sufficiently distrusted the others to feel obliged to keep up. The result of this phase of the conference was the so-called Five Power Treaty, which established a ratio of 20:20:12:7:7 among the capital ships respectively of America, Britain, Japan, France and Italy.

The Japanese disliked the inferiority the five-power accord imposed, even though Americans and British pointed out that their countries had global responsibilities while Japan's interests were merely regional. The Japanese were mollified by a Four Power treaty enshrining the status quo in the east, recently tilted in Tokyo's favor with the Japanese grab of Germany's Pacific possessions, by largely forbidding the construction of new fortifications. A third treaty, the Nine Power agreement—adding China, Portugal, the Netherlands and Belgium—pledged the signatories to observe the open-door principles in China.

The treaties of the Washington system, especially the five-power and four-power pacts, had particular significance for the position of the Philippines in American strategic planning. The five-power limits forestalled a navy-building contest in the Pacific, which, given the historic reluctance of the American people to fund peacetime military forces, the United States might well have lost. But despite granting American, and British, superiority over Japan in global numbers of ships it effectively conceded regional dominance to the Japanese. The four-power restriction on fortifications saved Americans the trouble of reinforcing the Philippines. But it left the islands vulnerable to Japanese attack should Tokyo decide to break out of the Washington system.

At best the Washington conference bought time for the United States in dealings with Japan. It purchased precious little good will. What it afforded of that dissipated two years later when Congress, under the usual pressure from anti-Japanese elements in California, included in an immigration reform measure a ban on Japanese entry to America. That the ban also applied to other Asians did nothing to soften its impact. Japan exploded in mass protests. The Japanese government proclaimed a day of national humiliation and launched a hate-America campaign. Subsequent efforts to narrow the breach between the two countries failed. Although Japan adhered to the American-sponsored 1928 treaty of Paris ostensibly outlawing war, almost no one took the accord seriously. At London in 1930 both countries accepted an extension of the Washington system, yet eviscerating reservations rendered the arrangement nearly meaningless.

As a consequence the United States possessed scant influence with Japan when the Kwantung army occupied Manchuria in 1931. The Japanese did not value America's good opinion, and with the depression deepening America's isolationist inclinations they did not much fear America's displeasure. Secretary of State Stimson urged an embargo of oil, the fuel of the Japanese war machine, but both the international community and Stimson's own president considered an embargo excessively provocative. In their favor those urging caution noted that the Kwantung army's actions in Manchuria lacked official approval. To stigmatize Japan, they contended, might simply strengthen the militarists. As Stimson himself conceded in his diary, "My problem is to let the Japanese know that we are watching them and at the same time do it in a way which will help [Prime Minister] Shidehara, who is on the right side, and not play into the hands of any nationalist agitators." Thus began the search that would occupy American policy-makers throughout the 1930s: for Japan's elusive moderates.[13]

Moderates grew scarcer when Japan attacked Shanghai at the beginning of 1932. The bombardment of China's principal city and the center of western influence in the country, occurring in the context of the takeover of Manchuria, signaled an intention to expand the Japanese sphere further, a total contempt for China's sovereignty and a challenge to the west to do something about it. As Tokyo anticipated, the powers acquiesced. The most the United States could muster was an announcement that it would not recognize changes in the status quo achieved by force. To this Tokyo responded that the status quo no longer obtained in China, that after twenty years of revolution and warlordism China had ceased to exist. "The Japanese Government do not and cannot consider that China is an 'organized people' within the meaning of the Covenant of the League of Nations. China has, it is true, been treated in the past by common consent as if the expression connoted an organized people. But fictions cannot last forever."[14]

III.   Casey at the bat

Not even the most sanguine Filipino leaders could view the ominous events in Asia with unconcern. Near the end of 1931 Dwight Davis, Stimson's successor as governor-general, wrote to Patrick Hurley, Hoover's secretary of war, "The recent troubles in Manchuria have had a marked effect on Filipino sentiment here. . . . The apparent aggression of the Japanese makes them feel that the danger from that source is more real than they had thought. Altogether I think it has made them pause and think."[15]

Filipinos had been pausing and thinking, and rethinking, for some time. Although immediate and complete independence remained the rallying cry of the dominant Nacionalistas, in private Quezon and other party leaders continued to hesitate. Their diffidence provoked a mutiny in the ranks, and in the elections of 1928 Isauro Gabaldón, formerly resident commissioner in Washington, campaigned for a seat in the house of representatives on a platform of noncooperation with the Stimson administration. Gabaldón joined hands with prominent Democratas, including Teodoro Sandiko and Claro Recto, and denounced Quezon and the Nacionalista leadership for betraying the cause of independence.

The dissidents' effort came to naught when the elections returned overwhelming majorities for the Nacionalistas: 71 of 94 seats in the house and 20 out of 24 in the senate. The Democratas found the results so dispiriting that they considered disbanding. A slight improvement in their fortunes in the elections of 1931 was followed by increased distress when three of their officeholders—one senator and two representatives—died shortly after the balloting and were replaced by Nacionalistas. Led by Senator Recto, who remained convinced of the need for a vigorous opposition yet conceded that the Democratas had lost credibility, the party dissolved itself in January 1932.[16]

The disappearance of the Democratas returned the focus of Filipino politics to the Quezon-Osmeña quarrel, quiescent since the formation of the common front against Wood. To some degree the outcome—victory for Quezon, defeat for Osmeña—was preordained. In the early Taft-Forbes days, when the nature of American rule had narrowly circumscribed Filipinos' freedom of maneuver and placed a premium on parliamentary skill and backstairs politicking, Osmeña's artfulness and command of detail had made him invincible. But the opening up of Filipino politics following the arrival of Harrison and the passage of the Jones bill favored the charismatic Quezon, whose genius lay in his ability to appear all things to nearly all people.

Quezon's triumph also registered high water in America's impact on the islands' political culture. In 1898 the predominant class in the country had been the ilustrados, Filipinos educated in Spain's way of life and governance. Osmeña early acquired fluency in Spanish, and throughout his career he appealed strongly to Hispanicized elements among elite. But as the years of Spanish rule faded into memory, those elements became increasingly anachronistic. A survey in the late 1930s showed that not 3 percent of the islands' population spoke Spanish. Meanwhile the influence of America grew, and with English being the language of government and power, young, ambitious and upwardly mobile types adopted it as their second tongue. In this regard Quezon's years in Washington benefited him greatly. He learned how Americans spoke and thought, and he demonstrated an unparalleled ability to play by the American rules of the political game.

Quezon cultivated American liberals, conservatives and anyone else he thought might prove helpful. His American correspondents included politicians, opinion-makers, academics, military leaders and the merely rich and famous. His tone was respectful or intimate as occasion demanded. To demonstrate his appreciation for what America had done for the Philippines he Americanized his name—to Casey—in dealings with American friends. Osmeña would never have stooped to such a thing—Ozzie? Yet what would have appeared pandering in Osmeña seemed simply further evidence of the irrepressibility that made Quezon Quezon. To any Filipino looking to get ahead during the middle years of the American period, it was clear who had more to offer.[17]

Although Osmeña realized the disadvantage he labored under, he was not prepared to surrender the prize of leadership to Quezon without another tussle. In February 1930 an "independence congress" gathered in Manila to demonstrate the solidarity of the Filipino people on the independence question. The conference had been precipitated by fresh evidence of retentionism in the United States. Stimson, for all his good will toward the Filipino people, suggested that at least another generation must pass before they could manage their own affairs. War Secretary Hurley declared that American interests could sustain "no diminution of American control in the Islands." Hurley, whose later experiences in China would reveal him as one of America's great ignoramuses on Asian affairs, added that "it would be inexpedient and hazardous to attempt to anticipate future developments by fixing any future date for ultimate independence." To signal their rejection of such views, two thousand Filipino delegates met in Manila to listen to speeches for four days before endorsing an independence resolution. Shortly thereafter the Filipino legislature commissioned another delegation to Washington. Heading the group were Osmeña and House Speaker Roxas. Quezon, ailing with the tuberculosis that would claim his life fourteen years later, stayed home.[18]

He remained there only a short while. Recognizing the political benefits that would accrue to Osmeña if the Osrox mission, as it was called, succeeded—or even if it failed, so long as Osmeña cast himself as the defender of Filipino freedom—Quezon he decided he must join Osmeña and Roxas in Washington. "My conscience bids me to go," he announced. "Duty calls me." How long would he be gone? He could not tell for sure. "I propose to stay in the United States until this uncertainty is cleared up, until I shall be able to tell my countrymen what it is that the United States really plans to do with us."[19]

Unfortunately for Quezon his health lapsed once more. On doctor's orders he retired to a California sanatorium. During the next two years Osmeña claimed center stage in Washington, while Quezon shuttled among California, Manila and the American capital. Usually on his own and as independent-minded as ever, Osmeña interpreted instructions from the Philippine legislature more or less as he chose. Eventually Quezon could stand this comeuppance no longer. He attacked the Osrox mission as "imprudent" and ordered its funding slashed.

Mutual recriminations followed, and when Osmeña returned to the Philippines the contest seized the legislature. Osmeña delivered a long speech in the senate claiming that Quezon "knew very well the injustice of his accusations." He denounced Quezon for efforts "to cast doubt upon the good name of the mission and to heap discredit upon its work." When Quezon forced the issue by threatening to resign, Osmeña reviewed two decades of dealings with his opponent:

> My personal relations with President Quezon date from long ago. During the days of our youth, we were always together; we loved each other and called each other brother. Through the long struggle for liberty for our people, we mutually counselled

each other, and worked always together in unison. During the first difficult days of a representative regime in the Philippines, when undeservedly I was chosen leader in the Assembly, President Quezon was my principal support. I supported him in the same manner when later on he was elevated as our leader. There is nothing that I could have done which I did not do to strengthen that leadership. I have followed Mr. Quezon wherever I could, but I can follow him no longer without failing in my duty towards our country.

Reciting a charge that would gain currency during the years ahead, Osmeña blasted Quezon for constructing "a political regime which seeks to establish a personal relationship achieved by secret machinations instead of a responsible leadership won in the light of day." He warned that if Quezon's designs succeeded the Philippines would face a "new state of things wherein nothing remains of democracy except the name."[20]

Osmeña's oratory fell short. Quezon controlled the party and the votes. The legislature refused Quezon's resignation and restated its confidence in his leadership. Quezon organized a new mission to Washington. When he set forth he traveled alone.

IV.   The triumph of American nationalism

The offstage presence in the confrontation between Quezon and Osmeña was the American Congress, which in 1932 passed the Hare-Hawes-Cutting Act providing for Philippine independence at the end of a ten-year transition period. In the interim the islands would enjoy increasing self-rule under what the act styled a commonwealth government. During the commonwealth decade the United States would defend the Philippines against aggression. After independence America would retain rights to such military base facilities as the president considered desirable for American security. The act would take effect upon acceptance by the Philippine legislature.

At first glance the Hare law seemed to represent a step in the direction Filipino nationalists had been pointing. To be sure, the ten-year transition left the urgentistas among the nationalists dissatisfied, but with Quezon in control the urgentistas exercised little influence. As for America's retention of base rights, few realistically expected Washington to settle for less.

Yet Filipinos were wary, with reason. The negotiations that produced the Hare act indicated that its passage owed less to American wishes to achieve independence *for* the Philippines than to a desire to gain independence *from* the Philippines. In an era of attempted isolationism the Hare act typified American legislative thinking. Despite the debilitating hangover from the Hawley-Smoot tariff, American commodity producers decided a cure required more of the same, and they looked upon the Philippines as a competitor to discriminate against. During the 1920s, while the American farm economy had precociously slumped,

Philippine exports to the United States climbed significantly. Sugar sales quintupled. Coconut oil and derivatives leaped to three times their former level. Abaca, or hemp, cordage gained 500 percent. Although the absolute levels remained low relative to the size of the American market, American producers blamed Philippine imports for aggravating their pain and agitated for protection.

They failed the first time around to persuade the Hawley-Smooters to throw the Philippines over the American tariff wall. Discrimination against an American dependency was more than even Republicans could countenance. But lobbyists are paid to be resourceful as well as persistent, and before long a phalanx of flacks—speaking for Colorado beet-sugar producers, who fought to save America from cheap Philippine cane; for Wisconsin dairymen, who stood for honest butter against coconut ersatz; for Mississippi cotton planters, who held the line on behalf of cottonseed oil against the copra-derived grease that would gum up America's industrial works; and for New York bankers, who contended that unfairly priced Philippine goods threatened the American standard of living, as well as their own investments—figured out that if Congress would not discriminate against a *dependent* Philippines, it might do so against an *independent* Philippines.[21]

Independence for the Philippines also promised to solve the problems of other influential pressure groups. The 1920s witnessed a resurgence of American racism and nativism. One manifestation was the new vogue of the Ku Klux Klan, whose agenda of intolerance now included foreigners, particularly those of dark complexion. Another outgrowth was the immigration reform of 1924, which installed strict limits on the number of arrivals from abroad and barred entry of almost all Asians. As in the case of tariffs, the Philippines occupied an anomolous position in respect of immigration, and even after the golden door had closed to Chinese, Japanese and Indians, Filipinos entered the United States freely. Between 1920 and 1929, the net increase in the Filipino population of the American mainland and Hawaii amounted to some eighty thousand. The nativists took alarm and insisted that the Philippine loophole be closed. The onset of the depression, by sharpening economic competition between Filipino immigrants and the already-here, amplified anti-Filipino arguments and broadened their appeal, especially among labor unions. Like the protectionists, the exclusionists realized that one way to achieve their goal was to grant the Philippines independence.[22]

The demand for Filipino exclusion, as for Chinese and Japanese exclusion, was strongest on the West Coast. California has never suffered a dearth of demagogues on the issue of the Asian peril. V. S. McClatchy of the California Joint Immigration Committee, adopting a stance of no-fault racism, declared,

> There is a basic racial or biological difference which does not permit of assimilation or absorption of one race by the other, and therefore the presence in either country of large groups of the other race must create friction and possible international diffi-

culty. The fault in such cases lies with neither race. The usual dislike of one race for another, frequently assumed to be purely a matter of prejudice, is perhaps really a wise provision of Nature, acting as a safeguard against miscegenation.

Another Californian, Senator Samuel Shortridge, asserted, "We already have enough race problems now in the United States: the Negro problem, the Chinese problem, the Japanese problem." Backing a ban on Filipino immigration, Shortridge said it was his purpose "to prevent the growth of the Philippine problem."[23]

Not all opponents of Filipino immigration confined themselves to oratory and the advocacy of legislation. The months surrounding the stock crash witnessed several outbreaks of physical violence against Filipinos in the United States. In October 1929 a mob of Anglo farm laborers near the California central valley town of Exeter went from ranch to ranch demanding dismissal of all Filipino workers. Owners refusing to oblige suffered considerable property damage. In January 1930, following trouble between Filipinos and Anglos near Watsonville, a local chamber of commerce adopted a resolution calling for the expulsion of Filipinos from the area. Shortly thereafter rioting against Filipinos broke out, leading to many injuries and the death of one Filipino. A week later a meeting hall of the Filipino Federation of America was bombed in Stockton. In May the White River valley of Washington, just south of Seattle, erupted in fighting as whites attacked a Filipino labor camp. The summer of 1930 brought clashes between Anglos and Filipinos in several counties of northern California. A bombing in the Imperial valley of southern California resulted in the death of one Filipino and injuries to several. Less violent demonstrations against Filipinos took place in Idaho and Utah.[24]

Such was the background to the measure Congressman Butler Hare of South Carolina introduced in the House in March 1932, following similar action in the Senate by Harry Hawes of Missouri and Bronson Cutting of New Mexico. Hearings in the two chambers brought arguments in favor of independence by lobbyists for the sensitive producer groups and from the American Federation of Labor. Opponents of independence included representatives of Philippine producers, who pressed for continued access to the American market; of importers of Philippine products, who argued, among other claims, that coconut oil made the best soap in the world; and of Hawaiian sugar growers, who did not wish to see their supply of Filipino labor curtailed.

The most serious opposition came from the Hoover administration. "The political chaos in the Orient today is such that, in my opinion, this is no time to deal with Philippine independence," War Secretary Hurley told the Senate insular affairs committee. "The present legislation directed to that end would serve the interests of neither the Filipino people nor the United States." The Filipinos, Hurley asserted, remained far from economic independence, without which "political independence would merely invite chaos and revolution." Accounting himself "the best friend the Filipino people have in Washington today," Hurley accused Harry Hawes to his face of trifling with their destiny. The senator's proposal, Hurley said, would tear down "what has been built by the United States by its treasure and blood over thirty years" and would "destroy the possibility of the Philippine Islands ever becoming a nation among the family of nations in the world." The Philippines, Hurley asserted, were "totally incapable" of fielding an army sufficient for their defense. They had no industries of war. A naval fleet was "completely out of the question." Independence "would ultimately be followed by domination of the Philippines by some foreign power," with grave implications for the security of the United States.[25]

Filipino leaders, represented in Washington at this point by Osmeña and Roxas, backed the Hare and Hawes-Cutting bills, although not without hesitation and not without recognizing the bad company they were keeping. Despite repeated professions of sympathy toward the Philippines and of support for Filipino aspirations, speakers at the hearings on the independence measures made clear that the primary backing came from groups intent on easing their own pain at the expense of the Filipinos. The American approach to the Philippines had always been motivated by self-interest. But until this point progressives and other reformers had managed to gloss self-interest with idealism of varying sincerity. Now American officials were preparing to drop the pretense and cut the islands loose.

America's turning away from the Philippines was part of the general parochialization of American outlook during the 1930s. At the beginning of the century the impulses that gave rise to progressivism had also contributed to the outburst of imperialism, with each movement reflecting the confident notion that the condition of the human race could be made measurably better by the actions of enlightened Americans. The world war had gone far toward killing this whiggish optimism, as the American unilateralism of the 1920s demonstrated. What the war missed the depression didn't. Unilateralism became isolationism.

Franklin Roosevelt would resuscitate the reforming spirit, but in a significantly altered character. The progressives were inspired by hope, drawn to a vision of a better future. The New Dealers were driven by despair, repelled by a disastrous present. Where contemporaries of the first Roosevelt looked outward, intending to remake the world in America's image, those of the second Roosevelt looked inward, desiring to shut the world out. Shortly after entering office Franklin Roosevelt scuttled a major economic conference in London summoned to forge a multilateral remedy to the international crisis. The Democratic president, summarizing American attitudes toward the world during the 1930s, declared that the United States would find its own way out of the depression. Two years later Congress passed a sweeping neutrality law that caught the same mood.

It was this retreat to a narrow nationalism more than anything else that accounted for the passage of the Philippine independence legislation. Writing the legislation involved some of the most tortuous maneuvering, on both sides of the Pacific, in the entire history of Philippine-American affairs. The first phase of manuevers, described above, led to the passage of the Hare-Hawes-Cutting bill during the lame-duck session of Congress in December 1932. Hoover, by then thoroughly rejected by American voters, nonetheless vetoed the measure. Hoover did not repudiate the notion of Philippine independence. No American president ever did. But he reiterated Hurley's message that the United States must not depart the islands in such manner as to "project them into economic and social chaos." Like Hurley he predicted dire consequences for American interests in the Far East from a premature severing of the American connection with the Philippines. Turning the islands loose would encourage aggressors—meaning Japan, although Hoover was too diplomatic to specify. "This legislation," he concluded, "puts both our people and the Philippine people not on the road to liberty and safety, which we desire, but on the path leading to new and enlarged dangers to liberty and freedom itself."[26]

Hoover's eleventh-hour appeal cut no ice with this hard-hearted Congress. American ejectionists overrode the president's veto. The fate of the Hare act then passed to the Philippine legislature, which had to concur for it to take effect. The issue immediately became wrapped up in the Quezon-Osmeña conflict. Osmeña, supported by fellow Osroxian Roxas, acknowledged that the measure fell short of perfection and conceded that it had passed the American Congress for all the wrong reasons. Even so, he argued, it represented the best Filipinos could hope for under present circumstances. Quezon opposed the act, partly from a desire to deny Osmeña credit, partly from concern that independence under the terms of the Hare act would lead to the closing of the United States to Philippine products and Filipino immigration, partly from worries about Japan and uncertainty whether the Philippines would be ready for independence in ten years, and partly from objection to the provision of the Hare measure allowing the United States to retain military bases after independence even without Filipino consent.

Quezon was joined in opposition by others among the Filipino elite, especially property owners and those connected with export industries. In the two decades since the passage of the Payne tariff, free trade between the Philippines and the United States had led, as both supporters and critics had predicted, to the economic dependence of the former upon the latter. American imports came to dominate the Philippine market, rising from less than one-tenth of total imports in 1899 to more than six-tenths in 1929. In the other direction the trend was even more significant. The last year of the nineteenth century saw the United States purchase less than one-fifth of Philippine exports. By 1929 Americans bought three-quarters of what the islands sold abroad. During the next five years this figure jumped to nearly nine-tenths. The importance of the last number lay in the fact that it measured, especially in time of worldwide contraction, the economic addiction of the Philippines to the American market. Deprived of access to this market, the Philippine economy faced tremors and convulsions.

A fair number of Filipinos appreciated their fix. Some said so privately to American officials. As early as November 1929 Governor Davis reported, after meeting with various groups of Filipinos, that "many of the more thoughtful people, and particularly those who own property, are beginning to consider what the effect of immediate independence would be on the progress of the country." Davis described "a consensus of opinion that if it came immediately it would mean a very serious disaster to the country which it would take many years to get over." In a postscript Davis added, "The unfortunate thing is that no one is able to advocate anything publicly short of complete, absolute and immediate independence."[27]

Events of the first years of the depression reinforced the ambivalence Davis described. Declining markets elsewhere increased Philippine dependence on the United States, but the rough treatment Filipino interests, and Filipinos themselves, received at American hands rankled more than ever. The violence against Filipinos in the United States especially touched a nerve. Davis described an increase in "racial antagonism" in the islands, characterizing it as far greater than most Americans knew—which was just as well, since knowledge would only feed American animosity. Like economic matters, he said, the race question was "bound up with the independence agitation." He hoped for a quick resolution of the independence issue one way or the other, believing that this would do more than anything to defuse the race problem.[28]

But the independence debate dragged on, now inseparable from the personal battle between Quezon and Osmeña. Osmeña's faction became known as the pros, Quezon's as the antis. The two locked in struggle through the short tenure of Governor Theodore Roosevelt, Jr., who remarked with reasonable accuracy that while the Filipino elite wanted "internal liberty but not independence," they were willing to accept the latter if necessary to achieve the former.[29]

The pros and antis were still bickering when Frank Murphy became governor in the summer of 1933. The wisdom of Murphy's appointment was one of the few issues the two sides agreed on. Quezon quickly developed an effective relationship with Murphy, while Roxas remarked, "We consider him a capable man and believe he will make a good governor." Each side sought to enlist Murphy's support; but Murphy, having survived some bruising labor-management battles as mayor of depression Detroit, knew when to keep still. "The situation is a rather delicate one here at present," Murphy reported to the White House, adding that he intended to stay "entirely neutral."[30]

Eventually the antis prevailed, rejecting Hare and knocking the independence issue back to the start. The rejection momentarily placed Quezon in the uncomfortable position of opposing independence. To remedy the problem he once more traveled to Washington, where he raised his complaints about the Hare act in conversations with members of Congress and with the Roosevelt administration. He explained his reservations regarding military bases. He questioned trade provisions that would have established quotas for Philippine sugar, coconut oil and abaca during the commonwealth period. He registered his country's resentment at restrictions on Filipino immigration.

When Quezon presented his brief in an interview with Roosevelt at the beginning of 1934, the president responded with a warning that the interest groups that had lined up behind the Hare bill remained strong. Filipinos, Roosevelt said, should forget completely about softening the measure economically. "If you insist upon better economic considerations, you may get your independence in twenty-four hours." But Roosevelt, typically noncommittal, made no objection to Quezon's trying to arrange the best deal he could for the Philippines.

Quezon then met with Millard Tydings of Maryland, chairman of the Senate insular affairs committee, who was proposing simply to reintroduce the Hare measure. Quezon's personal charm glanced off the tough Democrat. Tydings at one point told his visitor, "You want to play draw poker, but I'm playing showdown." Following Roosevelt, Tydings cautioned Quezon not to make noises about Hare's economic provisions, since a surly Congress, more committed than ever to a strict construction of the national interest, would change the provisions only to damage the Philippines further.

Tydings did hint at room for maneuver on the issue of military bases. Though bases had been a pet project of the Hoover administration, especially of Hurley, the new Congress could hardly have cared less. Indeed, far from insisting on retention of American bases in the Philippines, many in Congress would have been happy to hand the islands to Japan, the better to keep the United States out of trouble. Roosevelt, preoccupied with his domestic agenda and tight-fisted with his political capital, indicated he would not make a fuss over the bases. "After all," the president explained to Quezon, in what at the moment was something of a throwaway line but would prove dismayingly true later, "the American military force in the Islands is too small to protect the Philippines against foreign invasion, and after we have been in the Islands all these many years, it will be impossible to induce Congress to appropriate the necessary funds for the military defense of the Islands and the maintenance of an army of sufficient size to keep any enemy at bay."[31]

The next several weeks found Quezon engaged in negotiations shading sharply to intrigue. He struck an agreement with Tydings specifying that if the insular affairs chairman would consent to forgo army bases in the Philippines and make naval stations a matter of discussion at the end of the commonwealth period, he would work for acceptance of a thus-amended Hare act in Manila. Yet at the same time Quezon led Senator William King of sugar state Utah, who offered a substitute conferring independence at once, to believe he supported *his* plan. In addition Quezon spoke with Theodore Roosevelt, Jr., and suggested that what he really sought was some sort of dominion compact, such as Canada had with Britain. Finally, Quezon was reported in the *New York Times* as favoring an arrangement under which independence would come within two to three years, but free trade between the United States and the Philippines, excepting generous quotas on sugar, coconut oil and abaca, would continue for an additional decade.[32]

In keeping his options open Quezon proved almost too clever. At the beginning of March Roosevelt sent Congress a bill patterned on Hare's though without the army base clauses and making naval reservations conditional upon joint agreement between the United States and the Philippine republic. In an accompanying message the president said that if the law proved less than satisfactory he would rely on the good will existing between Americans and Filipinos for remedies. "I do not believe that other provisions of the original law need be changed at this time," the president declared. "Where imperfections or inequalities exist I am confident that they can be corrected after proper hearing and in fairness to both peoples."

The House accepted the administration's bill, as introduced by John McDuffie of Alabama, without significant complaint. But the Senate, confused by Quezon's juggling of alternatives, balked. Utah's King wanted to convey sovereignty as soon as the islands could organize a government. Michigan's Arthur Vandenberg recommended a variant of Quezon's *New York Times* proposal, calling for a rapid transition to independence followed by a gradual phasing-in of tariffs. Iowa's L. J. Dickinson argued for shortening the commonwealth period to five years.[33]

The administration's strength finally told, however, and the Senate approved Roosevelt's measure, which had been entered under Tydings' name. Quezon appropriated the triumph as his own, returning to the Philippines with the prize of independence.

For Quezon the timing could not have been better. Two months after Roosevelt signed the Tydings-McDuffie bill into law the Philippines held elections. Osmeña and Roxas, having seceded from the Partido Nacionalista Consolidado, ran at the head of a new group, the Partido Pro-Independencia Nacionalista. During the previous half-year, while independence legislation had languished in Washington, the Osmeña party's prospects appeared promising, and its leaders made a plausible case that by vetoing the Hare act Quezon had sold out the independence movement. But the passage of the improved version refurbished Quezon's popularity. Although Osmeña and his allies grumbled that the Tydings law was merely Hare warmed over, Quezon expressed full satisfaction. "I am very happy," he announced. "I got everything I wanted."

In fact both parties were right. The distinction between Tydings and Hare was not as great as Quezon claimed. Each specified the quick creation of a commonwealth government with general responsibility for domestic affairs. Under the terms of each, independence would come after ten years—and, unless Congress changed its views in the interim, would make imports from the Philippines subject to the same American tariff schedule applicable to other countries. The only important difference was that the Tydings act did not guarantee army bases to American forces after independence.

Small though the difference was, it sufficed to accomplish Quezon's immediate goal: the final defeat of Osmeña. One astute and thoroughly skeptical observer analyzed the situation for the *Philippines Free Press:*

> If Mr. Quezon had merely wanted to get enough ammunition to knock Sergio Osmeña, Manuel Roxas and Camilio Osias into a cocked hat, then he has gotten everything he wanted. But history will record that the victory of their hero is a pyrrhic victory of the people of the Philippine Islands. One more such victory and we are undone.

Undoing lay in the future. For the present the majority of Filipinos were pleased to reward their hero. The Philippine legislature unanimously approved the Tydings Act. The June elections confirmed the vote. The Quezonistas and their allies captured overwhelming majorities in the Philippine house and senate and won 44 of 48 governorships. Quezon easily retained his position as president of the senate. In the process he made himself the prohibitive favorite to become the first president of the Philippine commonwealth.[34]

9

The Datu and the Proconsul
1935–1941

I. Murphy's law

The Tydings-McDuffie Act propelled the Philippines on the path to independence at a most unpropitious time. Of course, if times had been more propitious there would have been no such act, at least not in 1934. The depression continued, essentially unrelieved, and the Roosevelt administration concentrated on solving America's domestic problems. Overseas affairs rated relatively little American consideration. What consideration they got inclined Americans inward even more. Hitler was ranting in Berlin and Mussolini in Rome. If one took the two fascists at face value—a problematic question—Europe seemed bound for another war.

Of more direct concern to the Philippines, the militarists in Japan were consolidating their control over that country's governance. The resulting high-pressure military-political system centered on Tokyo had already sent storm waves across Manchuria and into China. Now it threatened to combine with the low-pressure system over the Philippines consequent to the impending American withdrawal and produce an outright typhoon in the western Pacific. Absent timely precautions and farsighted leadership—in both Washington and Manila—the Philippines might well be swamped.

The wind was rising but the tempest was still a good distance off when Frank Murphy had assumed the governorship in Manila in 1933. Murphy succeeded Theodore Roosevelt, Jr., whose cameo role left little impact in the islands beyond the desegregation of Manila's Central High School. This accomplishment won him the respect of Filipinos if the disdain of the Manila Americans. "I have had numberless people tell me that I am the only Governor-General since you who really got to know the people," Roosevelt modestly told Cameron Forbes. Like his father, Roosevelt was a man of enormous physical energy. After resigning he took the long route home, traveling via India, the Persian Gulf and the Mediterranean. Stopping in Baghdad—where his son Kermit would make a name as Middle East expert for the Central Intelligence Agency—Roosevelt astonished American officials by playing several sets of tennis and five games of squash in the punishing heat of a Mesopotamian July, then winding down with an hour's swim in the Tigris. "An extremely active man," an exhausted onlooker commented.[1]

Murphy brought solid liberal credentials to Manila, which reassured some observers and worried others. From the time of Wood's troubles with the cabinet Americans had not infrequently perceived disloyalty to the United States beneath Filipino political opposition. Wood remarked that Quezon's actions during the cabinet crisis "bordered on sedition." Under Hoover, War Secretary Hurley, who in 1932 called out the cavalry in Washington to smash demonstrators on grounds that the "Bonus Army" threatened the survival of the republic, directed Governor Davis to look out for subversives. In the wake of the violence against Filipinos in California in 1929 and 1930 Davis reported that malcontents were "trying to stir up anti-American feeling using the Watsonville riots particularly as a talking point." Davis did not think communists posed a great challenge to American rule in the islands, but he thought they bore careful watching. "The influence of the red agitators is not very serious here," he reported to Hurley, "although the leaders are very active and there is well-defined suspicion that they are being paid from Moscow."[2]

The red-hunting eventually resulted in indictments for sedition against several particularly anti-American individuals. In the bargain it aroused the attention of the American Civil Liberties Union. The ACLU reminded the Hoover administration of the Supreme Court's decision that even if the entire Constitution did not follow the flag the Bill of Rights did. With other liberal organizations the ACLU applauded the appointment of Murphy as governor. One spokesman from the New York office described Murphy as "a long-time friend and member of the Union" and predicted that under a Murphy administration "there will be a considerable let-up of the anti-radical campaign on the Islands." Reactively, conservative groups viewed Murphy's appointment with concern, though after the great Republican repudiation in the 1932 elections their complaints echoed unheard.[3]

Murphy scored an immediate hit with Filipinos, confirming Roxas' prediction that he would make a good governor. The editor of the *Philippines Herald* lauded the appointment, describing Murphy as "a man of liberal views, a passionate champion of the liberties of the common man, and an enemy of materialism." One of Quezon's assistants visited Malacañang to relay his boss's high opinion of the governor. Quezon, the aide said, considered Murphy "a great man." He added, "He is the first Governor-General who ever dared to come out openly for Philippine liberty. Others have ignored it, or referred to it in such veiled language that none could understand. This man talks so we all could understand what he meant." On another occasion Quezon said simply that Murphy was "the best governor we have had so far." Osmeña was more effusive still. Speaking of Murphy, Osmeña declared, "He possesses the constructive genius of William Howard Taft; the sympathetic understanding of James F. Smith, under whom Filipinos first received the boon of representative government; and the liberalism of Francis Burton Harrison."[4]

To some degree Murphy's success lay in his individual magnetism. An American associate remarked that Murphy had "one of the most attractive personalities I have ever met in public life." Yet the real secret of his success in Manila was his rule of strict neutrality in matters of Filipino politics. While the Quezon-Osmeña battle raged, Murphy kept quiet, with the result that he managed to win the respect of both the winner and loser in the contest. Before sending Murphy off to Manila Franklin Roosevelt warned the new governor of the complexity of the situation he would be entering. "But I have great confidence in your good sense," the president said. Murphy vindicated Roosevelt's confidence. As Murphy explained to George Dern, Roosevelt's first secretary of war, he was "scrupulously careful" to avoid being drawn into partisan debates in the islands. Although he let the Filipinos know he wished them well and would support their efforts at advancement, he left to them to lead the way.[5]

Maintaining neutrality did not always come easily. One of Murphy's friends described the difficulties inherent in the governor's job. "If the Tagalogs like you, the Moros want your blood. If you manage to appease all the natives, the Americans want you drawn and quartered." Writing in the latter part of 1933 this individual added, "Thus far Murphy has been very popular with the Filipinos. He has been walking on paths of roses. Presently he will hit the thorns."[6]

Murphy managed to avoid most of the thorns. His neutrality with regard to the Filipinos reflected not merely expedience but a recognition of America's obligation to Filipino political development. Like Harrison he thought experience provided the best education. He respected Filipinos sufficiently not to try to meddle in their affairs. At the same time he believed that they would learn more from making mistakes than from being shown how to govern by him or any other outsider. Filipino leaders appreciated his views and reciprocated his respect.

It did not hurt Murphy's chances of staying above the Filipino fray that the Tydings law diminished the power of the governor, decreasing the incentive of Filipino politicians to solicit his support against their opponents. As commonwealth status approached, the ranking American in Manila lost importance relative to the ranking Filipinos. Busy establishing their ranking, the Filipinos lost much of their interest in the governor's office.

Creating the Philippine commonwealth kept them busy too. The Tydings Act specified that the people of the islands should follow American precedent and hold a constitutional convention to draft a charter. In the summer of 1934 voters selected 202 delegates, who met at the end of July. After the fashion of the American convention of 1787, the gathering in the Philippines was supposed to be a supragovernmental affair. For this reason Quezon remained in the background— after guaranteeing that Osmeña would too. But few doubted Quezon's influence among the delegates. A writer in the *Philippines Herald* remarked, "No matter what we may say, this Convention is being held under the auspices of the Philippine Government, and the disgruntled foes of Mr. Quezon to the contrary notwithstanding, he is the head of the Filipino participation in the government."[7]

At the opening session of the convention, which Murphy, maintaining his low profile, declined to attend, the delegates chose Quezon's current protégé, Claro Recto, as convention president. Under Recto's—and indirectly Quezon's—guidance, the delegates produced a document during the next six months that drew upon the constitutions of the United States and the Malolos republic. Malolos provided a unicameral legislature, certain clauses of a bill of rights and restrictions on land ownership. The American influence showed in the separation of executive and legislative powers. To some extent the American influence resulted from an honest preference for American forms. It also reflected the stipulation of the Tydings law that the Philippine constitution pass muster with the president of the United States.

The convention completed its work in February 1935. Roosevelt approved the constitution in March, and Filipino voters ratified it in a plebiscite in May. Elections followed for president and vice president and for representatives to the national assembly. To guarantee a smooth start and forestall any American second thoughts about the commonwealth experiment, Quezon fabricated a unity ticket, with his name for president and Osmeña's for vice president. The coalition easily swept to victory over a runner-up slate led by Aguinaldo, who emerged from political retirement for the occasion.

II.   Head man

As George Washington invented the American presidency, shaping the office defined in Philadelphia to suit his temperament and proclivities, so Manuel Quezon essayed to do with the position of chief executive of the Philippines. Where Washington brought the background of eighteenth-century America to his newly created post, Quezon carried the customs of Filipino society and culture of the first part of the twentieth century. Americans of Washington's day, at least those who wrote the American constitution, accepted the rationalism of the Enlightenment. They deliberately designed a "machine that would go of itself," a government of laws rather than men. The Enlightenment never had the impact on Iberia it had on the countries of the chilly north, and by the time it reached the Philippines its effects had attenuated nearly out of existence. Given this circumstance, and given the personalist orientation of Filipino village life—which was not so different from village life in any number of other preindustrial countries—the fact that the presidency Quezon created and the pattern he established for those who followed looked different from the American model should have come as no surprise.

The Philippine constitution gave Quezon a head start in fashioning his office in a characteristically Filipino mold. The Philippine president possessed an explicit item veto over revenue, tariff and appropriation bills, and because other measures were limited to single subjects this operated in practice as a generalized item veto. American presidents could only wish for such power. The Philippine president served for six years rather than the American four, and although the constitution initially barred reelection, the relative ease of amendment allowed Quezon to rectify this error before his first term ended. The most portentous difference between the Philippine presidency and the American involved section 16 of article 6, which opened the door to an enormous increase in presidential control of the government. "In times of war or other national emergency," the section read, "the National Assembly may by law authorize the President, for a limited period and subject to such restrictions as it may prescribe, to promulgate rules and regulations to carry out a decided national policy."

At first Quezon contented himself with working the ordinary levers of politics to strengthen his position. He freely solicited contributions from leading members of the Filipino business community and the landed aristocracy. They rarely failed him. The general manager of the tobacco firm Tabacalera made a habit of sending Quezon signed but otherwise blank checks, which the president filled in with amounts as high as 10,000 pesos. Another well-to-do individual was honored by being named godfather of Quezon's son. When Quezon needed cash he would ask, "Don't you have a gift for the education of your godson?" Quezon named the millionaire Joaquín Elizalde resident commissioner in Washington. No one thought the position came free. Credible reports, including one by the American journalist John Gunther in the *Atlantic Monthly*, had Philippine sugar interests delivering payments to Quezon of as much as 50,000 pesos at a time.[8]

Quezon employed his connections and power to neutralize opposition. Under the rubric "partyless democracy," which sounded alarmingly like what Mussolini was building in Italy and Hitler in Germany, the president chased from office those who had defied him in the independence fight. He exiled to Washington rivals he could not break. He threw money and prestige against persons with the temerity to challenge his rule. Not content with having defeated Osmeña, he humiliated his longtime foe at a public gathering where, in Osmeña's presence, he put his arms around two other politicians and announced, "Here are two future presidents of the Philippines."[9]

So complete was Quezon's hold on the machinery of Philippine politics that following a reunification of the Nacionalistas the party won every seat in the 1938 elections to the assembly. Quezon, as leader of the party, personally dictated who most of the candidates would be. Of the 98 individuals elected, 72 were regular party nominees approved by Quezon, 21 ran in "free zones" where the party leadership took no position and 5 ran against the leadership, while still calling themselves Nacionalistas. Quezon made clear that the five rebels would be punished. They were.[10]

The emergence of what amounted to a one-party dictatorship in the Philippines, after thirty-five years of American tutelage, caused embarrassment in the United States, although the rise of really threatening fascism in Germany, Italy and Japan took some of the curse off Quezon. Besides, Washington was in no position to do anything about the political situation in the Philippines. Franklin Roosevelt had spoken accurately in a confidential meeting with congressional leaders during negotiations over the Tydings Act when he said, "Let's get rid of the Philippines—that's the most important thing. Let's be frank about it." Once rid, or at least on the road to riddance, neither the Roosevelt administration nor Congress wished to unrid itself.[11]

The desire to have done with the Philippines informed the administration's policy toward the commonwealth, and it was reflected in the lack of instructions Washington provided to Murphy, now titled high commissioner. War Secretary Dern blandly commented, "In view of your experience and demonstrated judgment, tact, and sympathetic understanding of the policies and aims of this Government, I am confident that you will be able to determine in a satisfactory manner any questions that may arise." Murphy found this charge unhelpful and asked for more specific guidance. Dern declined to elaborate.[12]

Murphy responded by retreating further from Filipino politics. The high commissioner concentrated on maintaining what he described as "harmonious relations" with Quezon, engaging in activities that kept him out of the president's way. As part of an effort to reconcile the Moros to Manila's rule, he unoriginally announced a "New Deal" for the Moros, whom he aimed to make "a permanent part of the Filipino people." The Moros weren't buying, but Quezon was pleased that someone else was undertaking this thankless task. In his spare time, of which he had an increasing amount, Murphy kept up on Michigan politics. In July 1936 he told Roosevelt he was resigning to run for Michigan governor. Until he left Manila, Murphy's dealings with Quezon remained, as Murphy put it, "friendly and cordial."[13]

III.   An American unique

Even had Murphy assumed a larger role in Filipino politics he would have encountered difficulty making his presence felt above that of the dominant American on the scene. During the decade that began in 1935—in some respects, during the entire first half of the twentieth century—no American was more closely identified with the Philippines than Douglas MacArthur.

Son of Arthur MacArthur, the military governor of the islands for the latter part of the Philippine-American war, Douglas MacArthur had spent a major portion of his career in the Philippines. The young MacArthur did not require the assistance of his prominent father to gain admission to West Point. Gifted intellectually and single-minded in the pursuit of his objectives, he scored high on the entrance examination for the military academy. He graduated four years later first in his class. By the time he took his commission in 1903 the fighting in the Philippines had ended and Arthur MacArthur had moved on to greater things. But the islands captured the young man's imagination, and he gladly accepted assignment there as engineer on a surveying team.

MacArthur's initial posting lasted only a year, just long enough for him to acquire a feel for the place, and malaria, which did not prove severe or bother him much in later life. Following several months in San Francisco, MacArthur joined his father, now commander of the army's Pacific division, on an inspection tour of Asia in the wake of the Russo-Japanese War. The journey carried him from Japan, where he met the heroes of the recent conflict—"those grim, taciturn, aloof men of iron character and unshakeable purpose," as he described them—to Afghanistan, where he encountered the "king of the Khyber," Sir Bindon Blood. What MacArthur saw on his journey convinced him that the fate of his country, and his own, rested with Asia.

> The true historic significance and the sense of destiny that these lands of the western Pacific and the Indian Ocean now assumed became part of me. They were to color and influence all the days of my life. Here lived almost half the population of the world, with probably more than half of the raw products to sustain future generations. Here was western civilization's last earth frontier. It was crystal clear to me that the future and, indeed, the very existence of America, were irrevocably entwined with Asia and its island outposts. It was to be sixteen years before I returned to the Far East, but always was its mystic hold upon me.[14]

During those sixteen years, MacArthur served in Washington under chief of staff Leonard Wood, led a daring reconnaissance from Veracruz at the time of the 1914 American invasion, helped organize and commanded the celebrated Rainbow division of World War I, winning a clutch of medals, and superintended West Point.

In 1922 MacArthur returned to the Philippines as commander of the military district of Manila. Although he struck many observers as haughty and unapproachable, during this period he accomplished the difficult feat of maintaining good relations with both Wood and Quezon. Wood commended MacArthur to the war department for "great energy, courage and initiative." Quezon and MacArthur became fast friends and mutual admirers. Perhaps the two understood how useful each would be to the other.[15]

Following a brief stint on the mainland MacArthur returned to the islands in 1928 to assume charge of the army's Philippine department. The replacement of Wood by Stimson eased tension in Manila, allowing MacArthur more freedom in cementing relations with Quezon. So confident of Quezon's support did Mac-Arthur feel that when Stimson returned to Washington MacArthur asked Quezon to recommend him, MacArthur, for governor-general. MacArthur went so far as to draft a letter for Quezon to send to Stimson, in which Quezon would declare that "all shades of Filipino thought" were in "almost unanimous agreement on General MacArthur." MacArthur then would have Quezon say, "His appointment would be a master stroke of statesmanship and diplomacy. It would not only insure harmonious cooperation but would give promise of constructive accomplishments which would transcend anything which these Islands have ever known."

Quezon apparently never sent the letter, and Hoover appointed Dwight Davis instead. MacArthur took the news hard. "I recall the incident connected with the death of Stonewall Jackson," MacArthur wrote Quezon, "wherein one of his officers—bloody and disheveled, from the tragic field of Chancellorsville stood for the last time before his dead Chief and gave utterance to those epic words: 'If you should meet today with Caesar, tell him we still make war.'" Already Mac-Arthur was portraying himself in mythic terms.[16]

As consolation MacArthur received the post of army chief of staff. His assistance to Hurley in the trouncing of the Bonus Marchers of 1932 contributed to MacArthur's visibility but did little for his career chances in a Democratic administration. In fact the staff chief position marked what in the normal course of events would have been the apex of a career in the regular army. From there it seemed downhill to retirement—or to politics. MacArthur never met a man he didn't think he was more qualified than, almost regardless of the task in question, and his opinion in this regard certainly did not exempt Franklin Roosevelt. At least from this period the general had his eye on the White House. Yet he had enough sense to recognize that Roosevelt was unbeatable for the present, and he looked elsewhere for a fresh challenge.

Quezon obliged by offering MacArthur employment as principal military adviser to the Philippine commonwealth. From Quezon's perspective MacArthur was the ideal man for the job. Few individuals anywhere in the world possessed MacArthur's combination of talents and experience. No one could match his military knowledge of the Philippines. Most important were MacArthur's political connections. MacArthur may not have enjoyed the confidence of the current administration in Washington, but as one of America's top soldiers he wielded considerable clout with the officer corps and the permanent officials at the war department. When MacArthur spoke, Roosevelt and Congress listened, even if they did not always agree with what he said. Though MacArthur had enemies he also had powerful friends.

Clearing the way for MacArthur's appointment required special legislation, to wit, an amendment to an existing law allowing American officers to serve as military advisers to specified foreign governments without resigning their commissions. Roosevelt, wondering what mischief an underemployed MacArthur might get into in America, informed Quezon that nothing would give him greater pleasure than making the necessary arrangements. Congress cooperated, and the general set off to create a Philippine army.

The nature of MacArthur's task depended on what the Philippine army was expected to do. As a commonwealth bound for independence, the Philippines fell between two stools in American strategic planning. Had it been an unambiguous part of the United States, American military and political leaders would have been required to arrange for its security. Had it been a fully independent nation, American officials might have—and in the isolationist atmosphere of the 1930s, almost certainly would have—left the islands to fend for themselves. On military grounds the Philippines were too exposed and too distant from the United States to justify an all-out defense. The war and navy departments, already pinched by a stingy Congress, could make better use of their meager resources reinforcing a Pacific perimeter that ran from Alaska through Hawaii to Panama.

Americans could not bring themselves to abandon the Philippines entirely, but neither could they summon the will to protect them adequately. In the years before 1941 American leaders never resolved this ambiguity in their relationship with the Philippines. Dealing with it formed a primary part of MacArthur's job.

The ambiguity complicated Quezon's job as well as MacArthur's. If the Americans aimed to defend the islands the Philippine government might not have to bother. Revenues earmarked for defense could be spent elsewhere. On the other hand, if the Americans planned to retreat in the face of a challenge two choices presented themselves. The Philippine government could prepare to defend the islands, or it could pursue a policy of appeasing potential aggressors, particularly Japan.

Quezon's appointment of MacArthur reflected his accurate belief that the United States could not be counted on to protect the Philippines. The Filipinos, he believed, would be on their own. The first question Quezon asked the general, when broaching the subject of service in Manila, was whether the Filipinos could defend themselves against outside attack. MacArthur replied, "I *know* they can." Filipinos might never overawe potential aggressors, he said, but like the Swiss they could threaten such resistance as to make invasion unappealing. "If you have a small regular force as a nucleus to be expanded by employing the citizen army in time of peril, no nation will care to attack you, for the cost of the conquest will be more than the expected profits."[17]

MacArthur sailed for Manila in the autumn of 1935. On arrival he established residence and headquarters on the top floor of the Manila Hotel, recently renovated and air-conditioned. Following the inauguration of the Philippine commonwealth he and staff officers Dwight Eisenhower and James Ord prepared a plan for the defense of the islands. The plan took Switzerland as its model and envisioned an army of citizen-soldiers. The country would be divided into ten military districts, each of which would assume responsibility for conscripting 4,000 men annually, who after six months' training would return to the civilian population. At the end of ten years, the expected life of the commonwealth, the Philippines would greet independence with a trained reserve force of 400,000. A small regular army of full-time officers and enlisted men would provide the leadership cadre around which the reserves would mobilize in case of emergency. A coast guard, consisting primarily of 50 torpedo boats, would complement the army, as would an air force of 250 planes. Procurement of these and other weapons would take place over several years.[18]

In the Philippines, as in the United States at the time, money for the military came hard. Budgetary constraints placed severe restrictions on the pace of implementation of MacArthur's plan. In fact the proposal MacArthur laid before Quezon stopped considerably short of what Eisenhower and Ord thought the Philippines' situation required. Before leaving Washington the two staff officers had drawn up a blueprint based on military requirements rather than politically available resources. Their initial program projected annual costs of 50 million pesos. MacArthur, however, had told Quezon he could build an army on 16 million pesos per year. The general ordered the two colonels back to work. With grave misgivings they sliced their program to fit MacArthur's needs, if not the Philippines'. They trimmed the proposed training schedule from twelve months for each recruit to six. They canceled the creation of artillery divisions. They stretched the procurement timetable. They cut soldiers' pay. They eliminated the purchase of new weapons in favor of cheaper castoffs from the American military.[19]

Despite the doubts of his staff MacArthur supported the program with gusto. He promised Quezon it would produce defenses that would "give pause even to the most ruthless and powerful." He declared that upon completion of the buildup "no chancellery in the world, if it accepts the opinions of the military and naval staffs, will ever willingly make an attempt to willfully attack the Philippines." He pointed out the "enormous defensive advantages" the islands enjoyed: geographic separation from the Asian mainland, rugged terrain, dense forests, narrow beaches, lack of roads and other transportation lines. The main island of Luzon possessed few areas where an invading force of worrisome size might land, and "each of these is broken by strong defensive positions, which if properly manned and prepared would present to any attacking force a practically impossible problem of penetration." Once the Philippine fleet of fast torpedo boats and its air force of fighter planes and bombers came into being, invasion would be more difficult still, as the boats and planes would harass an attacker and make landing of troops prohibitively dangerous. In all, he pledged that by 1946 the Philippine military would be in a position to repel "any conceivable expeditionary force."[20]

Quezon approved the essential features of MacArthur's plan, and in its first piece of legislation the commonwealth assembly did likewise. The president gave a stirring speech calling on potential conscripts to acknowledge their responsibility to defend the homeland. United and mobilized, he declared, Filipinos would put the world on notice that an assault on their country "would involve such staggering costs to an aggressor, both in blood and gold, that even the boldest and the strongest will unerringly mark the folly of such an undertaking."

Yet Quezon was not willing to hand full authority over such an important area of government as national defense to MacArthur, or to anyone else for that matter. Contending that military preparations would have to reflect the Philippines' peculiar circumstances, he modified the program to suit his interpretation of these circumstances. He resisted MacArthur's efforts to shift resources to the army from the Philippine constabulary, which he needed to guarantee internal security. He set aside, "for the present at least," construction of part of MacArthur's fleet of torpedo boats. He emphasized those elements of the program that were of a "passively defensive"—that is, inexpensive—character. He told the legislature that the necessity for centralized administration of the program required a broad new grant of responsibility to the executive.[21]

When the assembly concurred, control of the pace of the buildup passed into Quezon's hands. Initially the president and MacArthur stayed on good terms, and no insuperable problems developed, although Eisenhower and Ord encountered frustration at the staff level. Eisenhower recorded "quite a shock" at discovering the extent to which Filipino politics shaped strategic decisions. Administrative lethargy repeatedly snarled relations. Eisenhower remarked, "We—at least Jimmy and myself—have learned to expect from the Filipinos with whom we deal a minimum of performance from a maximum of promise." Eisenhower found his counterparts capable enough, but they lacked the will or capacity to take action. Eventually he recognized that the difficulty resulted from Quezon's calculated monopoly of authority and the Philippine president's assessment of what was politically prudent. (Regarding the effect of politics on military decisions, Eisenhower judged Quezon not unlike Roosevelt. Early in 1936 Eisenhower complained in his diary, "We must never forget that every question is settled in Washington today on the basis of getting votes next November.") Eisenhower suggested to MacArthur that the general and Quezon meet regularly to work out differences. MacArthur, considering it undignified to go calling on the Philippine president more often than absolutely necessary, preferred the aloofness of his penthouse suite. Upon Eisenhower fell the burdens of the go-between.[22]

This arrangement worked well for a time. In the summer of 1936 Quezon proposed making MacArthur a field marshal in the Philippine army. Eisenhower thought the proposal ridiculous, even after MacArthur offered to promote Eisenhower to Philippine general. The colonel reminded MacArthur of his distinguished career under the American flag. "General," Eisenhower said, "you have been a four-star general. This is a proud thing. There's only been a few who had it. Why in the hell do you want a banana country giving you a field-marshalship?" Yet MacArthur, persuading himself that titles impressed Asians, and intrigued by the notion of holding a rank no other American had attained, accepted the offer. MacArthur designed his own uniform: sharkskin in black and white, replete with stars and braid. On the appointed day he received his gold baton and gave an appropriately pompous speech, which struck one listener as "a Sermon on the Mount clothed in grim, present-day reality."[23]

IV.   Caveat emptor

A short while into the commonwealth period Quezon defined Philippine security in terms of two governmental tasks, one relating to attack from abroad, the other to domestic strife. "If we are prepared to defend our country," he said, "we are free from foreign molestation. If we are just to our people, we will be free from internal rebellion. That is the whole problem—the club in one hand and the bread in the other."[24]

Quezon had reason to fear internal rebellion. In May 1935, two weeks before the plebiscite to ratify the Tydings Act, more than sixty thousand peasants rose in revolt in the hinterland of Manila. The rebels, known as Sakdalists—from the Tagalog *sakdal:* to accuse or strike—captured three communities and laid siege to several others. The revolt was violent but brief. After skirmishes with units of the Philippine constabulary, in which more than one hundred persons were killed or seriously wounded, the rebels put down their weapons and melted back into the population.[25]

The timing of the Sakdalist rising quite plainly demonstrated political considerations. The leader of the Sakdalists, Benigno Ramos, charged Quezon with betraying the Filipino people by means of the Tydings Act. But more fundamentally the Sakdalists drew upon profound dissatisfaction among the masses in the countryside. The ravages of the worldwide depression did not spare the Philippines, whose prosperity depended heavily on the export of commodities that now formed a glut on the international market. In parts of central Luzon daily wages were as low as fifteen cents per day, for those fortunate enough to find work.[26]

The Sakdalists were not alone in attacking the status quo. The Communist Party of the Philippines, descended from the Unión Obrera of 1902, the Congreso Obrero of 1913 and subsequent leftist organizations, regularly denounced Quezon—the "acknowledged leader of the Filipino bourgeoisie," according to one 1935 Communist broadside—for betraying the masses by conferring favors upon the big capitalists of the islands—"the Elizaldes, Sorianos, Ossorios and those others in whose hands he has entrusted the Philippine National Development Company and the Government Ice Plant, and whom he has favored with shipping contracts and other business interests."[27]

In the middle and late 1930s neither the Communists nor the Sakdalists posed a serious threat to Philippine stability, but they served as reminders that the upper class that governed the country in cooperation with the United States did not represent the entire populace. J. Weldon Jones of the high commissioner's office described a conversation with the chief of the Philippine constabulary, during which the latter assessed the situation confronting the government. The recent disorders, he said, posed "no immediate danger" of getting out of control. Even so, "the communistic influence" was "slowly gaining headway."[28]

Not for the last time, concern regarding the activities of radical challengers to the status quo disposed Washington to overlook authoritarian tendencies in Manila. The Roosevelt administration, for the reasons cited previously, was already disinclined to meddle in domestic Philippine affairs. But the threat of popular radicalism added an argument to those militating against political intervention. Jones registered a sentiment widespread among American leaders when he expressed satisfaction that the government of the Philippines was "in strong hands." So long as it was, he said, there was "no cause for apprehension here."[29]

Although Quezon appreciated the vote of confidence, the Philippine president was astute enough to recognize that strong hands alone would not solve the problem of peasant unrest. His government also needed to deal with the country's daunting economic troubles. The obvious place to look for help was the United States, but in light of the legislative history of the Tydings Act handouts from Washington appeared unlikely. Quezon spoke correctly, indeed too mildly, in a meeting with Secretary of State Cordell Hull when he suggested that "the Congress of the United States is not very friendly" toward the Philippines. Quezon hoped to temper the unfriendliness. Specifically he aimed to modify the terms of the Tydings law to cushion the Philippines' landing on the far side of the American tariff frontier after independence. In 1937 he persuaded Roosevelt to agree to the appointment of a joint Philippine-American commission to study the matter. The commission held hearings in both countries, took testimony from a wide spectrum of interested parties and produced a four-volume report detailing its recommendations. Chief among the latter was a call for an extension of the period allowed for adjustment of the Philippine economy to independence. Instead of full tariffs being levied in 1946 they should phase in gradually over fifteen years, reaching 100 percent in 1961.[30]

Unfortunately for the Philippines the lobbies that had induced Congress to approve the Tydings bill in the first place remained strong. In addition the state department, led by the free-trading Hull, hesitated to negotiate preferences for the Philippines. In the words of an interdepartmental working group, a phase-in scheme would be "out of harmony with the general commercial policy of the United States." Consequently a resolution comprising the recommendations of the Philippine-American commission died in congressional committee. A substitute measure eventually passed, but it was so diluted that Quezon predicted bleakly that the most important industries of the islands would probably not survive the transition to independence.[31]

The sobering outlook for the Philippine economy, combined with the increasing political turmoil in Asia, prompted reconsideration on both sides of the Pacific of the basic idea of Philippine independence. In 1934 Roy Veatch of the state department's economic advisory office had declared that "a great many Filipino leaders of the first rank would welcome an offer from the United States that would give them now, or in the near future, autonomous political control accompanied by definite assurances that mutually advantageous economic relations between the two countries should be continued." At that time the idea of a kind of dominion-status for the Philippines had proved acceptable neither to Quezon nor to American legislators. Yet after Congress indicated that it would not readily relent on the issue of trading preferences for an independent Philippines the dominion plan gained adherents.[32]

The most vocal was Paul McNutt, who succeeded Murphy as high commissioner. Where Murphy had cultivated a low profile, McNutt took pains to make his presence felt. He let it be known that foreign countries should route all communications intended for the government of the commonwealth through his office. While some countries complied, others, notably Japan, refused but adopted the device of telephoning Quezon and his subordinates, leaving no embarrassing paper trail. McNutt stood on protocol at diplomatic receptions, insisting that he, as representative of the president of the United States, should enjoy precedence over Quezon. Quezon circumvented this problem by absenting himself from receptions he expected McNutt to attend. McNutt plainly expressed his view that the Tydings Act was a mistake that ought to be remedied. Independence under present circumstances of international economic depression and regional political turmoil would end in disaster. "If our flag comes down," he said, "the Philippines will become bloody ground and the center of war within war for a generation." A dominion arrangement, by contrast, would allow the continuation and further development of "a complementary and reciprocal economy" between the United States and the Philippines and would assure the largest measure of political security and individual liberty to the Filipino people.[33]

Quezon did not dislike McNutt personally, describing him to a friend as "a regular fellow." Nor did the Philippine president deny the merits, especially economic, of McNutt's argument. Quezon recognized that severing ties to the United States would disrupt the Philippine economy. In this fear he had the com-

pany of export-oriented Filipino firms that looked forward with genuine trepi-
dation to independence and the inauguration of tariffs. Yet to turn away from
independence would exact an unbearable political price, and this without any
guarantee Congress would go along with a dominion deal. Quezon refused to risk
such a scheme. He told McNutt, "I am positive that the Filipino people will not
agree to it and I myself could not advocate it."[34]

As the future of the Philippine-American economic connection grew more
tenuous, the islands began forming significant commercial and financial ties in
another direction. Since the turn of the century Japanese merchants and investors
had demonstrated interest in the Philippines. This interest intensified during the
1930s as Tokyo deliberately set about extending its economic empire. By the latter part of the decade the Japanese all but monopolized the fisheries of the archipelago. They controlled two-thirds of abaca production. They had secured more
than one-third of retail trade. They were making sizable inroads in the lumber
industry.

The Japanese influence showed most clearly in Davao province on Mindanao.
There Japanese nationals numbered 18,000 and paid half the taxes collected in
the province. They directly employed 12,000 Filipinos and indirectly provided
jobs to many thousands more. In an allusion to the Japanese penetration of Manchuria, many Filipinos took to calling the Japanese-dominated province "Dava-
oquo."[35]

The trend worried American officials, for reasons economic and strategic.
American firms resented competition in markets they previously had dominated.
Textile producers particularly complained about their loss of exports to the
islands. In response the state department attempted to negotiate a ceiling on Japanese sales. Assistant Secretary of State Francis Sayre met regularly with representatives of the Japanese embassy in Washington in an effort to conclude an
agreement whereby Japanese producers of cotton, wool and synthetic-fiber goods
would voluntarily restrict sales to the Philippines. The discussions proved mad-
deningly convoluted. In a typical instance, Japanese negotiators accepted a cap
on products shipped from Japan to the islands, at which point Japanese companies
began routing their merchandise through third countries. Tokyo then claimed
that such transshipments did not fall under the accord.

Most maddening of all was the knowledge that the United States could do
nothing about the problem. Congress was as isolationist as ever, and the Roosevelt administration did not feel it could afford to provoke the Japanese. Neither
could it conveniently ask the government of the Philippines to look after American firms, considering the cold shoulder Congress was giving the commonwealth. As Sayre explained to representatives of the cotton industry, "The present is not an auspicious time to request favors from the Philippine
Government."[36]

The effect of Japan's insinuation into the Philippine economy on the strategic balance in the Pacific worried American observers even more. Should Japanese influence continue to grow at the current rate the islands might become in essence a Japanese colony without the bother of a military invasion. It seemed entirely possible that by independence in 1946 Japan would enjoy such an economic stranglehold over the Philippines that Tokyo could dictate terms—economic, political or military—to Manila. In 1936 an American writer in *Harper's* magazine asserted flatly, "Japan is the only beneficiary of Philippine independence." This author added, "The Japanese conquest of the Philippines, unlike the American, will probably not be sudden or sensational. It will take the form of step-by-step economic penetration." Three years later a correspondent for the *American Mercury* announced that the process of economic colonization was nearly complete. "In all but name," he declared, "the Philippines already are in large measure under the sway of Japan." Writing in the aftermath of the Czech crisis of 1938, he went on to predict an "Oriental Sudeten movement," by which the Japanese community in Davao would agitate for attachment to Japan. The swallowing of the entire archipelago might well ensue.[37]

Quezon shrugged off such forecasts as alarmist—prompting some of his more fervent critics to charge him with complicity in the Japanese takeover. The *American Mercury's* writer noted Quezon's half-Spanish ancestry and the support Quezon received from the Spanish community in the Philippines. He pointed out that most of the important Spanish families in the islands supported the fascist Franco government in Madrid, which in turn favored the militarists in Japan. Beyond citing this circumstantial chain, the writer adduced indirect evidence that the "Malacañang Palace crowd" had already been corrupted by Japanese money.[38]

Charges of incipient fascism elicited predictable support from the Communist party and other elements of the radical left. Less predictable, and therefore more significant, was the concern the growing Japanese influence triggered among groups closer to the center of Philippine politics. Perhaps, as numerous Americans had warned, early independence would simply mean trading one master for another. Claro Recto warned of an Asian version of the Monroe Doctrine. Referring to the Japanese threat, Recto said,

> The real danger for us, the danger that impends and against which the Filipino people must be ready to muster all their resources as well as their statesmanship and patriotism, is not the economic collaboration of America which we should foster and stimulate but such other economic ascendancy, such Monroeism which in view of geographic factors will mean for us and our posterity our economic pauperism and our political extinction.

The editor of the *Philippines Herald* agreed with Recto. Referring to Japanese expansionism, the editor asserted, "The law of necessity is forever exacting its terms. Many millions of human beings, multiplying beyond control, with scant

means within their borders to supply their needs, and unwelcome in other
lands—these are the law, the inexhaustible energy behind Asiatic Monroeism,
the monster that is capable of crushing any people that may obstruct its course."
Political commentator Salvador Arenata described the likely future in ominous
terms:

> Bluntly speaking, the issue that we have before us is to decide whether or not to have
> independence. A Japanese economic penetration throughout the whole line,
> planned to the very last detail, will take place. With the important industries in the
> hands of the Japanese, with our foreign commerce entirely controlled by Japan, with
> Japanese skilled labor controlling the key and best positions in our economic life, our
> laws will be dictated from Tokyo.

Tokyo would allow Filipinos to maintain their "apparent sovereignty," Arenata
concluded, only as long "as our national assembly continues acting as a mere rubber stamp of Japanese interest and welfare."[39]

V.   Orange squeezed

As the 1930s wore on, American strategists had to deal with a fundamental mismatch between their country's political obligations and its military capabilities.
American officials from the time of Theodore Roosevelt had recognized the vulnerability of America's position in Asia, especially in the Philippines. The initial
Orange plan for war against Japan had represented an attempt to address the
problem, although for lack of resources it amounted to little more than a statement of principles. The Washington conference of 1921–22 signified another
effort to narrow the distance between political responsibility and military reality,
but while the diplomats praised the nine-power pact as guaranteeing the open
door in China, military men thought considerably less of the four-power and five-
power accords preventing the fortification of American positions west of Hawaii
and limiting the strength of the American fleet. Leonard Wood, writing from
Manila, offered an analysis of what the agreements meant for the Philippines:

> As I see it, we were badly crippled at the Washington Conference in everything
> which pertains to completing the Manila defenses. The Navy has no adequate ter-
> minal station in the Far East; and it must have one. The only place we can now
> secure is Manila Bay. The bulk of the work has been done, and we must hold on as
> strongly as possible to what we have. We are prohibited from strengthening in any
> way our land defenses. We can develop the air defense, and defense through sub-
> marines, but on these lines little, if anything, is being done; consequently we must
> be secure as far as possible in our garrison.[40]

The collapse of the Washington system, culminating in the Japanese seizure
of Manchuria, demonstrated more than ever the need for a strong position in the
Philippines. Yet the depression and the isolationism it spawned in America pre-

vented the requisite buildup. Indeed the Tydings Act demonstrated that congressional opinion was moving in just the opposite direction, toward dropping the Philippine burden. Acknowledging this fact, the Roosevelt administration's military secretaries in the autumn of 1935 directed the joint army-navy board to reconsider the basic premises of American strategy in the Pacific. So grave did they consider the threat in the area and so thoroughly mixed up with the politics of diplomacy that they took the unusual step of inviting Secretary Hull to send a representative of the state department to take part in the discussions. The letter including the invitation captured their attitude. "The cumulative effects of successive developments during the past two decades have so weakened our position vis-à-vis Japan that our position in the Far East is one that may result not only in our being forced into war but into a war that would have to be fought under conditions that might preclude its successful prosecution." More forthrightly: We could lose.

In the interdepartmental negotiations that followed, the army advocated concentrating American forces on the triangle formed by Alaska, Hawaii and Panama. The Philippines should be considered expendable, and following independence the United States should withdraw entirely. The navy rejected this proposal, not least because pulling back from the western Pacific would give it little to do in that ocean. The navy eventually won this round of corridor skirmishing, though incompletely. While the 1936 revision of the Orange plan called for defending the Philippines, the defense would be halfhearted. No pretense was made that if war came soon the American garrison, then numbering 10,000, assisted by Filipino forces, could protect the entire archipelago. The plan did not envision holding even the region of Manila Bay. Instead the army should concentrate on defending Corregidor at the bay's entrance, thus depriving the Japanese of the harbor's use for further operations. Previous plans had specified a timetable for reinforcing the Philippine garrison after war broke out. The 1936 version, perceiving that Japan's growing fleet strength and its dominance in the western Pacific would require an American relief mission to fight its way through to the Philippines—an operation that might take two or three years—made no provision for reinforcement. Troops of the garrison would have to fight as long as they could, then surrender or be killed.[41]

Needless to say this was not what MacArthur, preaching the defensibility of the Philippines, had in mind. Part of the discrepancy consisted in timing: the Orange planners had to allow that war might break out imminently, while MacArthur's building program assumed a ten-year grace period. But even taking this into account many outside observers considered MacArthur's optimism unwarranted. In 1933 the commander of the army's Philippine department stated, "It is not within the wildest possibility to maintain or to raise in the Philippine Islands a sufficient force to defend it against any probable foe." The military balance tilted more unfavorably in the subsequent years. Congress demonstrated less inclination than ever to strengthen the Philippine garrison, and delays and lack of funding slowed the creation of the Philippine defense force. Critics pointed out that MacArthur's "mosquito fleet" of torpedo boats would scarcely slow the Japanese navy, which could afford to match destroyers two-for-one against MacArthur's flimsy 65-footers. The critics also claimed that MacArthur grossly overstated Filipinos' home-water advantage, since Japanese fishermen— easily convertible to sailors—knew the channels of the Philippine archipelago as well as the natives did. Finally, MacArthur's air force could never stand up to Japanese planes based on Formosa, less than 200 miles from Luzon, or on aircraft carriers.[42]

MacArthur was self-confident to the point of arrogance. He may have been megalomaniacal. But he was no fool in military matters. He could read intelligence estimates and orders of battle as well as his critics. Therefore one must assume that his strategy was as much political as military. A thoroughgoing Pacificist, MacArthur was convinced the Philippines had to be defended. They controlled the position where five empires met: the Japanese empire to the north, the French to the west, the Dutch and British to the west and south, and the American to the east. The Philippines would play a vital part in the defeat of Japan, should war come. Control of the Philippines might prove the key to keeping China in such a war, and it would greatly facilitate an ultimate invasion of Japan's home islands.

In addition the Philippines were important to MacArthur personally. His father had been military governor. He was now field marshal. He felt an individual and a familial obligation to defend the Filipino people. They counted on him. He would not let them down.

MacArthur did not hide his disdain for the Orange plan, which, he told an associate, was antiquated before it was written. Fortunately a forceful leader could change in the event what the planners predicted in advance. "The man who is in command at the time will be the man who will determine the main features of the campaign," MacArthur declared. "If he is a big man he will pay no more attention to the stereotyped plans that may be filed in the dusty pigeon holes of the War Department than their merit warrants."[43]

MacArthur, like many great historical figures, tended to believe what he needed to believe. The single-mindedness that gives rise to such self-persuasion is often a prerequisite to large accomplishment. Because the Philippines *must* be defended, they *could* be defended.

Beyond this, MacArthur's enthusiasm for Philippine defense constituted an effort to keep America interested in the islands' defense. The war and navy departments and the Congress certainly would not spend money and resources preparing to defend the Philippines if the commonwealth's leading military officer doubted the possibility of success. Neither, for that matter, would the commonwealth government. Moreover, by spurring the Filipinos to strengthen the islands' defenses MacArthur was playing to the American conscience. If the crisis came the American people would be more willing to rescue a country that had strained to protect itself than they would be to help a country that had followed a path of less resistance. How much America's conscience counted for was open to question. Yet any edge might prove crucial.

Discounting conscience, American planners in Washington projected the worst. Indeed, they projected worse than the worst, to the extent of drawing scenarios in which Japan was joined by Britain in war against the United States. This nightmare—the so-called Red-Orange script—was recognized to have a low probability, but Britain and America had verged on war within living memory, and a revival of the Anglo-Japanese alliance could not be wholly ruled out. Its consequences were appalling: a full-scale conflict in both Atlantic and Pacific and a possible invasion of the United States proper, on the pattern of the War of 1812. Reassuringly, developments in international politics rendered this scenario extremely unlikely, and the planners spent most of their time considering Japan alone. As for the Germans, they seemed still a distant threat.[44]

Within months of its formulation the 1936 Orange plan required revision. In the summer of 1937 the Japanese army carried its war against China farther south. Following a manufactured incident like that preceding the seizure of Manchuria the army marched on Peiping. As before, the officers in the field acted without approval of the government in Tokyo. As before, they received no reprimand.

But *not* as before, the Chinese resisted stoutly. A regular war erupted. The heavy fighting surprised the Japanese. The invaders captured the major coastal cities and penetrated some distance into the interior, but then the troops bogged. Tokyo had to consider what to do next.

The chief international consequence of the outbreak of the Sino-Japanese war was an increase in the alarm felt by western nations with stakes in the Pacific. Until now Americans could persuade themselves that Japan, while perhaps pushy, did not really intend to take over the Far East. By merely puppetizing Manchuria—rather than annexing it, for example—Tokyo wisely left room for those in the United States and elsewhere who desired to deny the increasingly obvious. But the latest thrust against China was impossible to overlook, especially for Americans who at least since the Open Door notes had taken a particular interest in China. Further, the invasion indicated that the militarists had definitely gained the whip hand in Tokyo. If they were willing to move against China, the largest country in the area, where might they not go?

Franklin Roosevelt recognized the Japanese challenge, yet recent domestic reverses—the failure of his proposal to enlarge the Supreme Court, a series of damaging labor strikes and a relapse of the economy following encouraging improvement—made this most political of presidents reluctant to take on the isolationists who still controlled Congress. After careful thought he decided on a speech, delivered in Chicago in October 1937, calling for a "quarantine" of aggressors. Just what this meant was uncertain, perhaps even to Roosevelt. A reporter, trying to pin the president to specifics, commented that foreigners were saying that his address indicated "an attitude without a program." Roosevelt responded, "It is an attitude and it does not outline a program, but it says we are looking for a program."

The president did not look far. When the American public responded to his quarantine speech with overwhelming uninterest, he let the notion die. Despite pressure from Britain and France he refused to take the lead in chastising Japan, rejecting economic and other sanctions.[45]

For its part, Japan demonstrated a desire to avoid confrontation with the United States, for the present at least. In December Japanese warplanes sank the American gunboat *Panay*, which was engaged in evacuating the American embassy in Nanking. The sinking was no accident. In the same engagement Japanese planes destroyed three American merchant ships and killed or wounded more than thirty Americans, some who were machine-gunned swimming from the wrecks. But Tokyo immediately apologized and agreed to pay $2 million in reparations.

Neither apology nor reparations, however, altered the balance of forces in East Asia, which continued to dip against America. At the beginning of 1938 the war and navy departments produced a new Orange plan, which predicted, as had all such plans since the Russo-Japanese War, that a conflict with Japan would begin with a surprise attack rather than a war declaration. The 1938 plan called for strengthening the American naval station at Guam. Not only would a fully equipped fleet base at Guam facilitate counterattacks against Japan, it would make possible a defense of the Philippines. Only a third as far from Manila as Pearl Harbor, the Guam base would allow the reinforcement of the garrison in the Philippines before the American and Filipino forces fell.[46]

But Congress refused to appropriate the needed funds. As parsimonious and unwilling to risk provoking Tokyo as ever, American legislators effectively torpedoed the new Orange plan. In doing so they eliminated any reasonable chance of defending the Philippines in event of war. Although American leaders declined to admit it in public, and although the government made no positive decision to this effect, Washington's inaction resulted in the Philippines' being pushed beyond the American strategic perimeter. If war came the islands would shortly be on their own.

V. The roots of collaboration

Few foreigners have possessed a better feel for American politics than Manuel Quezon, who had no difficulty reading the portents of American apathy regarding the Philippines. Quezon also recognized the growing strength of Japan, especially after a personal trip there in 1937. MacArthur accompanied the Philippine president to Tokyo. The general described the Japanese government's treatment of Quezon as "cordial"—while noting that his own reception displayed "a thinly veiled hostility." Japanese officials assured Quezon of Japan's peaceful intentions toward his country. They said they only wished the opportunity to buy the islands' products and sell Japanese goods there. Quezon agreed that trade would benefit both nations. He affirmed that he shared the desire for friendly relations. While he did not say so, Quezon understood that Japan would determine whether relations would be friendly or not. "We are at the turning point," he told an acquaintance. "Once Japan dominates China, she can stand against the whole world."[47]

Quezon's visit to Japan occasioned comment in the United States. Some observers suggested that the Philippine president had attempted to strike a deal with Tokyo for the security of the islands. Quezon disavowed all such ideas, vigorously reiterating his loyalty and devotion to the United States. The rumors stilled awhile, but two years later, following another visit to Tokyo, Quezon contributed directly to the charges of appeasement. By this point war in Europe had broken out. Filipinos had watched while first the Sudetenland, then the rest of Czechoslovakia, then Austria, then Poland disappeared under the onslaught of the aggressors. Only the last move had prompted the democratic states, and only Britain and France of them, to a declaration of war. So far this declaration had accomplished nothing. It certainly had not helped the inhabitants of the lesser powers crushed beneath the blitz of the attackers. Meantime America continued to find excuses for not getting involved.

Quezon returned from Tokyo to relay the shocking news that Filipinos could not defend their homeland even if all able-bodied persons took up arms. Japan was too powerful, he said, as the Spanish and Americans had been before. Filipinos' strength, he continued, lay in their endurance. They had endured subjugation for three hundred years. They must prepare to endure for three hundred more. He went on to announce curtailment of the military preparedness program. "Developments in the European war," he said, "have convinced me of the futility of spending money to carry on our program of defending the Philippines from foreign aggression, and this objective cannot be attained with the limited resources of the country for many years to come."[48]

MacArthur refused to accept Quezon's change of policy. "The Filipinos can defend themselves if they want to," MacArthur insisted. "These islands can be made so costly to conquer that no enemy will be willing to pay the price." To the Filipino people he proclaimed, "Courage! You can be what you will be. Go on and you will not go under."[49]

Quezon meant what he said. To demonstrate his seriousness he created a new department of defense over which he, rather than MacArthur, possessed direct control. From the new department he issued orders suspending or eliminating important parts of MacArthur's military program. He halted conscription. He placed military construction projects and weapons procurement on hold. He sliced the army's budget by three million pesos. He halved the number of reserves in training and canceled mobilization scheduled for 1940.

Quezon's about-face raised further questions in the United States regarding his loyalty. It created particular difficulties for Frank Sayre, the new high commissioner. Sayre had known Quezon personally for a few years and by reputation for considerably longer. In his transfer from the state department to the Philippines Sayre did not lack advice on dealing with Quezon. Both Frank Murphy and Paul McNutt warned against Quezon's efforts at self-aggrandizement. Murphy—who also advised Sayre to watch out for MacArthur, a "lone horse" and a "growing menace"—told Sayre to guard against Quezon's inclination to "dictatorship" and his "dangerous tendency" to encroach on American prerogatives. McNutt commented, "There is a concentration of power at Malacañan which makes for a totalitarian state rather than a free one."[50]

Shortly after Sayre arrived in Manila he encountered fresh evidence of Quezon's aggrandizing. In July 1940 Quezon summoned a special session of the national assembly and requested the extraordinary powers the constitution allowed in emergencies. The assembly obediently complied.

Sayre worried that Quezon's action would not sit well with the American Congress and people and would reduce further the chances of defending the islands. Sayre reported to Roosevelt "the pronounced drift here in the Philippines away from democracy and in the direction of totalitarianism and dictatorship." Citing a recent instance of this drift, Sayre explained that he had obliquely questioned Quezon's monopoly of power by suggesting in a speech that genuine democracy required a healthy system of competing parties. To this Quezon had responded, "I am not surprised that High Commissioner Sayre disagrees with me on the need of a party system. That is the orthodox view. We, the Filipinos, have to do our own thinking and learn from the lessons of contemporary history or bust."[51]

Quezon chided Sayre at greater length some months later. Although statutorily Quezon possessed the emergency powers, at Roosevelt's urging he had agreed to hold them in abeyance. By April 1941 he was impatient of waiting. To prepare Sayre for his next move Quezon lectured the high commissioner on the background to the assembly's conferral of his special powers, focusing particularly on America's failure to provide for Philippine security. Quezon said events had convinced him America would be dragged into the current war. To this possibility Filipino leaders could not remain indifferent:

> As the Philippines is the weakest and most exposed territory under the American flag, I thought it most likely, if America should become involved in the war, that the first point of attack by the enemy will be the Philippines. Although I have always been of the opinion that while the United States maintains its sovereignty over this country, the defense of its territorial integrity and the protection of the Filipino peo-

ple in case of war is the duty of the United States, I felt that we could not expect to receive at an early date all the necessary aid from the United States, because while President Roosevelt was evidently alive from the beginning to the dangers of the situation, the predominant opinion of the American people was that the war did not concern the United States.

This being the case, Quezon continued, he had believed it necessary to assume, by completely constitutional means, emergency powers. Not long thereafter Roosevelt had sent a cable questioning the action. Quezon blamed Sayre for Roosevelt's disapproval. Quezon asserted that the American president would have accepted his, Quezon's, decision "if he had been properly apprised of the objectives of the Government of the Commonwealth in enacting the emergency powers law." Against his better judgment he had deferred to Roosevelt's wishes and agreed to await the high commissioner's signal before putting the emergency program into effect. What had the delay accomplished? "As you know, I have kept my word and, much to my regret, sat idly by for many long months unable to do anything for the protection of my people." Recently the high commissioner had appeared amenable to measures to enhance the security of the islands. Quezon applauded the sentiment but feared it came too late. "I only wish you had felt that way when the Emergency Powers Act was enacted, and that you had so informed the President of the United States. We would not be finding ourselves in the situation in which we are now, having done nothing as yet for the protection of the civilian population of the Philippines."[52]

In light of his own decision to slice spending on preparedness, Quezon's complaint has to be read partly as an exercise in buck-passing. As always, it was easiest to blame America for the Philippines' problems. But Quezon's bitterness was not without foundation. It grew increasingly obvious that Washington had judged the islands expendable. In April 1941 Quezon reminded Sayre of the United States' "primary responsibility" for the safety of the Filipino people. What, he asked, was Washington doing to guarantee this safety? He received no satisfactory reply. Washington had none to give.[53]

"There is considerable uneasiness here over a possible Japanese invasion," Sayre told Roosevelt a short while later. The summer of 1941 witnessed Japanese advances in Southeast Asia, which brought the threat closer to the Philippines and revealed more clearly than ever the brutal nature of Japanese conquest. Sayre thought he detected a turning toward the United States—if only because the Philippines had nowhere else to turn. "There is growing sentiment here in the Philippines of loyalty to the United States, and I believe that in the event of trouble the Commonwealth Government will whole-heartedly support American activities." Yet even Sayre, who like MacArthur had a vested interest in overstating Philippine pro-Americanism, declined to predict what the Filipinos would do. "The situation here keeps changing with kaleidoscopic rapidity."[54]

III

UTANG NA LOOB?

10

Retreat
1941–1944

I. Japan comes

By midsummer 1941 few could doubt that the United States and Japan were headed for collision. In April Tokyo concluded a treaty of nonaggression with Moscow. Treaties being the uncertain things they are, and especially were in those deceitful days, the pact hardly secured Japan's position in northeastern Asia against Russian assault. But Hitler's double-cross of Stalin in June—the German invasion of Russia—did. Japan now felt free to move south. On July 25, following the landing of Japanese troops in Saigon, Tokyo announced the establishment of a Japanese protectorate over Indochina, to which the Vichy government of France acquiesced. Because the United States had cracked Japan's diplomatic code, Roosevelt had time to weigh his response. On July 26 the administration announced the freezing of Japan's financial assets in the United States. The action lacked the publicity and provocativeness of a formal embargo, yet it amounted to the same thing. Japan's reliance on American products, especially oil, left Tokyo two choices: to cease and desist in Southeast Asia, or to strike out farther in an effort to end Japan's economic dependence on America and the west. "If the present condition is left unchecked," General Teiichi Suzuki of Tokyo's military planning board told his colleagues, "Japan will find herself totally exhausted and unable to rise in the future." Suzuki predicted that the American blockade, which Britain and the Netherlands joined, would result in Japan's collapse within two years. Unwilling to accept such a fate, the Japanese high command laid preparations for war.[1]

Washington also made ready. In June Secretary of War Henry Stimson had decided to recall MacArthur to active service as American army commander for the Far East with headquarters in Manila. A month later, on the day after the announcement of the assets freeze, the war department made the appointment official. Unimpressed with MacArthur's Philippine rank of field marshal, the department named him a lieutenant general. Meanwhile Roosevelt issued an executive order integrating Philippine armed forces into the American military.[2]

These actions abruptly reversed the power relationship between Quezon and MacArthur. A week previous MacArthur had been an employee of the Philippine government, albeit one of stature. Now he wielded the sword of the United States in Asia. Washington's moves also forestalled, at least momentarily, any further neutralist maneuverings by Quezon. By this point MacArthur's military program had trained more than 100,000 Filipinos. With the amalgamation of these men into the American army the Philippines would constitute a threat to Japanese operations in Southeast Asia. Tokyo would have no choice but to eliminate the threat before striking against the oil fields of the Dutch East Indies.

Quezon, flexible as ever, quickly adapted to the change in circumstances. He became the most loyal of American patriots and the most enthusiastic of MacArthur's supporters. He and other Philippine officials conspicuously applauded MacArthur on his new appointment. MacArthur accepted the surrender with olympian grace. In August the Nacionalistas nominated Quezon for a second term. Quezon earlier had engineered a constitutional amendment allowing his reelection, adroitly timing ratification to coincide with Roosevelt's precedent-flouting run for a third term in the United States. As Quezon anticipated, Roosevelt declined to veto. MacArthur responded to Quezon's nomination with warmest best wishes, calling the Philippine president "the Champion" of the islands' destiny. An effusive note from MacArthur to Quezon soon found its way into the Manila press.

> I feel the Philippines should be congratulated, the United States should be felicitated and the world in general gratified, at what has occurred. It is to you personally, however, in the bond of adopted brotherhood which has united us for so long a time, that I wish to express the thrilling elation that I feel. My love and affection for you is such that not even your immediate family can feel a greater surge of pride and happiness than that which animates me.[3]

The renewal of good relations between Quezon and MacArthur eased but did not solve the problem of how to defend the Philippines. In fact the problem was in some ways worsened, since the United States faced the strong probability of war in two theaters. Although the Red-Orange scenario had long since been shelved, the exercise had not been a complete waste of energy. Many of the resource-allocation problems anticipated in a war against Japan and Britain seemed likely to arise in a war against Japan and Germany. Three months before the German invasion of Poland the American army-navy board initiated planning for the latter war. Variously numbered "Rainbow" plans summarized the results of the process. Of the several versions Rainbow Five came closest to predicting what actually occurred during the next thirty months, although even this one failed to forecast the sudden collapse of France and the eventual alliance of the United States and Britain with the Soviet Union. Of greatest lasting importance, Rainbow Five established the Europe-first principle that guided American strategy during the war. The plan stipulated that if the United States became involved in a conflict in both Europe and the Pacific, American forces should wage a "strategic defensive" in the latter theater while projecting forward as rapidly as possible into Africa and Europe. The primary goal would be the "decisive defeat" of Germany and its European allies. Although the Nazi-Soviet pact, the fall of France, the battle of Britain and the German invasion of Russia caused American planners to reconsider several times, the emphasis on Europe persisted.[4]

What Rainbow meant for the Philippines no one could immediately know. On one hand the greater complications and demands on American resources Rainbow entailed seemed to confirm the assumption of expendability Orange had made regarding the islands. This assumption appeared to underlie the first orders the war department sent MacArthur in the wake of the Japanese occupation of Indochina. The department told MacArthur it had no plans for major reinforcement of the Philippines. MacArthur should expect the arrival of only four hundred reserve officers to assist with training Filipinos. But then Washington reversed course. Following meetings at the highest levels of the Roosevelt administration, Chief of Staff George Marshall informed his subordinates, "It is the policy of the United States to defend the Philippines." Marshall cabled MacArthur to this effect, adding that preparations were being made for the dispatch of significant reinforcements to the islands.[5]

To some degree the shift in policy reflected changes in military technology since the mid-1930s. The army believed its new bomber, the B-17, could go far toward blunting a Japanese offensive toward the Philippines. To some degree the policy shift signified Washington's confidence in MacArthur, who although a prickly prima donna was recognized as an incomparable tactician and leader of fighting troops. MacArthur radiated optimism, which he transmitted not only to those below but to many of those above.

In largest part, however, the shift represented wishful thinking. Japan's advance into Indochina indicated Tokyo's intention to break out of dependency on America by seizing the resources of Southeast Asia. If the Japanese succeeded, there might be no stopping them. But Japan must be stopped. To do so, it seemed, the Philippines must be held. Therefore they would be held.

Between August and December Washington spared no effort providing for the protection of the Philippines. In September Marshall informed MacArthur, "I have directed that United States Army forces in the Philippines be placed in highest priority for equipment including authorized defense reserves for fifty thousand men." Although Congress had limited the size of the American army, no legal ceiling applied to Philippine troops. MacArthur might raise as many soldiers as he could feed and outfit, using increased monies from Washington and promises. By the beginning of December the active forces in the Philippine army numbered 100,000, in addition to 12,000 Philippine Scouts. The American contingent had risen by 8,500 to more than 30,000. Aircraft in the islands included 35 B-17s at Clark Field and 107 P-40 fighters scattered about Luzon, as well as more than a hundred other planes, giving the Philippines the greatest concentration of American air power in the Pacific. Naval forces comprised 3 cruisers, 13 destroyers and two score smaller fighting and service vessels, in addition to 29 submarines. Supplies continued to pour in as December began. In the first week of the month a large convoy bringing 70 warplanes, 600 tons of bombs, 9,000 barrels of aviation fuel, 48 75-millimeter guns and several million rounds of ammunition steamed west from Hawaii, bound for Manila.[6]

In the area of civil defense the American and Philippine governments made less headway. Difficulties of terrain complicated matters. The high water table around Manila rendered construction of underground shelters nearly impossible. Differences of opinion as to which direction the Japanese would attack from hindered efforts to devise evacuation plans. As events turned out, some of the designated relocation points were smack in the path of the enemy's advance. Diversion of resources to the military created shortages of items, such as gas masks, necessary to protection of civilians.

The division of authority between the office of the Philippine president and that of the high commissioner did not help the situation. Where MacArthur commanded all military forces in the islands, both American and Filipino, neither Quezon nor Sayre had full authority over preparations for civil defense. Facing a huge task with insufficient resources, each sought to shift responsibility to the other, or to anyone else plausible. Sayre said he was "far from satisfied" with the efforts of commonwealth government. Quezon blamed Sayre for preventing him from assuming emergency powers when the crisis grew apparent. Though not speaking directly to the high commissioner, Quezon evinced his feelings when he declared, "If war breaks out soon and our people die here, unprotected, by the bombs, those men who have stopped me from doing what I should have done ought to be hanged—every one of them on the lamp post."[7]

The Japanese attack on the Philippines on December 8—December 7 east of the dateline—demonstrated the essential inadequacy of both military and civilian preparations. At 3 a.m. the head of MacArthur's signal corps received a report of the assault on Pearl Harbor. A few minutes later an aide awakened the general, who found the news hard to credit. "Pearl Harbor!" he declared. "That should be our strongest point." By 4 a.m. confirmation of the strike against Hawaii arrived. Shortly after 7 a.m. the war department in Washington transmitted a radiogram summarizing the situation and directing MacArthur's response:

> Hostilities between Japan and the United States, British Commonwealth and Dutch have commenced. Japanese made air raid on Pearl Harbor this morning December seventh. Carry out tasks assigned in Rainbow Five so far as they pertain to Japan. In addition cooperate with the British and Dutch to the utmost without jeopardizing the accomplishment of your primary mission of defense of the Philippines. You are authorized to dispatch air units to operate temporarily from suitable bases in cooperation with the British or Dutch. Report daily major dispositions and all operations. You have the complete confidence of the War Department and we assure you of every possible assistance and support within our power.[8]

By this time MacArthur's air commander, General Lewis Brereton, was pressing for permission to launch air strikes against Japanese bases on Formosa. MacArthur's chief of staff, General Richard Sutherland, refused to allow Brereton to speak with MacArthur, claiming the boss was busy. But Sutherland told Brereton to proceed with preparations for sending out his planes pending MacArthur's approval. For reasons that remain unclear, gaining approval consumed three hours. Not until nearly 11:30 did orders go out to Clark Field to ready aircraft for takeoff. Fueling and loading required another hour. Noon came and went with the B-17s and P-40s still on the tarmac.

At 12:20 the first wave of Japanese attackers arrived from Formosa. More than fifty bombers and three dozen state-of-the-art Zero fighters swept in and destroyed two squadrons of B-17s and one of P-40s. Another squadron of P-40s, returning from patrol, encountered a second Japanese attack group at the airfield at Iba, forty miles away. Only two American planes survived. Before the smoke cleared, half of MacArthur's air arm had been amputated.[9]

For the next several years the principals to this fiasco played musical blame. Brereton charged Sutherland explicitly and MacArthur implicitly with responsibility for not letting his bombers take off. Sutherland asserted that Brereton should have relocated to Mindanao, beyond range of the Japanese bases on Formosa. Brereton, on orders from MacArthur, had begun relocation, but most of his planes remained on Luzon when the Japanese arrived. MacArthur said Sutherland had failed to inform him of Brereton's request for permission to hit Formosa, and he indicated that if Brereton had really desired such permission he should have insisted on an interview with the top man. MacArthur declared in addition that raids on Formosa would have been "suicidal," which may have been true, given the lack of American intelligence about the island and considering Japan's overall air superiority. But MacArthur also described his air group in the Philippines as "hardly more than a token force," which was patently untrue.[10]

Regardless of where blame lay—there was enough for all—the possibility of defending the Philippines evaporated on the first day of the war. The destruction of the major portion of American air strength in the islands precluded prevention of Japanese landings. The crippling of the Pacific fleet at Pearl Harbor rendered reinforcement of the Philippine garrison impossible. The Americans in the islands and the Filipinos would have to fight with what they had, which had never been enough but now was not even close.

II.   America goes

In the days following the initial assault on the Philippines the Japanese attempted to eliminate the American naval forces in the islands, as well as the rest of the air force. On December 9 a small group of Japanese bombers attacked Nichols Field near Manila. The next day a larger formation hit Nichols again, in addition to Del Carmen Field near Clark and Nielson Field outside Manila. On the same day more than fifty bombers struck at Cavite, opposite Corregidor, crippling the naval installation there, damaging vessels in the harbor and destroying a large stockpile of torpedoes. Bad weather over Formosa gave the Philippines a day's respite to fight the fires that still blazed at Cavite, but on December 12 and 13 the Japanese flew hundreds of sorties over Luzon. By the evening of December 13 the American air force had been so reduced that MacArthur chose to withhold his remaining planes from combat to save them for reconnaissance.

With the United States knocked out of the sky over the Philippines, the commander of the Asiatic fleet, Admiral Thomas Hart, decided that preservation of his forces required withdrawing from Manila Bay. On December 14 he ordered most of his ships and officers to the southern portion of the archipelago. Of the craft that remained the most important were 27 submarines, which made more-difficult targets for Japanese bombers and could flee later if necessary.[11]

Japanese landings started while the air raids continued. The first landing took place on Batan island in the Luzon Strait south of Formosa on December 8. On the 10th Japanese troops came ashore at two locations on the northern coast of Luzon itself. On the 12th a detachment from Palau to the east invaded Legaspi in southern Luzon. On the 20th another group from Palau entered Mindanao at Davao.

These first attacks had the objective of securing beachheads and providing bases from which short-range aircraft could cover larger landings. The larger assaults began in earnest on December 22, with two Japanese divisions splashing to the beach at Lingayen Gulf and pushing south toward Manila. Although the defensive forces, consisting of units from the Philippine army and the Philippine Scouts, offered spirited resistance, they were overmatched against the better organized and better trained Japanese and had to retreat. Two days later another Japanese force landed at Atimonan on Lamon Bay on the east coast of Luzon and commenced driving west toward the capital.[12]

By this time the strategy of General Masaharu Homma, the commander of the Philippine invasion, had become apparent. MacArthur afterward explained:

> It was obvious he sought to swing shut the jaws of a great military pincer, one prong being the main force that had landed at Lingayen, the other the units that had landed at Atimonan. If these two forces could effect a speedy junction, my main body of troops would have to fight in the comparatively open terrain of central Luzon, with the enemy to the front and to the rear. The Japanese strategy envisaged complete annihilation of the Luzon defense force within a short period. With the principal island of the archipelago under their control, they could look forward to an easy conquest of the remainder of the islands. It was a perfect strategic conception.

Although MacArthur was not above magnifying the advantages his enemies enjoyed, this analysis got the essentials right.[13]

While MacArthur scrambled to avoid annihilation American leaders in Washington tried to figure out where the Philippines fit in America's overall strategy. At the end of December Roosevelt broadcast a speech to the Filipinos proclaiming, "The people of the United States will never forget what the people of the Philippine Islands are doing this day and will do in the days to come." The president added, "I give to the people of the Philippines my solemn pledge that their freedom will be redeemed and their independence established and protected. . . . We are engaged in a great and common cause. I count on every Philippine man, woman and child to do his duty. We will do ours." But Roosevelt declined to specify what America's duty entailed, and his use of the term "redeem," as if Filipino freedom had already been lost, had unnerving overtones.[14]

From Manila, amid protestations of loyalty came cries of distress. Sayre wired the president, "We on the firing line are back of you to a man," although the high commissioner went on to recommend a propaganda campaign to counter Filipino defeatism. Quezon declared, "My people are already shedding their blood side by side with American soldiers and the civilian population are cooperating unto death." For many months the Philippine president had been trying to persuade Washington to release monies held in various accounts for the Philippines in the United States. His pleas intensified. "I am in dire need of funds for public relief and protection of our civilian population."[15]

MacArthur, while taking a less alarmist tone, likewise called for assistance. Two days after the first assaults he urged Washington to do whatever it could to get the Russians to hit Japan from the north while Japanese forces were deployed in the south. "Definite information available here shows that entry of Russia is enemy's greatest fear," MacArthur cabled. "Most favorable opportunity now exists, and immediate attack on Japan from north would not only inflict heavy punishment but would at once relieve pressure from objectives of Jap drive to southward. . . . A golden opportunity now exists for a master stroke while the enemy is engaged in over-extended initial air effort."[16]

MacArthur's recommendation indicated an acute attack of theateritis, a malady that chronically afflicted the general. Although Russia's armies had finally managed to stem the advance of Hitler's troops, Stalin could hardly be expected to take on another foe. Nor was MacArthur's subsequent suggestion of carrier-based air attacks against Japan much more realistic. "The enemy appears to have a tendency to become overconfident," MacArthur asserted at the beginning of January. "The time is ripe for a brilliant thrust with air carriers." After Pearl Harbor the navy thought it would be doing heroically to hold the line against further losses. It was not about to commit its precious remaining ships in the Pacific to such a high-risk endeavor as MacArthur advocated.[17]

Yet Washington did not believe the Philippines could simply be abandoned. Without going into specifics Marshall informed MacArthur he could expect "every possible assistance within our power." Secretary of War Stimson, no doubt influenced by his personal experience in the Philippines, argued, "We must make every effort at whatever risk to keep MacArthur's line open." Beyond the question of what America owed the Filipino people, Stimson contended that writing off the islands would demoralize pro-American groups throughout the world and "paralyze the activities of everybody in the Far East." Stimson found the navy's caution dismaying, and he decided to appeal to the top. In his diary he described how he rehearsed his brief with assistants:

> I laid before them the issue which was now pending before us, namely as to whether we should make every effort possible in the Far East or whether, like the Navy, we should treat that as doomed and let it go. We all agreed that the first course was the one to follow; that we have a very good chance of making a successful defense, taking the southwestern Pacific as a whole. If we are driven out of the Philippines and Singapore, we can still fall back on the Netherlands East Indies and Australia; and with the cooperation of China—if we can keep that going—we can strike good counterblows at Japan. While if we yielded to the defeatist theory, it would have not only the disastrous effect on our material policy of letting Japan get strongly ensconced in the southwestern Pacific which would be a terribly hard job to get her out of, but it would psychologically do even more in the discouragement of China and in fact all of the four powers who are now fighting very well together.[18]

MacArthur continued to demand reinforcements. In the process he challenged the assumptions of three years of American strategic planning. "The Philippine theater of operations is the locus of victory or defeat," he asserted. "If the Philippines and the Netherlands East Indies go, so will Singapore and the entire Asiatic continent." If America refused to make a stand in the Philippines, it would be risking a "fatal mistake."[19]

Roosevelt accepted Stimson's and MacArthur's arguments in principle. The president agreed that the Philippines were crucial, and he directed the navy to explore "every possible means" of relieving the islands, adding, "I realize great risks are involved, but the objective is important."[20]

Yet for all his good wishes toward the Philippines, Roosevelt could not ignore the other demands crowding upon him. On December 24 American and British officials began discussions for the optimal use of allied resources against their common enemies. Suspecting that the bloody nose the United States had just received in the Pacific might have weakened American resolve to pursue a Europe-first strategy, the British sought reassurances. Some American officers worried that the United States would be tricked into a defense of the British empire at the expense of American interests. "The whole god-damned thing is cockeyed," General Joseph Stilwell of the war plans division said, referring to the priority allotted the fight against Germany. "We should clean the Pacific first and then face east." But Stilwell and the Pacificists lost the argument. Roosevelt refused to buck the British, whose full cooperation he considered essential to the defeat of the Axis. By the time British prime minister Winston Churchill left Washington in mid-January the president had confirmed America's primary commitment to Europe.[21]

Roosevelt's decision meant that while minor help might find its way to the Philippines—and during January a small amount did slip via submarine through the Japanese blockade—there would be no major relief. The American and Filipino troops on the islands must fight as long as possible, with the object of slowing Japan's further advance. They would not be rescued.

As the realization of this fact dawned in the Philippines, complaints understandably arose. MacArthur continued to gripe, while Sayre, even as he professed "supreme confidence" in the president's leadership, called for reconsideration. "Although I am no military strategist," the high commissioner wrote, "I am convinced that a smashing attack now, while the Japanese lines are overextended and while Corregidor and Singapore are still in our hands, will be worth more than ten victories later on." Quezon, writing Roosevelt "with utmost diffidence," said he hoped reports of America's preference for Europe were simply "British propaganda intended to influence action in that direction." Quezon entreated the president to direct that the United States "use all the materials at her disposal to crush the Japanese forces at this time."[22]

Washington had not expected Quezon to applaud the decision to concentrate on winning the war in Europe, but American officials hardly anticipated Quezon's next move. On February 8 the Philippine president wrote a long letter to Roosevelt castigating the American government for neglect and abuse of the people of the islands. "While enjoying security itself," Quezon asserted, "the United States has in effect condemned the sixteen millions of Filipinos to practical destruction in order to effect a certain delay. You have promised redemption, but what we need is immediate assistance and protection." This said, Quezon proceeded to propose a seven-point plan for saving the Philippines from a dire fate. First, the United States should grant the islands "immediate and complete independence." Second, Washington should arrange with Tokyo for neutralization of the archipelago. Third, all American and Japanese troops should be withdrawn. Fourth, American military bases should be removed. Fifth, the Philippine army should be disbanded. Sixth, negotiations should commence for peaceful trade relations between the Philippines and other countries, particularly Japan. Seventh, the United States and Japan should assist in the evacuation of their nationals who desired to leave.[23]

Had Quezon's proposal arrived alone it would have provoked a considerable reaction. That it came with MacArthur's endorsement quadrupled its shock value. "So far as the military angle is concerned," the general wrote, "the problem presents itself as to whether the plan of President Quezon might offer the best possible solution of what is about to be a disastrous debacle." MacArthur continued,

> Since I have no air or sea protection you must be prepared at any time to figure on the complete destruction of this command. You must determine whether the mission of delay would be better furthered by the temporizing plan of Quezon or by my continued battle efforts. The temper of the Filipinos is one of almost violent resentment against the United States. Every one of them expected help and when it has not been forthcoming they believe they have been betrayed in favor of others.

MacArthur, in contradiction of his earlier insistence on the vital importance of the Philippines, went on to say that neutralizing the islands would not affect the outcome of the war one way or the other. America would win or lose the war elsewhere. He also suggested that acceptance of the principle of immediate independence would win political support for the United States among Filipinos and other dependent peoples.[24]

Stimson, receiving the two letters, could not believe what he was reading. "It was a wholly unreal message," he confided to his diary, "taking no account of what the war was for or what the well-known characteristics of Japan toward conquered people were." Marshall thought so too, as did Roosevelt, who rejected Quezon's proposal out of hand. The president directed Stimson and Marshall to draft appropriate responses to Quezon and MacArthur. Marshall passed the task along to Dwight Eisenhower, now Marshall's chief assistant.[25]

By this time the last of Eisenhower's once considerable admiration for MacArthur had vanished. Eisenhower accused his old chief of "losing his nerve." Eisenhower said that both MacArthur and Quezon were acting like "babies."[26]

The letter Eisenhower drafted and Roosevelt sent to MacArthur left the general no room for doubt regarding his mission. MacArthur might arrange the surrender of Filipino troops "when and if in your opinion that course appears necessary." But as for the Americans under MacArthur's command:

> American forces will continue to keep our flag flying in the Philippines so long as there remains any possibility of resistance. . . . The duty and the necessity of resisting Japanese aggression to the last transcends in importance any other obligation now facing us in the Philippines.

There has been gradually welded into a common front a globe-encircling opposition to the predatory powers that are seeking the destruction of individual liberty and freedom of government. We cannot afford to have this line broken in any particular theater. As the most powerful member of this coalition we cannot display weakness in fact or in spirit anywhere. It is mandatory that there be established once and for all in the minds of all peoples complete evidence that the American determination and indomitable will to win carries on down to the last unit.

Roosevelt's answer to Quezon was more diplomatic though no less firm. "I am not lacking in understanding of or sympathy with the situation of yourself and the Commonwealth Government," Roosevelt said. The crisis in the Philippines indeed appeared desperate.

But such crises and their treatment must be judged by a more accurate measure than the anxieties and sufferings of the present, however acute. For over forty years the American government has been carrying out to the people of the Philippines a pledge to help them successfully, however long it might take, in their aspirations to become a self-governing and independent people. . . .

By a malign conspiracy of a few depraved but powerful governments this hope is now being frustrated and delayed. An organized attack upon individual freedom and governmental independence throughout the entire world, beginning in Europe, has now spread and been carried to the southwestern Pacific by Japan. The basic principles which have guided the United States in its conduct toward the Philippines have been violated in the rape of Czechoslovakia, Poland, Holland, Belgium, Luxembourg, Denmark, Norway, Albania, Greece, Yugoslavia, Manchukuo, China, Thailand and finally the Philippines. Could the people of any of these nations honestly look forward to true restoration of their independent sovereignty under the dominance of Germany, Italy, or Japan?

You refer in your telegram to the announcement by the Japanese Prime Minister of Japan's willingness to grant to the Philippines her independence. I only have to refer you to the present condition of Korea, Manchukuo, North China, Indo China, and all other countries which have fallen under the brutal sway of the Japanese government, to point out the hollow duplicity of such an announcement. . . .

By the terms of our pledge to the Philippines implicit in our forty years of conduct towards your people and expressly recognized in the terms of the Tydings-McDuffie Act, we have undertaken to protect you to the uttermost of our power until the time of your ultimate independence had arrived. Our soldiers in the Philippines are now engaged in fulfilling that purpose. The honor of the United States is pledged to its fulfillment. We propose that it be carried out regardless of its cost.[27]

Roosevelt's refusal to consider a separate peace in the Philippines set the stage for the dramatic and tragic events of the next four months. At the end of December, unable to defend the capital against the encroaching Japanese, MacArthur had declared Manila an open city and evacuated his headquarters to Corregidor. American and Filipino troops continued to retreat before the Japanese advance, ultimately withdrawing to the Bataan peninsula west of Manila Bay. When they arrived they already lacked supplies. By the end of the first week on the peninsula they were down to rations providing but two thousand calories per day, half the requirements for an active man. They shot and ate their horses. They slaughtered any carabao they could find. Weak from hunger, many contracted scurvy, beri-beri, malaria and dysentery. "We could hardly crawl from the foxholes and aim our rifles," one survivor recalled. Uniforms, boots, raingear and medicine all ran or wore out. So did hope. "If we had had something in our bellies, some hope that we could expect help from the United States," General Jonathan Wainwright, the American commander, wrote, "things might have been a little more endur-able. But our perpetual hunger, the steaming heat by day and night, the terrible malaria and the moans of the wounded were terribly hard on the men."[28]

MacArthur made matters worse by raising false expectations. "Help is on the way from the United States," he announced in mid-January. "Thousands of troops and hundreds of planes are being dispatched." The promised aid never came. While MacArthur by this time should have known it would not, he still refused to believe that Washington would abandon the islands, *his* islands. The disappointment among the troops on Bataan led to denunciations of the general. Some sang of MacArthur, ensconced in a bombproof tunnel on Corregidor (to the tune of the "Battle Hymn of the Republic"):

> Dugout Doug's not timid; he just cautious not afraid;
> He's protecting carefully the stars that Franklin made.
> Four-star generals are as rare as good food on Bataan;
> And his troops go starving on.

The charges of timidity were unjustified. Throughout his long career Mac-Arthur demonstrated physical bravery to the point of foolhardiness. But one could forgive the "bastards of Bataan," as they called themselves, for resentment. The feeling increased, among those who lived to learn of the fact, when Mac-Arthur later received the congressional Medal of Honor for "heroic conduct of defensive and offensive operations on the Bataan Peninsula."[29]

By the beginning of April Bataan had become nearly indefensible. Wainwright reported the situation as "extremely critical." With adequate supplies the defenders might have put up a fight. But they were starving. Wainwright said, "Our troops have been subsisted on one-half to one-third rations for so long a period that they do not possess the physical strength to endure the strain placed upon the individual in an attack." That the Americans and Filipinos on the peninsula held out as long as they did was remarkable. They were not superhuman, though, and on April 8 they surrendered.[30]

Corregidor survived a few weeks longer. On February 22 Roosevelt had ordered MacArthur to leave the fortress for Mindanao where he might lay preparations for continuing guerrilla resistance after the surrender of regular troops. Thence he should proceed to Australia to assume command of combined allied forces in the southwestern Pacific. MacArthur hesitated to obey, arguing that a precipitate exit would exacerbate Filipino fears of American abandonment.

"These people are depending on me now," he radioed Washington, speaking immodestly but not inaccurately. "Any idea that I was being withdrawn for any other purpose than to bring them immediate relief could not be explained." Roosevelt insisted MacArthur do as told, although he left the date of departure to the general's discretion. On the night of March 12 MacArthur, his wife and son and various staff slipped out of Manila Bay aboard four PT boats. They reached Mindanao on the 14th. Two days later the group continued to Darwin, Australia, via B-17. With characteristic grandiloquence MacArthur reported on arrival, "This hazardous trip by a commanding general and key members of his staff through enemy-controlled territory undoubtedly is unique in military annals."[31]

Quezon likewise evacuated Corregidor. In mid-February MacArthur had written Marshall advocating that arrangements be made for the removal of Quezon and members of the Philippine government. "Their usefulness here is over and it is advantageous from every point of view that they do not share the destruction which now faces this garrison." Marshall concurred. A short while later an American boat took Quezon to the Visayas, where initially he hoped to seat his government and rally resistance against the invaders. In March, however, he received a letter from MacArthur, now in Australia, requesting that the commonwealth president join him there. Explaining that the United States was moving its forces into the southern Pacific area "in what is destined to be a great offensive against Japan," MacArthur asserted that Quezon could accomplish the most good outside the country. Partly from concern for Quezon's deteriorating health—life in the caves of Corregidor had aggravated Quezon's tuberculosis— and perhaps partly from a desire to make sure that he, MacArthur, received credit for the islands' deliverance, MacArthur wrote Quezon, "We have been completely identified together for many years, and you have been at my headquarters since the beginning of the war. It is the natural and proper thing for you to do to rejoin me at my headquarters in Australia in the great drive for victory in the Philippines." The next day Quezon radioed acceptance of the offer. On the 18th he left Negros for Mindanao. After a brief delay there he arrived in Australia on the 27th.[32]

A curious incident accompanied the evacuation of MacArthur and Quezon from the Philippines. In January, following MacArthur's withdrawal to Corregidor, Quezon issued an executive order authorizing payment of $500,000 to the general. Smaller amounts would go to members of MacArthur's staff.[33]

Although the order proffered the money as an expression of gratitude for exemplary efforts in defense of the Philippines, Quezon's motivation seems clear enough. At a moment when America's willingness to protect the Philippines appeared doubtful, to say the least, Quezon wished to do whatever he could to increase the attachment of important American officials to the islands. The first principle of Filipino politics has always been personal gratitude and loyalty, and money is as good a currency as most others for expressing such feelings. Nothing would have been more natural than for Quezon to offer a tangible measure of thanks to the American general for services rendered in the past and simultaneously to try to increase the likelihood of similar services in the future.

Why MacArthur accepted the gift is harder to explain. Maybe he felt he could not with grace turn down the offer—although Eisenhower had no difficulty declining a similar proposal after Quezon arrived in the United States. Maybe MacArthur's long service in the Philippines had caused some of its political culture to rub off. Maybe he just wanted the money. He doubtless thought he deserved it after all he had done, and on account of all he intended to do, for the Philippines. In justifying acceptance to himself MacArthur could contend that the payment was deferred compensation for his work as field marshal in the Philippine army, during the period between 1937 and 1941 when he had been on the American inactive list and eligible to take other employment.

In any event MacArthur left the Philippines richer by half a million dollars. On May 6 the Corregidor garrison capitulated.

III. To resist or collaborate

The surrender of American and Philippine army forces in the Philippines left Filipinos with a dismal selection of alternatives. The most obvious were variations of two: resistance and collaboration. Many determined individuals chose the former. Among the resisters a relatively large group, centered around Manila, joined the *Hukbo ng Bayan laban sa Hapon* (People's Anti-Japanese Army) or Hukbalahap. To a certain extent the Hukbalahap traced its lineage to the same radical nationalism that had inspired the Katipunan and much of the resistance to the American occupation two generations earlier. "I had no choice but to fight against the Japanese," one member of the guerrilla organization declared. "I believed that the Philippines should be independent. The Japanese had no more right to my land than the Americans did." To some degree as well the Huk resistance reflected a natural response to Japanese excesses. The least gracious of conquerors, Japanese troops treated locals with contempt. "Every time you went to market in the bayan and a Japanese passed by," a resident of Talavera later recalled, "you had to bow down to him. . . . If an official stopped you on the road and you didn't have a pass, you could be held for interrogation." The smallest sign of opposition provoked summary treatment. "Anyone who moved or objected in any way could be shot, no questions asked. . . . Anyone whom they suspected was hauled off and detained indefinitely, frequently beaten up and tortured."[34]

Resistance also developed in northern Luzon, where some stranded American and Philippine regulars formed the nucleus of a guerrilla force; in southern Luzon, where Quezon loyalists created an organization called President Quezon's Own

Guerrillas; and in the Visayas and on Mindanao. Throughout the war members of the resistance succeeded in allowing the government-in-exile to keep touch with the situation inside the country. The news usually was not good. "Terroristic methods terrible; compelled many civil officials and civilians to surrender," one of Quezon's informants reported early in 1944. Taken together the guerrillas did not substantially upset Japanese war plans, but they helped preserve Filipino self-respect and they provided intelligence that would prove important when the reconquest of the Philippines began.[35]

In most wars the courage of active resistance to occupation is given to few. The Second World War in the Philippines was no exception. On January 2, 1942, the Japanese commander-in-chief in the Philippines, General Homma, issued a warning: "Offering resistance or committing hostile acts against the Japanese forces in any manner will lead the whole Philippines to ashes." The next day Homma declared American sovereignty in the islands ended, and he ordered inhabitants "to sever their relations with the United States, to obey faithfully all commands of the Japanese army, to cooperate voluntarily with the army in its stationing and activities in the Philippines, and to supply to it all its military needs when demanded." Filipino officials were required "to remain in their posts and to carry on their duties as before." Failure to comply would be punishable by death.[36]

The Japanese complemented coercion with a policy of attraction. They carpeted the country with propaganda, turning the Americans' accomplishment in raising the literacy rate against the United States and prompting American Interior Secretary Harold Ickes to remark to William Donovan of the Office of Strategic Services that Japan's current success suggested a covert Japanese role in "a great deal of anti-American propaganda" in the islands "for many years back." Speeches, pamphlets and newspaper articles trumpeted the line of Asian solidarity against western imperialism. "Like it or not," one Japanese officer reminded the population, "you are Filipinos and belong to the Oriental race. No matter how hard you try, you cannot become white people." Another extended the argument, declaring, "The time has come to assert yourselves as an Oriental people."[37]

The combination of threat and encouragement was remarkably effective. The Americans had not even surrendered Bataan before collaborators began lining up to speak with Japanese officers. Shortly after Japanese troops entered Manila, Homma's chief of staff, General Masami Maeda, interviewed prominent Filipinos in the area, including Claro Recto, the Nacionalista leader; Jorge Vargas, recently appointed mayor of Manila; Quintin Paredes, formerly a Quezon lieutenant in the legislature; Benigno Aquino, a close associate of Osmeña and a Nacionalista campaign manager; and José Laurel, past secretary of the interior and acting supreme court chief justice. Maeda directed the group to tell the Filipino people to cease struggling, since resistance was hopeless. He added that their help would be vital to the restoration of order in Manila and the prevention of further public suffering. Initially Recto and the others suggested that Maeda contact Quezon, then on Corregidor. Maeda rejected this idea on grounds that Quezon had abandoned the capital and thereby his office.

The Filipino group then met separately. Paredes and Aquino advocated cooperation with the Japanese but only in exchange for Tokyo's recognition of an independent Philippine republic. Others opposed this plan, pointing out that the Chinese had fared poorly under a nominally independent government. Independence under Japanese auspices did not warrant the risks of disloyalty to the United States the scheme entailed. The group compromised on a proposal whereby Japan would recognize a new provisional executive, consisting of a president and vice president, chosen under the authority of the existing Philippine commonwealth.

When Maeda scotched this proposal, making plain he did not intend to deal with the Philippine commonwealth, the Filipinos thought again. Confronting a choice for the islands between direct military rule by Japan or indirect rule softened by Filipino intermediaries, Paredes and the others announced the formation of a provisional council of state headed by an executive commission. Vargas, chairman of the commission, broadcast the news to his compatriots. "Our crops have to be harvested and our fields cultivated, our roads and bridges reconstructed," Vargas said. "These we cannot accomplish under a reign of terrorism and lawlessness." The sooner the country, working with the executive commission, began reconstruction, the less its people would suffer.

General Homma responded by offering his "hearty thanks for the endeavors of many eminent Filipino citizens who with a true understanding of the aims of our new forces have devoted themselves to the task of establishing a new Philippines."[38]

Observing these events from Corregidor, Quezon had difficulty criticizing. He protested anew his attachment to the government of the United States, but he told MacArthur,

> It seems to me questionable whether any government has the right to demand loyalty from its citizens beyond its willingness or ability to render actual protection. This war is not of our making. Those that had dictated the policies of the United States could not have failed to see that this is the weakest point in American territory. From the beginning, they should have tried to build up our defenses.

Regarding the members of the executive commission, Quezon asserted that all of them had wished to accompany the government to Corregidor, but space had not allowed. He continued,

> They are not Quislings. The Quislings are the men who betray their country to the enemy. These men did what they had been asked to do, under the protection of their Government. Today they are virtually prisoners of the enemy. I am sure they are

only doing what they think is their duty. They are not traitors. They are the victims of the adverse fortunes of war and I am sure they had no choice. Besides, it is most probable that they accepted their positions in order to safeguard the welfare of the civilian population in the occupied areas. I think, under the circumstances, America should look upon their situation sympathetically and understandingly.[39]

Sympathy and understanding ran short in America in the months after Pearl Harbor, the more so as news arrived of the determined but doomed struggle of the defenders of Bataan. When Americans learned of the horrendous treatment the prisoners captured at Bataan received, their sympathy for Philippine collaborators disappeared entirely.

Regardless of American opinion the Filipinos had to survive as best they could. After pacifying the islands, or nearly so, the Japanese sought to integrate the archipelago into Japan's sphere of influence. In September 1942 Tokyo established a Greater East Asia Ministry charged with mobilizing the resources of the conquered territories, including the Philippines. The Japanese military claimed first call on the islands' produce. Rice fields fed Japanese soldiers. Sugar plantations were converted to cotton or had their output made into fuel alcohol. Abaca production became a military monopoly. Schools taught Japanese instead of English, and favored Filipinos were sent to Japan to college. Tokyo sponsored cultural exchanges, mostly one way. It ordered the "voluntary" dissolution of political parties and their replacement by a "non-political" national service organization known as the Kalibapi.[40]

To demonstrate Japan's good intentions toward the Filipino people, as the Japanese said, Tokyo at the beginning of 1943 announced plans for granting Philippine independence. In May Premier Hideki Tojo visited Manila and reiterated the message in person. Needless to say Tojo had ulterior motives. The war had begun turning against Japan the previous summer. At the battles of Midway and Coral Sea American forces had broken Japan's momentum, and during the next half-year they commenced the long but relentless drive back across the Pacific. From the outset of the war the principal question had been the Americans' willingness to fight a protracted conflict. Would they insist on total defeat of the Axis or settle for a negotiated peace? By January 1943 it was clear the Americans would fight to the finish. It was equally clear, to most objective observers at least, that in light of America's overwhelming advantage in productive capacity the American side would win.

The Japanese were hardly ready to give up. They prepared to resist the American counterattack. By granting the Philippines independence Japan hoped to undercut resistance in the islands and lessen demands on the Japanese troops stationed there. Some of these troops could then be redeployed. At the same time, independence for the Philippines would improve Japan's political credibility elsewhere in Asia. With luck Tokyo might yet enlist the forces of Asian nationalism against the American and European imperialists.

In any event Japanese officials in Manila summoned members of the Filipino elite in July 1943 and directed them to draft a constitution. Colonel Naonori Utsunomiya of the Japanese military administration specified that the document should embody the principle of "hakko ichiu," or universal concord. It must embrace the requirements of contribution to the Greater East Asia Co-Prosperity Sphere. While it ought to establish a republic it must not allow democratic quibbles to diminish efficiency of administration. A drafting committee did as told, and upon completion Tojo invited Laurel, Aquino and Vargas to Tokyo for congratulations. There Tojo delivered one further demand. He insisted that the Philippine republic declare war on the United States.

"It was a shock to all three of us," Laurel wrote later. "I silently prayed and said the Pater Noster." The three requested time to consult their colleagues. Tojo consented, citing a poetic Japanese epigram to convey his understanding of the Filipinos' predicament: "I have a mixed feeling of joy and sorrow as I walk in the morning frost for your sake." Tojo also offered the three men one million pesos to expedite matters. Laurel declined for the group, although on at least one other occasion he accepted Tokyo's money. Despite the cordial tone of the meeting Laurel and the others left with no doubt that Tojo would not tolerate noncompliance with his demand.[41]

During the next several weeks the collaborationists did their best to dodge the bullet. In September Laurel, recently elected president of the Philippine republic, summoned his cabinet and council of state. The latter failed to obtain a quorum, with most members lying low. To the braver—perhaps because more visible— cabinet ministers Laurel outlined four options: to refuse Tojo's demand outright, to head for the mountains, to commit suicide or to accept but try to waffle. The cabinet recommended the last. During subsequent discussions Laurel and the others searched for a formula that would diminish their responsibility for a war declaration. They took care to leave a trail showing they were acting under duress. Significantly, their decision to declare war turned on a belief that the Americans would be more forgiving than the Japanese. One of the discussants put the question to Laurel, "Would the sufferings of the people be greater if the Americans or the Japanese considered us hostile?" Laurel replied, and the rest agreed, "I prefer that the Japanese do not consider us hostile." In September 1944 Laurel announced a state of war between America and the Philippines. He called on all Filipinos to demonstrate their "unswerving loyalty" to the Philippine republic in this hour of trial.[42]

The war declaration underlined the impossible position confronting the Filipino leaders who remained in the country during the occupation. "I was in the government against my wishes," Laurel said later. Quezon concurred in this explanation when he argued to MacArthur that the collaborators were "victims of the adverse fortunes of war" and had "no choice" but to do what they did. The collaborators indeed were victims, although Laurel's self-interest tainted his testimony and Quezon exaggerated in saying they had no choice. They had as much choice as those individuals who refused to work with the Japanese and who either retired to their homes or joined the resistance.[43]

In a group sense, however, the Filipinos had no choice. As did persons in other countries under occupation, in this and other wars, Filipinos faced the necessity of mitigating the enemy's presence. If Filipino leaders did not come forward, as Laurel and Aquino and Vargas and the others endlessly told themselves and anyone else listening, the iron edge of Japanese rule would fall directly on the people at large. By going along, by yielding to force majeure, those who cooperated with the Japanese attempted to soften the blow. Laurel explained his thinking in a letter to a friend:

> Leadership, after all, is not a matter of choice but one of necessity. While there are many men who are fit to lead the nation in times of great crises, there are only a few who are willing to take the risks involved. I consider my present position nothing more than a surrender to the inevitable. . . .
>
> We who are at the helm of government can only conceive of our position as a form of service in much the same way as the soldiers who answered the call to arms because they were convinced in the cause they were fighting for.[44]

There was a good deal to this argument, though one did not have to be a member of the resistance to question the parallel between those who took arms in the defense of the Philippines and those who took office under the invaders. Sometimes the collaborators carried things further than necessary, as when Laurel congratulated a Japanese captain on the "invaluable services you are rendering my country." But persons who simply dismissed the collaborators as traitors ignored the genuinely agonizing alternatives the collaborators confronted. American dismissers also conveniently overlooked their own contribution in placing Filipinos in such a fix.[45]

The questions of collaboration and resistance, conjoined with the violence and repression of the war years, rent the social fabric of the Philippines. The period of the occupation was a grim time for most of the country's inhabitants, with Filipinos fighting Filipinos as often as they fought Japanese. Two Filipino historians later conceded candidly that "the Japanese occupation was infamous not only because of the ferocity of the military conquerors, but also because the Filipinos as a whole had lost their social and moral balance."

After MacArthur's designation of Manila as an open city, yet before the arrival of Japanese troops, looters had ransacked shops and stores for merchandise that had been and would remain scarce. Police, disarmed to prevent conflict with the invaders, joined the scramble. Throughout the occupation profiteering bled many to enrich a few. Because the Japanese expropriated much of the production of the country, people spent inordinate time trying to find the necessities of life. Lack of hard currency placed a premium on gold. Along Azcarraga Street in Manila passersby were accosted, "Baka may gintong ngipin kayo riyan! Baka may gintong ngipin kayo!"—Do you have gold teeth with you? Do you have gold teeth?" The demand grew so great that gold-seekers mined the graveyards to relieve the dead of their dental work.[46]

The fighting forced the populace to choose sides. The guerrillas of the resistance preferred voluntary support from the masses, but when voluntarism fell shy they coerced. In some instances the guerrillas adopted tactics more draconian than those of the Japanese. Yet to aid the guerrillas opened one to ubiquitous informers who, from belief in Japan's cause or to settle scores, were willing to denounce their neighbors. Neither party took particular pains to spare the dishonestly maligned. Better the innocent should suffer than the guilty go free.

Economic dislocation contributed to uncounted thousands of excess deaths by disease and malnourishment. Seeking food or medicine, for themselves or their families, honest persons turned to theft and corruption. "Morality cowered before the relentless onslaught of economic forces that the war had marshalled and unleashed," wrote the leading Filipino chronicler of the occupation. Among the humble, even more than among the leaders of the collaborationist government, survival required compromise.[47]

11

Return
1944–1946

I. Liberation

Japan's insistence on a war declaration by the Laurel government reflected the increasing pressure Tokyo felt at the beginning of 1944. Following the momentum-breaking battles of Midway and Coral Sea in the summer of 1942 the allies began the drive back to the Philippines. In August 1942 American marines landed at Guadalcanal in the Solomons. The ferocity of the fighting gave indication of the magnitude of the task ahead. Six months were required to root out the Japanese defenders. MacArthur then inaugurated his "island-hopping" strategy—although island-skirting would be a better term, since the idea was to bypass positions stubbornly held by the Japanese. He pushed from the Solomons to the Gilberts, Marshalls and Marianas. By mid-summer of 1944 allied forces were ready to strike at the Palaus, five hundred miles from Mindanao.

In July 1944 Roosevelt traveled to Hawaii to discuss strategy for the Pacific with his commanders there. Just weeks earlier the allies had landed at Normandy, and while many bloody miles separated Omaha beach from Berlin, few persons could not see the end of the war in Europe. For the first time the president could turn most of his attention to the Asian theater. To be sure, part of the reason for Roosevelt's trip was the approaching election. Photographs of the candidate with winning generals and admirals always warm a campaign manager's heart. But Roosevelt also had to settle a dispute among American strategists. Admiral Ernest King, chief of naval operations, wanted to alter the original design of retaking the Philippines on the way to Formosa and the Japanese home islands. King instead advocated skipping the Philippines and striking directly at Formosa. A persuasive individual, the admiral had half-succeeded in winning George Marshall to his point of view.

MacArthur would not even consider the plan. The Philippines remained as vital as ever, he said. No less than before they were the strategic fulcrum on which the southwestern Pacific balanced. Of even greater importance, MacArthur contended, was America's obligation to the Filipino people. The archipelago was American territory, and the United States owed the Filipinos a debt of honor to rescue them from enemy occupation as soon as humanly possible. MacArthur had made his case by cable before Roosevelt left America, and he did so with greater energy in person when the president arrived in Honolulu. Roosevelt may have been leaning to MacArthur's side before reaching Hawaii, but the vehemence of the general's presentation shredded the last of the president's hesitance. "Give me an aspirin before I go to bed," Roosevelt told his doctor after deciding in favor of MacArthur. "In fact, give me another aspirin to take in the morning. In all my life nobody has ever talked to me the way MacArthur did."[1]

After capturing the Palaus in relatively short order MacArthur prepared for an invasion of the Philippines. In September planes from American carriers began bombing the American-built airfields of central Luzon that the Japanese had converted to their own use. The American pilots achieved surprise comparable to that the Japanese had enjoyed at the war's beginning, and they wreaked even greater destruction. In two days they crippled four hundred Japanese planes while losing less than a score.

In mid-October MacArthur gathered an enormous armada for an assault on Leyte at the eastern side of the Visayas. More than seven hundred ships carrying 160,000 troops, thousands of big guns and hundreds of planes massed for the landing. On October 20 the invasion began. At dawn the battleships, cruisers and destroyers commenced a four-hour barrage against enemy positions on and behind the beach. At 10 a.m. four divisions of troops went ashore. As anticipated they encountered only light opposition—the real fighting was expected to occur on Luzon—and by day's end they had secured a beachhead and captured a nearby airstrip.

For MacArthur the landing fulfilled his 1942 vow to return to the Philippines. He played the moment for all it was worth. Before boarding a landing craft from his command ship *Nashville* he packed a revolver into his pocket, telling an aide, "It's just a precaution, just to make certain that I am never captured alive." When the general joined the third assault wave in the landing barges he took care to leave room for his company of correspondents. He ordered the coxswain to swing by the transport *John Land*, which carried Sergio Osmeña, now Philippine president after Quezon's recent death from tuberculosis, and Resident Commissioner Carlos Romulo. Clapping Romulo on the shoulder, MacArthur boomed, "Carlos, my boy! How does it feel to be going home?"

MacArthur's landing barge hit bottom fifty yards from shore. "Lower the ramp," he ordered. Through the surf, with bullets from Japanese snipers sizzling overhead, flanked by photographers, assistants and the top officials of the Philippine commonwealth, in sunglasses and trademark crushed-brim cap, clenching corncob pipe, shortly after noon on October 20, 1944, the conquering hero returned to the Philippines.[2]

As soon as the signal corps could rig a transmitter, MacArthur announced his arrival to the people of the islands:

> I have returned! By the grace of Almighty God, our forces again stand on Philippine soil—soil consecrated in the blood of our two peoples. We have come, dedicated and committed to the task of destroying every vestige of enemy control over your daily lives, and of restoring upon a foundation of indestructible strength, the liberties of your people. . . .
>
> Rally to me! Let the indomitable spirit of Bataan and Corregidor lead on. As the lines of battle roll forward to bring you within the zone of operations, rise and strike! Strike at every favorable opportunity! For your homes and hearths, strike! For future generations of your sons and daughters, strike! In the name of your sacred dead, strike!
>
> Let no heart be faint. Let every arm be steeled. The guidance of Divine God points the way. Follow in his name to the Holy Grail of righteous victory![3]

A short while later MacArthur apprised Washington of his unfolding triumph. "The operation is going smoothly," he wrote Roosevelt, "and if successful will strategically as well as tactically cut the enemy forces in two." The Filipinos, he declared, were reacting "splendidly." MacArthur went on to urge the president to make the most of the moment by pledging independence to the Filipinos at the earliest possible date. "I feel that a successful campaign of liberation if promptly followed by a dramatic granting to them of independence will place American prestige in the Far East at the highest pinnacle of all times." If the president himself could travel to Manila to inaugurate Philippine independence, such a step would "electrify the world and redound immeasurably to the credit and honor of the United States for a thousand years." With affected humility MacArthur closed, "Please excuse this scribble but at the moment I am on the combat line with no facilities except this field message pad."[4]

Establishing a beachhead proved the easiest part of the Leyte operation. The Japanese, recognizing that American control of the Philippines would lead to the severing of their fuel line from the East Indies, threw their best forces into the battle for Leyte. The Americans, hoping to deliver a decisive blow to the Japanese navy, lay in wait. On October 24 the greatest sea battle in history commenced. During the next forty-eight hours the Americans battered the outnumbered Japanese with everything from carriers and battleships to PT boats. As the fighting turned against them the Japanese launched kamikaze attacks against American ships. Impossible to stop, the suicide bombers did horrifying damage to the vessels they hit. But there were too few Japanese planes and too many American ships for the kamikazes to alter materially the contest's outcome. During the three-day engagement the Japanese navy virtually disappeared as a military factor. The phase of the war that had begun at Pearl Harbor ended at Leyte. Attrition remained.[5]

The Philippines witnessed a substantial portion of the attrition. Invalids at sea, the Japanese resisted on land and in the air more fiercely than ever. Tokyo's high command dispatched to Luzon fresh aircraft from Formosa and Japan. With these General Tomoyuki Yamashita mounted a succession of assaults on the American position on Leyte. At the same time Yamashita sent 50,000 troops to Leyte to defend what was called the "Yamashita line," in an effort to keep the Americans from creating a safe base from which to invade Luzon. But neither the air attacks nor the ground reinforcements prevented the Americans from driving across the island. Enjoying naval superiority and the maneuverability it implied, MacArthur outflanked the defenders. After a landing at Ormoc on Leyte's west coast MacArthur reported, "By this maneuver we have seized the center of the Yamashita Line from the rear and have split the enemy's forces in two. . . . Both segments are now caught between our columns which are pressing in from all fronts."[6]

The Japanese fought to the last. While 80,000 Japanese troops were killed, less than 1,000 surrendered. Yet by the end of December American forces had secured Leyte and were looking across the San Bernardino Strait to Luzon. In order to provide air support for a landing north of Manila, MacArthur sent a task force to Mindoro, whose northern coast was scarcely one hundred miles from the capital. The selection of Mindoro caught the Japanese looking the wrong direction, toward Panay and Negros, and the task force got ashore without a single casualty. In the days that followed, Japanese planes contested the foothold, but by the beginning of January the Americans had placed two airfields in operation.

Hoping Yamashita was expecting a move from the south, MacArthur circled to the north. In the second week of 1945 he sent troops ashore from the Lingayen Gulf—whence the Japanese had begun their conquest of the islands three years before. It was a hazardous undertaking, as MacArthur was happy to point out. In his memoirs he wrote,

> The plan of attack was regarded by some in Washington as too daring in scope, too risky in execution. The assault convoy was to sail on January 4th through narrow straits, by-pass the enemy-held islands, then steam up the China Sea, passing Manila, and boldly looping around fortified Bataan and Corregidor. At no time would the convoy be moving more than twenty minutes flying time from enemy airfields, which, for the past week, our air force in unrelenting sweeps was attempting to neutralize. The enemy's strength on Luzon was known to be heavy; his suicidal fanaticism, the last ditch of the defeated, was fully comprehended.

In fact the Japanese did detect the invasion force, and kamikazes and midget submarines accomplished considerable damage before the bulk of the American troops got to land. As at Leyte and with only slightly less theatrical flair MacArthur splashed onto the beach. This time he allowed Osmeña to deliver the arrival message, although the words may well have come from MacArthur's pen. Leaflets scattered across the countryside by American planes carried the Philippine president's statement:

> In a series of brilliantly conceived blows, General MacArthur's forces of liberation
> have successfully, in but a short span of time, destroyed the enemy army defending
> Leyte, seized firm control of Mindoro, and now stand defiantly on the soil of Luzon
> at the very threshold to our capital city. Thus are answered our prayers of many long
> months; thus is the battle for the liberation of the Philippines fully joined and the
> hour of our deliverance at hand.[7]

The Lingayen landing achieved tactical but not strategic surprise. Yamashita anticipated an approach from the north, although he expected it would not come for another two weeks. Now the Japanese commander confronted the kind of obstacles MacArthur had faced in 1941. Yamashita lacked sufficient supplies and men to defend Luzon successfully, and because of the enemy's superiority at sea and the priority Tokyo granted other areas he could not expect further reinforcements from home. As a result he found himself required, as MacArthur had, to conduct a fighting retreat from Lingayen. Like MacArthur, the Japanese general chose not to try to hold the central Luzon plain or Manila. He divided his force into three parts and withdrew to the mountains: toward Baguio and northern Luzon, into the Zambales mountains west of Clark Field, and down the Bicol peninsula to the southeast.[8]

Consequently American troops reached Manila at the beginning of February without having met the bitter-end opposition they were encountering on Iwo Jima and elsewhere. Within the next ten days American units encircled the capital and isolated it from the country around. At this point the bitter-ending began.

It lasted two weeks, and it proved most bitter for the Filipinos. One thousand Americans died in the battle for Manila. The Japanese lost 16,000. Filipino deaths, nearly all of noncombatants, numbered as many as 100,000. At the conclusion the city smoked in heaps, as a result partly of Japanese-set fires but equally of American artillery barrages. Water, sewage and electrical systems operated intermittently or not at all. The six bridges over the Pasig River were down. The city's hospital was beyond repair. The University of the Philippines was a wreck. Central government buildings were a shambles, port facilities flattened, factories rubble, residential neighborhoods uninhabitable.[9]

Not surprisingly, many survivors of the onslaught greeted their deliverers with something less than celebration. One Filipino woman recalled the period with emotion more than twenty years later:

> I spat on the very first American soldier I saw that unspeakable day in February 1945.
> A few seconds before, he had shouted at me from behind a tree in the Malate street:
> "Hey you! Wanna get yourself killed?"
>   I crossed over from the middle of the street where I had been walking and I saw
> that his features were flushed with fright as he hunched behind tree, rifle, steel hel-

met, dusty uniform and large wooden rosary beads which he wore like an amulet around his neck. Damn you!, I thought. There's nobody here but us Filipino civilians, and you did your best to kill us. . . .

Our home had been ransacked, put to the torch, its ruins shelled again and again. I had seen the head of the aunt who had taught me to read and write roll under the kitchen stove, the face of a friend who had been crawling next to me on the pavement as we tried to reach the shelter under Ermita Church obliterated by a bullet, a legless cousin dragging himself out of a shallow trench in the churchyard. . . .

I had seen all the unforgettable, indescribable carnage caused by the detonation of bombs and land mines on the barricaded streets of Ermita and the carpet-shelling by the Americans which went relentlessly on, long after the last Japanese sniper was a carcass on the rubble. . . .

And this precious American, awaited desperately for the last three years, pink-cheeked and overfed, tall and mighty, wanted to know, his dear Americanese idioms rising over the crashing of the bullets and the shells, whether I wanted to die. . . .

So this was Liberation. I was no longer sure what was worse: the inhumanity of the Japanese or the helpfulness of the Americans.[10]

On the whole Filipinos welcomed the Americans back. MacArthur's return represented the end of the most difficult period in the lives of the majority of Filipinos, and they were happy to have done with it. Yet those who lost friends and relatives in the fighting could not but wonder, with this woman, whether the Americans had to be so destructive about returning. Those who looked forward to independence, scheduled for 1946, had to ask what independence would mean for a shattered country.

MacArthur put the best face on affairs. Once more he proclaimed that the United States had honored its commitment to the Filipinos. "The girded and unleashed power of America, supported by our Allies," he said, "turned the tide of battle in the Pacific and resulted in an unbroken series of crushing defeats of the enemy, culminating in the redemption of your soil and the liberation of your people. My country has kept the faith."

Osmeña, who accompanied MacArthur into the smoldering city, had little choice but to assume a similar mood. In words MacArthur certainly vetted and probably wrote, the Philippine president likened the general to his father, Arthur MacArthur, "who on August 13, 1898, successfully led another American Army to free Manila." Speaking on his own, Osmeña would hardly have described the 1898 American occupation of Manila in such terms. History and the Filipino people, Osmeña continued, would remember Douglas MacArthur for his devotion to the highest standards of democracy. "He has been faithful in his role as liberator in the truest American tradition."[11]

Retaking the rest of the Philippines required several months. The Leyte landing had given heart to the various guerrilla groups in the islands, which by the middle of 1944 comprised perhaps 180,000 fighters. In advance of the Leyte operation the guerrillas had provided valuable information regarding the size and disposition of Japanese forces. Their reports, combined with information gleaned by the Office of Strategic Services from interviews with former Philippine residents outside the islands, were instrumental in the success of the American air raids on Luzon and of other attacks. After the Leyte landing the guerrillas increased their harassment of the Japanese, cutting telephone wires, mining roads and bridges and attacking patrols, convoys and supply stations. As in Europe at about the same time the activities of the partisans behind enemy lines lightened considerably the task of the re-occupiers. Yet the job remained far from easy, as the Japanese refused to surrender even against hopeless odds.[12]

From a strategic perspective the battle for the Philippines ended in April 1945, by which time American forces had secured the central Luzon plain, the air bases needed to cut Japan off from the East Indies, and staging areas for the projected invasion of Formosa and Japan. Fighting continued, however, in the outer portions of Luzon and elsewhere in the archipelago into August, when Japan surrendered following the atomic devastation of Hiroshima and Nagasaki. On August 15, the day the emperor announced Japan's capitulation, more than 100,000 Japanese troops and civilians remained at large in Luzon and on the other islands. Most quit within a few weeks, happy to see the war over if not won. Stragglers and disbelievers stayed out longer.[13]

II.   Quezon to Osmeña to Roxas: Rehabilitating the collaborators

The end of fighting in the Philippines raised the issue of restoring civil government. Beyond its effect on the Filipinos, Japan's rapid conquest in 1941–42 had knocked the American Philippine administration into disarray. High Commissioner Sayre, acting on orders of the White House, had departed Corregidor at about the same time as Quezon, arriving in Australia in March 1942. Other American officials had been left behind and were interned by the Japanese. In comparison with the treatment accorded American prisoners of war in the Philippines, the American civilians fared well. In January 1942 Consul-General Nathaniel Davis, who remained in Manila until the Japanese occupied the city, wrote in his diary,

> We have now been one week in internment, and gradually we are getting our menage in shape for reasonably comfortable living. We now have a cook with two helpers, two boys to do heavy cleaning and housework, one boy to go out and buy supplies—a full time job—and three laundresses who are kept fully occupied doing the laundry for twenty-eight people.

Davis wrote poetry, which he gathered under the title *Internment Interludes*, to keep spirits up. To the same end he organized activities in the camp, including a croquet tournament. In April 1943, after fifteen months in confinement, he reported to the Swiss diplomat charged with checking such things, "The condi-

tions under which we live here are as good as could be expected in the circumstances. . . . We continue to enjoy good health and receive adequate food and
the basic comforts of life." Six months later Davis and the other Americans were
removed to Tokyo. From there they were repatriated to the United States.[14]

Most of the records of the American administration in Manila—as well as most
of those of the Philippine commonwealth—did not survive the Japanese occupation, destroyed by their custodians before fleeing, by the Japanese or by accident. Sayre succeeded in salvaging a large amount of Philippine currency and
securities. Working with the American treasury department, the high commissioner cabled serial numbers and other forms of identification to Washington
where the notes were reissued. He then burned the originals. Sayre also managed
to smuggle 12,500 pounds of Philippine gold and 350 tons of silver from Manila
to Corregidor. The gold made its escape by submarine from Corregidor, serving
as the most expensive ballast the American navy ever knew. The silver apparently stayed behind.[15]

Following the flight of the American and Filipino officials, administration of
the islands reverted to Washington. There Sayre joined Quezon who, realizing
he could accomplish little good in Australia, had taken leave of MacArthur and
continued on to the United States. Possibly because of Quezon's demonstrated
neutralist tendencies, perhaps simply because its director, J. Edgar Hoover, liked
to poke about other people's affairs, the Federal Bureau of Investigation kept
watch on Quezon and reported his movements to the White House. But there
was not much interesting for the agency to report and less for Quezon to do. He
offered to send an envoy to Spain in an effort to guarantee the continued neutrality of Franco. Secretary of State Hull politely declined the offer. Quezon
requested that the Philippines be among the signers of the declaration of the
United Nations. This idea the Roosevelt administration accepted. Quezon asked
for a seat on the allied Pacific war council, taking his case to White House intimate Harry Hopkins. Hopkins remarked of Quezon after the interview,

> He presented a rather pathetic figure. He obviously hasn't anything to do here, and
> is thoroughly deflated and wants to get in the limelight some way or other. . . . He
> clearly can't contribute anything to the business by being a member of the Pacific
> War Council, but for political reasons it seems wise to include him.

Roosevelt agreed. Saying that the notion of Philippine membership had "a great
deal of merit," the president insisted on a place for Quezon. Quezon responded
with his "heartfelt gratitude."[16]

In June 1942 Sayre resigned as high commissioner. Quezon, more jealous than
ever of his prerogatives now that they had diminished so greatly, advocated leaving the post unfilled. After all, he argued, the American president hardly needed
a representative to the Philippine government while the head of that government
resided in Washington. Following receipt of a recommendation from Hull to

avoid any precedent-setting public commitments on the matter, Roosevelt quietly acquiesced to Quezon's wish.[17]

Quezon repeatedly implored Roosevelt to move quickly to rescue the Filipino people. Roosevelt assured Quezon he shared his concern for the suffering of the Filipinos. The president said he would do "whatever is in my power to free them from the bondage and unhappiness now being imposed upon them by an invader who is a total stranger to right and justice." Yet despite such assertions, Roosevelt never wavered from his Europe-first strategy.[18]

After a time Quezon became something of a pest. That he was a sick pest—tuberculosis had reduced him to a hacking shell—did not assist matters. Equally unhelpful was the fact that he again wanted to tamper with the Philippine constitution to allow his continuance in office. The amendment that had made possible his earlier reelection specified two four-year terms for the commonwealth president in place of the original nonrenewable six-year term. Quezon's eight years would end in November 1943. In October Quezon broached with Roosevelt the possibility of a special wartime waiver of the time limit.[19]

Quezon's request set the Roosevelt administration to weighing the legality and desirability of an exemption. Interior Secretary Harold Ickes' lawyer Abe Fortas gave the opinion that because the war blocked the normal process for amending the Philippine constitution a waiver might be obtained through special legislation by Congress or through an executive order by the president. E. D. Hester, an adviser to the high commissioner's office, thought that regardless of the legal possibilities of extension the administration would err to let Quezon stay in office. Hester argued, in fact, that the administration should dump Quezon while the dumping was good. Characterizing Vice President Osmeña as "the real workhorse" of the Philippine government, Hester labeled Quezon a "pooh-bah" who had demonstrated a "perhaps pathological inability to step down from office." Hester knew both Osmeña and Quezon from Manila, and he deemed the former far preferable. Hester asserted—on dubious grounds—that Osmeña was a thorough "Americanista." Quezon's loyalties were less certain:

Quezon is pro-Spanish and has surrounded himself, particularly in the government-in-exile, with persons mainly of Spanish blood, including at least two who were nationalized for purposes of taking office. These Spaniards hate the United States, President Roosevelt, and our program of education and democratic processes for the Philippines.

Beyond castigating the Quezonistas for crypto-fascism, Hester contended—inaccurately—that Osmeña was "vastly the more popular" of the two leaders in the Philippines.[20]

Looking to the return of the United States to the islands, Hester predicted that American forces would liberate the Visayas, Osmeña's stronghold, first, and only later move into Luzon, Quezon's area of greatest influence. This, Hester contended, would facilitate a transition from Quezon to Osmeña. More significantly it offered a unique opportunity to effect needed reforms in the islands.

> The great mass of the Filipinos *taos* (the common people) are still loyal to the United States. We have ample evidence of this. It is only the very wealthy class, the landlords, the "usurers," the top-drawer Quezon-politicos, and the Spanish party in the Philippines (which is part of the top drawer), and the remaining Spanish subjects, who have become traitorous and seditious. . . . The Filipino *taos* under the control of the enemy are not worrying about independence—they don't want it now—they don't want it immediately after we come back. They want us to return, restore order, rehabilitate them, punish the puppetry, and reestablish United States markets for their export products.[21]

Hester lost the immediate argument. Roosevelt authorized legislation allowing Quezon to remain in office. In some respects, however, the legislation was superfluous, for Quezon, more ill than ever, had already named Osmeña acting president. Within several months Quezon was dead.

Yet Hester's memo did serve the purpose of raising three issues that grew more pressing as the war's end approached and Americans prepared to return to the Philippines. First, how should the United States deal with collaborators? Second, what, if anything, ought Washington to do about the undemocratic character of the government Quezon and his cronies had created? Third, in what manner should the Philippine economy be rehabilitated and to what degree should it be linked to that of the United States?[22]

The question of collaboration put Washington in a bind. Although the United States government could hardly approve the actions of individuals who cooperated with the Japanese, the Roosevelt administration hesitated to denounce them openly. In the first place, American officials could not help feeling guilty about their country's failure to defend the Filipinos. By neither granting complete independence, which might have allowed the Filipinos to negotiate a separate arrangement with Japan, nor providing sufficient manpower and resources to protect the islands from aggression, the United States had left the Filipinos vulnerable. In the second place, to speak out forcefully against Filipino collaborators might backfire, convincing the Filipinos they had no choice but to hope and work for a Japanese victory. Interior Secretary Ickes—who, interestingly, later would take a hard line against allowing collaborators back into the Philippine government—initially argued for sympathy. Ickes wrote to Treasury Secretary Morgenthau regarding Filipino collaborators,

> To condemn them publicly might be playing directly into the hands of the Japanese who would then be in a position to represent to these men that they had burned their bridges behind them, and that they must necessarily stand or fall with the Japanese. They may or may not be engaged in treasonable activities, but even if they are there is nothing we can do about it at the present time and nothing is to be gained by name-calling.

Ickes went on to say that the administration ought to withhold condemnation until all the facts were known. In any event Washington should "refrain from ex parte judgment of men who are faced with the harsh facts of enemy occupation and control."[23]

The simplest method of dealing with the collaborators was to ignore the government they created—much as Lincoln had officially ignored the government of the Confederacy—and to treat the actions of the individuals involved as treasonous or not on a case-by-case basis once sovereignty was restored. Ignoring the problem possessed the attraction of freeing the Roosevelt administration to worry about other, more urgent matters. It also allowed the administration to maintain the position it had adopted at the inauguration of the commonwealth: that Filipinos were the appropriate persons to manage Filipino affairs. By this reasoning the collaboration issue was one for the commonwealth government to handle. It could do so when it resumed control of the islands.

Finally, leaving the issue to the Filipinos and dealing with the collaborators as individuals rather than as a group enabled the administration to sidestep a problem few in Washington besides E. D. Hester cared to tackle: what to do about the undemocratic character of Filipino political life. Reforming types in Washington expected to have their hands full democratizing Japan and Germany. They had little energy to spare for the Philippines. Besides, for better or worse, the United States had handed home rule to the Filipinos. Perfecting their government was their problem.

Consequently, as MacArthur's invasion of the Philippines neared, the Roosevelt administration had no fixed policy regarding the collaborators. In July 1944 Roosevelt announced that "those who have collaborated with the enemy must be removed from authority and influence," but the administration neglected to formulate concrete plans for putting the president's declaration into practice. Washington operated on the assumption that Quezon would return with MacArthur to the islands and reestablish the commonwealth government as soon as military considerations allowed. Afterward would be soon enough for decisions regarding the collaborators.[24]

Quezon's death on August 1, 1944, threw American planning slightly askew. Osmeña, who had supported Quezon's successful bid for an extension in office, hesitated to join MacArthur for the Philippine invasion. He recognized his lack of a broad political base in the islands, and he could see that although Quezon was dead, most of the Quezonistas lived. They would not make him their first choice for a successor. Those who had cooperated with the Japanese would hardly embrace him, the returning head of the government-in-exile, while those who had resisted would probably feel resentment at having been abandoned. And if MacArthur might have shared the glory of the return with compadre Quezon, the general gave no evidence of similar generosity toward Osmeña. Osmeña would reenter Manila at American sufferance and in the American shadow.

Yet MacArthur insisted that Osmeña join him. When the war department concurred, and Roosevelt personally requested that Osmeña accept MacArthur's invitation, Osmeña reluctantly went.[25]

As soon as he touched sand at Leyte, Osmeña sought to gain the initiative in handling the collaboration question, as he did on other issues. In an early radio broadcast he expressed sympathy for the collaborators' dilemma. "Not all public officials could take to the hills to carry on the heroic struggle," he said. "Some had to remain in their posts to maintain a semblance of government, to protect the population from the oppressor to the extent possible by human ingenuity and to comfort the people in their misery." Adopting the collaborators' argument, Osmeña asserted that if the natural leaders of Filipino society had not stayed at their posts, "the Japanese would either have themselves governed directly and completely or utilized unscrupulous Filipino followers capable of any treason to their people. The result would have been calamitous and the injuries inflicted to our body politic beyond cure." Osmeña promised that his government would examine the motives of those who had held office under the Japanese and not rely simply on the fact of office-holding in assessing guilt or innocence. He concluded with a pledge that every case would be examined "impartially and decided on its own merits."[26]

But MacArthur was not about to surrender the collaboration issue to Osmeña. When American forces approached Manila the government of the wartime republic fled. As the Americans regained control of the rest of Luzon the high-ranking collaborationists pondered evacuating the country. President Laurel initially resisted the idea. He told Yamashita he belonged with the Filipinos:

> A true leader does not desert his people even in the face of the most adverse circumstances. . . . I have stated, times without number, that our national salvation can be achieved only through the closest solidarity among ourselves, that we should stick together through thick and thin, if we expect to survive as a people. The gospel I have preached, to which I adhere, is that "We die together or survive together."

But Laurel changed his mind as the Americans drew nearer. He fled first to Formosa and then to Japan, where he ultimately turned himself in to MacArthur. His associates scattered, some to Japan, others to different parts of Asia.[27]

Most lower-level officials of the wartime republic remained in the Philippines. MacArthur used the left-behinds to stake his claim to the collaboration issue. Citing military security, he ordered the arrest of all collaborators, announcing their detention until the end of the war.[28]

Had MacArthur stopped here, his action would have occasioned little complaint, especially since he said that upon conclusion of hostilities the detainees would be handed over to the Philippine government. Yet MacArthur went on to impose himself personally into the case of one of the most visible of the collaborators, Manuel Roxas. The former speaker of the Philippine assembly and general in the Philippine army had participated with distinction at the war's outset in the defense of Bataan and Corregidor. When the latter fell Roxas escaped to Mindanao where he later was captured. The Japanese understandably brought great pressure upon him to join the new Philippine government, for as Quezon's heir apparent he would lend the puppet regime instant credibility. Roxas agreed, but throughout the war he played a double game. He maintained contact with the guerrillas and with the Americans, providing useful information to both. Quezon worried about Roxas' safety. In June 1943 the commonwealth president wrote to MacArthur, "If you can send for Roxas nothing should be spared to get him out soon."[29]

MacArthur couldn't or wouldn't, and Roxas did not come out. For obvious reasons his actions on behalf of the resistance were not common knowledge. Therefore MacArthur's decision to treat Roxas, upon the latter's arrival at the American lines in April 1945, as a rescued prisoner rather than a captured collaborator caused considerable eyebrow-raising. But MacArthur's word was good enough for the new head man in the United States. Harry Truman, upon whom the presidency had descended days before, would not learn to distrust MacArthur for a few years yet. Roxas gained immediate rehabilitation.

MacArthur's move did not go uncontested in Washington. Harold Ickes had joined the legions of MacArthur critics not long after the interior department inherited responsibility for American Philippine policy from the war department, consequent to the inauguration of the commonwealth. Now Ickes condemned "the collaborationist Roxas" and blasted MacArthur's effort to cover Roxas' tracks "with a thick coat of whitewash." When Paul McNutt, whom Truman reappointed as high commissioner, indicated a disposition to acquiesce in MacArthur's action, Ickes added him to the collaborationist cabal. He ridiculed McNutt's statement to the effect that collaborators had to be judged by examining whether their hearts were on the side of the Japanese or of the Americans, by asserting that "it goes without saying that unless a man's heart were in it he would not be a collaborator."[30]

Ickes did not speak for the president. In fact he soon found himself out of a job, although for reasons having little to do with the Philippines. Facing endless other problems, Truman was happy to leave the collaboration issue alone. To have done otherwise would have required a positive decision to intervene in domestic Philippine affairs. Legally, of course, the president had the right to do so. Politically it would have gained him nothing and would have stirred a storm in the Philippines. So Truman let stand MacArthur's decision in the Roxas case, and he left the fate of the other collaborators to the Filipinos.

As his early announcements indicated, Osmeña was not inclined to vindictiveness. Had other things been equal he might have welcomed MacArthur's pardon of Roxas as a convenient way to get through a political thicket. For any Filipino leader, dealing with the collaborators would have been a thankless undertaking. "Unification of our people is the need of the hour," Osmeña told a friend, rightly. The war had divided the Filipino people as never before, with collaborators and members of the resistance locked in a murderous struggle. Naturally, many of those who had fought the Japanese wanted vengeance against those who had abetted the invaders. At the least they demanded that the government make a moral statement on the question of resistance versus collaboration. One of Osmeña's associates remarked that the collaboration issue had the Philippine government "sitting on top of a volcano." But the ranks of the collaborators, while including opportunists and other non-heroes, also comprised persons of conscience who considered their actions in the best interests of the Filipino people. Weaving a net fine enough to catch the former without snagging the latter would have taxed the abilities of the wisest and most astute government. Complicating the matter further was the fact that in a country with a relatively small educated class, wholesale disqualification of collaborators would render extraordinarily difficult the postwar reconstruction of the country. Finally, the most prominent collaborators came from the class that had traditionally governed the Philippines—the class that produced Osmeña. Quezon's successor had no desire to effect a revolution, to cause the volcano to erupt. He would need the collaborators in the future as much as they needed him now.[31]

On the other hand, MacArthur's rehabilitation of Roxas made Quezon's heir apparent a formidable contender for the office Osmeña currently held—a point MacArthur, who considered Osmeña unfit for the Philippine presidency, had not overlooked. Ever since his eclipse by Quezon in the early 1920s Osmeña had been one step too slow in the race for primacy in the Philippines. Yet he had held on doggedly, and if he had not succeeded in outrunning Quezon he ultimately outlasted him. Now Roxas threatened to snatch the prize before Osmeña had a chance even to try it on. And Roxas could expect the support not only of the Quezon machine but of all those tainted by collaboration in one form or another.

However Osmeña might have wished to proceed on the collaboration issue, Washington's acceptance of MacArthur's exoneration of Roxas made prosecution of any except the most blatant cases nearly impossible. In August 1945 Osmeña presented a measure to the Philippine assembly authorizing a special court to consider collaboration cases. The measure immediately tangled up in the developing political struggle between Osmeña and Roxas. Clumsy Harold Ickes fouled matters more by openly urging Osmeña to hold firm against Roxas and the collaborators. In a letter to Osmeña, Ickes went so far as to suggest that the United States would withhold relief assistance if the Philippine government failed to prosecute collaborators "diligently and firmly"; in doing so, he succeeded only in casting Osmeña as the tool of the Americans and Roxas as the candidate of Philippine nationalism. The Roxas forces in the legislature managed to gut Osmeña's resolution by limiting staff and funding for the court, guaranteeing delays of several years.[32]

Roxas' success in paralyzing the prosecution of collaborators generated some eleventh-hour concern in the Truman White House. On the recommendation of High Commissioner McNutt and Attorney General Tom Clark, Truman sent Walter Hutchinson of the justice department to Manila to investigate. Hutchinson filed a report describing even Osmeña's position regarding the collaborators as woefully weak and recommending that the American justice department bring charges of treason against the foremost of the collaborators. "They must not be permitted any loopholes of escape," Hutchinson wrote, "for they are America's Quislings." Hutchinson suggested that if such were necessary to secure deserved convictions, collaborators should be transported to America for trial.[33]

With the scheduled date of Philippine independence less than a year away, Hutchinson's proposal was politically absurd. Truman rejected it, although not before toying with the idea of delaying Philippine elections while prosecution proceeded. Truman's rejection destroyed what slim prospects remained for American intervention and essentially assured easy treatment for nearly all the collaborators. The special court convicted Teófilo Sison, Laurel's justice minister, in the first case brought before it, but when Roxas captured the presidency in April 1946 the wind spilled from the sails of the prosecution. Of more than five thousand cases considered by the special court a mere 156 resulted in guilty verdicts. Of these only Sison's involved an individual of particular prominence. And even Sison managed to keep his case on appeal until Roxas canceled the whole business at the beginning of 1948 with a blanket amnesty.[34]

III.   Bases, trade and the ghost of Forbes

If Washington refused to take on the collaboration question, it displayed considerably more willingness to get involved in matters relating the Philippines to the broad issues of postwar security. As during World War I when Wilson brought together America's best and brightest to form the "Inquiry" into the optimal form of a peace settlement, so the Roosevelt administration during World War II laid plans for what would follow the Axis surrender. Two fundamental principles informed American thinking about how to prevent a third armed disaster. Each reflected lessons learned from the failure to avert the second. The first principle involved the notion of collective security. Taking their cue from the world's wavering before Hitler at Munich in 1938, the proponents of collective security called for a commitment by the responsible countries, acting through a body like the League of Nations and led by the United States, to punish irresponsible aggressors. The optimistic among the proponents believed that the threat of reprisal would prevent aggression from happening at all. The more realistic thought an occasional object lesson might be required for emphasis. The most realistic asked troubling questions about who would define aggression and what would happen when the great powers disagreed, but no one much wanted to listen to them lest their warnings prove self-fulfilling.

The second basic principle of American planning for the postwar period rested on the conviction that lasting peace demanded widespread prosperity and that prosperity required access to foreign markets. Like all persuasive political philosophies this belief combined self-interest with idealism. Remarking the connection between the global economic collapse of the 1930s and the rise of militaristic fascism, American leaders thought prosperity would minimize the appeal of fanatics like Hitler. Further, they attributed much of the depression's severity and persistence to the thunderous closing of markets that followed the 1929 stock crash. Consequently they advocated an expansion of opportunities for trade and investment to prevent another depression and more Hitlers. Not coincidentally, such expansion would redound to the advantage of the United States, the country with the world's strongest economy.

These two principles formed the background to American postwar policy toward the Philippines. The first, involving collective security, figured centrally in the formulation of America's strategic relationship with the soon-to-be independent Philippine republic. Its most prominent focus was the issue of American military bases in the islands. The second principle, of openness to trade and investment, led to negotiations regarding terms on which American investors and exporters would have access to Philippine markets. Discussions involving the issues of bases and trade took place simultaneously, and the two often joined.

"Trade policy in the Pacific must be built along liberal lines," E. D. Hester wrote near the end of the war. "Practically all existing policies will require radical revision or repeal." As Hester's remarks applied to the Philippines, liberal lines were generally interpreted to imply free trade. In September 1945 Congressman Jasper Bell of Missouri introduced a bill calling for free trade between the United States and the Philippines for twenty years after independence. The measure appealed to the usual suspects—Philippine exporters to the United States and American importers of Philippine products—as well as to the larger number who, like Hester, embraced free trade as the solvent of longstanding international rivalries and the cement of a peaceful world order. Bell's proposal drew the expected criticism from those commodity-producers who benefited from protection. Anomalously, Bell's plan also elicited objection from the state department, which in the main stood for free trade. The state department, however, had undertaken multilateral negotiations for a broader reduction of economic barriers, and it feared that a bilateral approach to Philippine-American trade relations would upset those talks.[35]

Bell was a faint soul, soon orphaning his own bill. But his proposal touched off a lengthy set of political and diplomatic skirmishes. Trade measures are among the most complicated Congress considers, with numerous interest groups lobbying legislators to load the bills with favors and few outsiders caring sufficiently to read the thousands of pages the bartering generates. Trade legislation for the Philippines became more convoluted than usual because of its linkage to the negotiations involving the future of American bases in the islands. The linkage led to compromises on both the trade and base issues that made little sense in themselves, being comprehensible, and then not always completely, only in the larger context. To add to the confusion, the Truman administration requested from Congress a package of financial aid for the purpose of repairing war damage and reconstructing the islands' economy. This sweetener was used to facilitate and offset adjustments on the base and trade questions.

Hovering over discussions of both issues was the matter of Philippine independence. Although no one in a position of responsibility in Washington advocated reneging on America's promise of Philippine self-rule, more than a few thought the sea-change that had occurred in world affairs since the passage of the Tydings Act compelled the United States to exercise caution in handing over power. To ensure a pacific Pacific, America had to guarantee that its departure from the Philippines not open the region to the kind of anarchy the previous decade had produced. The best guarantee, many believed, was a pledge by the successor government to support America's born-again internationalism. Millard Tydings, still chairman of the Senate's insular affairs committee, saw Philippine independence and regional security as inseparable issues. "Siamese twins," he called them. The Filipinos desired independence. Americans sought security. One might purchase the other, with military bases serving as the medium of exchange.[36]

Between the economic leverage afforded by both American trade with the Philippines and the islands' need for reconstruction aid, and the potential political threat of footdragging on independence—these in addition to the provisions of the Tydings Act—there was never any doubt that the Americans would get their bases. The only questions were how many and where located. In September 1944 John McCloy, assistant secretary of war, remarked that the selection of sites depended on the precise nature of American policy after the war. A policy involving an ambitious projection of American power would require basing plans of one sort, a more restrained approach another. Speaking just prior to the Leyte landing, McCloy noted that the operation about to begin would shed much light on the advantages and disadvantages of various locations.[37]

In April 1945 Navy Secretary James Forrestal listed fourteen sites as potentially suitable for development as American bases. Forrestal did not anticipate developing all the locations, but he advocated obtaining rights to the lot as a hedge against an unpredictable future. In May, Secretary Stimson described to Truman the war department's plans to construct "major air centers" in central Luzon and northern Mindanao, with outlying fields for fighter planes and several staging areas for ground and amphibious operations. Like Forrestal, Stimson recommended that the administration keep its options open. He also urged the president to insist that the Philippine government agree not to allow third countries to establish bases in the islands without Washington's approval.[38]

Stimson delivered his advice in conjunction with a visit by Osmeña to Washington. Osmeña came principally to seek American assistance in righting his country's capsized economy. Under the circumstances he offered no resistance to the administration's request for generous base rights. Following a White House meeting in which a solitary Osmeña confronted the president of the United States, the secretary of war, the secretary of the navy, the acting secretary of state, the chairman of the insular affairs committee and a blinding display of military brass, Osmeña signed an agreement granting the United States the right to establish and develop bases at the fourteen sites submitted by the navy and a dozen requested by the army. The agreement included the no-third-country clause advocated by Stimson.[39]

On the economic side of the ledger, Washington had been considering reconstruction assistance since 1943, when the Roosevelt administration appointed a board for planning the islands' future. This body was succeeded by a Philippine rehabilitation commission, which like the planning board comprised Americans and Filipinos, held meetings and discussed general issues, but which suffered similarly from Roosevelt's unwillingness to commit resources in advance of the war's end.[40]

Reconstruction planning picked up after Roosevelt's death. In July 1945 Tydings introduced a bill to provide substantial economic assistance to the Philippines. Congress appeared to look favorably on helping the Filipinos rebuild their country. Yet before the Tydings resolution came to a vote it got mixed up with the Bell trade measure.

After Bell dropped his original proposal for twenty years of free trade the Missouri congressman offered a substitute specifying eight free years followed by a twenty-five-year period of progressively increasing tariffs. While the state department judged this version an improvement over the original, American firms competing with Philippine producers found the new Bell as out of tune as the old. After lengthy haggling the pros and antis reached accommodation: eight years of no tariffs, twenty of tariffs gradually increasing to full. In the process of dickering, though, the opponents managed to include absolute quotas—not simply duty-free quotas—for imports of sugar, cordage, rice, tobacco and coconut oil.[41]

The failure of the Bell Act to include any reciprocal quotas for American exports to the Philippines was not lost on the measure's many critics in the islands. But what most galled Filipinos was the so-called parity clause. This required the Philippine government to treat Americans as if they were Philippine citizens in economic matters. Because the Philippine constitution limited foreign investment, acceptance of the Bell Act required amending the constitution, which understandably seemed a significant infringement on Philippine sovereignty. Promoters of parity echoed comments Cameron Forbes and others had made forty years earlier: that political independence for the Philippines would mean little without economic development and that economic development required opening the country to American capital. Objectors judged parity a device for continued American economic control of the islands after Washington relinquished political power.

The neo-Forbesians carried the American Congress without difficulty. With slightly more trouble they persuaded the Philippine government. Obtaining Philippine cooperation was a straightforward exercise in economic coercion. While the trade act went forward so did the measure for American economic assistance. The latter turned out to include some $620 million in aid, but it also contained a provision effectively placing a large majority of the money in escrow until the Philippine government accepted the trade act. Confronting destruction and destitution on a nationwide scale, the Filipinos had no alternative. "Mr. President," Osmeña wrote Truman, "eighteen million people, whose homes and properties are in ruins and who face hunger and disease as a consequence of their participation in the war, look to you for help." The Filipinos got help, but only in exchange for accepting the American diktat. Uncuriously, some of them felt less than fully free.[42]

IV

BY OTHER MEANS

12

Cold War in Asia
1946–1952

I. Short change

On the one-hundred-seventieth anniversary of American independence the United States transferred political power in Manila to the government of the Philippine republic. Americans congratulated themselves on fulfilling the pledge American leaders had made repeatedly throughout the half-century of American rule: to prepare the Filipinos for self-government and to deliver control when the Filipinos proved ready for it. The congratulatory mood was not wholly without foundation. On July 4, 1946, the Filipinos were by most measures more capable of sustaining independence than they had been in 1898, and after Philippine independence day Filipinos did indeed exercise political control in their country. But neither were the kudos entirely warranted. Reality fell short of promise in two respects particularly.

The first involved the nature of the Philippine political system. Notwithstanding Americans' espousals of democracy the government Washington handed power to was far from democratic. For fifty years the Americans had relied on the services of a small group of privileged collaborators. When the Americans left, this group remained. The Philippines displayed the trappings of democracy—elections, party organization, mass rallies and the like—but effective control of the institutions of government rested with the few. Average Filipinos were probably better off in 1946 than they had been in 1898, although the devastation of the war left room for doubt. Yet as had been true for centuries the majority of the population was beholden to a narrow class of politicos, business leaders and landlords. This class, ever-resourceful, had outlasted the Spanish and survived the Japanese. Now it bade the Americans a fond farewell.

Or it would have, had the Americans quite left. The second deficiency of devolution related to the continuing economic dependence of the Philippines on the United States. Forbes and others had repeatedly asserted that without economic independence political independence would mean nothing. Forbes exaggerated. Political independence meant something. But he got the essentials right, for the fact that the Philippines remained tied to the American economic system rendered Philippine independence considerably less than complete. The negotiations over the Bell trade act demonstrated in crudest fashion America's continuing capacity for keeping the Filipinos in line. At the most obvious level, the Filipinos relied on the United States to rebuild their economy after the war—a war, Filipinos could not help thinking, they might have avoided had the islands not been an American colony. In other ways also Filipinos depended on the United States. As the major purchaser of Philippine products America could shatter the economic health of the Philippines by raising tariffs or cutting quotas. Even accidentally the United States might seriously damage the Philippine economy. A recession, a shift in American tastes, or technological changes could diminish demand for Philippine exports and throw the country into turmoil. That the Bell Act, in addition to requiring parity, setting quotas and establishing tariffs, pegged the peso to the dollar made the Philippine economy the more hostage to American actions.

Such was the nature of America's gift to the Philippines in 1946. During the succeeding two generations the United States would circumscribe still further the control of Filipinos over events that shaped their lives. As the confrontation between the United States and the Soviet Union sharpened, American leaders demonstrated how well they had learned the lessons of the 1930s. Convinced of the seamless nature of peace and the necessity of standing firm at the first sign of aggression—and perceiving communism as, if not quite monolithic, at least sufficiently coherent to require a comprehensive response—Washington essayed to contain the Soviet Union and its co-conspirators. American attempts at containment early took shape in the eastern Mediterranean, when Truman called for and received economic and military assistance for anticommunist governments in Greece and Turkey and announced a policy of opposing leftist aggression and subversion. The Marshall Plan and NATO extended and elaborated the containment theme.

But even as American efforts to shore up the western front in the contest with communism were succeeding, the east spectacularly gave way. In 1949 the army of the Chinese Communist party defeated the Nationalists of Chiang Kai-shek, allowing the establishment of a regime in the world's most populous state that was more red than the Kremlin itself. Scarcely six months later the communist troops of North Korean dictator Kim Il Sung smashed across the thirty-eighth parallel and very nearly drove South Korean and American forces into the Sea of Japan. By the end of 1950 China joined the war, and as American and Chinese soldiers bled each other in the snows of Korea the world trembled at the brink of nuclear catastrophe.

Humanity survived the shocks of 1949 and 1950, but what little had remained of American equanimity did not. At home the United States convulsed itself trying to exorcise the communist demons that had brought the planet to this parlous condition. Abroad American leaders searched frantically for allies who would assist in holding the line against further communist expansion. The Korean War was the exception that proved the Cold War rule of the inefficacy of the United Nations as an instrument for collective security. With the global body seized by the Soviet-American struggle, American leaders lowered their collective-security expectations to the level of mutual-defense alliances. The Second World War, by aligning Washington with Moscow, had demonstrated the ability of Americans to conquer democratic scruples in a necessary cause. The Cold War similarly reduced American foreign policy to geopolitical basics. In North America and western Europe the United States found allies whose devotion to democracy matched its own, but in the broad arc that stretched from Greece through Iran, Pakistan, Vietnam, Taiwan and Korea, the American government embraced regimes that shared little besides a professed abhorrence of the Soviet Union, China and their agents.

In America's scramble to hold tough against communist expansion the Philippines played a signal part. Strategically the archipelago formed a vital link in the Pacific island chain that formed America's fall-back line of defense against Asian communism. Politically the government of the Philippines served the useful purpose of supporting American initiatives in international forums like the United Nations. Ideologically America's Oriental offspring demonstrated the universal appeal of American values.

Such at least was the rationale behind America's consistent support of governments in Manila that hardly exemplified the best democracy had to offer. American leaders were not blind to the fact that their Filipino protégés were usually undemocratic and often corrupt, sometimes embarrassingly so. But while Washington remained convinced that communism posed a grave threat to the security of Asia and the peace of the world—that is, during almost the entire period since 1945—the United States was willing to overlook such defects.

II. Re-Filipinization

Though Douglas MacArthur did not singlehandedly make Manuel Roxas the first president of the postwar Philippine republic, the American general certainly facilitated Roxas' election. MacArthur's exoneration gave Roxas a head start toward Malacañang, and while Osmeña attempted to divert him by offering the post of resident commissioner in Washington and by other gambits, the rehabilitated collaborator could not be turned aside. The Philippine senate—a 1940 amendment having swapped the unicameral assembly for a bicameral congress—made Roxas its leader, from which position he conducted political guerrilla war against Osmeña. With Roxas' blessing the senate voted legislators three years' back pay. When other government employees complained, Roxas promised them like treatment if they helped elect him president.

Osmeña, facing the divisive issue of collaboration and the additional trials of postwar reconstruction, sought to devise a national-unity ticket for the elections scheduled for April 1946. He went so far as to offer to decline the nomination of the Nacionalista party in favor of Roxas. But anti-Roxas and anti-collaborationist forces in the party urged him to reconsider. When he did Roxas bolted, creating an organization calling itself the Liberal Wing of the Nacionalista party. In the campaign that ensued, Roxas enjoyed the understated but not unnoticed support of High Commissioner McNutt, in addition to that of MacArthur. At a moment when Osmeña's partisans were claiming that Washington would withhold assistance from a regime headed by a notorious collaborator, McNutt announced, "The United States Government will carry out its promised aid to the Philippine people regardless of whom they choose for their next president." Roxas also benefited from the good will of the American army, whose communications corps commanded the airwaves, reporting—perhaps creating—a last-minute surge for Roxas, and whose military police in some areas distributed Roxas campaign literature.[1]

Osmeña suffered from drawing much of his backing from the central Luzon region where the leftist Hukbalahaps had their stronghold. Not surprisingly the Huks preferred the incumbent to the Japan-tainted Roxas; with equal predictability Roxas' supporters slammed Osmeña as the candidate of the radicals. Osmeña was also hurt by the opposition of most of the Quezonistas, who opted for their fallen hero's annointee over his career-long rival. Finally, Roxas was simply the more attractive candidate. Osmeña, never a stem-winder, was old and weakening, and he chose to stand on his record of service to the Philippines rather than to campaign vigorously. Roxas, by contrast, ran in the charismatic tradition of Quezon. One observer, writing of the crowds attending the challenger's rallies, remarked, "They were transfixed by the fiery oratory of Roxas who promised to bring heaven to earth."[2]

Roxas did not bring heaven but he did bring out the vote. Following a campaign which a Filipino journalist described as "the bitterest in Philippine history," marred by "distortion and vilification and rank demagoguery," Roxas and running mate Elpidio Quirino—the latter chosen for a spotless record of noncollaboration rather than for any conspicuous ability—swept to victory on a wave that also carried Liberal majorities into both houses of the legislature.[3]

As a first priority Roxas moved to solidify his position vis-à-vis the United States. With American aid awaiting only Philippine acceptance of the Bell trade law, Roxas pushed the Philippine legislature to action. The Truman administration wished to delay agreement on the measure until after July 4, 1946, to blunt charges that the United States was extorting favorable treatment for American nationals as a condition of Philippine independence. Roxas desired to close the deal before independence, fearing that the Philippine supreme court would construe the arrangement as a treaty requiring a two-thirds' majority in the senate. Before independence it could not be a treaty since the Philippines lacked sovereignty. With the deadline approaching, Washington and Manila decided to finesse the issue: if Roxas could get a majority in the Philippine congress *before* July 4, Truman would sign *on* July 4, just after the formal transfer of power. This agreed, Roxas kept the legislature in session until the wee hours of the first days of July. Opponents, including some members of Roxas' Liberals, found the parity provision of the Bell Act utterly obnoxious, but eventually he broke them down with reminders that upon their choice hung American aid. "I vote yes," one late decider muttered, "because we are flat broke, hungry, homeless, and destitute."[4]

Amending the Philippine constitution to conform to the Bell Act created more problems. An amendment required the assent of three-quarters of the legislature, a larger majority than the Liberals could readily muster. To narrow the odds Roxas engineered the ouster of eight announced opponents of parity—including Hukbalahap leader Luis Taruc and five other members of his anti-collaborationist Democratic Alliance—on dubious grounds of electoral fraud and manipulation. The strong-arm tactic succeeded. Roxas got his three-fourths' majority. But the victory exacted a price, for the ejection of Taruc convinced him and his followers of the futility of working within the law and helped touch off the rebellion that wracked the country during the next several years.

When the parity amendment went to the people Roxas took the rhetorical offensive. He directly denied charges that parity constituted a sell-out. Instead, he asserted, it would unlock the wealth of the country. In a climactic rally before the March 1947 referendum the Philippine president declaimed,

> We have today our one big chance to convert our native land into an ideal of democracy. Our one chance is to grow and industrialize to reach the first rank of the nations of the world. We have this chance because of the heroism we displayed in the war; we have this chance because we have demonstrated by deed our love for freedom. We have earned the gratitude of mankind. We can and will show tomorrow that we deserve that gratitude by plunging courageously ahead in the great tasks we face.

The speech was vintage Roxas, promising prosperity, praising the people, touching only tangentially on the issue at hand. But it worked, with help from the party machinery. Filipino voters gave their assent and parity entered the constitution.[5]

As with the trade act, so the agreement on American military bases required confirmation by the independent Philippine government. In 1945 the American war and navy departments, uncertain about the future and desiring maximum freedom of maneuver, had grabbed more sites than they knew what to do with. By 1946, after American lawmakers made painfully—that is, financially—clear to the Pentagon an intention to demobilize as quickly as possible, American strategists were forced to select the fewer positions they genuinely aimed to improve. Negotiations with the Roxas government revealed several sticking points regarding American bases. A principal one involved location. Not even as friendly a regime as Roxas' could allow a major American base in Manila; the continuing affront to Philippine nationalism would be too great to bear. Roxas asserted, "When the national capital is the nation's greatest center of population and of the nation's economic life, the presence of alien military establishments becomes truly intolerable." Yet relocating away from the city would cost money American military leaders were not sure they could get.[6]

The difficulty contributed to a decision to review American thinking about the Philippines. In November 1946 Dwight Eisenhower, now in MacArthur's old job as army chief of staff, proposed that the United States withdraw all army personnel from the Philippines. War Secretary Robert Patterson concurred with the recommendation. As Patterson explained, the fundamental problem was a mismatch between American responsibilities and available funds. Keeping order in the occupied territories—Germany, Japan, Korea, Austria, Italy—required nearly all the troops America could field. "We cannot afford," Patterson said, ". . . to waste our strength by maintenance of a force of any considerable size in the Philippines." As to funds, Patterson noted the Philippine government's "quite understandable" objection to an American military presence in the Manila area and the fact that removal would require substantial expenditure on new facilities. "Such an expenditure would be one that the War Department could ill afford at this time or in the future." To underline his concern—and to make it known to the Philippine government—Patterson canceled military construction projects in the Philippines.[7]

If the Pentagon's conspicuous loss of interest was a bargaining device, it worked. Upon learning that the United States might not want Philippine bases after all, Roxas went out of his way to demonstrate his country's wish for the Americans to have them. He told McNutt that the Philippines and the United States enjoyed a "virtually absolute community of defense interests." In a January 1947 speech directed more at Washington than at his immediate Filipino audience, Roxas dismissed reports of local objection to an American military presence as disinformation. He personally had sounded popular opinion on the subject. "I polled the people in several of the base areas," he said. "In Guiuan there was unanimous and full-throated expression of approval. It was the same everywhere I asked." Roxas assured the United States that American troops were "welcome guests in our land." He discounted complaints of American misconduct. The troops, he asserted, were behaving "in a manner that reflects credit and honor upon the United States Government." He concluded by saying what Washington most wanted to hear then and for the next forty years: that American bases served the purposes of the Philippines and the world as much as those of the United States. "We must not be left undefended," he asserted. "I cannot in good conscience overlook the absolute necessity of guaranteeing our security by every and all means available to us. . . . The establishment of these bases, not for aggression but for defense, will guarantee our own safety and advance the cause of world peace and security."[8]

Roxas did not specify whom the United States would be defending the Philippines against. At the beginning of 1947 Japan was prostrate, China paralyzed by civil war and the Soviet Union far beyond any conceivable strategic horizon. American leaders could not see much threat either, which was why they were not pressing the base issue. But if the Philippine government offered a good deal they would be willing to listen.

In the end, Roxas, encouraged further by a pledge of American military aid, offered a very good deal. In exchange for pulling American troops out of Manila the United States would receive a ninety-nine-year lease on a huge area at Clark Field, on a site to be developed near Olongapo on Subic Bay, and on various smaller installations around the country. Washington readily accepted, with the arrangement concluded in March 1947.

The completion of the base negotiations tidied up the last of the major issues left over from the transfer of political power. Filipino leaders were now free to get about the business of governing the Philippines. As during the first era of Filipinization this business was based to considerable degree on the principles of private enterprise, particularly the principle of profit maximization for those in position to maximize. The problem of corruption grew slowly at first, and while Roxas remained president the situation did not get out of hand. The Liberal party cut corners and defined the prerogatives of power more broadly than sticklers might have desired, but the Roxas machine's transgressions would not have startled Quezon—or Thomas Pendergast of Kansas City, for that matter—and the administration of Pendergast's friend Harry Truman felt no great chagrin in maintaining close ties.

Chagrin would come soon enough. In the meantime the Truman administration, or at least certain elements of it, had other worries about Roxas. The Central Intelligence Agency feared that Roxas' soft policy toward collaborators might produce a resurgence of anti-American feeling in the Philippines. The collaborators had included most of those individuals most hostile to American influence. The CIA raised the possibility that amnesty would allow such individuals—"who play on extreme Philippine nationalism and are themselves secretly or avowedly anti-American"—to assume positions of authority, with damaging consequences to the United States.[9]

To a certain extent the CIA's judgment demonstrated the bureaucratically predictable tendency of the newly formed intelligence agency to miss on the side of caution in threat assessment. The ranks of the collaborators comprised more opportunists than convinced anti-Americans, although a few notable persons, like José Laurel, fell into both categories. Opportunists America could work with. To some degree the CIA's warning reflected an American administration working at cross purposes. Having backed Roxas' candidacy and tolerated lenience toward the collaborators, Washington was only getting what it had asked for.

On the whole the Truman administration found Roxas' performance acceptable, and American leaders viewed with genuine regret his sudden and unexpected but otherwise natural death in April 1948. Of his successor, Elpidio Quirino, American officials knew relatively little, although initial reports from the CIA characterized Quirino as "friendly toward U.S. interests." The more Washington learned of Quirino and those he gathered around him the less it liked them, for the new president and his associates quickly demonstrated an alarming inclination to what Claro Recto, with unaccustomed delicacy, called "extravagant vagaries." Beyond manipulating the legislative process to their advantage— by shifting the tax burden to the poor, for instance, through more-regressive rates and imaginative loopholes—the ruling Liberals illegally exploited their favored position by evading taxes, siphoning American funds intended for payment of Filipino veterans, black-marketing surplus American war materiel and engaging in a variety of other activities providing profit at public expense—and American. During the first four years of independence the Philippine government ran through more than a billion dollars of American assistance, and at the end of the period the country's economy was hardly better off than in 1945.[10]

Officials in the Truman administration begrudged Quirino the wasted money, but they worried more that the American Congress would refuse to continue funding a government engaged in such abuses, thereby diminishing American influence in Manila. They also feared a replay of events in China, where corruption, similarly at American expense, had contributed crucially to the fall of the Nationalists. On numerous occasions Washington attempted to get Quirino to see where his laxness was leading.

The Americans' efforts availed little. During a visit by Quirino to Washington in the summer of 1949 Secretary of State Dean Acheson showed the Philippine president a report by the World Bank outlining the tenuous condition of the Philippine economy. Acheson predicted a bleak future unless Quirino turned his government around. The secretary even threatened to cut off American aid. But Quirino displayed "little comprehension," as Acheson remarked in a memo, and he proceeded to launch into "a thirty-minute dissertation which added up to an expression of confidence that all was well in the Philippines." Shaking his head, Acheson could only note that "it is difficult if not impossible to get President Quirino down to brass tacks about the Philippine situation."[11]

Acheson had a bad habit of accounting as fools those who disagreed with him. In this case he underestimated Quirino. The Philippine president received regular reports on the level of the Truman administration's distress from Carlos Romulo, the Philippine representative at the United Nations—also president of the General Assembly, later ambassador to the United States, and subsequently foreign secretary. Romulo shuttled between New York and Washington, keeping close touch with American officials and speaking with them on various topics: the politics of the United Nations, France's troubles in Indochina, the rehabilitation of Japan. Romulo often reminded the Americans of Filipinos' attachment to "our common ideology." He missed few opportunities to stress the "urgency" of the Philippines' financial situation. But most important, Romulo tracked the blood pressure of Acheson and others in the American administration, and he issued warnings to Manila when apoplexy approached. The accuracy of his analyses was reflected in the fact that for all their fulminations the Americans always stopped short of pulling the plug on aid.[12]

Sometimes they came very close. John Melby, the state department's point man for Philippine affairs, found Quirino's attitude mind-boggling. Following the same visit that provoked Acheson's frustration, Melby asserted that while the Philippines offered "distinct possibilities" for economic development along democratic lines, the country also faced "distinct liabilities." The Philippine economy, Melby said, was "living on the borrowed time of American governmental expenditures." He noted that half the Philippines' dollar earnings came directly from the American treasury, while the other half derived from exports, especially of copra, that were grossly overvalued and bound to fall. The present administration in Manila operated "on the happy postulate that when conditions get bad the United States will bail it out." Quirino himself was "ineffectual, dilatory, and disturbingly corrupt. He does not seem to understand most of the problems he is facing, nor does he appear to have much intention of doing anything about those he does understand." His "main preoccupation" was getting elected.[13]

When Melby spoke, Quirino was in the middle of a contest for the Philippine presidency that set new standards for dishonesty. Quirino faced a double challenge, from fellow Liberal José Avelino and from José Laurel. Quirino neutralized Avelino by effecting his removal from the senate presidency—for corruption, of all things—and agreeing to reinstatement only when Avelino threw his support to Quirino's candidacy. Between Quirino and Laurel, Washington deemed the former less objectionable despite his enormous flaws. The CIA accurately described Laurel as "bitterly anti-U.S.," and, reiterating its concern about the collaborators, the agency predicted that a Laurel victory would encourage "extreme nationalists." To the Americans' guarded relief Quirino ultimately won. But victory required all the manipulativeness the incumbent could muster. Widespread violence marred the voting, and conservative estimates placed the number of fraudulent ballots at upwards of 20 percent of those cast.[14]

As Acheson, Melby and other American officials expected, Quirino continued to mismanage the Philippine economy. During the summer of 1950 a special economic mission dispatched from Washington reported that government finances "have become steadily worse and are now critical." The members of the mission found the Philippines' balance of payments "seriously distorted" and detected a "widespread feeling of disillusion" with the Quirino administration. The mission recommended a continuation of American aid but only if it was "strictly conditioned" on an end to governmental corruption.[15]

John Melby put the matter more emphatically. Melby said the recent hijacking of votes and the pervasive corruption demonstrated that, politically speaking, "the Filipinos are only one generation out of the tree tops." Quirino continued to display a "disturbing lack of comprehension" of his country's troubles. Without far more stringent supervision of American aid the United States faced the possibility of "economic chaos in an area which Asiatics look upon as the American show-window in Asia."[16]

The CIA considered Quirino's sins so shocking, even by Philippine standards, that the agency thought he might well be impeached. Agency analysts listed the causes of popular disenchantment with the government: "a corrupt and inefficient officialdom, lawlessness, arbitrary misuse of governmental power, the 1949 election frauds, disorganized political parties, and a variety of economic problems." To give Quirino his miniscule due, the CIA noted that these troubles could not be charged entirely to Quirino personally, although he deserved the largest portion of individual blame. They reflected, rather, a fundamental skewing of Philippine politics in favor of the wealthy and well-connected. The CIA provided a succinct analysis of the country's woes when it declared that "at the base of these is an irresponsible ruling class which exercises economic and political power almost exclusively in its own interest."[17]

III. Huks to the rescue

One group of Filipinos intended to do more than impeach Quirino. The Huks aimed to overthrow the government and the system of elite privilege on which it rested. To the much-debated extent the movement possessed a comprehensive ideology and political program it drew most directly on the legacy of the Philippine Socialist party, founded in 1916 under Manuel Carlos and vitalized during the 1930s by Pedro Abad Santos, and the Philippine Communist party of Crisanto Evangelista.

Before World War II the government of the commonwealth observed the activities of the Communists and fellow travelers with concern. In 1941 José Laurel, then secretary of justice, drafted a memo to Quezon advocating firm treatment of the Communists. "I am of the opinion that vigorous action should be taken to repress communism in the Philippines," Laurel wrote. "We cannot afford to give the impression of weakness on the part of our government, especially in this time of emergency in case of our involvement in the present world conflict." Laurel added that the government should provide "clear and categorical" warning that it was prepared to use force "if and when necessary, at the least sign of resistance or actual defiance."[18]

Quezon was not one to shrink from vigorous action against political challengers, but the war intervened before such action became necessary. As noted earlier, the Japanese invasion produced a variety of resistance groups, among which the most important was the Huks. During the war, radical ideology ranked behind anti-Japanese nationalism in Huk thinking. According to Luis Taruc, "There was no time to argue about such ideas as the dictatorship of the proletariat or the virtues of atheism versus those of religion. We were fighting a bitter, bloody battle and sharing the same dangers."[19]

While the fighting continued American leaders were willing join with the Huks in the common cause. As late as February 1945 a directive from American military headquarters stated, "Utilize those guerrillas which can be profitably employed." Yet American officials were suspicious of Huk motives and long-term objectives, and as the end of the war drew near their suspicions grew. An analyst with MacArthur's command characterized Huk goals:

> The Americans were to be allowed to liberate the Philippines but were then to be attacked if immediate independence were not granted. Political figures of the Commonwealth Government were to be accepted only insofar as they could furnish a government not dominated by the U.S.A, Japan or any other foreign country, either politically or commercially. The Hukbalahap has said in its manifestos that the right of private property will be guaranteed in their postwar government, as well as freedom of speech, press, assembly, residence. Although the Hukbalahap has maintained this propaganda line to the present day, reports indicate that their policy is definitely communistic and that their plans include the establishment of a communistic government in the Philippines after the war, on the early Russian model. It is probable that there are also connections with communistic elements in China.[20]

This reading of the Huks' objectives was reasonably accurate, despite an overstatement of the single-mindedness of the movement. The political leadership deriving from the Communist and Socialist parties indeed intended a thorough transformation of the Philippine political economy. But the rank and file, largely illiterate and unindoctrinated, had no such specific agenda. Even those inclined to keep fighting after the war against Japan ended were moved more by a generic feeling of protest against the inequities of life than by the teachings of Marx, Lenin or Mao.

Yet both the American military command and the Filipino upper class recognized the threat an armed insurgency posed to the restoration of the status quo in the Philippines. MacArthur, who had smelled Bolshevism in the 1932 Bonus March on Washington, was not the man to tolerate leftist rebels loose in his beloved islands. Many of the Filipino elite recognized that they were twice guilty in the eyes of the Huks: once for fostering the conditions of oppression that made peasant life miserable, again for collaborating with the Japanese. Consequently when MacArthur announced, just before the Leyte landings, that "the only political activity which is legal is political activity aimed at the maintenance of the loyalty of the masses to the established, legal government," members of the elite concurred completely.[21]

American forces allowed the Huks to assist in rooting out the Japanese, but once Japan was defeated they ordered the guerrillas to put down their weapons. Most refused. Many of those within the reach of American military law were arrested. Others headed for the mountains.

During the next several months members of the American Counter-Intelligence Corps (CIC) attempted to locate Huk leaders and liquidate the movement. The Americans employed a variety of schemes and ruses. To one contingent of Huks they promised new arms, which they would deliver as soon as the guerrillas turned in their old models. Of course the new guns never arrived. The Americans persuaded Luis Taruc to hand over a list of Huk soldiers as a measure of his good faith. The CIC used the list to facilitate its roundup. The Americans favored selected Huk groups over others, in an attempt, as an American officer said, "to divide and conquer and to make it appear to outside observers that there was dissension and diversity in the Hukbalahap, which would cause the organization to lose the support and trust of the people backing it."[22]

As life returned more or less to normal after the war, certain elements of the Huk leadership carried the organization's grievances to the voters. In the summer of 1945 a coalition of guerrilla leaders and others unwilling to choose between Osmeña and Roxas united under the banner of the Democratic Alliance. As Taruc explained the party's program,

> The DA was not revolutionary. It believed in the ballot and the peaceful petition as instruments through which the people's will should be expressed and achieved. It did not propose even the mildest socialization or change in the system of society as we know it. The path it proposed would have led no further than the development of a healthy industrialized capitalist country out of the feudal agricultural colonial condition that we had.[23]

Whether or not the Democratic Alliance would have achieved the prosperity it intended, its program—indeed its very existence—challenged the hegemony of the ruling groups. The Huks threw their energy behind Alliance candidates and helped the party succeed in electing, despite a campaign of intimidation and fraud by Roxas' Liberals, six congressmen, including Taruc.

Roxas responded with charges of intimidation by the Huks. He demanded and received the rejection of the Alliance candidates by the Philippine legislature, a move that triggered a new round of unrest in the Huk stronghold of central Luzon. Roxas attempted to calm matters by getting Taruc and two other spokesmen of the peasants to agree to a peacekeeping mission. But the government's military police insisted on more decisive action against the Huks. Asserting that "the stability of the Republic is being threatened," the chief of police declared, "We mean business. We are coming to knock them out." On August 24, 1946, one of the mediators, Juan Feleo, was kidnapped by armed men in the uniforms of the military police. A few weeks later his headless body was found floating in the Pampanga River.[24]

Feleo's murder, which was accompanied by attacks by the military police on barrios throughout central Luzon known to shelter Huks, touched off a full-scale revolt in the region. Taruc wrote an open letter to Roxas announcing his decision to cast his lot with the peasants against the president's "reactionary subordinates, blood-thirsty MP officers and mercenary guards." Taruc affirmed the honest intentions of his followers. "The peasants of Central Luzon are loyal to our country and to our Constitution. You know that. They are humble, peaceful and law-abiding." And what were they gaining for their patience?

> Even as I write this, your blood-thirsty subordinates are already making an all-out punitive campaign against the peasants. The MP's are shelling barrios and shooting innocent civilians. They are even threatening to use bombs. Suspects they catch (and they just pick up everybody) are subjected to all despicable tortures. Together with the civilian guards, they are virtually in control of all government machinery, conducting a reign of terror worse than the Japs. . . .
>
> You have your choice, Mr. President—be a real liberal and a true leader of Filipinos and rest assured of our cooperation. But be an imperialist fascist agent and you will find that there are enough Filipinos who have learned a lot in the last war and who will not give up in peace social gains acquired during that war.[25]

Roxas answered Taruc's letter with a pledge to stamp out the Huk insurgency within sixty days. Members of the government's military and police forces took this as a license to brutalize peasants almost at whim. "In 1946, 1947, actually the rest of the forties," one resident of San Ricardo in Nueva Écija recalled afterward, "civilian guards and the constabulary arrested anyone they wanted, burned houses, took food, and raped. These men were absolutely the worst." Even an enlightened government would have found the revolt trying, for as in most guerrilla conflicts—including the Philippine-American war—it was nearly impossible to distinguish fighters from noncombatants. The government led by Roxas and subsequently Quirino was far from enlightened. Results were predictable. Rebel raids provoked government reprisals, and vice versa. Those caught in the middle suffered most.[26]

American officials would have fretted over an uprising of any ideological coloration in the Philippines in the late 1940s. The violent breakdown of the political process spoke ill of America's half-century of tutelage of the Filipinos, and with the western position in Asia under attack from nationalist insurgencies in Indochina, Indonesia and Malaya, not to mention the civil war in China, trouble in the Philippines was the last thing Washington needed. The fact that the Huk rebellion was communist-inspired, if perhaps not communist-controlled, simply added to Washington's worries.

Paradoxically—but not unpredictably—the very danger the Huks posed to the status quo in the Philippines proved the quo's salvation. As the insurgency heated up, representatives of the Philippine government reminded Washington of America's obligations. "Philippine independence is the handiwork of the United States," Lucas Madamba, a Quirino spokesman, said. This handiwork was now under threat from the local representatives of the worldwide communist conspiracy. Washington must not weaken. To do so would betray five decades of American promises. If American assistance had been necessary earlier, now, in what Quirino called "the present unsettled situation," it was absolutely vital.[27]

Washington agreed. Economic aid to Manila had begun with independence in 1946. Military aid commenced with the 1947 bases deal. As the rebellion intensified, both increased. American assistance to the Philippines, like that of the same vintage to Greece and Turkey, had the immediate objective of enhancing the internal security of the recipient. An American advisory team accompanied the dollars and weapons to the Philippines to ensure their proper use, to train locals and generally to promote the pro-American orientation of the country.

American advisers in the Philippines concentrated on developing a counterinsurgency strategy against the Huks, who by now had changed their full name to Hukbong Mapagpalaya ng Bayan, or People's Liberation Army. In March 1949, after two and a half years of the rebellion, the CIA estimated Huk strength at nearly 10,000 men under arms, in addition to a far wider base of active supporters and sympathizers. Alarmed that Manila was making scant progress against the rising, the agency sent one of its top counterinsurgency specialists to join the American military advisory mission. Edward Lansdale had served with American army intelligence in the Philippines during the Second World War. He remained in the country for three years after the war, during which time he devoted much effort to studying the Huks. At the end of 1948 he was transferred out, but before long he returned with orders "to give all feasible help to the Philippine government in stopping the attempt by the Communist-led Huks to overthrow that government by force."[28]

Lansdale arrived in the summer of 1950, when Manila's political and strategic value to Washington was reaching unprecedented levels—a point Filipino leaders fully appreciated. Several months earlier, while the Chinese Communists were completing their rout of the Nationalists, Truman had announced an increase in military aid to the Philippines. Quirino responded with an expression of gratitude that also contained an implicit warning. "Your speech," he told Truman, "has undoubtedly brought the United States closer to the hearts of people like ours whose national security is presently threatened by the advance of communism." As the east turned ever redder, Quirino's spokesmen reiterated this double message of Philippine support and Philippine danger.[29]

After the Communists' capture of Beijing the Philippine government stood by, and often in front of, the American delegation at the United Nations. Citing what Carlos Romulo described as "our common ideology and close association with the United States," the Philippine delegation adamantly opposed the seating of the Chinese People's Republic in place of the American-backed Nationalist government of Taiwan. At the same time the Filipinos made plain that cooperation must be reciprocal. Romulo summarized the strategy, and its success, in a note to Quirino. "Our stand in the General Assembly on major political and security questions has been such that the United States expects and even depends on the Philippines to take the lead in defending their cause," Romulo wrote. "In return, our support has caused the United States to view our requirements for financial assistance with the utmost sympathy."[30]

The outbreak and initial setbacks of the Korean War drove Washington nearly to panic, a condition Manila was only too happy to capitalize on. Driven by fear equally of Asian communists and American Republicans, the Truman administration moved to guarantee the security of Chiang Kai-shek on Taiwan and to fortify the French in Indochina. The administration also quit nagging Quirino about the deficiencies of his government. Instead American officials concentrated on fortifying Quirino against the Huks. Reporting a visit to the state department, Romulo noted with pleasure that Acheson could talk of little else. Acheson took pains to pass along President Truman's determination that America "must act quickly" against the insurgency. Spotting an opening, the Philippine diplomat remarked that the Korean invasion confirmed what his government had said from the start, that the Huk rebellion was not the result of Manila's mismanagement but was part of a "pattern of communist aggression."[31]

Through the following months Quirino and associates cleaved to the Americans, hauling Washington's water at the United Nations and acting, in Romulo's words, as "a bridge between America and Asia." As recompense the Truman administration assured Quirino that America would not let him down in the Philippines' hour of trial. Economic and military aid continued, all thoughts of a corruption-provoked cutoff banished. George Marshall, now in charge of the Pentagon, told Romulo, "Philippine defense is of major importance to the United States."[32]

At the moment Philippine defense, as Marshall used the term, needed work. The Huk insurgency had gathered momentum as government forces proved unequal to the task the rebels posed. In March 1950 an officer of the American military advisory group warned of an impending Huk takeover of portions of central Luzon. Following an especially damaging series of attacks, this officer predicted, "Should the Hukbalahap-Communists continue their strikes of the past few days, local control of the affected area will undoubtedly dissolve into a chaotic state." Against the hapless Philippine army troops the rebels struck at will. "The law and order situation in Luzon is definitely out of hand."[33]

The insurgents continued to gain ground through the summer of 1950. In September General Leland Hobbs, chief of the American military advisory group, told Quirino that Manila must adopt a tougher line in dealing with Huk sympathizers. Hobbs recommended laws proscribing activities of leftist groups. Quirino need not worry that such measures would upset Washington. The American Congress itself had recently considered outlawing the Communist party in the United States. In any event Americans would understand the necessity of vigorous anti-radical measures. "You and your people," Hobbs said, "are so much closer to the heart of Oriental Communism that action against a possible Communistic underground engulfment should be more drastic than has been the policy in America."[34]

These developments and this thinking lay behind Washington's dispatch of Edward Lansdale to Manila with instructions to stamp out the Huk rebellion. Lansdale immediately joined forces with the most promising member of Quirino's cabinet, the newly appointed minister of defense, Ramón Magsaysay. Lansdale had known Magsaysay when the latter, then a Liberal representative from Zambales province, had headed a congressional committee on national defense. Magsaysay's understanding of the nature of the Huk threat, as well as his no-nonsense approach to the insurrection, impressed Lansdale and other members of the Truman administration. Ambassador Myron Cowen especially appreciated Magsaysay's support when the ambassador drew fire from Filipino critics charging him with excessive influence in Filipino affairs. Magsaysay asserted, "An unwarranted attack against a benefactor is the bitterest dreg of ingratitude." Magsaysay warmed hearts in Washington with a speech before the Philippine congress in which he declared the existence of a "special relationship" between the United States and the Philippines.[35]

That Magsaysay was honest enhanced his attractiveness, and American leaders began thinking he would make a fine replacement for Quirino. Quirino read their thoughts and worried. When the Truman administration suggested that Magsaysay take charge of the anti-Huk campaign Quirino reflected carefully. On one hand, promoting Magsaysay would raise his visibility and increase the potential danger he posed to Quirino's position. On the other, Magsaysay might botch the job, and the Americans seemed set on the appointment. Preferring not to oppose Washington in the matter, Quirino went along.

Magsaysay and Lansdale collaborated famously. "We were so close that we thought and spoke of each other as brother," Lansdale remarked later. After conferring with various Philippine and American officials in Manila, Lansdale sought out the presumably more objective opinions of journalists in the capital. "The gist of what they had to say was ugly," Lansdale wrote.

> They told me that the Quirino government was rotten with corruption; that it had won the 1949 presidential election by extensive fraud ("even counting the birds and flowers in Mindanao as votes"); that the president's brother Tony had a staff of thugs to scare the critics into silence; that Magsaysay might be an exception—a "good"

man in the government—but would be powerless to change an entrenched officer corps in the army; that arrogant behavior had caused the military to be hated and feared by the people; that Huk "atrocities" were matched by what the government was doing; that there were bright men among the Huk leaders; and that the Huks were going to win before long.

Lansdale then set off for a firsthand inspection of the countryside, where he discovered much sympathy for the Huks. He claimed afterward that this discovery came as a "rude jolt." Such a statement is hard to credit, given Lansdale's familiarity with the background of the insurgency. But he was known to stretch or shrink the truth, depending on circumstances. At the time he concluded that any effort to stop the Huks would require more than the military repression the Quirino government currently relied upon.[36]

Returning to Manila, Lansdale established an office in Magsaysay's headquarters. Magsaysay set to cleaning up the officer corps. The defense secretary began making surprise visits to barracks and military installations around the country, explaining the purpose of the visits as "not only to see actual conditions for myself" but also "to be sure that the relations of the army with the civilian population are improved." He disciplined corrupt individual officers while he praised, and raised, the performance of the army as a whole. "It is unfortunate that there are a few individuals in the AFP [Armed Forces of the Philippines] who are besmirching the reputation of this fine organization," he said. As the besmirchers were weeded out, the reputation rose.[37]

Lansdale meanwhile formulated a policy of psychological warfare, then the rage in counterinsurgency. Drawing on his experience as an advertising executive, Lansdale developed a sales pitch on behalf of the government. His work dovetailed with Magsaysay's, for the decline of corruption in the armed forces increased the credibility of Lansdale's public relations efforts. Central to Lansdale's campaign was a program pledging farms for peasants, designed specifically to undercut the Huks' promise of land for the landless. The farms offered were located in public tracts, to avoid upsetting the landlords who formed the base of the ruling class and who could have vetoed the program. Because the homesteads were on Mindanao, the program promised the added benefit of separating Huks who accepted the offer from the territory from which they drew strength. To ensure that retiring rebels not spread revolutionary ideas to new territory, each group of homesteaders included ex-soldiers and civilians specially chosen, in the words of one sympathetic observer, "to leaven the community with loyalty and good citizenship."[38]

In addition Lansdale employed negative reinforcement. Making use of popular fears of night spirits he sent a "combat psywar" team into an area to plant stories that a vampire, or *asuang*, haunted the region. A few days later a small government force laid an ambush for a Huk patrol. The soldiers silently jumped the last Huk in the line, punctured his neck in two places with a fang-like instrument and hung the body upside down to drain the blood. When the victim's friends discovered him missing and returned, they found what appeared to be the work of the asuang. As Lansdale related the story, the Huks quickly abandoned the neighborhood.

Another operation involved what Lansdale called the "eye of God" technique. A spotter in an airplane, briefed with informants' reports on the membership of a local Huk unit, flew overhead and announced through a bull-horn that the members of the unit, identified by name, were doomed. The army knew everything about their activities and government troops were closing in. They might as well surrender. The speaker concluded with a comment on the order of "Thank you, our friend in your squadron, for all the information," a remark designed to set the Huks against one another as they tried to determine who had turned informer. Of one such operation Lansdale commented proudly, "Three of them were singled out and executed on the spot. The words had inflicted as many casualties on the enemy as troops could have done in a running fight."

Lansdale helped institute a practice intended to curb the illegal sale of government ammunition to Huks, by arranging for the introduction of sabotaged bullets into the supply stream. "Government troops reported a curious new phenomenon on the battlefield," Lansdale wrote. "Huk rifles were exploding from the use of the faulty ammunition." Lansdale did not record the reaction of the government soldiers whose own rifles blew up in their faces, nor of those who tried to use grenades that detonated in the user's hand. He did say, "It came as small surprise that the illicit sale of ammunition to the Huks ground to a halt. Dirty tricks beget dirty tricks."[39]

Other American tricks included providing napalm for attacks on suspected Huk positions. Ambassador Cowen initially declared himself "unalterably opposed" to the advisory mission's request for napalm. "The Philippine Armed Forces are not qualified to use this kind of equipment," Cowen wrote, "and, furthermore, I can see only the most unfortunate repercussions if it were used and innocent Filipino citizens were killed or badly burned. The result could only be to make more Huks than would be eliminated." Cowen eventually retreated in the face of pressure from Lansdale and advisory chief Hobbs. The ambassador finally insisted in July 1951 only that delivery be deferred "until after the November elections." By year's end the napalm had arrived. It soon was put into action.[40]

Washington meanwhile tried to get Manila to adopt measures that would render napalm and exploding ammunition unnecessary. The Truman administration did not feel in a position to hector Quirino, but American officials thought some friendly advice was not out of bounds. Dean Acheson wrote the embassy suggesting a number of points on which improvement in Quirino's performance was in order. The first was elections, always a sensitive topic with Americans on account of America's claims to have nurtured democracy in the Philippines. "We believe it essential," Acheson told Cowen, "that the Philippine Government and people realize that the United States will be watching very closely both the 1951 and 1953 elections." Acheson went so far as to indicate that a repeat of the 1949 fraud might provoke reconsideration of America's aid policy. Second, Quirino should do better at curbing corruption. Acheson suggested installing American technical advisers in various positions in the government. These persons would not be expected to halt dishonest dealings entirely, but "they should be able to make graft and corruption at least more difficult." Third, the Philippine government ought to extend its land-redistribution program. Although the resettlement scheme on Mindanao was a start, Acheson thought Quirino would have to go further—or rather, less far—and deal with the problem of tenancy closer to home. "The Department would appreciate any information the Embassy might have on the cost of buying up and redistributing estates in central Luzon," Acheson wrote to Cowen.[41]

The Philippine government responded to the first of Acheson's recommendations, although not entirely by choice. Quirino might have ignored the efforts of a citizens' group called the National Movement for Free Elections, or NAMFREL, to monitor the off-year elections of 1951 had Magsaysay not prevented the army from taking part in vote-stealing. This novelty caught Quirino by surprise, and when the president's cronies discovered that the returns were not rigged and were not producing the desired results, they ordered stuffed ballot boxes loaded onto army airplanes for delivery to key polling places. Magsaysay countermanded the order. Learning that one plane had already taken off, the defense secretary radioed the pilot saying he had a defective engine. The couriers of the fixed forms agreed to turn back.[42]

IV. America blinks

Running a clean election was one thing, and even in this case the improvement was only relative. Yet Washington thought the performance warranted congratulations. "The American people have been immeasurably heartened in watching the Filipino people practice the ways of democracy," Truman told Quirino.[43]

Progress toward ending corruption and in the direction of genuine land reform was something else. The Filipino governing groups could accept the replacement of some of Quirino's Liberals in the legislature by opposition Nacionalistas without undue distress. Party labels have never meant much in Filipino politics, and the challengers' social origins did not differ materially from those of the incumbents. But the upper classes drew the line at measures that might seriously undermine their privileged position in the country's political economy.

Whether an American government steeled to do so could have forced systemic changes upon the Filipino ruling classes is an open question. In the event Washington wilted. In November 1950 Truman approved a National Security

Council paper defining American policy toward the Philippines. Written against a background of the communist victory in China, the ongoing Korean War and the deepening troubles in Indochina, the paper described the Philippines as crucially important to the United States. The Philippines formed an "essential part" of the Pacific island chain that constituted America's vital defensive perimeter in the Far East. If retreat from the Philippines had once been conceivable, it was no longer so. American positions in the Philippines were required to project American power throughout the East and Southeast Asia region.

Accordingly, the NSC paper continued, it was "imperative" that the Huks be defeated. To this end American officials should concentrate on three objectives in the Philippines: maintaining a government that would preserve and strengthen the generally pro-American orientation of the Filipino people, developing a Philippine military capable of ensuring internal order, and creating a stable and self-supporting economy. The NSC authors recognized a role for actions designed to lessen popular discontent, such as land reform and a campaign against corruption. But for the moment beating the Huks came first. Not only would a Huk victory "discredit the United States in the eyes of the world and seriously decrease U.S. influence, particularly in Asia," it might make the Philippines "the key to Soviet control of the Far East." Despite Quirino's faults the ruling regime was preferable to any ready alternative. The collapse of the present government would probably lead to a seizure of power by the communists.[44]

Washington's fear of further slippage in the Asian status quo eviscerated American efforts to reform the Philippines. American officials repeatedly backed away in the face of elite intransigence, despite the potential leverage provided by American economic and military aid. As often as the state department and the White House resolved to curtail assistance to the Philippines unless Manila shaped up, events in China, Korea and elsewhere intruded to weaken this resolve. In 1949 Acheson told Truman a cut in aid to the Philippines "might raise serious consequences." Later that year the secretary of state remarked that the situation in China made the Philippines "more important than ever." Acheson went on to say, "We should have a Philippine policy which would do everything possible to keep the Philippines not only friendly to the United States but close to the United States." Truman concurred.[45]

Manila made the most of its heightened value to America. In the wake of the communist victory in China the Truman administration decided to work on rebuilding Japan. The decision raised fears among Japan's Asian neighbors, recently the objects of Japanese aggression. In the Philippine case it posed a fiscal threat as well. Filipinos had counted on payments of reparations from Japan to repair damage done during the war—and to line the pockets of well-placed officials. American leaders initially supported the idea of the Japan-to-Philippines transfer, but as Washington came to conceive of Japan as a friendly counterweight to a hostile China—reversing completely the earlier notion of bolstering

China against defeated Japan—they began to think that Japanese resources would yield greater returns invested in Japan. As a Truman administration insider explained in a letter to Manila: "The more reparations taken out of Japan, the less the economic potential of Japan."[46]

The issue was perfect for Filipino politicians opposed to reform. It provided an opportunity to throw the Americans' idealism back in their faces, to play on American guilt at having failed to protect the Filipinos from the Japanese, and to wave the banner of Philippine nationalism. One of Carlos Romulo's advisers admonished him not to give in to the Americans:

> I pray for your success in this your greatest fight—to establish our right to demand reparations from Japan in the name of justice and equity, in the name of our boys who fought in Bataan, Corregidor and other battlefields, in the name of our countless dead, victims of Japanese brutality. Let it never be said that we do not have the courage to choose the proper course between loyalty to an avowed friend, such as America is, and duty to ourselves and our posterity.[47]

Romulo hardly needed the encouragement. On a visit to Washington he announced that "it would be a patent distortion of the firm purpose of the Allies" to place Japan's recovery ahead of reparations due Japan's victims. Romulo said he found extremely distressing the willingness of the United States to allow such a perversion of allied policy. Should Washington follow through on this misguided venture he and his fellow Filipinos would be forced to live with the fear that Japan "will menace us once more."[48]

Manila did not derail American plans for Japan. Washington proceeded with its shift toward Tokyo. But by raising a stink on the Japanese question the Philippine government further deterred the Americans from making a fuss over the corruption and lack of democracy in the Philippines. A progress report written for the National Security Council at the beginning of 1952 asserted that America's Japanese policy required American leaders to exercise "the greatest tact" in relations with the Philippines. In handling the Filipinos, Washington would have "to lead rather than push." While the situation in East and Southeast Asia remained unsettled the United States must not risk allowing President Quirino to feel he was being placed "in an untenable position."[49]

13

A Special Relationship
1953–1957

I.   Ike and My Guy

Washington's solicitude for the political health of Quirino reflected a concern for stability in the Philippines rather than any preference for Quirino personally. When a respectable replacement, namely Magsaysay, presented himself, and when it seemed that the transition would not threaten the basic pro-American orientation of the Philippine government, American officials were only too happy to assist in Quirino's removal.

Before they had the opportunity to do so the United States itself underwent a change of leadership. Dwight Eisenhower and John Foster Dulles took command of American foreign policy at the beginning of 1953 committed, to a greater degree than the Democrats had been, to the defense of Asia against communism. Dean Acheson, America's ultimate Europeanist, considered Asia a distraction from the main business of American foreign policy: the establishment of European security. Although he certainly felt its effects, Acheson never quite understood the ruckus Republicans raised over the reverses America suffered in China and Korea. Eisenhower and Dulles knew Europe, to be sure, but both had experience of Asia their Democratic counterparts could not match. Eisenhower's time with MacArthur in Manila had sensitized him to the issues of the Asian balance of power, as well as to the particular difficulties of Philippine security. Dulles had negotiated the Japanese peace treaty and shepherded it past the suspicions of Japan's neighbors—including the Filipinos, who offered a variety of suggestions for improving the package that finally terminated the state of hostilities in the Far East.[1]

Of equal importance, Eisenhower and Dulles headed a party traditionally more committed to Asia than the Democrats. From William Seward, who gave America Asian frontage with the purchase of Alaska, through the Republican young turks of the 1890s—Roosevelt, Lodge, Beveridge—to Charles Evans Hughes of the Washington conference of 1921–22, the Republicans demonstrated consistent interest in the affairs of the Pacific and beyond. Republicans of the mid-twentieth century paid particular attention to China, partly because of the longstanding attraction of the semi-mythical China market to the business classes, partly because of the influence in the GOP of children of missionaries like Walter Judd and Henry Luce, partly because of the fact that the more conservative party took more seriously the communist victory in China, and partly because they perceived in China—and Asia generally—a blunt instrument for use against the Democrats. The last consideration figured centrally in Eisenhower's 1952 campaign, during which the candidate and Dulles harped on the failures of the Truman administration in China and Korea. Adlai Stevenson, an older and balder version of the John Kennedy who would scarcely squeeze to victory in 1960 past the utterly charisma-less Richard Nixon, may never have had a chance against the reassuring war hero Eisenhower, a Ronald Reagan with brains, though he often kept them hidden. But most observers reckoned that Eisenhower iced the contest with his campaign-climaxing pledge to "go to Korea" and right the botch the Democrats had made of America's Asian policy.

Ironically—and unfairly, in the Democratic view—the Republican's success in criticizing the Truman administration on Asia owed much to the Democrats' success in stabilizing Europe. By the early 1950s the central front of the Cold War had essentially achieved the permanence it would retain for forty years. So stable had the European situation become, in fact, that subsequent confrontations in the area were usually intramural affairs on one side or the other of the Elbe—the Suez flap among Britain, France and the United States in 1956; the Hungarian and Polish rebellions of the same year; France's defection from NATO in 1966; the Czech rising of 1968. Berlin would continue to irritate, but after the 1948 blockade and airlift its status as a soapbox outweighed its potential as a pillbox.

The turning to Asia that marked the Eisenhower years also followed from a heightening of American awareness regarding the importance of the emerging third world. The stalemate in Europe combined with growing restiveness among the colonized and otherwise dependent peoples of the planet to shift the superpowers' attention to Asia, Africa and Latin America. The late 1940s carried the Cold War to China and Asia's east coast. During the 1950s and 1960s the contagion spread, despite the strenuous prophylactic efforts of the coalescing nonaligned movement, through the rest of Asia, across the Red Sea to Africa, and across the Atlantic to Central America and the Caribbean.

Holding to the policy of containing communism they had embraced in the years just after the Second World War, American leaders might have been forced to make a stand in any of several locations along the shifting boundary between ideological east and west. As bad luck would have it, Indochina became the principal testing ground of the American interpretation of collective security. During the middle and late 1950s American leaders increasingly committed their country's prestige to the defense of South Vietnam. During the 1960s the commitment fell due, and America once more went to war.

In focusing American attention on Indochina, events there increased the value to the United States of a cooperative government in Manila. At the least Washington required stability in the Philippines. Victory in mainland Southeast Asia would avail little if the communists succeeded in a flanking maneuver offshore. More desirable was active involvement on the part of the Philippine government in support of American actions in Vietnam. Logistically the Philippines could serve as a staging ground for American operations across the South China Sea. Ideologically the Philippines' backing demonstrated the solidarity of the camp of democracy. Politically Manila's approval countered charges that the conflict in Vietnam was simply another imperialist war. Americans heard the charges so often that some came to doubt their own country's motives. They found Filipino refutations reassuring.

Not long after the 1952 American election an associate of Quirino wrote the Philippine president, "I do not believe that the new regime will be less friendly or sympathetic to our country than the old one." This prediction proved accurate. The Eisenhower administration soon demonstrated that it was fully as solicitous as the Democrats of the health of the Philippines. Unfortunately for Quirino the friendliness of the Republicans did not extend to the Philippine president himself.[2]

More than any administration before or since, Eisenhower's allowed the Central Intelligence Agency latitude to indulge its covert inclinations. In Iran and Guatemala the CIA staged operations that proved instrumental in the overthrow of governments. The agency laid plans to assassinate Cuba's Fidel Castro, the Congo's Patrice Lumumba, and perhaps Egypt's Gamal Abdel Nasser. Closer to the Philippines, the CIA fomented an armed revolt against the Sukarno regime in Indonesia in 1958. From 1954 onward American agents in Vietnam—including Edward Lansdale—engaged in activities designed to bolster Ngo Dinh Diem in the south and harass Ho Chi Minh in the north.

In the Philippines the CIA concentrated on two related objectives: winding up the war against the Huks and installing Magsaysay in Malacañang. The first goal was in sight when the Republicans arrived in office, thanks primarily to blunders on the part of the Huk leadership. In 1948 the brothers José and Jesus Lava had succeeded in gaining control of the politburo of the Philippine Communist party. A hard-core dialectical materialist, José Lava produced "An Analysis of the Developing Situation and Our Tasks," which purported to show that popular revulsion against the Quirino regime, fueled by the continuing economic crisis and the massive fraud and violence of the recent presidential election, had created a "revolutionary situation." The Communist party, as the vanguard of revolution, and the Huk army, as the military expression of the people's will, must strike while the opportunity existed.[3]

Lava got it wrong, falling victim to what a later writer on the left labeled "the impetuous petty bourgeois line of quick military victory." In the jargon, he mistook a "revolutionary mood" for a "revolutionary situation," meaning that although masses were upset with the status quo they were not ready to mount the barricades and storm the citadels of power. During the first half of 1950 the Huks achieved the series of military successes that had so alarmed the American advisory team, but the campaign failed to ignite the broad revolution Lava anticipated. When an informant in October 1950 tipped Magsaysay to the identities and whereabouts of the Communist and Huk leadership in Manila, Philippine intelligence forces essentially decapitated the urban wing of the insurgency, capturing several score rebels, including José Lava and the entire "PB In," the politburo inside the capital. Magsaysay complemented his Manila coup with increasingly successful forays against Huks in the countryside. As his military reforms proceeded the army grew more adept at tracking the insurgents, who were captured or killed in greater numbers every month. The leftist writer cited above described the eventual result: "The José Lava leadership was criminally responsible for the almost total obliteration of the People's Army within the short period of two years and for the most wanton sacrifice of the lives of Party cadres and Red soldiers in the entire history of the Communist Party of the Philippines."[4]

By the beginning of 1952 the rebellion was clearly dying. Following the Manila roundup the remaining Communist leadership—principally the "PB Out"—named Jesus Lava to succeed his brother as party secretary-general. The elevation of Jesus Lava indicated to Luis Taruc, commander-in-chief of the Huks since 1942, that the party hierarchy had learned nothing from the fiasco in Manila. Taruc had never been convinced of the prudence of a full-scale military effort. Now he grew more alienated by the party's support of kidnapping and murder of civilians. Recalling the situation afterward, Taruc remarked,

> The Huks began to lose the support of some of the barrio people in several regions where they had recently gained control. One reason was that when the peasants grew tired of giving away food, the Huks suspected them of having turned hostile and confiscated their rice and vegetables. Uncooperative peasants were often accused of associating with the enemy and treated as informers. Some of the "informers" were killed. And so the peasants' sympathy and loyalty began to turn into fear.

Sensing Taruc's softening attitude, Jesus Lava orchestrated his ouster from the military command. After Taruc called for a peaceful solution to the problems of the peasantry, the party suspended him. When he heard he was to be court-martialed for crimes against the people, Taruc decided he would be safer with his enemies than with his friends. He walked out of the mountains and turned himself in to the government.[5]

With the defeat of the Huks all but assured, Magsaysay entered the election campaign of 1953 in the enviable position of having saved the status quo from communist subversion, thereby gaining the approval of the ruling groups, and of having cleaned up the government, or at least his portion of it, thereby winning the plaudits of the people at large. That he ran against Quirino and the Liberal party machine added to his credibility as a reform candidate.

The campaign began in earnest in February when Magsaysay resigned as defense minister. "Under your concept of my duties as Secretary of National Defense, my job is just to go on killing Huks," Magsaysay complained to Quirino in quitting. "But you must realize that we cannot solve the problem of dissidence simply by military measures. It would be futile to go on killing Huks while the Administration continues to breed dissidence by neglecting the problems of our masses. The need for a vigorous assault upon these problems I have repeatedly urged upon you, but my pleas have fallen on deaf ears."[6]

Magsaysay's decision to try to tackle the masses' problems personally threw the country into an uproar. "Manila and the country are seething with politics," the American ambassador, Raymond Spruance, reported to the state department. "Rumors, plans, charges, and countercharges are heard from all quarters." With the polling still eight months away, Spruance anticipated significant rhetorical escalation. "The campaign will undoubtedly be tough and dirty, with no holds barred." It would probably be crooked as well, despite improvements the last time around. "The possibilities for coercive action and fraud are still strong."[7]

Although Spruance publicly denied a preference, saying the embassy would observe "strict neutrality" in the contest, Washington had no doubt whom it wished to win. American officials still held their noses in dealing with Quirino, and though they supported him against the Huks they did so only because he seemed the lesser of the two evils. Magsaysay, for a refreshing change, they could back with enthusiasm. He was honest, by Philippine standards certainly and even by the measure of American politics. He was young, energetic and personally appealing. "Magsaysay's My Guy" buttons became as popular in the Philippines as "I Like Ike" in America, and in the local pronunciation rhymed equally well. Best of all he was thoroughly pro-American.[8]

Fearing fraud by the Liberals and intending to leave nothing to chance, the CIA preempted efforts by Quirino's backers to steal the election by helping nail it down well in advance. Lansdale, with the firm support of CIA director Allen Dulles, acted as the candidate's de facto campaign manager. (Allen Dulles later reminisced to Lansdale about this period, when "we were working so closely together.") A first problem involved neutralizing opposition among the Nacionalistas. In fact the problem was only apparent, for Lansdale took the precaution ahead of time of gaining the agreement of Nacionalista leaders José Laurel and

Carlo Recto to support Magsaysay. Lest either man have second thoughts Lansdale got the agreement in writing and locked it in the embassy safe. Because the former collaborators Laurel and Recto were known to be strongly anti-American, the pact with Magsaysay made little apparent sense. Recto later explained his reasoning. "I thought it amusing to arrange a deal with the American military who spent most of their time unjustly defaming me. As for Ramón, he was so dumb I knew I could handle him." Events demonstrated the inaccuracy of Recto's estimate of Magsaysay, but not before Recto and Laurel delivered him the Nacionalista nomination.[9]

To offset the shake-down potential of the incumbent Liberals, Lansdale assisted Magsaysay in raising funds. Lansdale subsequently admitted to having access to $1 million for use in the campaign. He said he spent less than $60,000. (Reports of much higher figures he dismissed as a "fantasy" and a "fairy tale," although he commented that Magsaysay was partly responsible for spreading the story, as a device "to scare the opposition.") If Lansdale was telling the truth about his frugality, this simply indicated he thought Magsaysay did not need any more money. The candidate received a considerable amount, reportedly $250,000, from American businesses desiring strong Philippine-American ties. The American contributions contravened Philippine laws, and the ban cost Lansdale some effort. Speaking of the American money, Lansdale wrote former ambassador Myron Cowen, "One of the difficulties is getting the funds into the Philippines (which I think I can solve). Another is that local managers of U.S. firms want to help, but are damn afraid they will be found out." Lansdale added, "This is a real political battle going on out here and you don't win battles by sitting around." In the event Magsaysay did not lack cash. Philippine sugar interests, once convinced of the heft of his candidacy, contributed generously, eliminating money problems.[10]

Nor did Magsaysay lack angels of another sort. CIA analysts worried that Quirino intended to gain reelection, as an agency report put it, "by any means." Should the Liberals rig or otherwise disrupt the balloting, trouble might ensue. "There is a possibility that Nacionalista leaders, seeing the election stolen or about to be stolen, would ask for some form of American intervention." By coincidence—sort of—at this very moment the CIA was receiving Eisenhower's approval to stage a coup against the Mossadeq government in Iran. There, though, an eager successor had been identified. In Manila the situation appeared more problematic. "Magsaysay apparently has no intention or desire to head a rebellion or attempt a coup d'etat." Yet events might force his hand. "Should he be cheated of victory," the CIA report stated, ". . . a violent reaction is very likely and he could scarcely escape involvement in it."[11]

To obviate the need for a coup American officials set about guaranteeing a fair election. The CIA channeled money to NAMFREL, which pledged to supervise the balloting and guard against fraud. Agency operatives and the American embassy coordinated a public-relations offensive designed to elevate American interest in the election and ensure careful news coverage. The American military advisory group kept conspicuous watch on members of the Philippine army, making clear that ballot-stuffing or intimidation of Nacionalista voters would not go unnoticed. As a final reminder that Uncle Sam was watching, a group of American warships arrived off Manila just before the election.[12]

The effort achieved its dual objective: an honest count and a Magsaysay win. In fact the effort succeeded almost too well. Magsaysay buried Quirino by better than two to one, and while the magnitude of the margin demonstrated that Magsaysay's victory owed to considerably more than American machinations, observers were fully aware of the existence, if perhaps not the precise nature, of the American role in the outcome. Quirino complained of the activities of an unnamed "American colonel." The Indian ambassador in Manila told correspondents after the tally that the results "should cause a certain American colonel to change his name to 'Landslide.'" Claro Recto regularly applied the sobriquet to Lansdale, especially after Recto discovered that Magsaysay was harder to manipulate than he had anticipated. Even some of Lansdale's Filipino friends joined the fun, secretly changing his uniform nameplate to "Landslide," an alteration he did not immediately notice. "The nickname dogged me for some years," Lansdale half-complained afterward.[13]

II.   Manila contra Munich

After years of expecting little from Philippine leaders, American officials had great hopes for Magsaysay. Lansdale was elated at the victory of the man he considered the hammer of the Huks and the broom of Philippine politics. Spruance concurred, telling José Laurel that with Magsaysay now in charge of the entire government rather than merely the defense ministry, the few Huks still causing trouble did not stand a chance. The ambassador added that he knew Magsaysay would not countenance the graft in government that had made Quirino infamous.[14]

American officials in Washington were no less pleased at Magsaysay's triumph. Eisenhower, who had called the Philippine election a "vital test of democracy" and had been regularly apprised of campaign developments by CIA director Allen Dulles, read the results with satisfaction. Eisenhower expressed hope that Magsaysay would select "a really dedicated cabinet of honest and patriotic men" and instructed John Foster Dulles "to do everything possible" to help the Philippine president. CIA analysts declared, "Prospects for good government are brighter than ever." Allen Dulles described Magsaysay's election as "one of the most important and favorable developments for the United States in the Far East for a long time." The intelligence chief told the National Security Council that

Magsaysay's victory offered "the means of developing a much greater solidarity among the free countries of the Far East against Communism."[15]

Magsaysay soon fulfilled American expectations. He snuffed out the last significant smolderings of Huk resistance, so that by the beginning of 1954 the chief of the American advisory group could write the Pentagon that the insurgency had declined to the point where the Philippine military could leave the problem to civilian law-enforcement authorities. On the score of resistance to foreign communism, Magsaysay proved even more reliable than the Americans had guessed. Claro Recto snidely but not unjustifiedly described Magsaysay's diplomacy as "paul-revering all over the Western free world to awaken it to the menace of Asiatic communism." Carlos García, Magsaysay's vice president and foreign minister, naturally adopted a more favorable view. In García's words, the Philippine president displayed a "steadfast and unflinching allegiance to the banners of the free." At a time when much of Asia was distancing itself from the United States, Magsaysay refused to be swept along. García declared,

> For him none of the deviousness of the opportunist or the equivocality of "neutralism." For him and his people the only course to follow was the course of honor and sincerity; the only path to tread was the path of friendship and alliance with the free forces of the free world, particularly the leader and champion thereof, the United States of America.[16]

Magsaysay's administration missed few opportunities to demonstrate its solidarity with the United States. Washington received consistent Philippine support in the United Nations. At the 1955 Bandung conference of Asian and African countries, Philippine delegates refused to accept the nonalignment promoted by India's prime minister Jawaharlal Nehru, so irritating Indian delegate V. K. Krishna Menon that he charged Carlos Romulo—perhaps accurately—with deliberately leaking unsavory stories about Nehru. During the Taiwan Strait crisis of the same year, which cast Washington, in most Asian eyes, as a warmonger, Magsaysay announced forthrightly, "We stand squarely behind the United States." An assurance by Romulo to John Foster Dulles encapsulated the position of the Magsaysay government. "You can always depend on the Philippines," Romulo said.[17]

During the middle 1950s, what Washington most depended on the Philippines for was political support in Southeast Asia. Earlier, with the help of other United Nations members, including the Philippines, the United States had succeeded in securing South Korea against communist encroachment. But no sooner had the cadres of Kim Il Sung and Mao Zedong accepted a ceasefire in Korea than the followers of Ho Chi Minh put the French to flight in Vietnam. Although the Geneva conference of 1954 stilled the guns in Indochina and separated Vietnam into communist and noncommunist zones, the division was supposed to be temporary. All involved and watching anticipated that the struggle would continue.

The Eisenhower administration prepared for the next battle by attempting the extension of the American network of anticommunist alliances into Southeast Asia. Unfortunately for American plans, few of the likely Southeast Asian candidates for partnership wished anything to do with Washington's scheme. Manila was a notable exception, and from the American perspective a crucial one. From the time of the signing of the North Atlantic treaty in 1949 the Philippine government had expressed interest in what Quirino called a "parallel safeguard for Asia." Washington initially responded with skepticism. Indeed Romulo reported that American officials were "greatly disturbed" over Manila's efforts to talk up a Pacific pact. At a moment when the Truman administration was doing its best to divert attention from China, it found Quirino's assertion of a "pressing and urgent" need for action to prevent further communist advances in Asia decidedly unhelpful.[18]

Through the end of 1949 the Philippine quest for an American security guarantee continued to be what Romulo described to Quirino as "a difficult and uphill fight." That Quirino opened discussions with Chiang Kai-shek on the subject of a Pacific alliance without consulting Washington did not make the fight easier. As an official at the state department told Romulo, "Nobody will believe the United States had nothing to do with it." Yet in one sense the Truman administration's discomfiture gratified the Filipinos, who expected an uneasy Washington to be more pliable on the issue that lay at the heart of Manila's interest in a security organization: American aid. Writing to Quirino, Romulo remarked, "Your conference with Chiang has placed the initiative in your hands."[19]

The outbreak of the Korean War pushed Washington in the direction of a Pacific pact. The impetus Korea provided was indirect but threefold. In the first place, it prompted American officials to speed the diplomatic rehabilitation of Japan by the negotiation of a prompt and mild peace treaty. As payment for the acquiescence of Japan's neighbors in such a settlement Washington agreed to underwrite their security. The ANZUS accord with Australia and New Zealand formed one part of the payoff. Increased American aid to Manila and a 1951 U.S.-Philippines mutual defense treaty formed another.

The second aspect of the push Korea provided toward a Pacific pact had to do with the significance American officials read into the North Korean invasion. Taking their cue from the failure of appeasement during the 1930s, Washington determined to stand fast against aggression, however small the immediate stakes or remote the location. In the American mind a direct path connected the Sudeten crisis of 1938 to the German invasion of Poland the following year. The process of aggression was now repeating itself in the Pacific, or at least it would if the democratic powers did not act decisively. Decisive action might include a Pacific pact.

The third connection between Korea and a Pacific pact followed from Truman's decision, upon the commencement of fighting in Korea, to step up American aid to the French in Indochina. From 1950 the defense of Indochina against the communists increasingly became an American responsibility. Before long the United States was funding the major portion of France's vain endeavor to halt the insurgency. A Pacific pact would help shore up Indochina.

Although a Pacific security treaty, or something fulfilling the same purpose, was implicit in the actions of the Truman administration, not until Eisenhower and Dulles assumed charge of American foreign policy did the implications take concrete form. The delay was not the Filipinos' fault. Romulo repeatedly asked Acheson for what he called "the firmest and broadest arrangements for Pacific defense." During one conversation of August 1952 Romulo reminded Acheson how the Philippines had "endeavored to mediate between the West and the embattled East." He added, "On the basis of this record, the Philippines feels that it has a natural and primordial interest in the planning and organization of a collective security system in the Western Pacific."[20]

"We are working on it," Assistant Secretary of State John Allison told Romulo ten days later. The work went slowly, though, and the Democrats left office with little progress made.[21]

The advent of the Republicans gave Manila new hope. Recognizing the Eisenhower administration's greater interest in Asian affairs, the Filipinos lost no time promoting their plans for a broader American commitment to Southeast Asia and the Philippines. Romulo did not even wait for Eisenhower's inauguration before raising the issue of a "Pacific NATO" with Dulles. Romulo told the secretary-designate that President Quirino was "vitally interested" in the matter and hoped Washington would agree to move ahead swiftly. In January 1953 Romulo repeated the message to Eisenhower.[22]

At this stage Washington was interested but not vitally so. Opposition came principally from American military leaders who resisted having to deal with another bureaucracy of the sort NATO was producing in Europe. The Pentagon preferred bilateral arrangements with the countries of the Pacific rim, a strategy that ensured America's freedom of action by allowing Washington to treat each small partner individually. For exactly this reason the government of the Philippines, joined by Australia and New Zealand, desired a more comprehensive organization, one in which the lesser countries might make common cause.

As the French position in Indochina slowly crumbled, and with most countries of Asia keeping their distance from the western colonialists and their American allies, the Eisenhower administration decided to compromise on the issue of a Pacific pact. While the French continued to struggle against the Viet Minh at Dienbienphu, Eisenhower and Dulles attempted to line up support for multilateral military action, especially with Britain, to assist France. The British proved unenthusiastic about attempting a military solution to the Indochina problem. So did the American Congress, which desired to avoid another Korea. Yet London did agree to a joint diplomatic approach, in the form of a security guarantee for whatever portion of Southeast Asia remained noncommunist after a French defeat. A strictly American-British-French arrangement for Southeast Asia, however, smacked too much of continuing colonialism for Washington's tastes. Consequently the Eisenhower administration now accepted Manila's standing proposal for a multilateral Pacific pact.

This time it was the Filipinos' turn to be coy. On different occasions the Philippine government had tossed up various Asian candidates for inclusion: Taiwan, Japan, Indonesia, Burma, Thailand, India and Pakistan, among others. When most of the candidates withdrew or were disqualified Manila faced the likelihood of appearing a token Asian country in a security system dominated by the westerners. In August 1954 Magsaysay expressed to Dulles his concern at the political difficulties this would cause in the Philippines. Magsaysay did not say he wished to back out, but he did insist on a "clearer definition" of America's commitment to the Philippines, something he could use to counter his critics. In particular he hoped for an American pledge to an organization modeled on NATO.[23]

No one in Washington intended to go all the way to a Pacific NATO, with its joint military command and planning apparatus. Some questioned the necessity for any multilateral organization. Charlton Ogburn of the state department asked, "How, for example, could such an organization have contributed to the defeat of the Communist threat in the Philippines in 1950? Could it have added anything to the highly successful joint efforts of the anti-Communist Filipinos and Americans?" Ogburn thought not. He feared that in the rush to throw something in the way of further communist expansion the United States was buying bills of goods from the British, who were more worried about preserving their imperial enclave of Hong Kong than about safeguarding democracy; from the French, who wanted American backing for a continued sphere of influence in southern Vietnam and Laos and Cambodia, and who could be relied upon for cynicism in any diplomatic endeavor; and from the Filipinos, who while genuinely fearing a communist takeover of mainland Southeast Asia looked upon Washington chiefly as a never-ending source of military and economic aid.[24]

Dulles disagreed. Judging multilateralism a symbol of free-world unity, the secretary of state accepted Magsaysay's offer to host negotiations for what became the Manila pact, or, informally and misleadingly, the Southeast Asia Treaty Organization (SEATO). The discussions were tedious. The American delegates attempted to commit themselves to as little as possible. The representatives of the other countries—the Philippines, Britain, France, Australia, New Zealand, Thailand and Pakistan—sought to pledge the United States to much. Dulles, whose personal memory stretched back to the 1919 debate over the League of Nations and who repeatedly avoided provoking Congress, resisted any automatic war trigger. War declarations, he said, must be in accord with the constitutional processes of the signatories. Carlos García complained that such narrow legalism was dangerously outdated. With the world war and the Japanese occupation still evident in the Philippine countryside, Filipinos needed to hear an unequivocal American promise.

> Those of us who are, so to speak, or are likely to be, in the frontline in case of war, as shown in past experiences, must insist that when we are attacked, that attack shall be repelled by all and instantly, because, during these times when the atomic and hydrogen bombs and other weapons of that type will be likely used, if we are to depend on constitutional processes, we may all be wiped out in this Archipelago before action is taken.[25]

Dulles refused to accept the Philippine position, although he privately reassured Magsaysay that "an attack on the Philippines is an attack also on the United States." Neither did Dulles accede to Filipino wishes to extend the multilateral defense treaty into a NATO-style organization—hence the misleadingness of the label SEATO. In addition, he made clear that the United States was pledging itself only to resist communist aggression and did not intend automatic involvement in other quarrels signatories might get into. (He particularly wanted to disabuse Pakistan that it would come to Karachi's aid in another fight with India.) But Dulles did agree to a proposal by the Philippine delegation to annex to the accord a "Pacific charter," analogous to the Atlantic charter of 1941, calling for self-determination of peoples in the Pacific area. The result, embodied in a treaty signed in September 1954, satisfied Filipino demands for a greater role in Pacific planning. The Americans likewise thought it sufficient to their needs. "We got what we wanted," Dulles remarked upon returning to Washington.[26]

III.   Parity repairs

While Washington applauded Magsaysay's defeat of the Huks and generally appreciated his handling of Philippine foreign policy—"There is not in the whole world a more vigorous champion of liberty as against the menace of Communist despotism," Dulles declared of Magsaysay—American officials had reservations regarding certain Philippine domestic issues. A report written for Eisenhower's National Security Council at about the time of the Manila conference remarked, "The election of Magsaysay has not resulted in an area of wide agreement or mutual good feeling as had been anticipated by some observers." In a case similar to one of three decades later, when another corrupt incumbent fell to a popular challenger, the buoyant optimism of election day had given way to the hard reality that removing the crook at the top effected little change in the system that made his thievery possible. Quirino was gone, but the elite of entrenched privilege remained. Magsaysay could beat Quirino in a fair election. Transforming the status quo was another matter entirely.[27]

To a certain extent Magsaysay had himself to blame. A CIA analyst writing some while afterward remarked, "It is an axiom of Philippine politics that a presidential candidate cannot win on an anti-American platform. At the same time, no Philippine president wishes to be accused of not protecting the national interest, especially where the United States is concerned." The first part of the analyst's statement gradually lost force as years passed, although even in the 1980s and early 1990s the ability to deliver American good will, and American aid, counted for something, often much, on the hustings. The second part of the statement has admitted of no exceptions since the days of the commonwealth. Magsaysay, failing to heed it sufficiently, found himself charged with subservience to Washington. From the American ambassador and from other American advisers he sought advice that even a staffer for Eisenhower's NSC said "he properly should obtain from leaders within his own administration." Washington did not help matters by allowing Lansdale, since reassigned to Saigon, to visit Manila. Claro Recto, now an ardent opponent of the Magsaysay administration, hooted at the return of "General Landslide"—the colonel having been promoted. John Foster Dulles acknowledged the blunder to Eisenhower. "We let him go experimentally for a vacation from Vietnam, which he needed," Dulles said. "The result, however, has been counterproductive."[28]

If Magsaysay's critics complained when he looked to the Americans for advice, none objected when he turned to Washington to seek redress of Philippine grievances against the United States. A primary irritant involved the perennial sticker of economic relations between the two countries. In the aftermath of independence the Philippines had seemed well positioned to prosper. War damage needed to be repaired, of course, but the United States had committed itself to major rehabilitation assistance. Further, the Japanese threat that during the 1930s had forced the Quezon government to divert resources away from the productive sectors of the economy had vanished. To the degree challenges to Philippine external security developed Washington appeared primed to deal with them. The parity provision of the Bell trade act chafed, yet it also opened the country to the foreign investment that would facilitate growth.

Unfortunately prosperity did not materialize. Part of the failure resulted from complications in assessing war damage and processing claims for payment from the United States. Filipinos considered stingy a clause in the rehabilitation agreement by which the American Congress set payments for destroyed property at face value or replacement value, whichever was *less*. Part of the failure owed to the Huk rebellion, which distracted the Roxas and Quirino administrations from economic matters. More important, by challenging the legitimacy of the system of landlord-tenant relationships the rebellion caused the landlords to circle their wagons and resist the sorts of reforms that might have spurred productivity in the agricultural sector. In greatest part the economic stagnation followed from the corruption and mismanagement that marked Liberal rule. The government spent as though its revenues were limitless, yet taxed as though it had no expenses. The taxes it did legislate it often failed to collect. At one level the consequence was an enormous and growing government deficit: 461 million pesos by 1950, or nearly twice the average annual tax take during the postwar period to date. At another, more serious level the result was widespread loss of confidence in the ability of the political process to deal with the problems of the country's economy.[29]

A balance-of-payments crisis in 1949, combined with the increasing inroads of the Huks, convinced Quirino that action was necessary to stem the slide. He agreed to American demands that he allow a visit by an American advisory mission, no doubt hoping that further aid would follow. The Bell mission—named for mission chairman Daniel Bell, not Jasper Bell of the trade act—arrived in June 1950 with pencils in hand and eyeshades on brow. After five months studying the Philippine economy in field, shop and library, the Bell group filed a report that put the matter in undramatic but unmistakable language. "Economic conditions in the Philippines are unsatisfactory. The economic situation has been deteriorating in the past two years and the factors that have brought this about cannot be expected to remedy themselves." The report called for swift action. "Whatever is to be done to improve economic conditions in the Philippines must be done promptly, for if the situation is allowed to drift there is no certainty that moderate remedies will suffice." The problem had reached the stage where it could soon transcend economics. Absent rapid amelioration "political disorder will inevitably result."[30]

The changes the Bell report advocated included tax increases, controls on transactions in foreign currencies, a minimum wage law, various administrative improvements and land reform. The enticement it offered was $250 million in American aid.

Within weeks Quirino accepted the deal. He delivered a portion of his side of the package. In the first half of 1951 he persuaded the Philippine legislature to approve a new corporate income tax, a tax on certain currency transactions and a minimum wage. He also accepted the appointment of an American advisory group to oversee improvements in administrative efficiency.

But on the issue of land reform, ever the crux of Philippine economic, political and social troubles, nothing happened. The landholding elite could go along with certain of the Bell requirements with relative equanimity, if only because taxes and minimum-wage laws might be evaded. Redistributing land, however, struck at the foundation of the elite's power. On this question the landlords and their political allies stoutly resisted pressure for change.

Washington declined to force the issue. American officials recognized, as they had since the days of Taft, the usefulness of the Filipino upper class. At a moment when communism had just swallowed half of Asia and seemed set to gobble the rest, Washington had little inclination to alienate the most reliably anticommunist group in the Philippines.

Luckily for the landlords and Washington both, the Philippine economy revived in the early 1950s even without land reform. The revival had less to do with implementation of the other aspects of the Bell report than with the Korean War and the strong market it created for Philippine exports. Aid from America— Quirino got credit, and grants too, for what Washington deemed a good try on the Bell deal—did not hurt either. The collapse of the Huk insurgency and the election of Magsaysay improved investor confidence. As in the case of the roof that leaks only in the rain, the return of prosperity eased pressure for land reform and other fundamental fixes. American and Filipino officials could and did turn to less testy issues.

These included revision of the 1946 Bell trade act. The 1950 Bell report claimed that the act placed artificial and now outdated restrictions on trade and investment, to the mutual disadvantage of Filipinos and Americans. Quirino agreed, at the instance of business interests in the Philippines benefiting from American investment and seeking extended preference for Philippine exports in American markets. The Truman administration consented in principle to trade revision, but the distractions it faced in other areas prevented progress, and the Democrats departed with the job unbegun. Quirino quickly took the matter up with the incoming Eisenhower administration. An election approached, and Quirino desired presents to deliver to his supporters. Yet as with the Pacific pact, Washington did not get around to serious discussion of the trade issue until the crisis in Indochina alerted American officials to the immediate need for friends in the South China Sea. Although the dawdling of Eisenhower and Dulles on trade revision had little to do with their preference for Magsaysay over Quirino, a reasonable inference by interested Filipinos that the candidate obviously preferred by Washington might make a better bargain on trade certainly did not hurt the challenger's chances.[31]

When talks began, Magsaysay's chief negotiator, José Laurel, once more proved his flexibility. Laurel worked on influential American officials, providing gift-wrapped samples of the Philippines' products, especially cigars, to legislators, cabinet members and bureaucrats. He sent Eisenhower birthday greetings. He hosted dinners and receptions for administration notables. He caused many in Washington to wonder how such a nice fellow could have collaborated with the Japanese and said those nasty things about the United States.[32]

Laurel was no nicer than before, merely as calculating. He laid out his strategy for dealing with the Americans in a letter to Magsaysay. The Philippine position now, he said, as on more than one occasion in the past, must be to play competing American factions against each other. In addition the Philippine government should remind the Americans what Philippine economic health meant for them:

> The powerful industrialists of the East will again be facing the no less powerful farm bloc of the West and the cotton and oil interests of the South, in a manner similar to the fight which was waged when the Jones Act and later the Tydings-McDuffie

Act were being discussed. . . . It should be our strategy to cater to the interests which might favor our cause for their own sake and to the independents who hold the balance of power. . . . It will require the right kind of publicity on such topics as our stand on communism and our requirements to have a sound and healthy economy.[33]

The negotiations went slowly, with issues beyond trade falling onto the table. Laurel pressed for larger payments for war damages, for interest charges on Philippine gold stored in America since before the war, for arrears due Filipinos who had enlisted in the American army and for American assistance in collecting reparations from Japan. Laurel himself felt the influence of Philippine sugar producers who insisted on extension of the free-trade provisions of the Bell Act. Philippine supporters of American investment in the Philippines sought guarantees for American capital. J. M. Elizalde, the wealthy Quezonista, looked past the current negotiations and told Laurel, "The thing, to my mind, that should be uppermost in our overall planning after the passage of the bill updating the Bell trade act is the scheme to attract more American investment to the Philippines." Prudent handling of the matter, Elizalde said, "might well mean future prosperity for our country and people."[34]

Laurel sought to wrap trade and other issues into the more fundamental question of Philippine independence. In numerous and usually amicable discussions with his American opposite number, James Langley—"a good man," Laurel remarked privately—Laurel stressed the connection of trade issues to the matter of independence. "The United States cannot grant independence and at the same time deny it," he told Langley; and to strengthen independence he sought removal of the parity clause. But parity and Philippine independence were both collateral to the immediately essential "$64 question," as Ambassador Spruance phrased the matter. "What is the ultimate situation envisaged for July 1954?," Spruance asked, referring to the end of free trade as specified by the Bell Act. "Is the Philippines then to continue to have some special trade relations with United States, or is it to be entirely divorced and to receive most-favored-nation treatment only?"[35]

Negotiations leading to the Tydings Act had demonstrated that when agents of American businesses started to work on American Philippines legislation their demands carried more weight than those of the Filipinos. For this reason Laurel moved cautiously. He acted according to Elizalde's advice: "Too much interference in Congress, particularly by American lobbyists, may prove detrimental to our interests." Success, Elizalde said, would result from working "very quietly and smoothly."[36]

If nothing else Laurel was smooth, and the negotiations eventually produced an agreement that afforded quietly significant advantages to Philippine vested interests. The principal changes the Laurel-Langley accord specified in the area of trade were a deceleration in the rate at which Philippine exports to the United

States would be subject to American tariffs and an acceleration in the rate at which American exports to the Philippines would be subject to Philippine imposts. Both provisions benefited Philippine producers.

Other clauses were more cosmetic. The absolute American quotas on Philippine goods other than sugar and abaca cordage were replaced by duty-free quotas. This concession to Philippine producers came at little cost to Americans, since actual imports had yet to reach quota levels. On those items—namely sugar and cordage—that quotas had restricted, absolute ceilings remained. The peso was detached from the dollar, allowing Manila to set the exchange level for itself. In practice, however, foreign constraints, as from the American-dominated International Monetary Fund, discouraged devaluation.

On the emotional question of parity the two sides succeeded in defusing the issue without substantially altering the status quo. Although Laurel had desired parity's elimination, he ultimately accepted retention provided that parity be applied to Filipinos in the United States as well as to Americans in the Philippines. This solution satisfied those Filipinos like Elizalde who desired to encourage American investment while eliminating the onus of nonreciprocality. Magsaysay and his associates could defend the accord as a blow for Philippine nationalism, and they did. Magsaysay publicly congratulated Laurel for accomplishing a goal "most necessary and vital to the future of our country." Because Filipino investment in the United States was very small compared with American investment in the Philippines, in practice reciprocity cost Americans almost nothing.[37]

The significance of the Laurel-Langley agreement, which the Philippine legislature ratified at once and the American Congress more slowly, consisted in the indication it provided of American willingness to satisfy the demands of Filipino elites so long as those demands did not carry an inordinate price tag. To the degree the Filipinos came out ahead in the bargain, the accord represented payment for the cooperativeness of the Magsaysay government.

14

The Ground Softens
1957–1964

I. Regression to the mean

Washington and Manila have never got along better than during the years of the Magsaysay administration. In foreign affairs the Philippine government consistently supported American initiatives, from the Manila pact through the Taiwan Strait crisis and the Bandung conference and on numerous lesser issues. Magsaysay was the epitome of what Washington was looking for in an Asian leader, the model it held up for its other client countries. Edward Lansdale reported from Saigon in 1954 that President Diem and his South Vietnamese associates were taking the lesson to heart. "To them, you are the really great man of Asia," Lansdale wrote Magsaysay, "way above Rhee or Chiang." American officials had a few quibbles regarding Magsaysay's handling of domestic Philippine matters. They might have wished less conspicuous reliance on American advice, which made both governments look bad, and a firmer hand on the economy. But they recognized the boundaries of Magsaysay's freedom of action. As Washington's approval of the Laurel-Langley accord demonstrated, the Eisenhower administration was willing to make concessions to help keep him popular.[1]

For this reason Magsaysay's sudden death in an airplane crash in March 1957 came as a double tragedy. The Philippines lost a promising leader, one who though not perfect was several cuts above the norm in the country's politics. The United States lost a reliable ally who could proclaim his adherence to the ideals of democracy without making Americans wince. Eisenhower's assistant secretary of state for East Asia, Walter Robertson, had not had to exaggerate much to tell Magsaysay, after a visit to Manila, "It is obvious even to a casual observer the bond of confidence and affection which binds you to your own people. And you must know from the innumerable testimonies given you both in person and in the press of the universal esteem and confidence in which you are held in the outside world." The *New York Times* mourned Magsaysay's death in terms indicating the highest respect and deepest sorrow:

> With good reason the Filipinos have often called him "Our Abraham Lincoln." They have recognized those same homely virtues, that massive integrity, that humble warmth of heart that make a man able to lead because he is both honored and truly loved. . . . It is not only the Philippines but the whole free world that has been bereaved.[2]

A giant would have found Magsaysay's place difficult to fill, not least since that place grew with each tearful telling. Giants are never plentiful, in the Philippines or elsewhere, and Magsaysay's vice president, Carlos García, was not among them. At the time of García's nomination for the number-two position on the Nacionalista ticket a rival stepped aside with the comment, "Everybody knows a Vice President's job is to wait for the President to die. I am afraid Magsaysay is a very healthy man and would make a healthier President." The remark, as it pertained to the vice presidency, missed the point. A vice president's first and most important job is to become vice president by getting the president elected. García, a Nacionalista regular, added party respectability to the arriviste Magsaysay. He was also known to deliver the votes, which he did with a flair, running half a million ahead of the Liberal vice-presidential candidate.

In recognition of García's polling-day service Magsaysay appointed him foreign secretary. The nomination followed a precedent established when Roxas made his vice-president, Quirino, simultaneously foreign secretary. Nor did the choice lack logic. García had served on the Philippine delegation to the United Nations, and as a member of the Philippine senate he had taken an active interest in international affairs. Whatever his qualifications or experience, García in office had little to do with the foreign relationship that mattered most to the Philippine government. When Magsaysay had matters to discuss with the Americans he usually dialed direct to Washington, working through Romulo or special envoys like Laurel, or he brought the American ambassador to Malacañang, or he talked to Lansdale or other CIA personnel.[3]

As vice presidents accidently elevated are wont to do, in the Philippines as in the United States, García immediately pledged to carry on the work of the fallen hero. But because 1957 brought an election to the Philippines, others soon promised to do likewise, only better. Amid what a Philippines-watcher at the American embassy called "rampant" speculation regarding the succession there developed what another American analyst characterized as a "confused partisan political struggle." Although García had no difficulty claiming the nomination of his party, the Nacionalistas had considerably greater trouble picking a vice-presidential nominee. The convention failed to give the usually required two-thirds'

majority to any contender. Binding arbitration eventually delivered the nomination to José Laurel, Jr., son of the wartime president, not especially popular but
a wielder of major clout within the party.[4]

At the beginning of 1957 the Liberals, in disarray since their 1953 thrashing,
were not even sure they wanted to field a candidate in the fall. Magsaysay's death
changed their minds. For president they nominated José Yulo, a sugar planter
and lawyer. For vice president they picked Diosdado Macapagal, a self-made politician in the Magsaysay mold who despite being in opposition had strongly supported many of Magsaysay's measures in the legislature. Other presidential candidates in a crowded field included Antonio Quirino, the younger brother of the
now-deceased Elpidio; Manuel Manahan, a journalist-turned-Magsaysay-pro-
gressive; and Claro Recto.

Election day brought no landslide, as in 1953, but it did produce a typhoon, a
spate of killings and utter confusion. García defeated Yulo for president by
600,000 votes of not quite five million cast, yet Macapagal defeated Laurel by
400,000. Because the vice-presidential candidates ran separately from the presidential nominees, as had been the case in America in the days of John Adams
and Thomas Jefferson, the result was a Nacionalista president and a Liberal vice
president. To confuse the issue further Macapagal garnered more votes than García, so if anyone could claim a popular mandate, it was the vice president.

In light of the fact that both victors stood in the Magsaysay tradition, a continuance of that tradition by the García-Macapagal administration surprised no one.
Unfortunately García inherited Magsaysay's problems without his predecessor's
prestige. By 1957 the Korean War–induced boom in the Philippine economy had
faded beyond effect. American aid was diminishing. The house-cleaning impetus
that had helped Magsaysay gain power had dissipated. As in the bad old Quirino
days the government's give exceeded its take by several hundred million pesos.
Once more an excess of imports over exports precipitated a balance-of-payments
crisis, yet a cursory glance at the life-style of the stylish indicated that the upper
classes were finding ways around conditions that put a pinch on everyone else.

In 1957 the Philippine legislature passed a measure that would have facilitated
imports by those who also produced for export. The putative justification for the
bill was the stimulus it would provide to the economy even as it retained overall
controls on imports. Skeptics judged it simply a device for those with pull to continue their spending spree. Opponents included García, who vetoed the measure.
García's veto followed partly from the fact that Magsaysay had pledged to kill
the measure before he died and partly from García's adoption of an attitude of
economic nationalism, what he called a "Filipino First" policy. This policy in
turn reflected García's dependence on that portion of the Filipino elite possessing
manufacturing interests—as distinct from the landed classes that had tended to
support Yulo—and which stood to lose from an increase in imports.

In addition, García's veto of the import-liberalization measure owed to a desire to keep import licenses and the sub rosa revenues they generated under his personal control. García could interpret the results of the 1957 election as well as anyone else. Accurately guessing that he would not be reelected, he chose to enrich himself while he could. Customs kickbacks soon merged with other schemes for private profit-taking, and before long his administration was breaking records for corruption established under Quirino.[5]

García knew that such shenanigans would not sit well with officials of the Eisenhower administration who, as García may or may not have known, were keeping abreast of the less obvious malfeasances of García's grafters with the assistance of none other than Vice President Macapagal, a regular informant for the CIA. To mitigate American distress García applied a proven pacifier. He made himself more anticommunist than the McCarthyites.[6]

As a first measure García took on the Philippine Communist party. For many years the Communists, now generally known by their Tagalog initials PKP, had inhabited legal limbo. Occasionally outlawed, at other times they engaged in normal political activities. After the war the party had even elected representatives to the Philippine congress, although the legislature refused to seat them. During the Huk rebellion and under Magsaysay, Communists had been prosecuted for seditious activities, but mere membership was not grounds for imprisonment. García remedied this oversight. He initiated legislation banning the party entirely, and the congress approved.

Upon signing the anticommunist measure into law García declared, "We are serving the cause of the Free World as well as our own best interests." The remark was intended for an American audience, as were assorted other statements and actions designed to demonstrate the value of the García administration to Washington. García embraced, literally, America's client in South Vietnam, Diem, on a 1958 visit by the latter to the Philippines. García lauded the man who had refused to allow elections specified by the 1954 Geneva accords for Vietnam and who was establishing an increasingly authoritarian regime in Saigon as "the liberator of his people and one of the recognized leaders of democracy in Asia." In a letter to John Foster Dulles the Philippine president spoke fervently of "our mutual endeavors to preserve our democratic ideals against the threats of international communism." On a trip to America García defended Dulles against European carping. "Some critics among our western allies have complained that he is too inflexible," García said of the secretary of state. "But we the small countries that have known at first hand the infinite capacity of the enemy for deceit consider this inflexibility as the very armor and shield of our freedom." When Eisenhower traveled to Manila in 1960 García presented the Philippines: "Here, Mr. President, is a nation that stands for all America stands for in the way of the greatest human values—freedom, democracy, and the brotherhood of men."[7]

García's representative in Washington, Carlos Romulo, besides lobbying legislators and administration officials on the usual subjects—American aid, sugar quotas, war damage claims—likewise tried to conjure a benign image to cover the grafting of the García gang. The Philippine ambassador highlighted and rebroadcast favorable comment in the press and in Congress, such as a statement by House Republican Joseph Martin describing García as "this pro-American Filipino who refused to surrender to Japan during the war and preferred to risk his life with the resistance movement." With the cooperation of friendly journalists he convinced Eisenhower that a presidential trip to the Philippines would be a personal triumph. It proved a success for García as well, who thanked Romulo for his efforts in producing the "glorious Eisenhower visit." Romulo cultivated relations with the retired but still influential Douglas MacArthur. Working the other side of the political fence, he arranged the burial in the Philippines of Francis Burton Harrison, whom García lauded as being to Filipinos what Lafayette was to Americans.[8]

While Romulo publicly endorsed the attachment of García and the Philippine government to American policies, the ambassador was not unable to question certain aspects of those policies. In the summer of 1959 a communist insurgency was bubbling in Laos, hinting at the broader turmoil that once more would convulse Indochina. Eisenhower pronounced Laos the principal trouble spot in Southeast Asia, and American officials were seeking to prevent Vietnamese communists and the indigenous Pathet Lao from destabilizing the country. Romulo wondered if the Americans knew what they were getting into. "Ever since 'The Ugly American,'" he wrote, referring to the book that featured a novelized Edward Lansdale, "the American mood has been that action of some sort in those outlying Asian regions is better than no action at all. Against the dynamism of the Communists there is certainly a need for some sort of Western dynamism, although the dangerous commitments the American representatives have made in Laos seem to be rather sad examples of it." Romulo did not doubt that communist successes in Laos would redound to the advantage of Moscow and Beijing, but he questioned whether the Americans understood the differing interests of the major communist powers or the degree to which the North Vietnamese acted independently of their communist allies. Romulo told Philippine foreign secretary Felixberto Serrano,

> My own view is that while the Communist world empire is still in the making, there are maneuvers for position within it. Laos, along with North Vietnam, is still an unclaimed area, in the sense that it has become neither wholly a Russian nor wholly a Chinese sphere of influence. Both, however, are jockeying for it, and neither dares to say to Ho Chi Minh, the boss of Vietnam, whether or when he decides to make a bid for a revolution-plus-civil-war-plus-invasion in Laos.

Romulo did take heart from the growing interest of the United Nations in the Laos affair—an attitude not surprising in a man who had served as president of the General Assembly. "If this had happened during the Czech crisis more than twenty years ago, the history of the world might have been different," Romulo asserted. "In all the vast darkness that engulfs us, there are glimmers of light, and the United Nations action is one."[9]

II.   Touching bases

At the same time that Romulo was wishing for greater American reliance on the United Nations to resolve the troubles of Indochina, Washington was moving in the opposite direction. Colonial devolution in the late 1950s and early 1960s wrought a sea-change in the composition of the General Assembly, which Washington—with signal help from President Romulo—had dominated a decade earlier. The successor states of Asia and Africa usually refused American guidance. With the Security Council, where the Russians wielded a veto, likewise useless as an instrument of American diplomacy, American policy-makers lost interest in the United Nations. In cases where they thought significant American interests at risk they preferred to make their own security provisions. This was the message of the Manila pact.

It was also the reason for America's insistence on maintaining a strong military position in the Philippines. The Cold War's arrival in East Asia in the late 1940s had erased from American minds the possibility of a pullout from the Philippines. The conflict's spread into Southeast Asia during the 1950s made American bases in the Philippines appear more vital than ever. An analysis produced by the office of the American chief of naval operations for the joint chiefs of staff summarized the Pentagon's attitude toward the bases in the Philippines. Reiterating the significance of the Pacific island chain in assuring a forward defense in Asia, the navy paper assessed the likely course of a war in the Pacific-Asian theater. Under the most probable circumstances the American bases in the Philippines would be "of extreme importance" in holding the chain together. The report concluded, "These bases are therefore an essential part of a worldwide base system designed to deter communism. Any reduction in this base system creates a point of weakness which invites communist aggression."[10]

Neither Truman nor Eisenhower contested the Pentagon's view on this point. Consequently both administrations resisted efforts by the Filipinos to revise the 1947 base agreement. But Filipino leaders could hardly do other than to agitate for greater control over the bases, since the American military presence seemed a stigma of continuing colonialism. Not even the reliable Magsaysay, who once declared of a series of naval exercises centered on the American base at Subic Bay that "Such a show of massive strength inspires in everyone confidence in the ability of the United States to defend democracy," could avoid the issue. Throughout the late 1940s and 1950s—and for three decades more—the bases issue provided the background to all aspects of U.S.-Philippine relations.[11]

Although the crux of the question was control—Who would control these three-quarter million acres of Philippine territory?—a variety of subsidiary matters were involved. What was the nature of American jurisdiction over Filipinos on the bases? What was the nature of Philippine jurisdiction over Americans off the bases? Which flag should fly above the installations? What compensation should the United States provide for the use of Philippine land and waters? Should it be called compensation, even rent? If, as Washington claimed, the bases existed as much for the benefit of the Philippines as for the security of the United States, should Manila have the right to alter the bases agreement if it decided the American presence no longer served Philippine interests? Had the 1947 pact been accepted by the Philippine government under duress? From a political, rather than a legal, perspective, should Washington stonewall on terms if the Filipinos demanded changes?

On the last question Eisenhower took the view that a narrow legalism would do neither side any good. He told Dulles he wanted to be "reasonable and understanding" regarding the bases. He said he did not want "to let our people get too demanding." Eisenhower's comments came in the context of a position staked out by the justice department that the United States had retained sovereignty over the bases at the time it transferred title to the rest of the islands to the Philippine government. The defense department liked this interpretation because it allowed greater control over access to the bases. American forces experienced persistent problems with pilferage, provoking Joint Chiefs Chairman Arthur Radford to mutter privately, "Filipinos are the most accomplished thieves in the world." Attempts to warn off intruders nearly always led to friction, not infrequently to violence, sometimes to tragedy. Every Filipino arrested or wounded or killed became, in the eyes of Filipino nationalists—who at the emotional level, at least, included the entire population—a victim of American imperialism.[12]

Eisenhower sought accommodation within the bounds of what he judged to be the strategic imperatives of the United States. He officially acknowledged that ownership of the land the bases occupied resided with the Philippines, and he agreed to negotiations to ease the annoyance the bases were causing. Personally he thought the United States would misstep seriously to raise a fuss over matters like flag-flying. Let the Filipinos raise their banner, he told the Pentagon's Reuben Robertson. Having watched the British come to grief over such items of detail in Egypt—Eisenhower spoke just after Nasser seized the Suez Canal, while the British were plotting the debacle that would end their career as an arbiter of the Middle East—he argued that the United States must avoid investing its prestige in an empty principle. Yet he refused to accept any Filipino demand that might diminish America's free use of the bases in emergency. "It would destroy the utility and one of the major purposes of having the bases there," he said, "and in such an event we would be better to pull out from the bases or make other arrangements." On this issue the president rejected compromise. "We should stand very firm."[13]

With this attitude in the White House, American representatives had scant cause for concessions in talks with the Filipinos about the bases. A judgment that Filipino complaints tended to the irrational contributed to the American reluctance to yield. The state department's Herbert Hoover, Jr., visited the Philippines in October 1955 and returned to say the Filipinos were "supersensitive" regarding the bases. The American naval attaché in Manila described the question as an "emotional issue." Joint Chiefs Chairman Radford was convinced the matter was being used by opportunistic Filipino politicians to gain votes. "We cannot give in to blackmail in connection with the base rights negotiations," Radford said. The admiral added that in any event there was no point cutting an agreement with the Filipinos before they cleaned up their corruption and learned the art of self-rule. "Until there is good government in the Philippines, no agreement will stand up." The American military attaché asserted that the tempest over the bases raged merely in Manila's teapot. "Provincial areas outside of Manila have all voiced a strong desire for the continuation of a strong and healthy relationship between the two countries, including the granting of whatever military bases may be needed by the U.S. to give security to Philippine sovereignty." Yet all Americans involved stressed the need for handling the bases question carefully. Air Force General Nathan Twining of the joint chiefs pointed to the importance of a "prevalence of an atmosphere of goodwill" between the two countries. Hoover called for the "utmost tact." Radford advocated secret negotiations. The military attaché in Manila remarked, "Nothing has ever been gained in the Philippines through direct dealing."[14]

To some extent the American belief that Filipino indignation over the bases was a contrivance mirrored reality. As had been true since the beginning of the American era in the Philippines, the Americans made convenient targets for politicians and others looking for an inexpensive way of demonstrating their solicitude for the welfare of the Filipino people. What Cameron Forbes and Leonard Wood had stood for during the period of formal American control, the bases became in the years after independence. If the bases did not exist Filipino leaders would have had to invent them.

Yet the troubles the bases and related American activities in the Philippines provoked were by no means entirely the inventions of manipulative Filipino leaders. Had Americans stationed at Clark and Subic comported themselves as exemplary guests, the mere fact of their presence would have grated on a people still attempting to define its place in the community of nations. Small countries in the shadow of great powers commonly feel required to demonstrate their independence of the shadow-casters. As it happened, Americans were not exemplary guests. The racism that had plagued American relations with the Philippines from the beginning had lost respectability since the turn of the century—Hitler, among other people, saw to that—but it still existed. The attitudes that inclined Americans to speak of "gu-gus" during the Philippine-American war would dispose them to think in terms of "gooks" in Vietnam. The Asians who inhabited the Philippines were conceived of as generally friendly, but a country that still practiced its own version of apartheid could not help producing many persons who considered nonwhites inherently inferior.

Racism aside, many Americans demonstrated distressingly little tolerance for a poor country attempting to solve the myriad problems that have confronted third-world nations during the last forty years. Arthur Radford's remark about Filipinos being the world's most accomplished thieves may have reflected a racist attitude. It may simply have demonstrated an inability to appreciate the plight of impoverished people living elbow-close to thousands of employees of the most profligate institution of the wealthiest country on earth. In his subsequent comment that the Filipinos were not fit to govern themselves, Radford seems to have ignored the fact that the United States had had half a century to instruct the Filipinos in the arts of self-government. Their deficiencies in this regard owed considerably to America's failure. In any event the Filipinos had as much right to run the Philippines as they saw fit as Americans had to run the United States to American specifications.[15]

From whatever causes–racism, cultural insensitivity, political amnesia— American actions exacerbated the difficulties that inevitably developed between the two peoples. The most innocuous events could easily swell into crises. In November 1956 an American military transport plane crashed on landing at the Manila airport. The wreckage and flames naturally drew a crowd of photographers and reporters. When American military police arrived on the scene they unaccountably became obsessed by the notion that the photographers might have caught something on film that would compromise American security. They brusquely handled the photographers and placed them under detention, confiscating cameras and film. No serious harm came of the matter, but to Filipinos the contretemps built on a long legacy of affronts and seemed just cause for complaint. American observers, forgetful of a past that touched them psychologically far less than it did the Filipinos, saw the event in isolation and could not understand the uproar it caused. The American military attaché blamed the Manila papers for all the trouble. "There is no doubt the press is bent upon making the incident something colossal," he wrote.[16]

Because American officials considered much of the objection to the bases manufactured, they did not try hard to satisfy the Filipinos. When Magsaysay once suggested to Dulles that the bases were worth more to the United States than America was paying, the secretary responded with a typically Dullesian lecture. He corrected the figures Magsaysay used in calculating American aid, saying the actual total came to nearly three times what the Philippine president recognized. He asserted that the United States had assumed "a very considerable part of the burden of defense which would otherwise fall upon the Philippines alone." The "full force of the United States," Dulles said, was committed to Philippine security. "This is no inconsiderable asset." It was true that other countries received more assistance than the Philippines—Magsaysay had mentioned Korea, Taiwan and Vietnam—but the others' greater aid followed from the fact that they lay more squarely on "the front lines" of the struggle against communism, where the danger was greater. On another occasion Dulles dismissed Magsaysay's efforts to raise the base-compensation issue as the work of "cheap politicians" who surrounded the Philippine president and who insisted that "the Philippines could get a lot more out of the United States if Magsaysay would only play a different game."[17]

The accession of García to the presidency reinforced the American view on "cheap politicians" angling for aid. They now seemed to have taken over Malacañang. During a visit to Washington in the summer of 1958 García explained to Eisenhower his dream of making the Philippines a "showcase of democracy." Unfortunately insurgents in the countryside desired to thwart this goal. García admitted that the communist insurgency was quiescent for the moment, that only "pockets of Huks" remained at large. "But there is a danger of recurrence unless something can be done for the masses." He suggested that the United States could help. Surely the American government did not wish to see a country so important to Pacific security fall to the communists. Eisenhower replied blandly that he would look into the matter.[18]

While the Huks remained quiet Washington deemed neither requests for increased aid nor demands for revision of the base agreement particularly pressing. Charles Bohlen, appointed ambassador about the time of Magsaysay's death, persuaded the Pentagon to accept a redrawing of the boundary of the Subic base to allow the transfer to Philippine jurisdiction of the 80,000 inhabitants of Olongapo. But beyond this the base question stayed stuck, and with it applications for more money. That Dulles and Eisenhower had assigned Bohlen, a Soviet expert, to Manila indicated the low priority the Philippines received in American planning during the late 1950s. Bohlen, like his predecessor, Homer "Three Putt" Ferguson, amused himself playing golf with the Manila country-club set.[19]

The García government might have gained greater American attention had it possessed more political credibility. The new marks it was establishing for corruption did not reassure American officials reluctant to diminish American control of the bases or jurisdiction over American soldiers and sailors in the Philippines. Yet mere corruption in Manila had never and would never much deter Washington from actions deemed in America's interest. García's greater liability, to the American way of thinking, consisted in his tenuous position vis-à-vis Macapagal and the Liberals. Despite the president's heroic efforts to utilize patronage and other perquisites of office to bolster his support, he was far from a sure thing in the next election. Any favors Washington might have been inclined to do García—few enough as it was—would have been lost on Macapagal in the not unlikely event the vice president defeated García in the 1961 election. Macapagal's continuing ties to the CIA did not increase García's chances of reelection.[20]

Philippine affairs, including the political maneuverings of García and Macapagal, did not at this juncture top the list of Washington's worries. Eisenhower, old and slowing, hoped to ease some of the strain of the Cold War through personal diplomacy with Soviet leader Nikita Khrushchev before becoming history. His failure, precipitated by an ill-considered U-2 spy flight over Russia, cast a pall over his last months in office and left him frustrated and distracted. When Macapagal arrived for a White House visit in the autumn of 1960 the acting secretary of state, C. Douglas Dillon, thought it necessary to remind Eisenhower that Macapagal was of the Philippine opposition party and could not speak for García. Eisenhower had little to say. The conversation consisted of pleasantries, the usual Philippine pitch for aid and an Eisenhower dodge.[21]

III. At sea

If Washington could at times ignore the Philippines, Manila enjoyed no such luxury with respect to the United States, and if the Americans looked forward to a change from García, the Filipinos watched the transition from Eisenhower to Kennedy with even greater interest. Ten days after the 1960 polling in America, García told Romulo, "This is about time to start cultivating the good will of President-elect Kennedy and the incoming Democratic administration." The Philippine ambassador replied that all was under control with Kennedy. "His two right-hand men Sorenson and Salinger are close friends of mine," Romulo wrote. "Also his advisers Schlesinger and Galbraith." Romulo added that he had set up an appointment at Kennedy's home on Thanksgiving Day, arranged "in strict confidence." He offered solid encouragement. "I assure you we will be closer to this new administration than to the previous one."[22]

Ambassadors have been known to exaggerate their intimacy with the governments to which they are accredited. It makes them important and their voices heard. Romulo was not immune to the temptation. Yet the Philippine ambassador's expectation of increased attention from the Kennedy administration was not without basis in fact. During the previous several years Senator Kennedy had taken a highly visible position on American assistance to the third world, especially to noncommunist Asian countries. Kennedy saw economic development as a key to American victory in the Cold War, and he viewed American aid as vital to Asian development. At the same time he recognized that aid alone could not defeat communism. The United States must be armed and vigilant, prepared to oppose force with force.

Such a policy could hardly have suited Manila better. Other Asian countries might stand in larger need of American development aid, but none exercised a more valid claim on American generosity, both historically and in terms of contemporary support against communism. García, in America in 1958, had spoken of the "mutual partnership" of the United States and the Philippines in building a strong, noncommunist Asia. At the same time he had warned against taking America's Asian friends for granted. "It is of the utmost importance that free Asia should not appear to be disregarded or ignored." For this reason he advocated a "joint program of mutually profitable economic development." No one had to guess where the money would come from.[23]

The incoming administration's loudly stated opposition to communist expansion afforded encouragement to Manila. Indochina's turmoil as yet did not approach the cataclysmic level of the Far Eastern crises of 1949–1950, which had caused the Truman administration to appreciate the finer traits of the Quirino regime, in particular its noncommunist character. But the problem of Laos had not disappeared, and if Ho Chi Minh tried to make good his pledge to liberate South Vietnam the United States once more might find itself up to its neck in Asia. America again would need, or at least would greatly desire, Philippine support.

García lost no time demonstrating the availability of such support. The Philippine president wrote Kennedy soon after the latter's inauguration to say that "the sacrosanct cause of freedom and democracy will always find among Filipinos defenders who are willing, if need be, to fight to the 'bitter end' as we did in Bataan and Corregidor." García added that the pledge of the United States, reaffirmed so eloquently by the American president, "to stand by its commitments in the Free World electrifies the Filipinos specially at this juncture when Communism is threatening to overrun the whole Asian continent."[24]

Yet the Philippine-American relationship did not immediately regain the momentum Manila anticipated. Part of the problem lay in Kennedy's personnel decisions. Romulo found the selection of Dean Rusk as secretary of state disappointing. Although the Philippine ambassador described Rusk as a "long-standing friend," the secretary, who had considerable experience in Pacific and Asian affairs, was too set in his ways for Romulo's taste. "He is a stubborn man when he thinks he knows the facts. I was hoping we would have a Secretary of State without fixed views on the Philippines as Secretary Rusk has." Romulo's reservations about Rusk did not prevent him from doing his duty as a diplomat and lying. "You are the ideal man for the Kennedy New Frontier policy," Romulo told the new secretary. Kennedy's choice of Eisenhower holdover Douglas Dillon as treasury secretary similarly seemed a vote for the status quo. Romulo concluded with disappointment, "The Kennedy cabinet does not offer what we in the Philippines hoped for when we hailed the advent of a Democratic administration in Washington."[25]

Part of the sluggishness of Philippine-American relations resulted from Washington's concern with other causes. Among Asian countries exotic and sometimes disdainful India possessed greater allure for the dashing types of the New Frontier than the plain old Philippines. Closer to home Kennedy was launching the Alliance for Progress in Latin America, which absorbed both money and attention that might have gone to the Philippines.

Finally, part of the lack of decided direction in relations between the two countries resulted from the unsettled character of Philippine politics. To no one's surprise Macapagal early announced his candidacy for president, further disrupting García's administration. García himself was sick, which may have been just as well for the country, considering the ends to which he applied his energy. The campaign was raucous and unprincipled, and although Macapagal won, the victory cost him an amount unprecedented in Philippine history. Money had long been the lubricant of Filipino politics as candidates and their supporters applied the advertising techniques of Madison Avenue to the traditional culture of the *barangay*. They bombarded constituents with balloons, T-shirts, bumper-stickers, food, drink, promises and cash in an effort to forge the ties of *utang na loob* (debt of gratitude) that would bring the voters to the polls on election day. Wise to the practice, leaders of churches, schools and fraternal and charitable organizations scheduled fund drives to coincide with campaigns, expecting and receiving large donations from candidates. One of the 1961 vice-presidential candidates, Sergio Osmeña, Jr., gave 10,000 pesos to every parish priest in a closely contested province, in hopes of a good word from the pulpit. Because candidates regularly jumped parties and fashioned temporary coalitions, village captains, called *liders*, distributed sample ballots indicating preferred combinations to puzzled voters.

Ironically, one of the consequences of improvements in administering elections, especially greater secrecy in voting, was an escalation of campaign costs, as *liders* resorted to ever-larger favors and higher bribes to ensure that bought ballots stayed bought. Double-dipping by voters became more common and harder to detect. Such practices drove the price of election up ten-fold between Magsaysay's 1953 victory and Macapagal's 1961 triumph. In the latter year candidates spent an amount equivalent to 13 percent of the national government's budget. Nor was this the peak. By 1969, the year of the last presidential election before Ferdinand Marcos declared martial law, the bill came to one-quarter of government expenditures.

If nothing else these numbers afford a useful corrective to notions that the American CIA ever bought Philippine elections. Considering the amount of money involved in campaigns, American funds did scarcely more than indicate which candidates the Americans favored. To the extent American support played a role in placing nominees in office, that role was far less financial than political. The American imprimatur went farther than America's cash.[26]

Facing such astronomical expenses, it was no wonder Filipino leaders looked to the United States for sustenance. Macapagal definitely did. Shortly after he took office he sent his new ambassador in Washington, Emilio Abello, to the

White House. Abello sought help from the Kennedy administration in stabilizing the peso, again under pressure, and he requested additional payments from the American government for war damages. The American Congress was then considering a bill authorizing such payments; Abello said he hoped the administration would back the measure, which would be "a great boon" to the Philippine economy.[27]

Although Kennedy expressed sympathy for the Philippine request, he did not push the matter, and the legislature rejected the claims bill. Macapagal responded to the rejection by scratching a scheduled visit to the United States. "The feeling of resentment among our people," Macapagal wrote Kennedy, "and the attitude of the U.S. Congress negate the atmosphere of good will upon which my state visit to your country was predicated." Macapagal also threatened to suspend negotiations on the American bases in the Philippines—a rather empty threat, since revision of the status quo mattered more to Filipinos than to Americans.[28]

Eventually Macapagal got over his indignation. In the spring of 1963 he told Kennedy he detected a "noticeable improvement" in Philippine-American relations. Yet the improvement amounted to little, and during the first half of the 1960s the relationship drifted without perceptible direction. American sugar interests attempted to eliminate Philippine quotas. Manila stood firm on the Laurel-Langley accord. Talks on the bases started, stopped and went nowhere. Manila continued to seek additional American aid. Washington dispensed some but not much.[29]

15

What Allies Are For
1965–1972

I. Deeper and deeper

Two events of 1965 halted the drift of U.S.-Philippine relations. During the first half of the year the administration of Lyndon Johnson sharply escalated the American role in the Vietnam war. In November Filipinos elected Ferdinand Marcos president.

As Carlos Romulo had predicted in 1959 the troubles of Laos did not lend themselves to ready solution. At the end of 1960, even as the Pathet Lao seemed nearly beaten, Romulo guessed that the world had not seen the last of the Laotian difficulties. "The apparent defeat of the pro-communist forces should not lull us into the belief that the problem of Laos is settled," Romulo wrote. "The fact is that all the essential ingredients of another Korea are present." Romulo concluded, "For us in the Philippines it continues to be a dangerous situation."[1]

Although Romulo got the country wrong, he got the part about the continuing danger right. Laos calmed down, but the trouble merely moved next door to Vietnam. As communists and other dissidents in South Vietnam took arms against the Diem government the United States grew more and more involved in defending that which America had created. Douglas MacArthur, retired and ailing yet still attentive to affairs touching the western Pacific and the Philippines, told Kennedy, "The chickens are coming home to roost, and you live in the chicken house."[2]

Kennedy immediately sent 500 American military advisers to Saigon to reinforce the several hundred already there. In the process he rendered the 1954 Geneva agreement, which capped such an advisory force at less than 700, deader than ever. Kennedy also dispatched Vice President Lyndon Johnson, who made a fool of himself, in the manner of American vice presidents, by dubbing Diem the Winston Churchill of Southeast Asia. Filipino leaders did not fault Johnson's rhetorical excess. They found it reassuring. During the same trip the vice president stopped in Manila, where García toasted him: "We like to look at your tour to the Philippines and Southeast Asia as a positive demonstration of the unwavering resolution of the American government and people to translate into living realities all the commitments of the U.S.A. to the emerging democracies in Asia."[3]

Emerging democracy or not, South Vietnam appeared to Kennedy to require substantially more American help. Kennedy rejected the Pentagon's worst-case scenarios, which foretold an imminent South Vietnamese collapse without a major infusion of American military power. But he agreed to send an additional 10,000 troops, then 5,000 more.

Diem did almost nothing to help his own cause. His increasingly authoritarian actions provoked massive protests and facilitated the recruiting efforts of the insurgent Viet Cong. When a conspiracy of South Vietnamese generals plotted Diem's overthrow the Kennedy administration gave the nod. The plotters killed Diem during the coup, bloodying America, at least morally, in the process. The spot would not out, and the staining drew America still more deeply into the unfolding tragedy.

When Kennedy's assassin arrived three weeks later, the American commitment became Johnson's to honor or repudiate. Johnson, though supremely self-confident, and rightly so, regarding domestic politics, was a foreign-policy agoraphobe, deathly afraid of being caught out alone. He demanded company, especially regarding Vietnam. Fortunately for Johnson's peace of mind, if not for the peace of Asia, finding company turned out to be no problem. His advisers, with exceptions few enough to spotlight their eccentricity, told him to stay the course.

Johnson likewise craved the support of America's allies, including the Philippines. From the beginning the new president attempted to secure the support of Manila for his administration's initiatives in Asia. Just before Kennedy's death Indonesia announced what Jakarta called its "confrontation" with Malaysia. American analysts and other observers feared that Indonesia's Sukarno would push his campaign of harassment to the point of war. In Washington just after Kennedy's funeral, Johnson asked Macapagal for assistance calming the situation. The United States, Johnson said, had little influence with Sukarno. The Philippines might be "of great help" in averting a major conflict. Macapagal, without committing himself to anything particular, agreed. "The Philippines can be a window for Sukarno to look at the West," Macapagal said, "and for the West to look at Sukarno." Johnson responded that it would be "a great achievement for us all" if Manila's mediation helped restore normal relations in Southeast Asia.[4]

Such help as the Philippines provided had little effect on the Indonesia-Malaysia dispute, but on the issue Washington cared most about—Vietnam—Macapagal accomplished somewhat more. Few Filipino leaders cared much about Vietnam per se. Nor did Philippine leaders worry inordinately over the possibility of communism spreading to the Philippines even if South Vietnam fell. A communist victory in Vietnam might hearten radicals in the Philippines, but whatever dominoes toppled in mainland Southeast Asia were probably not long enough to reach across the South China Sea. The Manila pact notwithstanding, most in Manila could not summon much enthusiasm for a Vietnam rescue. (Neither could SEATO as a whole, rendering the organization largely moribund.) Among many Filipinos, especially those of a nationalist bent, there existed positive resistance to taking part in what increasingly seemed America's war.

On the other hand, the United States still had favors to supply the Philippines if Washington so chose, and no Philippine government would lightly reject such favors. Macapagal assured an American visitor that if the chips were down and the United States needed assistance "the Philippines would forego its own feelings and support the United States." By the summer of 1964 the chips were down. The regime in Saigon was fading fast. Undersecretary of State George Ball wrote the embassy in Manila directing American officials there to tell Macapagal "as forcefully as possible" that the United States would appreciate a demonstration of Philippine backing. A contingent of troops would serve nicely. Lest Manila object on grounds of cost, Ball added, "We are prepared to pick up the tab for their Vietnamese package." On the same day Johnson contacted Macapagal personally. Humanity was watching, Johnson declared, to determine the attitude of the Philippines and other countries of Asia on the critical issue of democracy in Indochina. He trusted the Philippines would continue to adhere to the free world. Johnson commented significantly that the American Congress and the American people were following the question closely, hoping for reassurance that "one of their truest and most steadfast allies stands with them."[5]

While Macapagal considered his response, the Johnson administration raised the stakes in Vietnam further. In February 1965 the president approved the commencement of a major bombing campaign against North Vietnam. At the beginning of the summer Johnson ordered 50,000 combat troops to Vietnam. The American escalation led to additional pressure on the Philippine government. In July 1965 the state department warned the embassy in Manila to expect "greatly increased use" of the American bases in the Philippines consequent to the buildup in Vietnam, and it suggested preparing Macapagal for this development. Although there was little Macapagal could do formally to restrain American actions on the American bases—this being the point of the Pentagon's long insistence on maintaining freedom to use the bases as Washington desired—if he objected loudly he might create political roadblocks not easily overcome. On another issue the Philippine government possessed more leverage. American war strategists desired the right to fly American airplanes over the Philippines on whatever routes proved convenient. For this they required Manila's permission.

Ambassador William Blair put the matter to Macapagal in August 1965, request-ing blanket approval for overflights.[6]

Macapagal, with one eye on Philippine nationalists and the other on Wash-ington, tried to accommodate the latter without antagonizing the former. The strategy did not work. He managed to finesse the overflight issue, refusing the blanket approval Washington wanted but in practice letting the Americans fly where they chose. Neither did his acquiescence in the increased use of the bases trip him up, if only because the American comings and goings poured larger amounts of money than usual into the Philippine economy. Yet when he asked the legislature for funds to send a Philippine expeditionary force to Vietnam, the Johnson administration applauded but the nationalists exploded in derision. Leading the deriders was the president of the senate, Ferdinand Marcos.[7]

II.   The man who would be despot

The Marcos myth-making began early, with the protagonist directing the fabri-cation. In the late 1930s young Marcos had faced murder charges in the killing of a political opponent of his father. The victim had displayed the poor judgment not merely to defeat the elder Marcos but to taunt the loser in public. Convicted in trial court, Marcos appealed to the supreme court. By this time the case had attracted national attention, and when Marcos, conducting his own defense, suc-ceeded in having the conviction overturned, the Philippines Free Press placed his picture on the front page and declared the handsome twenty-three-year-old a "public hero."[8]

The second chapter began with the Japanese attack on the Philippines. Mar-cos fought at Bataan, was captured and subsequently released. By his own telling he raised and commanded a tough unit of guerrillas that made life miserable for the Japanese and aided materially in the liberation of the country. In the process he earned more than a score of decorations, including an American congressional Medal of Honor.

Such was the Marcos version, retailed at length during subsequent years. It was mostly false. Marcos did win one ribbon during the Bataan campaign, but his claim to guerrilla greatness evaporated under historical scrutiny, as did his Medal of Honor and the bulk of the rest of the tale.

Yet the scrutinizers came late to their task, and during the two decades after the war, when few in the Philippines cared to inquire closely into the period of Japanese occupation, Marcos' fictions convinced the majority of those paying attention. In 1949 he gained election as a Liberal to the lower house of the Phil-ippine legislature. His star rose slowly during the relatively honest Magsaysay years. Matching his politics to the period, he came to the attention of the Amer-ican embassy with a speech calling for close U.S.-Philippine ties. The "able young

LP Representative Fernando Marcos," in the embassy's description, acknowledged that current agreements between the United States and the Philippines might be improved. But Filipinos must never forget the "fundamental basis of interdependence and cooperation" that linked the two countries. Those who contended that the Philippines could break the link and go alone into international affairs practiced the "highest form of hypocrisy."[9]

In 1959 Marcos made a victorious run for the Philippine senate. Filipino legislators, even senators, have rarely had much impact on running the country. From the time of Quezon the executive has generally succeeded in drawing power to itself. Politically ambitious types—and whatever his other faults, none ever charged Marcos with lacking ambition—have commonly used the legislature as a forum for building reputations and alliances. Marcos certainly did. He switched affiliation to the Nacionalistas when the Liberal Macapagal changed his mind about abjuring a second term, and as president of the senate Marcos attacked Macapagal unmercifully. His challenge to the Philippine president regarding the troops for Vietnam formed part of the pattern. He surprised no one when he announced his decision to seek to replace Macapagal in 1965.

American officials viewing the Macapagal-Marcos campaign found little to choose between the contestants. The CIA described the incumbent as "barely a middle-weight in terms of political know-how, administrative ability, and intellectual capacity." Regarding the challenger, the agency said, "Marcos has a record as a brilliant lawyer and a reputation as a skillful but ruthless politician." The CIA noted that Marcos would probably prove more independent than Macapagal, but still it considered the Nacionalista candidate friendly to American interests.[10]

Ambassador Blair placed the campaign in the broader context of U.S.-Philippine relations. Regarding the issue of greatest importance to the Johnson administration, Blair wrote that most leading Filipinos supported the American venture in Vietnam. "Those few politicians who advocate outright U.S. withdrawal or who have taken similar extreme positions," Blair asserted, "are beyond the pale and so identified." The Macapagal government in particular was "fully behind U.S. Vietnam policy." Yet there remained in the country some reservations about the turn the war had recently taken, and with the escalation of the American role Blair detected a certain resentment "at the fact that white men are killing Asians." In addition, among those old enough to recall the events of the 1930s and early 1940s there existed doubts that the Americans had the patience and fortitude to see their commitment to Vietnam through to the end. As for the Filipino masses, they scarcely thought about Vietnam. They were "preoccupied with the problems of daily living" and would "go along with whatever the Government of the Philippines proposes."[11]

The 1965 campaign produced the usual mudbath of smears and flash floods of cash, although less violence than normal. The United States remained essentially neutral in the contest, to the dismay of Macapagal, who thought his support of Johnson's Vietnam policy had earned him better from Washington. Macapagal especially wanted an appearance by Johnson during the campaign. "My election would have been a certainty if President Johnson had come," he complained to Blair. In the end Marcos triumphed by somewhat less than 10 percent of the vote cast.[12]

Blair immediately approached the president-elect for soundings on his attitude regarding the United States. Marcos was noncommittal about the American bases. On Vietnam he expressed general but vague approval. Yet despite the lack of overt signs of opposition, Blair and other American officials sensed that Marcos might prove a more difficult partner than his predecessors had been. A trip by Secretary of State Rusk to Manila produced an accurate assessment of the Philippine president's position. Marcos had agreed to send a modest number of troops—an engineer battalion, as it turned out—and the Johnson administration issued an invitation for Marcos to visit Washington. "Although Marcos was very friendly and obviously has the highest esteem for you," Rusk reported to Johnson, "I have no doubt he will make every effort to parlay his visit and the troops for Viet Nam into pretty tangible returns."[13]

Marcos arrived in America in September 1966 with wife Imelda and a large entourage. The festivities exhibited the egregiousness characteristic of state visits by leaders of America's client countries. Marcos addressed a joint session of Congress, to which he pledged the Philippines' undying devotion to the cause of liberty in Asia and the world. The press lavished print and pictures on Imelda, who demonstrated the brilliance and charm she was capable of at her best. The Philippine first couple conjured memories of Jack and Jackie Kennedy, and many Americans congratulated themselves that their former colony could produce such a pair.

The substance of the visit turned out to be less impressive. Johnson wanted a larger Philippine force in Vietnam. Marcos desired greater American assistance. Marcos got the better of the deal, returning to Manila with a pledge of more than $80 million in American aid. Johnson received nothing beyond confirmation of Marcos' previous commitment to send two thousand troops to Vietnam.

Marcos' success with Washington, then and later, owed to his ability to apply a theme similar to one Johnson sought to use in the United States. Recognizing that he was the only Philippine president America had, Marcos spoke the part of a good and loyal ally, while privately he pursued his own interests. To a degree unknown before, Marcos diverted American aid monies into his own accounts and those of his friends and political allies. He continued the trend toward consolidation of power in the executive branch, utilizing patronage and money to entrench his loyalists in key posts. In a typical 1968 case he impounded billions of pesos appropriated by the Philippine legislature, releasing only those designated for projects and constituencies he thought would further his personal agenda.

Pork-barrel tactics worked even better in the Philippines than in America, since abstract issues mattered less to the millions of Filipinos correctly identified by Ambassador Blair as preoccupied with the daily struggle for survival than they did to more comfortable Americans. As one veteran legislator, whose longevity in office attested to his mastery of the ways of Filipino politics, explained the situation, "My constituents need me as long as I bring them the bacon: public works and jobs. As soon as I am unable, I am of no use to them." When opposition to the Philippine contingent in Vietnam developed in the legislature, Marcos ensured approval by promising to disburse funds to the districts of those who supported the measure, reportedly at a rate of 200,000 pesos per favorable vote.[14]

In October 1966 Marcos hosted what amounted in some respects to an effort to recapture the spirit of the 1954 Manila pact. Changing times and circumstances altered the attendance list. France, Britain and Pakistan, of the Manila pact signatories, stayed away, but Australia, New Zealand and Thailand came, as did South Vietnam and South Korea and of course the United States and the Philippines. The Marcoses outdid themselves directing the celebration, showcasing their country and the Marcos administration in an international coming-out party. Although Johnson still begrudged Marcos' unwillingness to expand the Philippine presence in Vietnam, the American president appreciated the opportunity Marcos provided to demonstrate the solidarity of noncommunist Asia behind the American war effort. The Manila summit produced nothing of substance, but as a symbol it allowed American officials to continue to portray their struggle in Vietnam as the latest expression of the ideal of collective security.

III. Revolutionary mood or revolutionary situation?

On matters unrelated to Vietnam, Marcos proved a distinct disappointment to Washington. To some degree the Johnson administration fell for the Marcos myth-making. Certainly American officials expected better from Marcos than from his immediate predecessors. In the 1960s Marcos had not developed corruption into the back-the-trucks-to-the-vault business it became later in his reign, and if he was, as Blair said, more ruthless than Macapagal, he also seemed more intelligent. American officials have rarely counted ruthlessness a disqualifying trait in clients and collaborators. From Iran to Korea to Vietnam to Nicaragua, Washington during this period helped prop regimes contemptuous of democratic processes and harsh in their treatment of those who disagreed. Yet American leaders expected their sons of bitches, to use Franklin Roosevelt's characterization, to exercise prudence and care in quieting dissent. Washington dumped Diem not for suppressing the rights of his opponents but for doing it so clumsily as to render himself an international disgrace, and tainting America in the process. Had Marcos been watching he might have learned something worth knowing.

American officials did not underestimate the seriousness of the problems confronting Marcos and the Philippines. Philippine rice production per hectare was among the lowest in Asia. Although the Philippines ranked in the middle of the noncommunist Southeast Asian nations in average individual income, distribution of income skewed heavily in the direction of Manila. Beyond the capital the typical person commanded but half the earnings of one living in the metropolis. That Manila's wealth was highly visible and concentrated in a few neighborhoods exacerbated discontent.[15]

Washington hoped Marcos would see the trouble the rift between rich and poor portended for the Philippines and that he would attempt to diminish the gap, out of self-interest if not magnanimity. At the beginning of 1966 the CIA listed the principal hazards to Philippine stability: "land hunger in the countryside, unemployment in the cities, and the grinding poverty of the overwhelming majority of the people." The situation, the agency asserted, had not yet turned critical, but it soon might in the absence of effective reform. Violence and crime spawned by dissatisfaction with the status quo grew more widespread with each passing month. So did corruption in government. Optimism came hard.

But even as Washington recognized the danger ahead, the Johnson administration could not bring itself to attempt to force remedies upon Marcos. The war in Vietnam mattered more to the American government than discontent in the barangays, and the Philippines, especially the American bases there, played a vital part in the war effort. "Marcos is an anti-Communist and supports the U.S. on most issues respecting the Communist world," the CIA remarked. The agency reminded, however, that Marcos was no pushover. "He is also a strong nationalist and will seek greater equality for the Philippines in its dealings with the U.S., particularly on those issues involving U.S. military bases and special U.S. economic privileges." On balance the Philippine president appeared a risk worth taking. "Marcos is unlikely to hamper effective U.S. use of its bases so long as he is satisfied that such uses do not run counter to Philippine national interest."[16]

Where Manuel Quezon had excelled in dealing with the United States by exploiting American sympathies and convincing the Americans he was one of them at heart, Marcos played on Washington's fears, threatening to deprive the United States of access to what the Americans thought they needed to prevent much of the world from slipping into the communist sphere. Quezon had assumed the presidency of the commonwealth at a moment of confluence of American isolationism and Japanese expansionism. With the Philippines needing the United States more than the United States needed the Philippines, Quezon operated from a position of weakness. Marcos took power three decades later, at a time when American commitments were outrunning American resources and when no outside power seriously endangered Philippine independence. America now needed the Philippines more than the Philippines needed America. Consequently Marcos acted from strength.

Yet that strength had its limits, as Marcos eventually would discover. Meanwhile he faced a growing challenge from the domestic left. Officials in the Johnson administration desired social amelioration in the Philippines primarily as a device to prevent a recurrence of the Huk rebellion. Initially they thought they detected signs of a reforming spirit in Marcos, but soon they recognized their error. James Thomson of Johnson's National Security Council staff wrote, with evident discouragement, "Marcos is acting more and more like a Philippine President than the far-sighted New Dealer/pragmatist that he appeared to be earlier." Americans could understand Marcos' wish to avoid the perception of being what Thomson called an "American errand boy" regarding Vietnam, and Marcos' efforts to extract "highly tangible goodies" in compensation for committing troops to the war came as no shock. But his failure to address the issues jeopardizing the stability of his government occasioned continual dismay.[17]

At the end of 1967 the CIA produced a midterm assessment of Marcos' first administration. Superficially, the agency's analysts said, Marcos seemed to be doing well. The Nacionalistas had scored significant victories in the off-year elections just held. Yet the polling also revealed incipient weakness. "The glow of victory was somewhat dimmed by the outstanding showing of the Liberal senatorial candidate, Benigno Aquino, ex-governor of Tarlac Province and a vigorous opponent of Marcos." Aquino's opposition indicated a split among the elites, with those not on the inside objecting to Marcos' excessive, even by Filipino standards, efforts to draw as much power as possible to himself. Whether Marcos interpreted the situation in the same terms the American analysts did was unclear. If he did, the interpretation did not show up in his actions. He continued to demonstrate what the CIA called a "need to control the game."

Below the level of partisan politics the desire for fundamental change was building. For now revolution remained a distant prospect, with popular discontent taking the form of sullen nonparticipation rather than armed revolt. But circumstances might change. "Unless the peasant farmer and the urban slum dweller are persuaded that the present system can respond to their needs," the CIA report asserted, "their growing apathy could in time turn to rebellion." Marcos displayed little realization of the danger. Beyond occasional concessions to nationalists demanding distance from the United States, he offered nothing in the way of basic change. The story read as usual:

> Efforts to institute the necessary reforms have been undercut by corruption, inefficiency, and nepotism in the political structure. Public office continues to be used to further personal or family fortunes. An official dispenses jobs and favors, not in the public interest but to satisfy obligations to those people tied to him through the complex familial or patronal relationships that characterize Philippine society.

Although economic development might do much to alleviate the strains in the Philippines, the entrenched powers rendered it impossible. "The problem facing any Philippine government is, in some way, to persuade or manipulate the conservative elite to accept the political and economic pressures necessary to stimulate the economy." So far Marcos had demonstrated neither will nor ability to overcome the resistance of the "powerful conservative oligarchy." Until he summoned some of both, the CIA concluded, the country's troubles would only get worse.[18]

Get worse they did. As under Quirino, so under Marcos: corruption in high places and a failure to offer hope of a better life to the millions of victims of the elite-dominated system contributed to the rise of a leftist insurgency. During the early 1960s the few remnants of the Huks were engaged principally in petty racketeering rather than militant resistance against the government. Yet a handful of burning-brights clung to the dream of popular liberation. One, Bernabe Buscayno, commonly known as Commander Dante, sought support from the emerging student movement in Manila. Dante formed an alliance with José Marie Sison, a recent graduate of the University of the Philippines who was convinced that the peasant-oriented approach of Mao Zedong offered greater promise than the stodgy Stalinism of the Philippine Communist party, the PKP. Sison determined to rectify the party's errors. In 1968, while the cultural revolution raged in China, Sison and a small group of followers split from the PKP to form the "Communist Party of the Philippines (Marxist–Leninist–Mao Tse-tung Thought)." Sison shortly thereafter called on Commander Dante to help organize a military wing for the CPP, which they dubbed the New People's Army, or NPA.

An NPA manifesto stated the movement's perception of circumstances in the Philippines:

> The basic condition of the Philippines today is that of a semi-colonial and semi-feudal country, dominated by the U.S. imperialists, the comprador bourgeoisie, the landlords and the bureaucrat capitalists. These vested interests mercilessly exploit the broad masses of the people.

The remedy was clear. "There is only one road which the working class under the leadership of the Communist Party of the Philippines must take. It is the road of armed revolution to smash the armed counter-revolution that preserves foreign and feudal oppression in the Philippines." In keeping with repeatedly invoked "Mao Tse-tung's thought," NPA leaders nominated the peasantry, rather than the urban proletariat, as the prime mover of the revolution. "From the countryside, the people's democratic forces encircle the cities. It is in the countryside that the enemy forces are first lured in and defeated before the capture of the cities from the hands of the exploiting classes."

Putting the manifesto into effect, the NPA commenced operations in central Luzon. Dante selected a site in western Tarlac for a training camp, located conveniently close to a gunnery range on the Clark reservation, where the sound of gunfire would occasion few suspicions. Recruits received strict instructions to respect the people. The NPA issued "Eight Points of Attention," which again reflected Maoist influence:

1. Speak politely.
2. Pay fairly for what you buy.
3. Return everything you borrow.
4. Pay for anything you damage.
5. Do not hit or swear at people.
6. Do not damage crops.
7. Do not take liberties with women.
8. Do not ill-treat captives.

Toward perceived enemies of the people the NPA exercised considerably less tolerance, employing sanctions running from expropriation of property to summary execution. Atop the list of enemies were government informants, followed by cattle rustlers, rapists, land overseers, abusive members of the Philippine constabulary, usurers and robbers.[19]

As if one revolution were not enough, the late 1960s and early 1970s also witnessed a resurgence of unrest in Mindanao, where the Moros were once again growing impatient with Manila's pretensions. Since the time of Leonard Wood the Muslims of the south had accepted what seemed to them the pretense of membership in a Philippine nation only as long as the other members, the infidels, trod lightly on their turf. During the 1960s, when population growth and efforts to alleviate tenant pressure in Luzon produced large-scale migration of Christians to Mindanao—with up to 3,000 arrivals per week—the tramping became unbearable. The fact that issues of land title fell subject to the same sort of grafting endemic to other areas of Filipino politics intensified the Muslim conviction of a conspiracy against their religion and culture.

Communal conflagrations, especially those touching confessions of religious faith, rarely require much kindling. A handful of incidents during the first years of the Marcos era more than sufficed to set the southern region ablaze. The most provocative involved the deaths under mysterious circumstances of two dozen young men from Sulu on the fortress-island of Corregidor. Exactly what they were doing there and how and why they were killed remained a puzzle a quarter-century later. The explanation that gained greatest contemporary currency in the Muslim parts of the country placed the men in a secret army created by Marcos for the purpose of invading Malaysian (and largely Muslim) Sabah, across the Sulu Sea, and converting it into his private plantation. When the would-be commandos complained of dangerous and demeaning training conditions, their Christian officers executed them.[20]

Beyond aggrieving kin and friends of the deceased, the Corregidor incident suggested a plot by the Marcos government to set Muslim against Muslim, and

when military courts acquitted the officers involved, renewed demands for sep-
aratism arose. In 1968 the governor of Cotabato province proclaimed the establishment of the Muslim Independence Movement. Gang warfare, never absent
from Mindanao, took on increasingly sectarian dimensions. By the middle of 1971
more than five hundred persons were known to have died in the fighting, with
the largest single group of victims perishing in the town of Manili where Christians out for revenge massacred several dozen men, women and children seeking
shelter in a mosque. Convinced that the conflict had become irrepressible, Muslim separatists established the Moro National Liberation Front, or MNLF.

The issues involved in the Moro rebellion often remained as opaque to officials
of the Johnson and Nixon administrations as Moro affairs had been to Leonard
Wood. Constitutionally agnostic, culturally assimilationist and congenitally mod-
ernizing, Americans as a people have never successfully fathomed the well-
springs of conservative religious communalism. Nor have they particularly cared
to, since until recently movements embodying the principle rarely touched
American interests. Washington largely ignored the Moro uprising.

The communist rebellion was an entirely different matter. The same vigorous
views that propelled American troops into Vietnam sensitized American officials
to the revival of the communist movement in the Philippines. Even before the
formation of the new CPP and the NPA, the Johnson administration kept close
watch on what seemed the rebirth of the Huks. In the spring of 1967 the CIA
asserted that while the Huks did not now constitute a genuine threat to Philippine stability, they might cause the Marcos government "serious political difficulties." The agency's report described the recent growth of Huk forces from a
nadir of a few dozen armed troops to a present level of three to four hundred.
Beyond this the rebels could expect the active support of nearly thirty thousand
noncombatants. Considerable question surrounded the Huks' connection with
the formal apparatus of the Communist party. The CIA analysts labeled current
Huk ties to the PKP as "vague and contradictory." To a significant extent the
Huks' appeal rested not on their doctrinal message but on their ability to serve as
an alternative to the government provided by Marcos and his allies in the provinces.

> Although there have been recent indications that recruits are again receiving Marxist
> indoctrination, among the peasantry the Huks maintain a "Robin Hood" image of
> assisting the poor. In fact, the Huks' separate system of justice in the areas they influ-
> ence, chiefly the rice-producing provinces of Central Luzon, appears to be more effi-
> cient than the government's slow-moving and often corrupt judicial system. The
> Huks' decisions, which do not always favor the peasants, seem to be accepted by
> many landlords as well.

Despite Marcos' avowed determination to eradicate the Huks, the American
intelligence agency did not anticipate early success. Assassinations had risen
sharply, from less than twenty during all of 1965 to more than seventy in the first

eight months of 1966. Government efforts to punish the assassins were hindered by the fact that increasing numbers of peasants preferred collaboration with the Huks to cooperation with the government. "This attitude can be expected to continue as long as local landlords block reform efforts, as corruption by officials diverts funds from development projects, and as legal redress remains slow and one-sided." The CIA concluded, "If not effectively dealt with, the Huk movement could again develop into a major insurgent threat."[21]

Ambassador Blair elaborated upon the causes of the failure of the government's anti-Huk campaign. Blair placed less emphasis on the Robin Hoodism of the rebels and more on their tactics of coercion. "One of the most powerful weapons in the hands of the Huks is terror," Blair said. "The executions, as they are calculated to do, send a shiver of terror through Central Luzon, enhancing Huk influence considerably." Unfortunately the government did almost nothing to counter this influence. "The spirit, enthusiasm and drive that marked the Magsaysay effort are missing in the contemporary Philippines; and anti-Huk operations of the Government are marked by a lack of imagination, limited means, and political embarrassment that hamper their effectiveness." Blair suspected the Philippine armed forces of not seriously attempting to track down Huk leaders, in the belief that a continuing rebel presence would lead to higher defense budgets and enhanced opportunities for graft. As for the basic reforms that alone could dry up popular support for the insurrection, Blair rated their probability near zero. "The Filipino leadership group is drawn from landowning families. Hence few Filipino leaders feel any strong commitment to major change in the countryside, since their family and personal interests lie in perpetuating the status quo." Blair ended on a note as pessimistic as the CIA's. "During the past year or so the Huk issue has emerged as a problem in the Philippines which, though no larger than a man's hand on the horizon, is still so potentially serious that it cannot be discounted."[22]

American foreboding notwithstanding, the communist rebellion at this point failed to catch fire. Assassinations continued through the end of the decade. In May 1969 eight jeeploads of terrorists tore through downtown Angeles spraying bullets, killing several civilians and wounding more, and trading fire with Philippine military units. Government counterterrorists called "Monkees," after a television pop-music band, conducted reprisals against the communists, as well as against other enemies of the government. In a twelve-month period beginning in November 1968, the death toll in Pampanga province mounted to more than 100, in adjacent Tarlac to nearly 150. But the peasant uprising the CPP hoped for did not materialize.[23]

Francis Underhill, counselor of the American embassy, attempted to explain why. Underhill, a career diplomat and Southeast Asia expert, served in Manila as chief political adviser to the ambassador from 1968 to 1971. During this period he watched the Philippines slip toward chaos. On receiving a new posting at the beginning of 1971 he summarized what he had seen. "Valedictory observations of officers leaving the Philippines have not as a rule made very cheerful reading," Underhill wrote.

> Almost all have found deterioration between their arrival and their departure. All have expressed concern about the lack of visible progress in dealing with the country's major problems: graft and corruption, peace and order, the widening gap between the rich and poor, "too much" politics, government inefficiency, and the inadequacies of top leadership.

Underhill concurred in the majority opinion. "Pollyanna herself would be hard put not to continue in the same vein today," he said.

Yet this was old news, as his comments indicated. What struck Underhill as especially significant was the fact that despite the decline the system as a whole appeared relatively stable and resilient. "If there is general agreement that the Philippine society is seriously ill, there is also an equally firm general agreement that a revolutionary situation does not exist." With the American position in Vietnam collapsing in the face of a revolutionary situation there, Underhill's comments were intended to reassure Washington regarding the fate of the Philippines. At the same time his message revealed Underhill as a perceptive student of Philippine affairs. It also went far toward explaining why despite almost constant revolutionary agitation the status quo in the country had never gone down (and still has not).

Underhill conceded the existence of a number of preconditions of revolution, including a "highly visible chasm" between rich and poor, a large supply of firearms readily available to anyone intent on trouble, and a "huge university student population (300,000 in Manila alone), economically exploited (higher education is a profitable business here), and living in teeming dormitory slums in downtown Manila." But prospective revolutionaries had not succeeded in pushing from precondition to actuality. Underhill cited several reasons for the failure.

In the first place, although the political status quo did not work particularly well, at least it worked.

> There is a political *system* in the Philippines. Except for the period of the Japanese occupation, they have a constitution which has been in effect for 35 years without being suspended by a coup d'etat or rewritten by a military strong man. Whatever its weaknesses or inadequacies, it has repeatedly survived the test which makes it a system: the peaceful transfer of power.

Marcos would soon force revision of this aspect of Underhill's argument, but the eventual reaction against Marcos showed him to be a rule-proving exception.

Second, where the biggest deficiency of the government of South Vietnam consisted in Saigon's inability to persuade the population to identify with it, no such deficiency existed in the Philippines. "If anything," Underhill claimed, "the people identify too much." Underhill described Filipino politicians as overwhelmed by individuals seeking help with problems. "The wife of a first term congressman from Laguna tells us she has an average of 50 constituents for breakfast (bread and coffee) every week-day morning. The House Majority Leader, a Manila congressman, says that he has constituents who come into his bedroom." Far from being aloof and unresponsive to voters, government in the Philippines responded personally in a manner Americans found hard to believe.

The political socialization process began early. In schools, on playgrounds, in clubs, Filipinos elected officers. As adults they continued electing, choosing leaders for civic and professional organizations and at all levels of government from the barrio to the nation at large. Whatever good the chosen accomplished or did not accomplish in office, the process served as a societal safety valve. "Winning an election is tremendously gratifying to the ego, and the successful candidate, hooked at a very early age, seeks continuing ego satisfaction on a wider and wider stage. The energy, competitiveness, and ambition of the most active, politically oriented sector of the society is absorbed therefore in this game of elections." Winners implied losers, of course, but with so many elections there always existed opportunities to try again. Besides, losers had sufficient company to make losing no disgrace, and the art of losing well was a matter of social virtue.

Underhill named the Philippine press as a third stabilizing influence. Manila papers told all, and then some.

This is a compulsively open society, where the life span of a secret is measured in hours. Scandal quickly becomes public knowledge, and is not merely aired in the press but hyperventilated. The columnists thunder, the President orders an investigation, and Congress promises a probe, but by the next week it is pushed into oblivion by some new outrage. This process produces after a while not indignation but boredom. Nothing is more tiresome than last week's scandal.

Underhill judged the relatively open nature of the Philippine economy a fourth factor lending to stability. To be sure, peasants could not readily become landlords, and the poor of Manila's Tondo shantytown faced high barriers to advancement. But compared with adjacent Asia and other parts of the third world where military leaders and handfuls of the mighty monopolized economic power, the road to riches lay relatively unguarded in the Philippines. "There is money to be made," Underhill said, "and no social stigma attaches to conspicuous consumption if you do strike it rich." Marcos later overstepped Underhill's bound on this score, as on political continuity. The negative response again revealed him as the exceptional rule-prover.

As a final, and the most important, inoculant against revolution, Underhill pointed to the fundamental character of Filipino society and culture. "This is a highly personalized and subjective society," he said. "The individual flesh and blood human being takes priority over all abstractions, principles, and institutions." The pervasive graft and corruption in the Philippines demonstrated a weakness of this tendency, although the Filipinos' relative tolerance of nest-feathering indicated it was less a problem for them than for American observers. But the emphasis on the individual and on the individual's connections to the surrounding society also inhibited the development of revolutionary personalities.

> Sheltered in his extended family system, linked by the dual ties of loyalty and obligation upward and downward in the social structure, the Filipino is almost never alone, either actually or figuratively. . . . The individual loneliness and alienation that is deeply troubling the societies of the West is almost unknown here. This is perhaps the central reason why the average Filipino is a happy, cheerful man, optimistic about the future. To the despair of the doctrinaire revolutionary, he has not lost his sense of humor, has not lost hope, is not desperate, sullen and bitter.[24]

IV.   The untimely end of the American century

First in 1898, when an anticolonial revolution in Cuba set the United States on the path to empire; then in 1929, when the Wall Street crash triggered the depression that turned Americans inward and generated the political and economic demands that resulted in the Tydings-McDuffie Act; again in 1949–50, when the communist capture of China and the eruption of the Korean War impelled the United States to carry containment to Asia, producing the commitments that gave rise to America's involvement in Vietnam—which is to say during the entire period of U.S.-Philippine relations through the mid-1960s—the events of greatest significance for affairs between the two countries happened elsewhere than the Philippines. The pattern repeated itself early in 1968, although few in either America or the Philippines immediately recognized the recurrence. Marcos was one of the few.

The Tet offensive in Vietnam, whatever its much debated military significance, broke the political back of the Johnson administration's Indochina policy. For the first time a decisive portion of the American electorate doubted the feasibility and wisdom of their nation's Vietnam undertaking. Their doubts drove Johnson from office and recycled Richard Nixon, who understood, if belatedly, that the fundamental premise of America's approach to Asia—the existence of an effective community of objectives between China and the Soviet Union—now did violence to both reality and American interests. The recognition that China might better be cultivated than contained dovetailed with the realization that North Vietnam could be neither, and it led to America's decision to cut losses and get out of Vietnam.

The war in Vietnam would not end for another seven years, but Marcos sensed the shift in tide at once. As soon as Johnson announced his March 1968 decision to pursue peace, the Philippine president wrote the White House to express deep pain and concern regarding the future of freedom in the Philippines' part of the world. He suggested that without the steadfast protection of the United States, democracy in Asia would be endangered. Johnson replied by assuring Marcos of America's unwavering commitment to the principles for which American and Philippine troops still struggled in Vietnam. Johnson hoped Marcos' worries would not result in the flagging of his government's resolve on this vital issue. "I look to you and to our other allies," Johnson said, "to join with us in continued efforts in Vietnam."[25]

Each president had reason to suspect the intentions of the other. Johnson feared a Philippine bug-out. The chief rationale for expending as much energy as the Johnson administration did on Vietnam was that otherwise America's allies would lose confidence in American pledges and seek their own accommodations with America's rivals. Marcos' letter indicated that already the Philippine president was questioning American resolve. Johnson had sense enough to realize that his own brave phrases in reply would not convince Marcos that American policy remained as before, which it did not. When the CIA station in Manila a short while later reported a decision by Marcos to reduce the size of the Philippine contingent in Vietnam, Johnson's fears were confirmed.[26]

Marcos' suspicions about America's commitment to Vietnam were genuine, although they had hardly anything to do with the fate of the South Vietnamese government. Instead they focused on the value Washington would place on the Philippines in a post-Vietnam Southeast Asia. The market for allies in the region could go either way. If Americans turned bearish on international obligations, Manila's value might decrease significantly. On the other hand, if Americans retreated from the mainland only to dig in on the offshore islands, the price they would pay for Philippine cooperation could reach record highs.

In fact the market did some of both during the next twenty years. Initially Marcos had cause to think the ticker would register gains. Johnson, hoping to reassure the Philippine president, replaced Blair as ambassador with G. Mennen Williams, former governor of Michigan and a Democrat of greater stature and larger influence with the White House than Blair. The appointment was greeted with broad but not unrelieved warmth in the Philippines. The *Manila Chronicle*, portraying Williams as "a veteran politician and diplomat and a respected liberal with known concern for developing nations," proclaimed the arriving ambassador a "vast improvement" over his predecessor, whom the paper deemed a dilettante. The *Evening News* several weeks into Williams' tenure announced "a good start." The *Cebu Advocate*, punning on Williams' nickname, asked, "Will relations be cleaner with Soapy around?" The *Manila Times* remarked wryly, "The U.S. has named its envoy to the R.P. Time to resume our unfriendly relations." Yet even the skeptics were mollified when Williams, following the shooting of a Filipino boy by an American guard at the Sangley Point naval station, immediately apologized and ensured that Washington turn the case over to Philippine authorities.[27]

Before sending Williams off to Manila the Johnson White House put together a summary of the contemporary condition of U.S.-Philippine affairs. "Our relations with the Philippines at this time are generally good," the report declared, but added, "There are minor irritations in the operation of our bases in the country and minor trade difficulties." Assistance to the Philippines was "relatively modest," totaling for the current year roughly $20 million each for military and economic aid, in addition to an Export-Import Bank credit of $3 million.

But trouble, as usual, lay ahead. "Probably the most disturbing aspect of the situation in the Philippines, for 1968 and succeeding years, is the continued low state of respect for law and order," the White House paper continued. "This inhibits investment, both foreign and domestic, contributes to the loss of confidence in the government and increasing disaffection among the mass of the people, and creates the danger that the present political structure will at some point no longer be considered as the most satisfactory means for evolutionary social and economic advance." Though the authors stopped short of predicting revolution, the evidence suggested that the downward spiral could not continue without end. Events would force someone to take extraordinary action to break the trend.[28]

The lack of respect for law and order the White House report referred to showed up especially during the election campaign of 1969. Four years earlier, when Marcos entered office, the Philippines had one of the highest homicide rates in Southeast Asia. During his first term it climbed even higher, attaining unprecedented levels with the election of 1969. To some degree the murdering merely reflected a violent society in which honor bound an injured party to avenge injury in kind. In this regard it demonstrated the continuing effects of the traumatic period of Japanese occupation, as blood feuds begun then were bequeathed to the second generation. In part it owed to the easy availability of American war-surplus weapons. Nor did the social strains that always accompany modernization help matters. Yet to a peculiar extent lethal violence in the Philippines became an expected adjunct of political activities, with killings mounting alarmingly just prior to elections. Money, dispersed more freely than ever, no longer had the effect it once did. Party leaders turned to gangs of enforcers to protect their territory from interlopers and ensure a favorable vote.[29]

Predictably and without difficulty, although not without expense and bloodshed, Marcos gained reelection in 1969. Whether the American government assisted in the victory is a matter of some dispute. Beyond question is that Marcos would have won without such help as Washington provided. But the excesses of the election simply compounded the turmoil in the country. In January 1970 tens of thousands of students demonstrated in Manila against the Marcos regime. Six were killed in a march on Malacañang. Radicals and sympathizers attempted to seize control of the University of the Philippines. When they proclaimed the establishment of the "Diliman Commune" in February 1971 the army intervened to break up the protests. In August of the same year bombs exploded at a rally of the opposition Liberals, killing several persons and seriously wounding one hundred, including a number of the leading Liberal candidates for the senate. Marcos blamed the attack on the communists. Evidence that surfaced much later indicated he was right, but few believed him then, and many judged the president's goons responsible.[30]

The Liberals, led by Benigno Aquino, benefited from sympathy and protest votes and scored a significant upset in the off-year elections. The result startled Marcos, who, thinking of the two-term limit the constitution placed on his political ambitions, had meanwhile agreed to demands for constitutional reform. The reformers hoped to clean up the political process, to diminish the scope for fraud and violence. Marcos, remembering Manuel Quezon's example, hoped to arrange a longer stay in office.

Unfortunately for the cause of good government, when a convention met to write a new constitution, its large size (320 members), the diversity of proposals forwarded, the lack of strong leadership and the susceptibility of delegates to the traditional temptations of money and influence all but paralyzed the proceedings. After a year of deliberation the end lay nowhere in sight. An original self-prescribed deadline of December 1972 had become a dead letter. By then, though, Marcos had figured out another way to remain in power.

16

Democracy Undone
1972–1983

I.   The man on the horse

While the constitutional convention argued the merits of presidential and parliamentary systems and pondered means, depending on the ponderers, of preventing or ensuring a Marcos succession to Marcos, violence in the country remained at a high level. Most acts of terror, sabotage and reprisal claimed humble victims, but one targeted Malacañang itself. During the first months of 1972 the Liberal leader Sergio Osmeña, Jr., devised a plot to assassinate Marcos. The plan aborted when Marcos' spies infiltrated the conspiracy, which included three American killers-for-hire. One of the potential assassins was jailed. Osmeña and the others escaped to the United States. The plot did not fit Marcos' continuing contention that communists lay behind the surge of crime and unrest in the country, and perhaps for this reason he did not publicize it. But it did contribute to his conviction that only firm action would save the Philippines and, more to the point, his position at the country's head.[1]

Following the bomb attack on the Liberal rally in August 1971 Marcos had suspended the writ of habeas corpus. Now in September 1972 he canceled most of the rest of the constitution and declared martial law. He forbade political demonstrations, announced a curfew, shut down newspapers and radio and television stations, and jailed prominent members of the opposition, including Benigno Aquino and more than a dozen anti-Marcos delegates to the constitutional convention. By the end of the year the number of political prisoners reached several thousand. Political debate quieted at once, then essentially ceased.

Marcos' decision to overturn what American governments for three-quarters of a century had officially been trying to foster came as no great surprise to Washington. Manila had rippled with rumors for many months. "You can hear most anything, depending on the person you are talking to," James Wilson wrote from the American embassy. By the beginning of September the talk was focusing on the possibility of martial law. A few days before the event the American ambassador, Henry Byroade, received a report that a proclamation was imminent. Byroade attempted to dissuade Marcos, less from devotion to democracy than from a belief that such a measure would prove counterproductive. Years later Byroade described his reservations to a journalist in Washington: "I could imagine protests against Marcos sweeping through Manila and back here, on Capitol Hill, demands that we cut off his aid for raping democracy."[2]

Yet Marcos, while not quite so proficient at reading American moods as Quezon had been, accurately guessed that the Nixon administration had things on its collective mind besides political rights in the Philippines. Marcos did not know of the Watergate affair and Nixon's role in directing a cover-up, but the Philippine president recognized Nixon's preoccupation with getting reelected and ending the war in Vietnam. Besides, neither Nixon nor National Security Adviser Henry Kissinger, the architects of America's embrace of the Chinese Communist government, had a reputation as a prominent civil libertarian. On the contrary, Nixon's preference for "law and order" was well known.

Washington quickly accommodated to the new situation in the Philippines. Four weeks after the martial law decree the state department produced an assessment of its impact on American interests in the Philippines. The paper dismissed Marcos' claim that martial law was necessary to prevent a communist takeover. "While the communist insurgency, if left unchecked, might have been able to overthrow the Philippine Government in another five years, it clearly does not have that capability at the present time." The true explanation was simpler. Marcos could not figure out another sure way to remain in power past 1973. As a further consideration the report's authors suggested that Marcos may have decided that only martial law allowed him sufficient freedom to effect needed reforms. Considering the Philippine president's previous apathy regarding reform, this argument sounded less like a counsel of sincerity than an effort by the authors to insure themselves against the not unlikely prospect that higher-ups in the Nixon administration would decide martial law was not such a bad idea.

While commenting that the martial law announcement had been a serious gamble, the state department analysts asserted, "Thus far events seem to be working out in Marcos' favor." The army had backed the president, the opposition was scrambling for cover, and the general public was not complaining particularly loudly. Whether Marcos' luck would hold remained an open question. The United States might have much to say in the matter. "Marcos personally will be very heavily dependent on continued U.S. military and economic assistance programs and upon support from American business circles in order to maintain law and order, achieve internal security and accomplish the economic and social reforms set out as objectives of his martial law regime."

The report acknowledged the tradeoffs involved in any policy now adopted toward the Philippines. The United States possessed "an interest in the preservation of individual rights and constitutional procedures." Support for Marcos would, on its face, contribute to repression of these rights and procedures. On the other hand America valued stability. Military aid enabled the Armed Forces of the Philippines to maintain stability. "Failure of the AFP effort to improve conditions of law and order and to suppress the dissident communist forces, now that the military establishment has committed itself to this martial law gamble, would of course result in a fairly rapid deterioration of internal security." American commercial interests also required stability. The report's authors deemed it worth mention that the American Chamber of Commerce in Manila had announced its support for martial law. Most important, the use of the American bases in the Philippines required the cooperation of the government, for better or worse currently in Marcos' hands.

On balance, the state department paper said, the United States should continue providing assistance to the Philippines. American officials should attempt to hold Marcos to his avowed reformist purposes in proclaiming martial law, to the end that "the achievement of these objectives, rather than the perpetuation of Marcos in power, becomes the criterion for the continuation or lifting of martial law." In any event the American government ought to go forward with a $50 million economic assistance package in the pipeline and with a proposed 50 percent increase, to $22 million for fiscal 1973, in military aid.[3]

This particular report was intended for the consumption of the White House, hostile territory for state department officers during the Nixon years. Within the department itself few gave the reforms Marcos professed to support much chance of success. A departmental intelligence analysis of what the analysts dryly dubbed the Philippines' "one-man democracy" noted that "Marcos' security measures so far appear aimed more at his own political opponents than at communists, and his 'reforms' have been little more than conventional bids for popular support which could have been initiated without martial law." His reform program was "largely hortatory," and nothing he had done had seriously touched "the entrenched economic interests of the country's oligarchy."

As part of what he was calling his "New Society," Marcos had announced the extension of a 1963 Luzon land reform law to the country as a whole, but, as the state department paper noted, he had yet to explain how a program that had not worked in Luzon, and which he had done almost nothing to implement, would fare better nationwide. He had said the country's 700,000 tenant farmers would acquire title to the land they worked within fifteen years, but the stipulated purchase arrangements were no bargain for the tenants and the whole program appeared highly susceptible to obstruction and mismanagement. He had pledged to streamline and "purify" the government and claimed to have sacked nearly 5,000 government employees, but with few exceptions most of those fired were "small fry." He had decreed the passage of a large flood-relief bill, which he blamed the opposition for having previously blocked, but his own party had controlled the congress that failed to approve the measure, and it remained uncertain where the money would come from to fund the program. He had promised to stamp out communism and insurgent activity, but he had made no meaningful progress attacking the basic problems that provided recruits to the CPP and NPA, and some of his actions, especially his proclamation against private possession of firearms, were likely to aggravate the Muslim insurgency in the south.

The state department report pointed out that martial law was producing a split in the ranks of the Filipino elite. Standing with Marcos were the military leaders, who desired to root out communism and considered martial law facilitative of this end, and government "technocrats," who hoped for genuine reform and were willing to accept Marcos' assurance that such was what he intended. Opposing Marcos, although silently at the moment, were the "oligarchs," especially the large landowners. Marcos' relations with this group were not clear-cut, for in significant respects he was one of them, having amassed one of the greatest personal fortunes in the country during his time in office. Yet many of the old elite resented the arriviste, and while he had done little to damage them economically his actions had engendered their hostility by threatening to cut them off from political power. Their enmity might yet prove the president's demise. "They intensely dislike Marcos and could mount the most formidable challenge to his ambitions."[4]

Marcos proved more clever than his rivals, at least for awhile. He struck a nice balance between those in position to support him and those poised to do damage. He cultivated the military by expanding the defense budget and increasing the number of men under arms. Appropriations for the army, navy, air force and constabulary tripled in real terms between 1972 and 1977. As a portion of the national budget the military's share doubled to 23 percent. Uniformed troops increased 100 percent to more than 110,000, and after Marcos announced plans to integrate municipal police with the constabulary and to expand "home defense units," a kind of militia, the total projected force came to a quarter-million.

One result of this buildup was the injection of military leaders into Filipino politics in unprecedented fashion. In countries that achieved independence through armed struggle—Indonesia and Vietnam, for example—the military had long played a major political role. The Philippines, by contrast, had until Marcos been spared. But under martial law the generals and their civilian associates gained influence, and despite Marcos' efforts to keep them under control such individuals as defense minister Juan Ponce Enrile and constabulary chief Fidel Ramos became powers in their own right.[5]

Marcos also worked to strengthen his political base among the masses. This was the point of his bold pronouncements on agrarian reform. Promises of land for the tiller had been a staple of Filipino politics since Quezon. Magsaysay, as champion of the common folk, and Macapagal, as floundering incumbent searching for a life preserver, had succeeded in persuading the legislature to approve impressive-sounding title transfer laws. Yet in the face of landlord resistance none of the schemes got far. Marcos, in martial-law decree 27, proclaimed the most sweeping program to date. Tenants whose landlords owned more than seven hectares would be able to purchase the land they farmed at a price equal to two-and-a-half times annual production, payable over fifteen years at 6 percent interest. In the interim each tiller would receive a certificate of land transfer specifying the land to be acquired.

Marcos' program accomplished some good. During his time in office more tenants came nearer to ownership than during any previous administration. Reality, however, fell far short of promise, in the process revealing the essentially political purpose of the whole business. Marcos concentrated on his opponents in determining where to commence expropriations. The estates of the Aquino family headed his list. Because Marcos and friends had a personal financial stake in sugar and other export crops, reforms focused on land planted to rice and corn. The government blithely equated certificates of land transfer with true titles, enabling it to proclaim to Washington, which conditioned aid on progress on the land question, that the program was proceeding swiftly to the desired goal. That Washington accepted Manila's figures, with the Reagan administration telling Congress in 1981, for example, that 88 percent of eligible families had received land titles—a vast overstatement—demonstrated the success of the ploy.[6]

In the longer term, though, Marcos' land scheme may have done the Philippine president more harm than good. An incomplete Machiavellian, he injured or frightened those members of the landed elite who already distrusted him, but he did not completely deprive them of power. Ultimately they would strike back. While Marcos improved the lot of thousands of peasants, his failure to deliver on his extravagant pledges left millions disillusioned and resentful. During the first years of martial law Marcos' support in the provinces probably increased. At the end the peasants abandoned him along with everyone else.

II. Washington as fiddle

In important respects Marcos' New Society achieved its greatest triumph in the United States. If human rights meant nothing to Nixon, Congress cared a bit more about the issue, and despite Nixon's efforts to seize control of the American spending process, via the same sort of impoundment Marcos practiced in the Philippines, the legislature largely determined what the Philippines would or would not receive in American aid. By espousing support for land reform, for breaking the grip of the oligarchy and for cleaning up the government, Marcos rendered his regime more palatable to the aid givers than it otherwise would have been. Washington was fairly tolerant in this area. American officials had fallen over themselves sending assistance to post-Sukarno Indonesia, despite the complicity of the Suharto government in the deaths of hundreds of thousands of communists and related unfortunates. Suharto's pledge of a "New Order" had reassured Congress, and Marcos calculated correctly that his own promise of a New Society for the Philippines would do the same. An American official of the Agency for International Development captured the attitude of many in Washington when he said of the agrarian part of Marcos' package, "I'm not too hot on supporting dictatorships, although we seem to be doing this more and more. But it makes it easier to do so when they have programs like the land reform that the Philippine government has."[7]

Of course, just as the real attraction to Americans of Suharto's New Order lay in its liquidation of the Indonesian Communist party, so the fundamental appeal of Marcos' New Society was the prospect it offered, at least initially, of quelling the revolt of the NPA. Had Marcos carried out the reforms he promised, perhaps he would have stolen support from the rebels. As matters turned out, martial law guaranteed the future of the revolution. From its founding in 1969 until the summer of 1972 the NPA had caused the government trouble, but not enough to genuinely threaten its overthrow. In outlawing dissent Marcos became the NPA's most effective recruiting officer. Hundreds of student dissidents and other opponents of the government, forced to choose between prison and the hills, opted for the latter. Where in 1972 the NPA was active in only a handful of provinces, by the end of the decade the guerrillas had spread from Luzon all across the archipelago, achieving particular strength in Samar, Negros, Panay and parts of Mindanao. In Samar the extent of NPA activities provoked the government to adopt the reconcentrado policy of the American pacifiers of the turn of the century, recently revived by the Americans in Vietnam. The uprooted peasants often turned against the government, swelling insurgent ranks further. Perhaps the most significant unintended result of the Marcos crackdown was the establishment of a CPP-NPA foothold in the cities. The communists, calling for a united front against the "U.S.-Marcos dictatorship," infiltrated student and labor organizations. Their emphasis on Marcos rather than Marx enabled them to attract even faithful members of the Catholic church.[8]

American leaders observed the intensified activities of the communists with concern, although initially they underestimated the seriousness of the rebels' challenge. Partly because they viewed the situation in the Philippines against the backdrop of the simultaneous utter disintegration of the South Vietnamese government, partly because they mistook for inactivity the CPP's emphasis at this stage on political organization rather than military attacks, partly because they had not learned to discount sufficiently Marcos' press releases, and partly because Washington wanted to hear that martial law was working, American officials reporting from the Philippines emphasized the government's successes in dealing

with the communists. An airgram from the embassy in late 1974 said the declaration of martial law had dealt "a serious blow" to the rebels, a blow "from which
they still have not recovered." At a time when NPA numbers and activity were
in fact increasing significantly, the embassy described the guerrilla troops as "hard
pressed just to replace their losses." It went on to predict comparable difficulty in
the months ahead.[9]

The following summer when Marcos, following Nixon's lead, traveled to Beijing and prepared to normalize relations with China, the embassy noted the dismay of what it called the "harried membership" of the CPP. The communist
paper Ang Bayan had spent three pages of "tortured logic" trying to explain away
the significance of Marcos' trip, being reduced in the end to the lame argument
that "a bad thing can at the same time be a good thing." The embassy forecast
failure in the rebels' effort to deny that "Uncle Mao may have sold them out for
a cheap mess of real-politikal pottage." The communist intelligentsia might
attempt to put a bright gloss on the matter, but they would not succeed with the
troops. "The guerrilla in his jungle lair is unlikely to be heartened."[10]

Three months later the embassy reiterated the message of government competence, present and future, to deal with the insurrection:

> The government will almost certainly be able to cope with the NPA threat at a min-
> imum cost in terms of manpower and equipment losses. While the AFP will not be
> able to totally eradicate the NPA, it will probably continue to effectively check the
> NPA's expansion efforts, except in its traditional bases or in areas such as Samar
> where the government presence is limited and where economic and social problems
> have created conditions favorable for exploitation by the insurgents. In short, the
> indications are that, while the NPA will remain a thorn in the government's side,
> the general peace and order situation—now generally favorable to the government
> in most areas—will not be adversely affected to any significant degree by NPA activ-
> ities.[11]

While Marcos managed to convince Washington of his ability to handle the
communist insurgency, he succeeded even better showing the Americans he was
the man to safeguard their military bases. The bases remained as sensitive a subject as ever. From the Filipino perspective the issues stood as always: critics
judged the American presence an insult to Philippine nationhood while supporters deemed it a guarantee of American interest and largess. From the American
viewpoint, though, things had changed. The fall of South Vietnam, which by the
second anniversary of martial law was a near certainty and by the third an accomplished fact, made the American bases either more necessary than ever or essentially superfluous, with the decision depending on the same considerations that
would determine the American assessment of the Philippines overall. If the
Americans took their failure in Vietnam as a signal for policy redesign, then the
bases counted for little. Before China became Asian enemy number one, the
United States had thought about abandoning the bases. Now that the Forbidden

City was no longer forbidden, they might think about it again. On the other hand, if the loss of Vietnam triggered a hold-what-we-have response, then the bases appreciated.

For a moment during the second half of the 1970s the redesigners gained the upper hand in American foreign policy. In 1975 Congress refused to allow American aid to anticommunist forces in Angola. The following year brought the election of Jimmy Carter, who pledged to avoid the excesses that produced the Vietnam debacle and the inordinate fear of communism that led to the embracing of dictators.

Taking courage from such straws in the wind, officials in the American diplomatic establishment uneasy with America's tolerance of Marcos pressed for rethinking of the base question. Francis Underhill, currently ambassador to Malaysia, summarized the arguments for a pullout. Underhill circled the subject gingerly, aware of the damage the national-security bureaucracy's inertial guidance system could do to the careers of careless dissenters. He began by merely raising the matter for review and offering a mild suggestion: "The necessity of maintaining bases should not be considered as obvious and self-manifest. Those that support a base agreement should be required to state and defend their case, as of course should those who question the need for this kind of presence." Underhill proceeded to list the principal tenets of the retentionists' position: that the United States required the bases in order to project power into the southwestern Pacific and mainland Southeast Asia, that the bases demonstrated the sincerity of American commitments and served as a stabilizing influence in the region, that they deterred Soviet and Chinese adventurism, that they supported the global balance of power, and that Moscow and Beijing did not object to America's presence in the Philippines.

Warming to his subject, Underhill dismissed the projection-of-power and counter-adventurism arguments as irrelevant at a time when neither the Russians nor the Chinese displayed an inclination to attack any of the noncommunist countries in Southeast Asia. Perhaps they would in the unforeseeable future, but such an uncertain event afforded no sound basis for present policy. "Do we need to furnish a live-in fireman and pay a handsome board-and-room fee to the householder on the possibility that the house may some day catch fire?" Against such a day the United States might negotiate an agreement allowing access to base facilities in event of emergency, similar to agreements America had with other countries.

Regarding the stabilizing-presence argument, Underhill contended that the Southeast Asian states were more interested in an American economic presence, in the form of markets and technical and financial assistance, than in troops on the ground and ships at anchor. The countries other than the Philippines did not dislike having Americans in the Philippines "as a kind of residual insurance policy," yet they were not sufficiently impressed by the importance of American bases to volunteer facilities in their own territories. Within the Philippines the bases exercised a net negative influence on stability by handing radicals and other anti-government groups an issue with which to flay the government.

As to the global balance of power, Underhill thought the bases of marginal significance at best. Now that the war in Vietnam had ended, the Philippines lay too far off the track of superpower competition for the bases there to count for much.

The final argument of the retentionists, that the Soviets and Chinese did not seriously object to the maintenance of the bases, struck Underhill as almost incomprehensible. Naturally the communist powers did not object to an opportunity to portray Americans as colonialists and militarists. Nor did Moscow and Beijing complain about something that enhanced the stature of communists in the Philippines. Underhill deemed the very fact of Soviet and Chinese acquiescence in America's staying in the Philippines prima facie evidence of the desirability of leaving.

These counter-arguments, Underhill held, should have prompted reconsideration of the need for bases even if keeping the bases cost nothing. But keeping them cost much, and the cost was growing. Beyond the economic and military aid the Philippine government extracted from the United States in lieu of rent, the United States paid dearly for the bases in dealings with the Filipino people. "Our relations with the Philippines can never be normal while our bases remain," Underhill said. "For the Filipinos they create contradictions and strains which twist and warp every aspect of their attitudes toward us." Filipinos long ago had persuaded themselves that the bases served only American and not Philippine interests. Consequently they saw the American presence as intrusive, a symbol of "imperfect independence and continuing dependency." They also judged the compensation they received insufficient payment for the criticism they suffered from other countries of the third world. The persistent problems of jurisdiction and the chafing that inevitably accompanied the presence of large numbers of relatively wealthy and mostly white-skinned Americans among larger numbers of poor Filipinos lengthened the list of complaints. Yet, conditioned by three generations of history to consider America their protector, the Filipinos could not bring themselves to tell the United States to leave. The ambivalence about the bases produced what Underhill described as "a neurotic, manipulative, psychically crippling form of dependency."

Washington would err, Underhill concluded, to cling to the bases until thrown out. If matters deteriorated that far, both the United States and the Philippines would be losers. Better to take the initiative, maximizing the possibility of friendly ties and cooperation in the future and ensuring that if war or other emergency required a return, there would be something to return to. "Rather than negotiating to remain, we should be negotiating for an orderly and gradual withdrawal that would maintain the physical facilities and reservoir of trained manpower and minimize the severe economic, social, and psychic consequences of our departure."[12]

Fortunately for Marcos, Underhill's argument did not go far. The defense department hunkered down, predictably contending that the fall of South Vietnam rendered the American bases in the Philippines more important than ever. The Pentagon held that the costs of remaining in the Philippines, while not insignificant, were manageable. The state department offered Underhill no support, concurring in the defense department's judgment that the American bases were "of high strategic value" and "irreplaceable."[13]

The White House also went along, though more reluctantly. Despite his initial advocacy of retailoring America's commitments to match the multipolar realities of the second generation of the postwar era, Carter soon smacked into the Democrats' dilemma: how to fend off charges of softness on communism without adopting the Cold Warriors' agenda. Carter succeeded in Panama, negotiating and persuading Congress to ratify a treaty specifying relinquishment of American control of the canal. He got halfway to a strategic-arms pact with the Soviet Union. But, recognizing the limits of his political capital, he chose not to make an issue of the bases in the Philippines.

This left the matter to Marcos. The Philippine president, correctly assessing the retentionist mood in America, played Washington like a virtuoso. Earlier talks, culminating just before Marcos' 1965 election, had resulted in reducing the length of the American leases from 99 years to 25. Marcos contended that the Philippines should not have to wait until 1991 to rectify the problems the bases caused, and in 1975, even as he assured Washington that "we believe in an effective presence of the United States in the Western Pacific," he hinted at abrogating the agreement unless the Americans offered satisfaction.[14]

In light of his cavalier attitude toward Filipinos' civil liberties, few in Washington at the time were surprised to discover that satisfaction for Marcos had less to do with extraterritoriality or other issues impinging on the rights of Filipinos than with increased American aid. For public consumption the American government consistently denied linkage between base rights and American assistance. The United States, according to the official line, did not pay rent for facilities that served Philippine interests as well as American. But everyone involved knew better, including President Gerald Ford, whose frankness on the issue prompted National Security Adviser Brent Scowcroft to send the Oval Office a gentle reminder "to avoid any implications of a quid-pro-quo relationship between our military presence and economic assistance."[15]

When negotiations began in 1976 the essential question involved how many quid Marcos would get pro his quo. Marcos' chief negotiator, the unsinkable Carlos Romulo, now foreign minister, suggested a few billion dollars as an appropriate neighborhood for a deal. The Ford administration held out for a lower-rent district. Secretary of State and geopolitician par excellence Henry Kissinger persuaded Ford to raise America's offer to Marcos by many millions per year, but the White House drew the line at that point. Preferring to try his luck with the arriving Democrats, Marcos suspended discussions.[16]

III. Debased or de-based?

During the numbered days of the Ford presidency various committees of the American Congress unearthed a considerable pile of information regarding the sordid doings of the CIA and other agents of the American government around the world. The CIA, it appeared, had attempted to assassinate foreign leaders, had disrupted economies, had rigged elections, had conducted secret experiments on unwitting subjects, including Americans, and had generally violated what most Americans hoped were the principles their government stood for. In this atmosphere of national soul-baring a closer look at the human rights record of America's Asian offspring was almost inevitable. That Jimmy Carter, alone of America's postwar presidents, deemed a foreign government's treatment of its citizens an important consideration in conducting relations with that government added to the impetus for scrutinizing Marcos.

Shortly after Carter's inauguration the president sent the assistant secretary of state for the Far East and the Pacific, Richard Holbrooke, to Manila. Holbrooke informed Marcos that the human rights situation in the Philippines was a matter "of personal importance to President Carter." Perhaps previously there had existed justification for short-cutting habeas corpus and other constitutional guarantees. But now the Philippine government was "clearly strong enough to take positive steps in the human rights field." Holbrooke cited the continued detention of opposition leaders, particularly Benigno Aquino, as an item generating "substantial interest" in the United States, and, speaking for the president, he called for "prompt and compassionate resolution" of these cases. Thus far the White House had been content to deal privately with Malacañang regarding human rights. It would not do so forever. "President Carter's willingness to remain reticent is limited," Holbrooke said.

Marcos at first indicated reluctance. If he released Aquino and the rest, he said, they would be "lionized" by the Americans. To this Holbrooke remarked that if Marcos' government was truly secure it could stand a little criticism in the United States. Marcos then told the undersecretary to assure President Carter that the Philippine government would take his advice to heart. "We really understand his views," Marcos declared. "We're really going to do something about Aquino and the others." Holbrooke answered that he would pass the message along, adding for good measure that the president would be watching the situation carefully. Progress, Holbrooke said, was "essential."[17]

Other Carter administration officials followed Holbrooke to Manila to repeat the message. Patricia Derian, occupant of the freshly created office of undersecretary of state for human rights and possessor of a personality rather at odds with the tactful style cultivated in the diplomatic corps, arrived at the beginning of 1978 and lectured Marcos on the abuses of his regime. She also attempted to embarrass the Philippine president, or at least encourage his opponents, by visiting Aquino in jail. Vice President Walter Mondale journeyed to the Philippines several months later. Like Holbrooke and Derian he proclaimed America's desire for restoration of civil liberties. Like Derian he met with leaders of the Philippine opposition.

Yet because Washington had failed to back its threats with sanctions, Marcos by this time sensed the emptiness of the American challenge to his authoritarian rule. The Mondale visit came just weeks after another patently fraudulent election. Derian argued for cancellation of the vice president's trip, contending that no matter what Mondale told Marcos the fact of Mondale's presence would indicate American acceptance of the hijacking of the vote. Holbrooke countered that a public slap would simply antagonize Marcos, that quiet diplomacy would prove more effective and that however desirable improvement in the treatment of dissidents might be, such improvement did not warrant jeopardizing the future of the American bases. Mondale agreed with Holbrooke and went ahead with his trip.[18]

This wasn't the last battle Derian would lose, and her defeat was symptomatic of the direction American Philippine policy was heading. Negotiations over the bases had resumed in 1977. The Carter administration was under attack for liberal wimpiness, blasted by the Committee on the Present Danger and other conservative pressure groups, and rather than encourage the critics the administration chose to concentrate on getting a new agreement. In November 1978 Ambassador Richard Murphy cabled from Manila that the talks were approaching a "particularly critical or delicate stage." The administration must exercise great care in getting past the "politically ticklish issues" of jurisdiction and compensation. Murphy worried about a report on human rights Congress required the state department to produce shortly. He forecast heavy fallout for the base negotiations from a negative evaluation of the Marcos regime. A previous report, and the attention it had received in the American news media, had made Malacañang difficult to deal with. This time the damage would be worse. "If the human rights report on the Philippines receives the same sort of media interpretation in 1979 as it did in 1978—an interpretation which put the Philippines at the bottom of the human rights barrel in East Asia—I fear there would be a very serious impact on base agreement prospects in both the U.S. and the Philippines." Should Marcos again be drawn as the bad boy of Asia, he might well be enraged to the point of cutting off talks or retracting agreements in principle already made. In addition, the support in the United States necessary to consummate a deal— that is, to fund the large aid package any deal would include—might dissipate.

"Either result would indefinitely delay our reaching an agreement and could have a destabilizing effect throughout this region where countries are watching closely whether we will succeed in these talks."

Murphy did not argue that the administration should lower its standards to the extent of ignoring Marcos' excesses entirely. And he recognized that the state department had limited control over the interpretation outsiders, in Congress and in the media, placed upon its reports. But he held that the issues involved were of such importance that American officials should make an "extraordinary effort" to avoid singling out Marcos for criticism. In particular he urged a "meticulous review" within the department of the human rights records of other countries in the area, to ensure that the report on the Philippines not lend itself to "invidious comparisons." He also recommended "an advance campaign with key media personnel" to remind them that the department did not array foreign governments in a "human rights pecking order" and that the department's reports did not cover many countries—China, Cambodia and Uganda, for example—with far worse records on human rights.[19]

Marcos intensified Murphy's concern with a calculated campaign of psychological warfare designed to demonstrate that the Philippines might do just fine without the United States. Americans after Nixon could not much object to Marcos' normalization with China, yet a subsequent cozying to Moscow and other countries of the communist sphere, as well as a variety of nonaligned nations, grated Washington's nerves. The crowning impudence occurred in 1978 when he joined Vietnamese Prime Minister Pham Van Dong in signing a nonaggression, nonsubversion pact. In the meantime he encouraged members of his government to denounce the American bases as symbols of neocolonialism—an action that did double duty in appeasing Filipino nationalists and raising the rent he would squeeze from the Americans.

American officials understood what the Philippine leader was up to. "President Marcos, like any master strategist, realizes that in any game it is wise to keep one's options open," Ambassador David Newsom wrote from Manila. "He therefore may flirt without compunction with the Third World, China, or the Soviet Union, if this suits his immediate purposes." Washington could do little to stop him. Newsom saw no great cause for geopolitical concern in the matter, since despite his brave posturing Marcos faced severe constraints, both domestically and in terms of international affairs, in adopting an explicitly neutralist position or one farther left. "It would take a severe jolt to dislodge him from his basically pro-American sentiments."[20]

Newsom's equanimity proved well founded. In the first week of 1979, before the deadline for the Carter administration's human rights report, Marcos' negotiators concluded a deal with their American counterparts. The new accord reduced the size of the reservations at Clark and Subic, although not sufficiently to hamper American operations. It explicitly labeled the facilities "Philippine" bases, requiring that the Philippine flag fly there. It specified review of the agreement every five years until 1991, when the twenty-five-year treaty expired. Most important, it obligated the American president to make his "best effort" to persuade Congress to deliver half a billion dollars in aid during the next five years.

As anyone could tell, the slippery part of the pact involved the president's "best effort." Human rights advocates in the Carter administration contended that a simple request to Congress, unaccompanied by vigorous follow-up, would fulfill the obligation. But Marcos cared little for legalism—obviously, considering his contempt for law in the Philippines. He wanted the aid, and if Washington failed to deliver he doubtless would scuttle the agreement. Carter understood this, and when Marcos' accusers in Congress attempted to slice even slightly the first installment of the administration's aid request, the president called out his crack troops—the secretary of state, the secretary of defense, the joint chiefs of staff—to overwhelm the opposition with arguments about the bases' essentialness and about American steadfastness and credibility.

Other administration officials, including the president himself, defended the policy of quiet diplomacy as having increased the responsiveness of the Marcos regime to complaints on human rights. The assistant secretary of state for congressional relations, Douglas Bennet, replied to a query from a skeptical legislator by noting that in the past several months accusations of torture and mistreatment of prisoners had become less frequent, "at least in the Manila area," that complaints of torture had led to investigations and courts-martial and in one recent instance to prison sentences for three constabulary personnel, and that the Philippine government had announced parole and amnesty programs affecting more than two thousand detainees. "We will continue to express our concern over the human rights situation in the Philippines and to urge further improvements in that situation, for so long as problems persist," Bennet pledged.[21]

Events continued to work on Marcos' behalf. Not for thirty years, since the defeat of the Chinese Nationalists, had an American administration come in for such concerted criticism for soft-minded naïveté in foreign affairs as Carter's did in 1979. To Russian gains in East Africa, consolidated by a Soviet-Ethiopian alliance, were added in the Democrats' debit column the victory of the Sandinista guerrillas in Nicaragua, the ouster of the shah of Iran and the subsequent taking of American hostages, and the Soviet invasion of Afghanistan. The last two events, which significantly altered the power balance in the Middle East, provided further arguments for retaining the American bases in the Philippines, since Subic in particular would help sustain an American naval presence in the Indian Ocean and Persian Gulf. In calmer circumstances Carter and Congress might have read the overthrow of Somoza and the shah as object lessons in the perils of supporting dictators. As it was they adopted the politically safer expedient of keeping Marcos fat and friendly.

IV.   The new old regime

Expedience forces political leaders into embarrassing positions. To secure the bases the Carter administration jettisoned its preference for human rights over geopolitics. Some administration officials later claimed credit for the 1980 release of Aquino from prison, and Aquino himself acknowledged Carter's role in the matter. Perhaps the administration's expressions of concern over human rights made Marcos more reluctant than he otherwise would have been to allow Aquino, who needed heart surgery, to die in jail. But if the Carter years demonstrated anything they showed that the American commitment to Philippine democracy remained essentially a matter of convenience, worth pursuing—as for eighty years—only after the narrower interests of the United States had been secured. The Carter administration's bailing out on human rights surely came as no surprise to anyone familiar with the events surrounding American annexation of the Philippines and the accompanying war—in which Americans were involved in repression directly, and not just as accessories—or with the complex of American decisions in the late 1930s that left the Philippines indefensible in the face of Japanese attack.

If expedience produces embarrassment, embarrassment requires self-awareness. Officials in the Carter administration were fully aware of the compromising position their embrace of Marcos placed them in. David Newsom explained the fundamental difficulty:

> In seeking to achieve our current goals and objectives in the Philippines, we face a serious but not unique dilemma. We have certain specific national security objectives, namely, the retention of our military bases, which we can only achieve by reaching agreement with a leadership considered by many in the United States— and in the Philippines—to be in violation of accepted norms of human rights.

There was no way to finesse the issue, and as long as the United States deemed the bases essential, improvements on the human rights front would be marginal at best. Newsom had no illusions that Marcos ever intended to restore democracy to the Philippines. "He will not risk his future in a truly democratic election," the ambassador predicted. American officials, including Newsom, had once hoped Marcos might become the reformer he initially pledged to be. "The tragic irony of martial law is that Marcos is probably the first Philippine President with enough power to seriously attack the twin abuses, extreme wealth inequity and corruption, which plague Philippine society," Newsom said. "Had he been so inclined, the last two or three years, when his power, prestige, energy, and intellectual faculties were all at high levels, would have been the time to do so." But Marcos was demonstrating daily that he was not so inclined, to state the situation mildly. All evidence indicated that Marcos' regime was "increasingly bent on perpetuating itself in power for power's sake alone."

Newsom wondered whether the problem ran deeper than Marcos, whether he was not more typical of Filipino politics than Americans wished to admit. "Do we delude ourselves to think that democracy existed or can exist? Are we destined to continue to reconcile our objectives with essentially Machiavellian, authoritarian Filipino leaders?" Newsom could not confidently supply answers to such questions.

Whatever the long term held, in a shorter time frame conditions in the Philippines would almost certainly continue to decline. Until the onset of martial law Marcos' greed had not seemed exceptional, by the standards of Philippine officials. But beginning in the mid-1970s it grew to breathtaking proportions. Newsom in 1978 thought Marcos had squeezed about as much as he could from the uppermost classes. The step below the top on the social ladder would be the next rung wrung. "The increased acquisitiveness of the Marcos financial empire and the government sector will put more and more pressure on the strong middle class," Newsom predicted. This, combined with the continued exigencies confronting the lower classes, portended instability across the social spectrum. "The population bomb is still ticking, although some progress toward control is being made. Land and forests are being consumed without adequate replacement. Food is in surplus, but other exports crops face uncertain futures. The gap between rich and poor is not lessening."[22]

American officials took particular note of what some called "creeping state capitalism" and others "crony capitalism." By the early 1980s the Marcos government acknowledged owning or directing nearly one hundred corporations. How many the regime held unacknowledged was anyone's guess. The American embassy in Manila regularly monitored this expansion of government influence, partly because, after the accession of the Reagan administration, the trend contradicted the free-market prejudices of the Republicans; partly because it limited opportunities for American investment, which, although now less talked about than in the days of Lodge and Beveridge, remained a significant consideration in Washington; and partly because, by closing economic doors in addition to the political ones already shut, it threatened to alienate Filipinos not already opposed to Marcos. In April 1983 the embassy analyzed the activities of three of the government's holding companies: the Philippine National Bank—that venerable sink of iniquity; the Development Bank of the Philippines, a more recent emulator; and the National Development Company. By various means, including taxpayer-financed "rescue" operations, these firms had attained control over scores of smaller corporations, filling the boards of the acquired entities with cabinet-level members of the Marcos government and members' relatives and running the corporations' affairs to suit the interests of the new overseers. The embassy report hesitated to predict whether the 600 percent growth of the three holding companies during the previous few years—a time of scant expansion of the Philippine economy as a whole—would continue at such a pace. But it hazarded the opinion that "the degree of government intrusion has reached a very significant and perhaps unhealthy level."[23]

To whatever extent Marcos and his henchmen augmented the ranks of the opposition by monopolizing political and economic opportunities, the regime would probably stand while the military held fast. Unfortunately—or otherwise, depending on one's view of Marcos—the uniformed officers appeared to be responding to their lately won stature according to what the American embassy called "time-honored tradition in the Philippines." In a paper entitled "The Day of the Generals," the embassy offered its assessment of the military's position. "The AFP is not the most corrupt organization in the Philippines; others are more corrupt. However, they are not as powerful at the moment as the AFP and are, therefore, not as interesting politically." The embassy report briefly summarized the pre-martial-law history of self-help in Philippine government offices, noting that what Americans deemed corruption reached so deeply into Filipino society that unless its practitioners carried their activities to especially flagrant extremes few Filipinos cared to condemn them. Before Marcos, "the politicians and the oligarchs" had enjoyed a lock on the dispensation of favors. For this reason the leaders of the army and the Philippine constabulary had been largely confined to unremunerative honesty. "The members of the Philippine military establishment were like the wall-flowers at a ball, invited but not dancing. They were outside the circle of the powerful. Even the PC were cast in the minor role of muscled amanuensi."

The declaration of martial law had altered the situation significantly. Now the vast majority of political power, and with it the opportunities for pocket-lining, flowed through Malacañang. This undermined the influence of the traditional elite and simultaneously fostered the rise of the military. Marcos could not rule alone, so he turned to the generals for help. The embassy explained: "The intimidation or dispossession of the oligarchs left a vacuum in the power structure which was filled by the military who inherited the responsibilities, power and all the associated benefits of the ancien regime." Even prior to martial law the unwritten rules defining unacceptable excess had eroded considerably, but the rise of the untutored generals, in an atmosphere conditioned by the example of Marcos and his inner circle, had produced a nearly complete breakdown of the ethical code. "With the restraints of a muck-raking press and competing interest groups removed, certain senior members of the AFP are diverting resources on a grand scale. They have, in effect, become a new elite whose paternalism extends no further than their own family and military colleagues."

Although Marcos recognized the problems his avaricious generals were causing the civilian population of the country, he chose not to pull them back. "He needs the AFP and doesn't want its most important leaders overly annoyed. At most, he rules the AFP leaders with a loose leash." The embassy report did not foresee the imminent development of insuperable difficulties resulting from the arrival of the military at the feeding trough. But it warned that if the corruption continued to spread, it might become an obsession with all involved and might "increasingly hamper the ability of the military and the government as a whole to carry out their duties."[24]

The duties referred to included, more than ever, dealing with the communist and Moro insurgencies. For a time during the 1970s Marcos appeared to have reached a modus vivendi with the Moros. Under pressure from various Muslim states, especially the oil-producing countries full of themselves and petrodollars, Marcos agreed to discuss expanded autonomy for the Moro provinces. The MNLF, beset by factional fighting, decided to try its hand at a negotiated settlement. The fact that the talks took place courtesy of the dubious good offices of Libya's Muamar Khaddafi did not bode well for the agreement that resulted, and which in the event fell to pieces within months. By 1980 the MNLF was more active in the field than ever. The AFP responded by recapturing individuals previously granted amnesty and stepping up anti-insurgent operations. Already the war in the south had claimed more than fifty thousand lives and left nearly one million homeless. Both numbers climbed sharply in the years that followed.[25]

Following the return from exile of Ayatollah Khomeini to Tehran and the establishment of the revolutionary Islamic regime in Iran, American policy-makers belatedly recognized the destabilizing potential of armed Muslims. Yet Washington accurately guessed that Moro nationalism was a less explosive force internationally than Shiite fundamentalism, and American worries regarding Philippine insurrections focused on the communists.

In January 1981 Marcos lifted martial law. The move was an essentially cosmetic gesture, since he retained all the powers he had arrogated to himself by decree during the previous eight and a half years. Also cosmetic, indeed farcical, was a presidential election the following June. The leading members of the opposition to Marcos, convinced he would steal the victory, refused to lend legitimacy to the exercise and called a boycott. Marcos responded by drafting the septuagenarian Alejo Santos, defense minister under García, to serve as his opponent and by directing a propaganda blitz reminding citizens of their legal obligation to vote, with violators subject to a minimum penalty of six months in prison. Not surprisingly Marcos won, although he evidently cooked the figures to produce an official 80 percent turnout and an 88 percent majority.

The façade of restored constitutionalism did not fool the the CPP-NPA, now twelve years old and gaining strength by the month. Nor did it reassure American officials in the Philippines. The embassy reflected on the failure of the Marcos regime to stem the communist rebellion, ostensibly Manila's prime objective for a decade. Under martial law, embassy analysts said, the government had devoted extraordinary military and economic resources to suppressing the communists. It had succeeded in capturing some key individuals, including Sison and Buscayno-Dante. Yet overall the anticommunist offensive had failed to achieve its goal. "The communist movement continued to expand, making deep inroads for the first time in rural areas outside Central Luzon's traditional belt of agrarian dissidence." Martial law had proved twice counterproductive: beyond adding to the weight of oppression on the masses, especially in the form of an increasingly brutal and scarcely checked military, it eliminated the safety valve of legitimate dissent. "With the enfeebling of Marcos' moderate political opposition, the CPP/NPA has probably gained greater credibility as a militant anti-government organization taking on the regime." This development, more than any specific success of the rebels to date, seemed to the embassy cause for worry. "The growth of the NPA as a credible opposition force may attract other anti-Marcos elements to its radical 'nationalist' position, with potentially far-reaching consequences for government stability, orderly succession, and U.S. interests."[26]

Americans had never treated the communist threat in the Philippines lightly. But the advent of the Reagan administration, which fashioned a doctrine out of actively supporting anticommunist movements, sometimes over the express prohibition of Congress, in locales as diverse as Nicaragua, Angola and Afghanistan, added weight to worries about NPA advances. The Republicans, guided ideologically by Jeane Kirkpatrick, a former academic now ambassador to the United Nations, drew a distinction between "authoritarian" and "totalitarian" regimes. Authoritarian regimes—in countries such as South Africa, Chile, South Korea and the Philippines—were said to be susceptible to suggestions for reform. Totalitarian regimes—in the communist countries—were not. A crucial task of the United States, Kirkpatrick said and Reagan believed, consisted of ensuring that the totalitarians not oust the authoritarians. In the Philippines this required supporting Marcos against the NPA.

The Reagan administration revived the notion of a Soviet global conspiracy, attributing much of the unrest in much of the third world to Moscow's machinations. Naturally Washington wished to know of possible Russian connections, for instance in the area of weapons, to the communist insurgency in the Philippines. The American embassy in Manila reported disappointingly that it saw "no evidence" of any logistical link. While a few east-bloc guns, probably from the international arms bazaar, had found their way to parts of Luzon, American M-16s rather than Soviet AK-47s were the weapons of choice among the rebels, selling for the equivalent of $125 each. The NPA's arsenal of American arms provided the guerrillas more than enough firepower to conduct their military campaign. The best the embassy could do in supporting the Reagan administration line was to repeat an unsubstantiated yet not improbable opinion expressed by a tame Filipino columnist that Soviet agents, if not active in the Philippines, were hard at work in the countries nearby.[27]

Even at the bargain per-barrel price the embassy quoted, the NPA's professed objective of a 25,000-rifle army would cost a lot of money. In the spring of 1983 American officials in Manila analyzed the means by which the communists generated funds. The rebels called the process taxation. The Americans preferred the term extortion, although they conceded that the communists' shakedown style sometimes did not differ greatly from that of the government. In fact the embassy remarked that in certain instances the persons taxed preferred dealing with the NPA. A rice merchant required to make payments to the NPA told an embassy official his company was content with current arrangements. The communists, he said, offered more flexible terms, accepting their levy in grain rather than insisting on cash. This businessman added that when the government offered to post an AFP unit nearby as protection against the insurgents, his firm and a large mining outfit in the area protested, desiring instead to keep the insurgents as protection against the AFP. The surprising part of the story was that the protest succeeded. The American analysts hesitated to put a precise figure on the rebels' take, but their best estimates indicated something on the order of half a million dollars per month. While this hardly challenged Marcos and the Malacañang crowd for the cash-flow championship, it suggested a network of influence and support sufficient to keep the NPA in the field for years to come.[28]

What the rebels expected to accomplish during that period was harder to tell. Common sense and a variety of sources revealed the NPA's general approach. Recognizing the political benefits they derived from contraposition to Marcos and understanding their incapacity to defeat the AFP in open battle, the communists were not pressing for an immediate takeover of the government. Rather, the embassy said, they aimed at "strategic stalemate," in the belief that the United States would dump Marcos once Washington concluded he could not liquidate the insurgency. Meanwhile they would expand their political base, preparing for the ultimate thrust against Manila. In addition, they would cultivate international opinion, and especially American opinion, in favor of restoring civil liberties and freeing political prisoners in the Philippines.

The insurgents' propaganda and other political work would benefit from the well-educated character of the party leadership. The embassy reported that most of those in positions of power had roots in the middle and upper classes of Filipino life. It was not unusual for leaders of the rebel forces to have close relatives in the government, the military or other influential sectors of society. Nearly all the most important communist leaders possessed ties to the colleges and universities, both the University of the Philippines and private religious institutions. Even the seminaries provided recruits, some who dropped out to pursue political goals before religious ones, some who stayed in and sought to reconcile Marx with Jesus.

The rank and file consisted of peasants and others from the lower classes. They rarely arrived at rebel ranks with strong ideological views. What they knew of the class struggle they had experienced in their personal dealings with landlords and corrupt government officials. Their grievances made them ready pupils for the ideologues at the top of the insurgency, and their presence in the NPA gave the movement a credibility it might have lacked. But their commitment to revolution remained open to question—most would be content with genuine land reform and correction of government abuses—and by no stretch could they be considered serious communists. To a large degree their continued adherence to the insurrection depended more on what the government did or failed to do than on the actions of their own leaders.[29]

17

Vox Populi
1983–1991

I.   The devil they knew

Left to his own prejudices Ronald Reagan would happily have supported Marcos through the eight years the Republican president occupied the White House. While the Carter administration's record on human rights in the Philippines demonstrated ambivalence at best, capitulation at worst, the Reagan administration was not ambivalent, nor could it be said to have capitulated, because it did not recognize any struggle. In 1981 the state department's Walter Stoessel briefed Vice President George Bush regarding an imminent visit by the latter to Manila, where Marcos was to be re-inaugurated as president. Summarizing the current condition of relations between the American and Philippine governments, Stoessel told Bush, "There are no serious problems outstanding." Stoessel remarked that during the last year of the Carter administration "human rights activists" in Congress had attempted to signal American dissatisfaction with Marcos' suppression of Filipino liberties by trimming aid appropriations. "This has not been a problem in 1981," Stoessel said, with evident relief.

Far from using the leverage they possessed with Manila—even Marcos would hesitate before spurning American assistance heading toward a billion dollars in the not-distant future—top Reagan administration officials took pains to let the Philippine dictator know all was right between the two countries. "Your presence at the inauguration," Stoessel told Bush, "will help reassure Marcos that the Reagan Administration regards him as a friend and continues to attach importance to a close relationship with the Philippines." During the past few years, Stoessel went on, critics in Congress and certain American-based Filipinos had raised questions in Marcos' mind about the steadfastness of the American government.

"He has become concerned about the ultimate goals of U.S. policy." The vice president's visit should quiet Marcos' doubts.

> We wish to assure him in the interest of our overall relations that these critics do not reflect Administration policy and that the Administration looks forward to working with the Marcos government. We think Marcos will be enormously pleased that you have come and he will welcome the opportunity to show the Philippine people the close ties that exist between his government and the Reagan Administration.

Stoessel identified five points for the vice president to make in discussions with Marcos. He should extend congratulations and greetings from the President and Mrs. Reagan to President and Mrs. Marcos. He should invite Marcos to visit the United States in 1982. He should convey the administration's pleasure at the close cooperation obtaining between Washington and Manila on various east-west issues. He should express the administration's commitment to carry out the 1979 agreement on military aid. And he should relate the administration's willingness to crack down on persons in the United States who supported terrorist activities in the Philippines. On this last point the Reagan administration was prepared to negotiate an extradition treaty designed to help Marcos prosecute persons in America the Philippine government charged with terrorism. Conspicuous by its absence from Bush's list was anything breathing the slightest hint of upset regarding Marcos' continued trampling of Philippine democracy.[1]

Defenders of the Reagan administration might have argued that a vice-presidential visit did not afford the most promising opportunity to raise troublesome topics like the abuse of Philippine citizens by the military—although Walter Mondale had at least mentioned human rights during his otherwise undistinguished 1978 journey to Manila. Yet when the administration's real diplomats traveled to the Philippines they too scanted the issue.

Reagan's first secretary of state, Alexander Haig, visited the Philippines shortly after Marcos' farcical 1981 election. Haig was a career soldier, one to whom American access to military bases counted for considerably more than Filipino access to the institutions of democracy. What Haig said to Marcos behind the closed doors of Malacañang is not known. But the tenor of the trip was summarized by the secretary's public congratulations to Marcos on a "wonderful victory."[2]

In 1983 Haig's successor George Shultz prepared to meet Marcos. The secretary of state received a briefing from Assistant Secretary Paul Wolfowitz along lines similar to those earlier drawn for Bush. Wolfowitz mentioned human rights, yet he placed it last on an agenda headed by the desire, as the assistant secretary said, "to provide visible evidence of the excellent state of U.S.-Philippine relations" and followed by such subjects as the recent Williamsburg economic summit conference and Washington's backing for the Association of Southeast Asian Nations.[3]

To the Reagan administration human rights in the Philippines hardly existed as an item worthy of discussion. When administration officials felt compelled to mention the subject they did so primarily in the context of, and on account of, what Wolfowitz called "the keen interest of the U.S. Congress" in the matter. The conservative geopoliticians who dominated foreign policy during the Reagan years had no time for liberal distractions like human rights. Instead they focused on tangible assets of direct and immediate importance to the United States. Wolfowitz delineated in terms of narrow American self-concern what amounted to the beginning and end of Reagan administration thinking on the Philippines. "Our relationship with the Philippines is dominated by our interest in the maintenance of unhampered use of our military facilities at Subic and Clark," the assistant secretary declared. "These facilities are essential for our strategic posture in the Far East as well as the Indian Ocean areas. We also have important economic interests in the Philippines, and the U.S. remains the chief foreign investor there."[4]

Reagan defenders cited recent history as evidence in support of the need to stick by Marcos. As Republicans in 1949 had blamed the Democratic administration for the fall of the pro-American Nationalist government in China, so Republicans in 1979 saddled the Democrats with responsibility for the overthrow of the shah in Iran and Somoza in Nicaragua. No more reality informed the argument in 1979 than had been the case thirty years before, but it made a good campaign theme. More troublingly, it subsequently served as a guide to policy. Just as the Republicans who succeeded to executive power in the 1950s determined to prevent a further erosion of American influence by supporting strongmen such as the shah and Somoza, so the Republicans of the 1980s insisted on restoring American credibility—as they defined it—by backing the likes of Marcos.

To be sure, the insurgencies Marcos faced in the form of the MNLF and especially the NPA did not appear about to topple the Philippine leader in the near future. But American intelligence had been surprised and chagrined by the suddenness of the Iranian revolution, and the Reagan administration chose to take no chances. Marcos must be reassured, cultivated and maintained in power. To criticize him threatened to weaken him. To weaken him threatened to weaken the American position in the Philippines. While a successor regime to Marcos' might better democracy's prospects among the Filipinos, it could hardly improve on the security for American strategic and economic interests Marcos had provided for most of two decades. As usual, American interests—measured in a harder currency than human rights or democratic values—came first.

II. Mugged by reality

Yet developments beyond the Reagan administration's reach ultimately made liberals, after a fashion, out of the Republicans. During the early 1980s Marcos' hold on the Philippine political system began to slip. The spread of armed insurrection provided the most obvious indication of slippage, but others ultimately turned out to be more damaging. The recession that slammed the United States and much of the industrialized world in this period floored the Philippines. Producers of commodities, particularly sugar, faced ruin. The preferential treatment accorded Philippine sugar in the United States by the Laurel-Langley agreement had run out in 1974. At first the winds of the open market blew softly upon Philippine producers and by extension upon their employees. But starting in the late 1970s the world price of sugar collapsed, falling from 65 cents per pound in 1974 to 4 cents in 1985. In the Philippines' best sugar-growing province, Negros Occidental, the cost of production stuck at 12 cents. Costs elsewhere were higher. "The more we plant, the more we lose," groaned one producer. As provincial economies stagnated, social distress intensified, leading one development official in Negros to predict, "If no decisive measures are taken very soon, this province will fall to the communists in six months."[5]

The contracting Philippine economy exaggerated the effects of the expanding corruption of the Marcos regime, which was antagonizing both those who felt the arm of Malacañang personally and those who witnessed its effects from afar—in other words, a large portion of the populace. More and more the members of the elite not blessed with partnerships in the charmed circle resented the monopolization of power and profit-making opportunities by Marcos and his gang. Imelda Marcos, once an asset to her husband's political ambitions, became a symbol of corruption out of control. Her spectacular grafting far exceeded any conceivable financial purpose and evidently served some hidden psychological need. Her highly visible spending sprees, which, she contended, brought vicarious pleasure to the Filipino people, in fact alienated millions. At the same time they stole, literally, resources from the rest of society, making economic recovery all the more difficult.

The pre-Marcos elites, as well as civilian officials in the government, also resented the growing influence of the military. The armed forces claimed an increasing share of government revenues, and the uniformed officers formed a center of power new in the country's politics. Even after the end of martial law they constituted a faction that promised to play a decisive role in any struggle for the succession to Marcos. That the military itself was split, with opposing groups gravitating toward Marcos loyalist and Chief of Staff Fabian Ver, on one hand, and Defense Secretary Enrile and constabulary head Ramos, on the other, added to the volatility of the situation.

The middle class and the general population of Manila remained uncertain factors in the political equation. Much of the city had originally greeted martial law with relief, as affording a respite from the crime and violence that marked the early 1970s. But the martial law regime outstayed its welcome, and when Marcos failed to deliver on his promises, committing and allowing abuses overshadowing those he had pledged to eradicate, many people previously moderate grew disillusioned. Lifting martial law did little for Marcos' popularity, since his firm control remained apparent. The contraction of the country's economy affected Manila less than some of the provinces, yet still it pinched. Perhaps more than any other factor the economy portended trouble for Marcos. Benigno Aquino described the situation in the spring of 1981. "If a ruler reduces political rights but is able to offer a measure of economic prosperity, he can get away with it," Aquino said. "But if there is no economic prosperity you have the reverse conditions. . . . This is the case in the Philippines."[6]

Disaffection among moderates showed in the increasing criticism expressed by the mainline Roman Catholic clergy, led by Jaime Cardinal Sin. For years priests had played a role in opposition politics in the Philippines, yet until the late 1970s political priests remained at the fringe of influence within the church. By then, though, the corruption of the Marcos regime had grown sufficiently serious that the leadership felt forced to speak out. In 1979 Cardinal Sin called on Marcos to lift martial law. In 1981 he told church members to follow their own consciences, rather than the government's dictates, in deciding whether to honor the election boycott. Throughout the early 1980s Sin and the country's bishops denounced the regime's abuses and warned that unless Marcos expanded the scope of popular political action the country faced civil war.

By 1983 Marcos counted few friends outside the clique of his cronies. Even so, the impetus for an overthrow did not yet exist. Although many members of the old elites detested him, he had largely succeeded in neutralizing them politically. Increasing numbers of peasants and student radicals identified with the NPA, but the insurgents could not claim the mass support necessary for a popular revolution, and the Philippine military effectively prevented an armed takeover of the government. While the lower and middle classes of Manila thought little good of Marcos, their disaffection remained inchoate.

In August 1983 the Marcos regime committed a doubly fatal error, fatal literally and immediately to Benigno Aquino, fatal figuratively and ultimately to Marcos himself. Following Aquino's release from prison in 1980 the Liberal leader had flown to the United States for heart surgery. The hegira constituted a victory of sorts for the Carter administration, which had been proposing exile to America as a means of persuading Marcos to let Aquino out of jail and thereby ease tensions. As Ambassador David Newsom said, "Aquino's peaceful departure to the U.S. would benefit the situation." Newsom added, "We should continue to work for this." Administration officials worked, and eventually Marcos decided to hustle Aquino out of the country rather than risk his dying behind bars. Marcos specified a condition in acceding to the Carter administration's request: that Washington not make a fuss over the exile. Carter himself stood by the pledge and paid no attention to Aquino. But in the administration's last month in office Aquino received an invitation to address a small group at the state department. When he accepted, Marcos screamed foul.[7]

During and after his convalescence Aquino chose to remain in the United States. He took up residence in Massachusetts, where his wife Corazon and their children joined him. Events more than once tempted him to return to the Philippines, but other events argued for postponement. Just prior to the 1981 election he told a reporter, "Marcos has contacted me three times and said, 'You come back after the elections and we talk. . . . You come back before and you go back to jail.'" Not for the first or last time Marcos welshed on his word. Even after he won the election he made plain that Aquino had better stay put.[8]

Yet Aquino had not spent a life in Filipino politics to end his days in exile. As the Marcos regime showed signs of unraveling he pondered more deeply returning home. Though Marcos did his best to hide the fact, news had spread that he was suffering from kidney failure. Aquino, fearing a takeover by Imelda in league with General Ver, among other possibilities, decided during the summer of 1983 to risk going back. Imelda tried to prevent the trip, alternately threatening and trying to bribe him. Juan Ponce Enrile warned of conspiracies against Aquino's life. Still Aquino determined to proceed, convinced, as he told an American journalist, that Marcos "won't shoot me." Salvador Laurel, who visited Aquino in the United States, later said he and Aquino had weighed the various fates that might befall Aquino in the Philippines and had concluded that the chance of assassination was at most 5 to 10 percent. A report by the American state department placed the odds higher. "Assassination is not Marcos's style," the paper asserted. "But it is not beyond the capability of some of his operatives."[9]

The state department got it right. Arriving at the Manila airport, Ninoy Aquino met his death at the foot of stairs from the plane. Confusion and great controversy surrounded the identity of the assassin. Was he the "man in blue" immediately gunned down by nearby soldiers, or one (or several) of the soldiers themselves? More confusion and controversy surrounded the architect of the assassination. Diverse theorists pinned the blame on Marcos, on Imelda, on Ver and on less obvious suspects. Marcos fingered the communists. Eight years later the case remained unsolved.

The Aquino assassination marked the beginning of the end for Marcos. Few doubted that the regime was responsible for the assassination, whoever might have given the precise order. Nearly all agreed that this time matters had gone too far. Until now Marcos' opponents had lacked a unifying element, a symbol they could rally round. In death Aquino provided the missing piece. Cardinal Sin presided at the funeral mass, placing the weight of the church squarely on the side of the opposition. The funeral procession was a day-long affair that brought as many as a million people from office buildings, schools and slums into the streets of Manila. The Philippine press, recently cowed by the regime and uncharacteristically quiet, was jolted by the brutality of the murder and heartened by the popular upwelling, and it began to resume its questioning and challenging role.

From the American embassy Ambassador Michael Armacost remarked on the striking show of popular feeling and attempted to figure out what it portended. He quoted a well-placed informant who declared of the torrent of emotion, "At a minimum it is an eloquent testimony to the appeal of Ninoy; at a maximum it is a serious indictment of the government." The magnitude of the reaction to Aquino's death surprised Marcos, as it did everyone else, but the Philippine president possessed sufficient presence of mind to attempt to defuse the crisis by hinting at reforms. Armacost could not tell what would come of the hints, which were not unlike many Marcos had made before.

It seems clear that the shock of Aquino's death and the massive outpouring of public sentiment on August 31 have had an impact on at least some of the government leadership. If the steps under consideration are implemented, they should achieve a positive, if moderate, alteration of the political process.

Unfortunately, while these kinds of steps may be undertaken in the name of reconciliation, their very modesty suggests they will not go far to dissipate opposition mistrust of the government.

Yet Armacost accounted Marcos "a very shrewd politician," and the ambassador guessed that if the Philippine president judged his political survival dependent on more-sweeping measures, as indeed it might, he would accept them.[10]

Marcos, however, perhaps from illness, perhaps from hubris, perhaps from the sort of simple miscalculation all politicians and other mortals are prone to, decided he could hold the ring as tightly as ever. Within the week Armacost reported another conversation, this with a government insider. The ambassador gave Marcos' man a gentle nudge toward liberalization. "I observed that the size of the crowd at the Aquino funeral and procession and comments of people around town regarding the responsibility for Aquino's assassination suggested the Government of the Philippines faced rather fundamental problems of confidence and credibility," Armacost wrote. "I noted further that with Aquino's demise the opposition appeared bereft of leadership, organization, and finances. I commented that under the circumstances it was my personal view that the government had both an opportunity and political need to adopt measures which would promote reconciliation and arrest the erosion of popular confidence in the regime."

The response of Armacost's interlocutor indicated a business-as-usual attitude at Malacañang. "He observed that the opposition would find it extremely difficult to translate the emotions of the funeral into a political base," the ambassador related. "He went on to deride major figures in the opposition as ineffectual politicians who had 'started at the top,' loved the hyperbole of the senate, but had never learned the nuts and bolts of politics at the grassroots level." The current excitement would pass, for it had shallow roots. "He said that the President had never been that impressed with what the Manila elite thought about key issues, preferring to rely on the sentiments of those 'up in the hills,' i.e., in the provinces.

He seemed confident that out in the provinces the residual support for Marcos was very strong and had not been that affected by Aquino's assassination." Armacost's contact went on to say he expected Marcos to run for reelection in 1987 and win, and perhaps repeat the process in 1993. "He appears very confident that the President will escape his current difficulties," Armacost concluded, discouraged.[11]

Others in the administration shared Armacost's discouragement. A state department analysis of the post-Aquino condition of Philippine politics asserted that the opposition leader's assassination, in conjunction with the continuing economic decline and various other troubles in the country, had administered "a crippling blow to Marcos' prestige" and probably also "a death blow" to the possibility of any dynastic maneuver by Imelda. The state department paper labeled the assassination "a national scandal" that had "traumatized elements of the Philippine power structure and perhaps rendered it less able to defend its interests with draconian means against either a democratic or a revolutionary opposition."[12]

Given a choice, of course, Washington would have opted for the democratic opposition over the revolutionaries. But as Marcos dug in, many in the Reagan administration feared he was delivering the Philippines to the communists. "The CPP has developed an effective organizational, financial and military network throughout the Philippines," the American country team in Manila reported in June 1984. "It has made mistakes and suffered losses but is stronger now than ever before." The insurgents daily increased the territory under their control. The government appeared unable to stem the advance. "Across the Philippine archipelago the CPP is moving in a ratchet-like manner to expand its influence. The Government of the Philippines still has running room to take effective action and reverse the trend of events, but the longer it delays in beginning to deal effectively with the problem the harder this will be." Although the embassy analysts recognized that the constituency for a reformist, noncommunist solution to the Philippines' problems still existed, they wondered whether the moderates could hold out for long. "Until the government demonstrates its awareness of discontent and undertakes to deal with its source, the communist threat will continue to grow." In a punch line guaranteed to grab attention in Washington, the embassy concluded, "The eventual outcome—ultimate government defeat, a communist takeover of the Philippines—thus becomes a very possible scenario."[13]

Intelligence officials in the state department took this analysis and combined it with material from other sources to elucidate what they called the "remarkable" success of the communists in the Philippines. By contemporary regional standards the phenomenon was nearly inexplicable. While communist movements in the other noncommunist Southeast Asian states languished, that in the Philippines flourished. "The NPA, without any foreign assistance"—a significant

statement in an administration noted for tracing most malevolence to the Kremlin—"has grown from a few roaming bands in Luzon at the beginning of the Marcos period, to an estimated force of 13–15,000 armed regulars and several thousand part-time guerrillas operating in 62 of 73 provinces." What made the NPA's
growth the more exceptional was the fact it was not the result to any significant
degree of anti-foreign nationalist sentiment. In China and Vietnam, the only
Asian countries where local communists had achieved control through their own
efforts—as opposed to North Korea, Laos and Cambodia, where communists had
won power largely as a result of external developments—the communists had
harnessed the force of rising nationalism. In the Philippines nationalism explained
only a minor part of the NPA's appeal. Anti-Americanism, the predominant
strain of Filipino nationalism, inspired the radical intelligentsia of the cities, but
it had not caught on in the countryside, the principal base of the NPA, as its
absence from communist provincial propaganda attested. In other countries—
Burma, Thailand, Malaysia—partial successes of communist insurgents had followed from ethnic tensions, in particular reflecting conflict between Chinese
minorities and indigenous populations. The NPA made no appeal to cultural
chauvinism. Nor could the growth of the NPA be attributed primarily to the low
standard of living in the Philippines. Several of the Philippines' neighbors suffered
lower standards but showed fewer manifestations of revolt.

Having ruled out the other likely causes, the state department's intelligence
bureau could only place the blame for the growth of the NPA on Marcos. The
increasing strength of the insurgency in the Philippines, the report asserted,
stemmed from the declining legitimacy of the regime and from disenchantment
with its authoritarian character and its ineffectiveness in dealing with the nation's
problems. The report specified four widespread causes of hostility against the
regime: the crony capitalism of the Marcoses and their favorites; the failure of the
government to relieve the ongoing economic crisis, a failure exacerbated by the
crony capitalism; decaying discipline of the armed forces, leading to abuse of the
citizenry; and the NPA's success—resulting from all of the above as well as from
Marcos' stifling of legitimate opposition—in casting itself as the only alternative
to the government.

The popular response to the Aquino assassination demonstrated the regime's
loss of credibility. The damage was probably beyond repair. The closest parallel
the state department analysts could find came not from Asia but from Central
America, and considering the outcome there it afforded thin reassurance. "As in
Nicaragua, a plundering of the country by the local oligarchy rather than foreign
oppression or simple poverty has united the Philippine middle class, the business
community, the church, and youth against the regime, while the decay of government institutions and a declining economy have sown the seeds of revolution
in the countryside." Marcos might struggle a while, but seemed unlikely to survive.[14]

And the longer Marcos struggled the greater the probability of a radical successor. For all the Republicans' castigation of the Carter administration for failing to stand by America's allies, they could read the lessons of Nicaragua and Iran. In each country the United States had contributed to the triumph of revolution by holding too long to the dictator. By no stretch of the MNLF's imagination would the Philippines become another Iran, but Nicaragua, as the state department paper made clear, was not out of the question. At this point—late 1984— the Sandinista script circulated principally in the lower echelons of the Reagan administration. Yet eventually the shudders it evoked would work their way to the White House. These shudders, more than concern for democracy for Filipinos, would produce the ultimate decision to cut Marcos adrift.

III. The final days

Arriving at that ultimate decision required time and no little doing. Marcos, aware of the injury Aquino's murder was causing the regime, had attempted to regain a measure of legitimacy by scheduling legislative elections for May 1984. To his discomfiture the opposition revived NAMFREL, the clean-election committee that had helped Magsaysay gain the presidency in 1953. Although the committee's chairman denied affiliation with the CIA—probably accurately, since CIA Director William Casey remained a Marcos loyalist almost to the last—the American embassy offered its moral support to the committee's activities. Marcos' American congressional critics, returning to life after two years under the spell of Reagan's conservatism, indicated a strong desire to see a fair polling. The stigma now attaching more than ever to Marcos caused cancellation of a scheduled visit by Reagan, although the American president assured Marcos of his continued unwavering support. "Our friendship for you remains as warm and firm as does our feeling for the people of the Philippines," Reagan wrote Marcos.[15]

As anticipated and by the means expected, Marcos' candidates won a majority in the election. But the government's fixers did not prevent the opposition from scoring sizable gains. The short-term outcome was a wash. Marcos' opponents achieved greater voice and credibility, while the president could point to the Philippines as a functioning democracy whose voters still had the good sense to support him.

The Reagan White House found Marcos' argument appealing, and in the 1984 American presidential campaign Reagan portrayed Marcos as America's principal safeguard against a communist Philippines. "What is the alternative?" the president asked. "It is a large Communist movement to take over the Philippines." Reagan continued, "We've had enough of a record of letting, under the guise of revolution, someone that we thought was a little more right than we would be, letting that person go and then winding up with totalitarianism pure and simple." The United States ought to concentrate on persuading Marcos and his associates to improve "rather than throwing them to the wolves and then facing a Communist power in the Pacific."[16]

Others in the administration, however, took a more skeptical view. Admiral William Crowe, the American Pacific commander, soon to become chairman of the joint chiefs of staff, and the man on whom the burden of defending the region of the Philippines fell most immediately, visited Manila shortly after the Philippine election. Observing the situation on the ground, Crowe joined those in the state department and the American embassy who had concluded that Marcos, far from being a safeguard against a communist takeover, might well prove the NPA's ticket to victory. An observer close to the scene paraphrased a Crowe report to the joint chiefs on the future of the Subic base vis-à-vis Marcos: "There is no hope for my naval base with that guy as president of that country. Choose between Marcos and that base." Crowe's disillusionment was crucial, though not yet.[17]

In the Philippines the legislative election solved none of the country's underlying problems. If anything it exacerbated them, for the regime spent nearly five billion pesos, or one-tenth of the national budget, attempting to influence voters. The expenditure fanned inflation, which topped 60 percent before the end of 1984. The government responded by tightening credit, pushing the prime lending rate to 40 percent. Businesses closed, throwing thousands of employees onto the streets. Busloads of farmers arrived in Manila from the provinces to protest high fertilizer prices. The gross national product fell by 6 percent in 1984 and by 4 percent the next year. Exports declined in the face of continuing low commodity prices. The depression in the capital set the population of Manila looking to Malacañang for solutions Marcos did not produce. In the countryside the depression gave the planter-landlords additional cause to hate Marcos and gave the peasants another reason to join the communists.

The slump also affected the Philippines' creditors. Economists for the International Monetary Fund and for various commercial banks estimated that the Philippines required an injection of $3 billion to $4 billion in new financing to right the economy. But the creditors hesitated to invest more money in a regime as crooked as Marcos'. The regime's decision to finance the 1984 election with freshly printed currency did not sit well with the bankers. Neither did a discovered discrepancy of more than half a billion dollars—in Marcos' favor, naturally—on the government's ledgers. The lenders eventually decided to deliver more cash, primarily to protect the stake they already had in the Philippines. The conditions they insisted on, however, included painful items like new excise taxes, which exacerbated popular unrest and triggered, among other responses, a paralyzing strike by Manila's jeepney drivers.[18]

The capital meanwhile sizzled with rumors. Marcos was sick. He was dying.

He was dead. He had lost his mind. Imelda and Fabian Ver were plotting a palace coup. They had carried it out. Ver and Fidel Ramos were marshalling their separate troops for a military shootout. The Americans would rescue Marcos. They would dump him.

The truth of some of the rumors lent plausibility to the others. Marcos indeed was sick, although Malacañang continued to deny the fact. Imelda and Ver doubtless were plotting, jointly or separately, but what they were plotting was impossible to know. The Ver-Ramos split was indisputable. It grew more visible with the formation early in 1985 of the Reform the Armed Forces Movement, or RAM, an organization of junior officers who had ties to Ramos or Enrile or both, and dedicated to thwarting any effort by Ver to seize the government.

Seeking to recapture the initiative, Marcos floated the possibility of an early presidential election. The plan had obvious attractions. By the end of Marcos' current term, which ran until 1987, the opposition might be unmanageable. Clearly the trend line of regime support tilted downward. An early election would take advantage of the fact that Marcos' rivals spent almost as much time quarreling among themselves as criticizing the government. If he could exploit their disarray and win, without excessive fraud or intimidation, he would enhance his stature within the country and overseas, especially in the United States.

It was a gamble, but Marcos thought it worth taking. On an American news program in November 1985 the Philippine president announced his intention to hold an election within the next few months. A short while later he set the precise date, February 7, 1985.

For a time it looked as though Marcos' gamble would pay off. The most prominent member of the opposition, Salvador Laurel, younger son of José Laurel, the wartime president, was a relatively late arrival to the challengers' camp. Laurel struck many oppositionists as too much the traditional politico to capitalize on this unique opportunity to oust the dictator. Laurel had a fair claim to the opposition candidacy: as the leader of the United Democratic Nationalist Organization, or UNIDO, he had been the one to stick his neck out farthest in the 1984 election. And if he represented the values of the traditional politician, of the compromiser and deal-cutter, he stood in the real-life footsteps of Ninoy Aquino.

But Aquino now walked in heaven, figuratively speaking—literally speaking, in the opinion of millions of Filipinos—and nothing would do except to draft his widow. For the purposes of the snap election, Corazon Aquino possessed the eminent virtue of having no political history and no prior existence apart from her martyred husband. A vote for Cory would be a vote for Ninoy—yet better than that, a vote for what Ninoy represented in death. That Cardinal Sin placed his imprimatur on Cory's candidacy added to its spiritual appeal.

Until the last moment it looked as though Laurel would not step aside. Nor did it appear Cory would run. But a petition of one million signatures urging her to make the race pushed her toward an affirmative decision, and the acquittal of

General Ver and other officers on trial for Ninoy's murder clinched the matter. Laurel, by this time under irresistible pressure from a wide array of opposition sources, consented to accept the second slot on the ticket.

The election campaign revealed the rifts in the American government on matters touching the Philippines. At the state department Michael Armacost, now undersecretary for political affairs, agitated for a pro-Aquino posture. Armacost and other Marcos critics had nearly succeeded in getting Secretary of State Shultz to agree. At the Pentagon Joint Chiefs Chairman Crowe likewise pulled for Aquino, convinced that if Marcos did not give way to moderates he would fall to more-dangerous radicals. In Congress backers of Marcos and Aquino were fairly evenly matched among those who took positions, with the balance to some degree in the hands of Republican Richard Lugar, chairman of the Senate foreign relations committee, a Reagan partisan but not an unthinkingly conservative one.

The White House withheld judgment. Reagan's chief of staff, Donald Regan, remarked that even if Marcos won by fraud the United States would still "have to do business" with him. The United States dealt with dozens of governments that made no pretense of holding elections. Diplomatic recognition did not imply approval, simply a decision to face reality.[19]

Under the circumstances the Reagan administration could hardly have taken a different stand. Smart—although not the smartest—money predicted a Marcos victory, by hook or crook. There appeared no percentage in antagonizing the likely winner. And in characterizing recognition as morally neutral Regan accurately described the historically customary, though not unbroken, practice of the American government.

Yet many observers thought President Reagan, out of prudence if not conviction, might have dissociated himself somewhat from the conservative ideologues who accounted Aquino a stand-in for the communists. Jeane Kirkpatrick, now a syndicated columnist and a widely heeded spokesperson for the Republican right, complained about all the criticism Marcos was receiving. "From reading the American press," she wrote, "one would think Marcos is the focus of evil in the contemporary world and that his government is the major threat to American interests in Asia." Conditions in the Philippines were not so bad. "The Philippines probably is governed better than at least 100 of the 159 member states of the United Nations." America might do far worse than Marcos—as it had done elsewhere. "This is not the first time we have seen a display of obsessive intolerance toward the government of a nation strategically important to the United States," she declared. She cited the regimes of Batista in Cuba, Diem in Vietnam, Somoza in Nicaragua and the shah in Iran as cases in point. "The failings of each were magnified by people who played on American political purism as skillfully as Iago played on Othello's doubts." The American government should leave Marcos alone. For all his demerits he was allowing an election, he remained reliably anticommunist, and, as he had demonstrated most recently in 1983 when he agreed to a renewal of the military bases agreement, he could be counted on to preserve American interests in the region.[20]

Almost certainly the White House desired a Marcos victory, if only from a preference for the known and tested. It hoped the election would afford at least a semblance of honesty, which would ease both the administration's Philippine problems and, presumably, Marcos'. Yet, as Donald Regan's comment revealed, it was quite prepared for more of what Marcos had been dishing out for two decades.

Others in America demanded more than a semblance of honesty. These persons took pains to force a fair tally on the Marcos regime. As the February polling approached, the Philippines grew crowded with observers from the American Congress, led by Senator Lugar; from American newspapers, magazines, and radio and television networks, as well as from media from countries besides the United States; and from religious and human-rights groups. The American embassy made plain it would be following the vote-counting closely, while the United States Agency for International Development contributed funds to the Filipino watch-group NAMFREL, which mobilized half a million poll watchers of its own.

Even under the international spotlight the Marcos machine undertook extraordinary actions to win. Thugs intimidated NAMFREL volunteers. Registrars purged millions of Aquino supporters from the election rolls. Ballot boxes were lifted and stuffed. The official Commission on Elections, or COMELEC, scored returns seriously at odds—consistently toward Marcos—with those reported by NAMFREL. The differences grew so glaring that three dozen COMELEC technicians in Manila walked off the job in protest, sensibly seeking refuge in a nearby church.

Marcos of course claimed victory, but no one with personal knowledge of the election took the government's announced results seriously. While the regime's figures gave the incumbent a 54 to 46 percent triumph over the challenger, CIA estimates called the race for Aquino by 58 to 42. An intrepid political scientist at the University of the Philippines, working from internal errors in the regime's totals, set the figures at 54 to 46 for Aquino.[21]

Marcos' attempted fraud was hardly without precedent in Philippine history, although in most cases rigging had affected only the margin of victory, not the identity of the victor. But times had changed, in this regard as in others Marcos failed to recognize. The officially proclaimed loser, Aquino, refused to accept defeat, and with the support of the Catholic bishops she called for a campaign of civil disobedience to force Marcos to heed the voice of the people. Boycotts of companies controlled by Marcos and his favorites would escalate to a general strike set for February 26.

The American policy-making apparatus remained split. The embassy in

Manila and the state department believed that the United States must sever itself from Marcos while the Philippine center might still hold. Delay would only strengthen the forces of the left, with eventual grave results for American security. The White House, to the lesser extent the president and his closest advisers were paying attention to the Philippine issue—this was the period of the soon-to-be-notorious Iran-contra operation, among other business—was unconvinced that a meaningful Philippine center existed. Reagan, whose feelings of individual loyalty more than once got him into trouble, preferred to stand by the person who had served American purposes for twenty years.

The division within the Reagan administration also reflected a broader debate about the nature of American interests in the Philippines, a debate that had been going on for eight decades. The embassy and the state department, by arguing that American safety lay in the cultivation of Philippine democracy, took the line set out during the Wilson administration in Washington and the governorship of Francis Burton Harrison in Manila. What Michael Armacost and Ambassador Stephen Bosworth advocated was essentially a modern version of Harrison's Filipinization approach. Like Harrison they believed that a truly democratic Philippines would make the most promising and reliable partner for a democratic America.

The position of the Reagan White House paralleled that of William Howard Taft, W. Cameron Forbes and Leonard Wood. This position was not anti-democratic in theory, but in practice it worked out that way. Reagan and his conservative advisers, hardly less than Taft, Forbes and Wood, did not consider the Filipinos competent to manage a democracy. The early Republican colonialists saw the choice for the islands as between American control and chaos, the latter likely including an eventual takeover by Japan. The late Republican neocolonialists perceived the alternatives as American influence, through Marcos, and chaos, the latter probably leading to a communist conquest.

Just as the Taft-Forbes-Wood philosophy had run aground when Quezon and the cabinet withdrew their cooperation from the Wood government, so the Reagan approach hit bottom when the Filipino middle class withdrew its support from Marcos. This second withdrawal was the fundamental message of the boycotts organized in the wake of the 1986 election. The embassy in Manila did its best to get the message across. While the votes were still being counted members of the opposition began visiting Stephen Bosworth, urging the ambassador and the United States to throw their support to Aquino. One visitor predicted that the legislature would ratify Marcos' claim to victory but added, correctly, that no one would believe that the president had really won a majority. Another implored Washington to speak out against the fraud. This evidently well-placed individual—whose name the state department deleted upon declassifying Bosworth's cable relating the conversation—said the United States had made a good start on restoring democracy to the Philippines by pressuring Marcos to hold the elections. Unfortunately, he added, referring to an initial statement by President Reagan suggesting fraud by both sides, the American government seemed to be getting "cold feet." Yet the situation might be saved. "Marcos is now mouse-trapped," he said. "It is important that we not let him out of that trap."

Bosworth's visitor described the present opportunity as "the last chance" for the Filipino middle class. "This city is not big enough for the middle class and Marcos. Either they rid themselves of Marcos or they must leave. The super-wealthy can survive until the Philippines slips into the abyss, but the middle class has no future in a Marcos-run Philippines." Marcos and his cronies had gained a stranglehold on the economy. The stranglehold would not be broken until Marcos quit office. Further, the middle class had staked its future during the last several months to the removal of the regime. Marcos' goons would exact revenge if he remained in power.

But Marcos would not remain in power. The election had thoroughly discredited him. "Marcos is through. He has clearly demonstrated that he cannot govern this place." The only uncertainty involved the manner of his departure. Here was where America came in. "The middle class can't get rid of the Marcoses by themselves. They require help. The question is who helps them." If the United States offered assistance Filipino moderates would accept it gladly. If America failed they would be forced to look to the radicals of the Philippine left. The course likely to cause the least damage to both Americans and Filipinos called for a quick departure by Marcos—within the next ten days. Should he linger longer the influence of the communists would grow, as would the possibility of a military coup. The economy would continue to disintegrate. Anti-Americanism would increase, rendering cooperation between any successor Philippine government and the United States more difficult.[22]

In his summary to Washington Bosworth cautiously judged these arguments "interesting but too categorical, too sure and too simplistic." All the same the ambassador deemed them sufficiently important to relate at length. In certain respects they did not differ greatly from his own opinions. While Bosworth was not convinced Marcos' days in power had reached their end, he agreed entirely that Marcos' continuance in office would darken the Philippines' future. Bosworth particularly worried about the direction of the Philippine economy, upon which all else hinged. He said that even assuming the best—that the current agitation dissipated quickly and without major violence—the country would remain stagnant while Marcos ruled. Small farmers, already close to the margin of economic viability, would not change their actions much, since they had almost no room for maneuver. But the larger producers of export crops, whether Marcos cronies, rival members of the elite or foreigners, would hesitate to invest in new palm trees, rubber trees, equipment and the like, fearing either further misman-agement by Marcos or his eventual ouster by radicals. Their plantations would run down, putting pressure on the individuals who worked the plantations and on the country's export earnings.

Something similar would occur in Manila and the lesser cities. Owners of businesses would continue to operate their enterprises, but they would not make the investments necessary to maintain machinery or expand output. Their operations would diminish, with serious impact on the urban working class. While Marcos' cronies would attempt to extend their hold on the economy, they would follow the predatory practices by which they had amassed most of their wealth. Rather than increase production of the firms they owned or create new ones, they preferred to take over existing companies and run them in a fashion designed to produce maximum short-term but ultimately unsustainable profits. Bosworth described the policy as a "bleed rather than build" approach.

The ambassador noted that private fixed investment in the Philippines—the basis for future growth—had declined by an astonishing 40 percent during the previous two years. Investors had either shipped their capital overseas or converted it to a form that lent itself to rapid withdrawal. The embarrassment of Marcos at the polls, combined with persisting concerns about his health, would aggravate the trend. A flight of human capital would probably accompany the withdrawal of financial resources. Many ambitious individuals, seeing opportunity blocked by the Marcos circle, would leave the country, taking much-needed talent with them.

As traditionally occurred after elections, the financial backers of the winning party would expect repayment. This could lead only to increased corruption. It might also provoke sharper competition between the principal antagonists among the Marcos cronies: the Romualdezes, including Imelda Marcos and her brother Benjamin Romualdez, commonly known as Kokoy; and the Cojuangcos, led by Eduardo, or Danding, Cojuangco—who happened to be a cousin of Corazon Cojuangco Aquino. As the Romualdezes and the Cojuangcos fought over the spoils of victory, their competition would spill through the government into society at large. "We should expect extraordinarily perverse behavior from all government and collective institutions," Bosworth said. The credibility of the government, such as yet remained, would dissolve, leading to what the ambassador called the "refeudalization" of Philippine society. As during the dark ages in Europe, individuals would seek protection wherever they might find it, in the Philippine case under local warlords who commanded private armies or, more likely, under the alternative government that already existed in much of the country. "This refeudalization will prove extraordinarily hospitable to the NPA," the ambassador predicted.[23]

In a narrow sense Bosworth's cable contributed little new to the debate within the American government over what to do about Marcos. By now the state department, including Secretary Shultz, agreed that Marcos had to go. But the ambassador's message, amplified in numerous cables and transpacific telephone calls, laid out most clearly the thinking that finally caused Washington to decide against Marcos and in favor of Aquino. Marcos was no more a dictator in February 1986 than during much of his tenure as president. If anything he had moved in the direction of democracy, certainly by comparison with the period of martial law. During all that time the American government had never seriously considered helping depose him, and from Nixon to Reagan American presidents—with a fleeting exception under Carter—had hardly pressed him to liberalize his rule. Only when Marcos' position became entirely untenable did Washington act to ease him out, and then with great reluctance. If Marcos stayed the Philippines might well collapse. If the Philippines collapsed the communists would be the probable winners. The United States would be the certain loser.

Had Marcos *succeeded* in stealing the election, the Reagan administration likely would have acquiesced. But Marcos failed. As the date of the scheduled general strike approached, Manila grew more turbulent than ever. The dam of popular opinion burst on February 22. The previous day military officers associated with the reformist group RAM and led by Enrile and Ramos had defected from the regime, setting up headquarters at Camp Aguinaldo in outer Manila. What began as an effort to stage a military coup turned into the focus for an enormous anti-government demonstration. With Cardinal Sin's encouragement hundreds of thousands of Aquino supporters filled the avenues leading to the compound, preventing loyalist forces under General Ver from attacking the defectors, convincing more military units to join the rebels—and eliminating what thoughts Enrile entertained of making himself president. Marcos threatened to attack the dissidents, but he could not find officers willing to fight their way through the mass of unarmed civilians. When he sent a squadron of helicopters to bombard the rebels from the air the pilots and crews went over to the opposition.

The people of the Philippines presented the Reagan administration with a stunning fait accompli. Had Reagan assured Marcos of America's continued backing—as the American president, until the last, was tempted to do—Marcos might have triggered a bloodbath. On the other hand, he might not have, being short on troops with the discipline and brutality to carry out his orders. But by this time Marcos had so disgraced himself with the Filipino people that even Reagan could no longer support him.

Reagan's supporters applauded the American president for deft policy management in the transition from Marcos to Aquino. The applause was hardly justified and certainly not for Reagan. American officials in the Philippines supported the Aquino movement morally and logistically, but the White House provided little more than the getaway vehicles: a helicopter to Clark Field and a plane to Guam. The president could not even bring himself to deliver the final message personally, delegating the chore to a friend in Congress.

IV. The morning after

It was ironic that following nearly a century of preaching democracy to the Fili-
pinos the American government had to be taught what democracy really meant.
The "People Power" movement of 1986 demonstrated the overwhelming desire
of Filipinos to rid themselves of the corrupt autocrat long favored by the United
States and to establish a government responsive to the wishes of the people.
Washington, far from leading the movement, only hopped aboard at the last.

Marcos' flight removed the single most important obstacle to the welfare of
the Filipino people. With his departure and the prudently simultaneous exit of
the closest of the cronies, the country could make a start on reversing the damage
his rule had caused. The despair of improvement that had marked the last years
of the Marcos era immediately gave way to a euphoria in which everything
seemed possible.

But the imprint of the Marcos regime was not to be erased so easily. Although
the Aquino government at once set about attempting to recover the loot the Marcos gang had acquired, determining the size and present location of the boodled
billions turned out to be an enormous task. Laying hands on the pile was harder
still. American prosecutors attempted to help out, bringing charges against Ferdinand and Imelda for embezzling and otherwise fraudulently acquiring hundreds of millions of dollars, but a New York jury refused to convict, evidently
unconvinced that perpetrators of a crime against the Filipino people ought to be
tried in the United States. Until Marcos' death in September 1989 (and until 1991
for Imelda), Aquino refused to allow the former ruling couple back into the Philippines, for fear of the political disruption the return might cause.

Nor could the deterioration of the Philippine economy during the first half of
the 1980s be reversed overnight. Though a fortuitous resurgence of commodity
prices afforded welcome relief in the provinces and led a return to positive economic growth, required servicing of the nearly $30 billion foreign debt Marcos
left behind deprived the economy of critical investment capital.

Perhaps the greatest cost of the Marcos years was the opportunity cost. In the
perennial race between economic development and population growth, the last
several of the Marcos years were a time when population significantly outpaced
development. With the Catholic church and the traditional culture tilting against
population-control measures, even a resuscitated economy would require considerable time to regain the ground lost under Marcos. In human terms the Marcos
legacy was more poorer Filipinos than ever before. Government statistics com-
piled after Marcos left office showed 60 percent of the population in 1986 living
under conditions of "absolute poverty."[24]

The injection of the Philippine military into the islands' politics under Marcos
created problems of another sort. Whether or not Enrile had intended to march

on Malacañang before the People Power movement rendered such action impossible, the defense secretary made little effort to disguise the fact that he considered himself better qualified to deal with the country's problems than Aquino. Enrile especially complained at the new president's conciliatory moves toward the NPA and the Communist party. Portraying himself as the strong-willed man of action, in contrast to the housewifely Aquino, Enrile declared that he was losing patience with those in the government who would not let him clean out the communists once for all. "When I lose my patience," he added, referring to the American movie hero, "I am like Rambo."[25]

Under Enrile's direction the Philippine military dragged heels in ceasefire negotiations with the rebels. As institutions, the army and the other services recognized that the fight against the insurgents constituted their principal claim upon the prestige and resources the government had to offer. Personally Enrile understood that it might provide his ticket to the presidency. Yet Aquino, showing greater dexterity than most observers, Enrile particularly included, had credited her with, succeeded in easing her chief rival out of the cabinet following reports of a planned coup.

Unfortunately for Aquino and the country, the military played Medusa. Decapitating one coup attempt caused more to appear. Of the five that reached the point of arms-raising during her first eighteen months in office, the most serious occurred in August 1987 when Colonel Gregorio Honasan, the spearhead of the mutiny against Marcos, led hundreds of followers against the presidential palace. The anti-Aquino forces captured parts of two military bases in the area of the capital and knocked out four of Manila's five television stations. Eventually Aquino stalwart General Ramos rallied troops loyal to the government and brought the situation under control. But Honasan escaped—and following capture four months later escaped again, evidently with the collusion of his captors—and the affair raised troubling questions about Aquino's ability to hang on.

The questions quieted for a time, as the troops remained in the barracks; but in December 1989 another revolt broke out, this the most serious of all. For more than a week rebels held positions in the Makati business district of Manila, with the fighting producing upwards of 100 deaths and prompting Aquino to declare a national emergency. In Washington, George Bush grew alarmed that the rebels might prevail and the Philippines revert to authoritarianism, and at a crucial moment ordered American jets from Clark air base to fly low over rebel positions in an unmistakable show of force. At the same time, the Bush administration threatened to cut off American aid in the event of a rebel victory.

The American actions, combined with those of Aquino loyalists, eventually succeeded in quelling the rebellion, although Aquino emerged weaker than ever. Even before the latest coup, Aquino had suffered from the perception that Washington was pulling her strings. A Manila columnist charged the Americans with acting as though "Corazon Aquino is their creation," adding that for influential American officials, underwriting Aquino had become "a matter of amor proprio and credibility." During and after the December 1989 uprising, Aquino's spokespersons downplayed the American role, with her national security adviser Rafael Ileto dismissing the overflights as merely an aspect of "psychological war" and not crucial to the government's victory; but many in the Philippines interpreted the episode as demonstrating once again Aquino's dependence on the Americans. The opposition Nacionalistas denounced the "naked American coercive intervention in Philippine internal affairs" and lashed Aquino for allowing the Americans to abuse their base rights so egregiously.[26]

The unrest in the military—which produced yet another coup attempt in October 1990, this in Mindanao—reflected wider disillusionment with Aquino's performance. Corruption among government officials once again became pervasive and increasingly obvious. Low-level bureaucrats openly padded their salaries, while relatives of the president saw their opportunity to make like the Marcoses and took it. One disheartened idealist in the government decried the "culture of corruption" Aquino condoned and went so far as to estimate that the situation under Aquino was worse than under Marcos. At least under Marcos, this critic said, the government was strong enough to prevent unauthorized corruption. The Aquino government was toothless and everyone knew it.[27]

Salvador Laurel did not quite fit the disheartened-idealist description, but the vice president seized on the corruption issue to defect from the administration, sort of. Denouncing Aquino for incompetence and her—decidedly not their—government for graft, Laurel declared himself in opposition. Yet because the vice presidency afforded a convenient forum for just such attacks, Laurel refused to resign. Instead he followed the example of Diosdado Macapagal a quarter-century earlier and prepared to wage a battle for the presidency from the office next door. With each opportunity he raked Aquino, portraying himself as the true nationalist, in contrast to the American-controlled president. When the United States government threw its support to Aquino during the December 1989 coup, Laurel hit both Aquino and Washington at once. "A true friend," he declared of the United States, "should not take sides in internal disputes, especially when the contending forces are both friendly."[28]

Opportunism ran in the Laurel family, from father to son, as did ambition, and Salvador's sabotage surely came as no surprise. Perhaps no more surprising but at least equally unsettling was the abandonment of the regime by members of the elite who had figured significantly in Marcos' fall. Enrique Zobel in 1982 had founded the Makati Business Club, an organization that had provided a focus for the complaints of the Manila financial and commercial community against the Marcos regime. The beginning of 1988 saw Zobel at the head of a similar group, this one labeled the National Movement for Economic Reconstruction and Survival. The National Movers, as they liked to be called, now leveled their criticism at the Aquino government. Significantly their ranks included both Enrile and Laurel.[29]

The reassertion of elite influence also stymied efforts toward land reform. Aquino had entered office pledging to enact and implement sweeping measures designed to deliver land to the tillers. Within several months, however, her enthusiasm began to wane. She reconsidered earlier promises to extend existing laws beyond rice and corn properties—to sugar, for instance—and to include her own family's estates among the first to be broken up. Her tardiness on the matter helped spark a protest march on Malacañang by peasants demanding action. The demonstration took a tragic turn when guards opened fire on the crowd, killing more than a dozen and wounding nearly one hundred.

Proponents of change called on Aquino to promulgate reform by decree before the new congress convened in July 1987. While she dithered, landlords mobilized to prevent reform, to the point of raising private armies. A sudden increase in world sugar prices, which returned many plantations to profitability, heightened their incentive to fight to hold their land. In the face of elite resistance Aquino issued a wafflish decree that though fulfilling her pledge to enlarge the scope of earlier laws left crucial questions of implementation—prices, timetables, and excluded categories—to the legislature to determine. On one fundamental issue the Aquino decree allowed landlords to appeal decisions to the courts, guaranteeing endless wrangling and ensuring deep-pocketed owners an advantage over strapped tenants.[30]

Potentially as disturbing as the opposition that mounted in Manila was the attitude of the American government. Aquino had watched Washington warily, rightly convinced that the Reagan administration's support of her People Power movement was no less opportunistic than that of Enrile and Laurel and hardly less liable to withdrawal. As ever, democracy in the Philippines and the general welfare of the Filipino people rated below continued security for American interests in the calculations of America's foreign-policy planners. As since the late 1940s, the primary American interest in the islands was the maintenance of the Clark and Subic bases. While Marcos had not hesitated to squeeze the last dollar out of the American treasury in compensation for the bases, few in Washington expected him to kill the goose that laid the golden eggs.

Aquino was a different story. Elevated to the presidency as the antithesis of Marcos, she faced strong pressure to distance herself from the Marcos policy of accepting a continued American presence. The most significant feature of the pressure was the broad cross-section of the populace from which it emanated. At times past, demands for an American withdrawal had come predominantly from the radical fringes of Philippine politics: from the communists and fellow travelers and from groups luxuriating in the irresponsibility of minimal prospects of gaining power. But the Marcos years had demonstrated more plainly than before the capacity for collusion between an unscrupulous Philippine regime and an American government preoccupied with holding the forts in the islands. By the time Marcos fled, questioning the fundamentals of the U.S.-Philippine relationship had become an activity well within the mainstream of Philippine politics.

Government officials and well-placed outsiders evinced the changed attitude. Aquino proposed a popular referendum on the future of the bases beyond the expiration of the present treaty. Foreign Secretary Raul Manglapus declared that the "American father image" must be reduced to "brotherly size" if the Philippines were ever to mature as a self-respecting nation. Narciso Reyes, president of the Philippine Council for Foreign Relations, commented that a generation earlier Manuel Roxas had expressed contentment for the Philippines to follow in the "glistening wake of America." Reyes remarked that the image doubtless still appealed to the Americans, since a wake looks lovely from the afterdeck of the ship creating it. "But if you are in a small boat bobbing along in the glistening wake you would not be in a position to admire the view. You would have your hands full, coping with all sorts of refuse from the big ship, with the pollution from its engine exhausts, and with a lot of turbulence not of your own making."[31]

Just as Aquino offered little assurance on the base issue, neither did she inspire confidence on the communist question. Despite the resistance in her own military ranks the Philippine president preached conciliation toward the rebels. In November 1986 her government signed a sixty-day ceasefire with the insurgents. Aquino hoped the truce would lead to a more comprehensive settlement that would bring the communists back within the fold of political respectability.

The Reagan administration, then devising stratagems for circumventing a congressional ban on aid to anticommunist forces in Nicaragua, believed that communists in the Philippines, like communists anywhere, would accept a peace accord only as a device for regrouping in preparation for further offensives, military or political. For attribution, the administration adopted a position described by Assistant Secretary of State Gaston Sigur, who told the Senate's armed services committee, "The coming to power of the Aquino government has dealt a political blow to the communist insurgents." On background, though, administration officials suggested that Aquino was not taking the communist threat seriously enough, hinting that new American aid would depend on a stiffer line against the rebels.[32]

Aquino confronted the issue directly during a September 1986 visit to the United States. Officially she remained the darling of the administration, Exhibit A in the effort to prove the continuing soundness of the Republicans' authoritarian-versus-totalitarian paradigm. The fact that Exhibit B, the successor regime to the Duvalier dynasty in Haiti, was rapidly losing its luster, added to Aquino's appeal. Liberals toasted her as the vindicator of their efforts to remove Marcos.

Invited to address a joint session of the Senate and House of Representatives, Aquino defended her policy of conciliation toward the communist rebels and made clear that she would not short-circuit the peace process merely to please Washington. At the same time she assured her listeners that her government had undertaken the search for peace with eyes fully open. Should the rebels reject the hand of friendship, that hand would not hesitate to grasp the "sword of war."

The speech brought a standing ovation. More concretely it furthered Aquino's efforts to secure American assistance. Senate Majority Leader Robert Dole congratulated her at the conclusion of her address. "Cory, you hit a home run," Dole said. Aquino, having just asked the legislators for a hefty increase in American help, responded, "I hope the bases were loaded."[33]

They were. The House immediately voted a $200 million package of new economic and military aid, and the Senate concurred, albeit more slowly. The Reagan administration, approving the assistance, also encouraged the Philippines' creditors to reschedule repayment of the country's foreign debt. In March 1987 the bondholders agreed to an easier timetable for nearly half the total, or more than $13 billion.

It may not have been coincidence that the debt agreement came just a week after Aquino announced a change in policy toward the communists. The ceasefire had lapsed in February, with government and rebels trading charges of bad faith. Aquino, bolstered by a big victory in a plebiscite ratifying a new constitution and consequently feeling less required to placate the left, declared that the time had come to secure the state by a military victory over the insurgents.

Washington applauded the move. The American government made a great show of giving the Philippine military ten helicopters for use against the rebels. Less publicly and less directly the Reagan administration supplied assistance to counterinsurgent vigilante groups operating in the countryside. John Singlaub, retired American general, CIA veteran and associate of National Security Council staffer and all-purpose bagman Oliver North, visited the Philippines, purportedly to search for "buried treasure." In fact Singlaub brought some treasure of his own. He met with various military officials who explained their desire to fight the NPA's guerrillas with guerrillas sympathetic to the government. The pro-government forces would welcome any assistance. The Reagan administration, already supporting anticommunist guerrillas in Nicaragua, Angola and Afghanistan, liked the idea. During the next several months the CIA apparently disbursed some $10 million to finance the campaign.[34]

Guerrillas are notoriously difficult to control, and when they receive money no one wants to admit giving them, control becomes nearly impossible. Before long the vigilantes, including the prototypical organization, Alsa Masa in Davao, were reported to be copying the NPA abuses they had banded together to eliminate. By the beginning of 1988 the situation had drawn the attention of the human-rights advocacy organization Amnesty International, which condemned the "rising cycle of killings and reprisals" in the islands. The vigilantes and the Philippine military were by no means solely responsible for the growing violence, the rights group said. The communists bore much of the blame. But the anticommunists certainly shared it.[35]

Amnesty International's reports did not top President Reagan's reading list. Having condoned worse elsewhere, and previously in the Philippines, Washington was not about to complain regarding overzealous anticommunists. Especially it would not complain if Aquino, having come around to the American viewpoint on the communist threat, proved amenable to American persuasion with respect to the bases. In 1987, Philippine and American negotiators began the second five-year review specified under the 1979 treaty revision. Although Aquino no longer spoke of bringing the base issue to a popular vote, her government made plain that should the Americans genuinely desire to keep the bases until 1991 they had better prepare to pay for the privilege. The Reagan administration countered by hinting that if pressed the United States might go elsewhere. "We have no plans to relocate our facilities from the Philippines," Assistant Secretary Sigur said, while adding, "As a great power, we must, of course, plan for contingencies. Evaluations of other possible locations are a regular feature of our strategic planning."[36]

The posturing and haggling went on for months. Some more-ambitious voices on the Philippine side suggested a debt-for-bases swap: the United States would pay the Philippines' foreign tab in exchange for continued access to Subic and Clark. But $30 billion, or a large portion of it, struck Washington as steep for what amounted to two years' rent—although that four-letter word never passed official American lips. Soviet leader Mikhail Gorbachev threw a wrench into the business by offering another trade: Cam Ranh Bay for Subic and Clark. Intent on trimming Moscow's military and foreign aid bill, Gorbachev said the Soviets would return their naval base at Cam Ranh, and perhaps an air field at Danang (both mostly built by the United States during the Vietnam War), to the Vietnamese if the Americans would hand Subic and Clark back to the Filipinos. The proposal possessed a certain plausibility, since the Pentagon had repeatedly cited the Soviet presence in Vietnam as justification for retention of the American position in the Philippines. But American military leaders wanted to stay in the Philippines more than they wanted the Russians out of Vietnam, and the Reagan administration politely told the Kremlin to mind its own affairs.

In October 1988 the two sides finally cut a deal. Manila consented to let the Americans remain until September 1991. Washington agreed to deliver nearly half a billion dollars in economic and military aid for each of the two years left on the treaty.

As everyone recognized, the bargain merely bought time—expensive time, and not much of that. Hardly another year had passed before American and Philippine officials were talking about what would happen after 1991. In the Philippine senate, opposition to an extension of the base treaty mounted, especially after the December 1989 rebellion. Enrile, speaking for the opposition Nacionalistas, asserted that American intervention from the bases had violated international law, the Philippine constitution and the bilateral treaties governing the use of the bases.[37]

The talks started, then broke down; they started again, then broke down again. The end of the Cold War, with its tacit admission by Moscow that the Soviet Union was dropping its pretensions to global influence, diminished the value of the American bases in the Philippines, and thereby undermined the negotiating position of the Philippine government. On the other hand, the Persian Gulf crisis and war of 1990–91 showed the continued importance of military facilities on the opposite side of the globe from North America, thereby restoring some of Manila's lost leverage.

By the spring of 1991, the general shape of a deal had become evident. The United States would phase out Clark and Subic over perhaps ten years, during which period Washington would continue to provide the Philippines with billions of dollars of aid. Like the proverbial sinner who prayed to be saved, though not just yet, Philippine nationalists would gain the satisfaction of ejecting the Americans, but would retain the benefits of collaboration a while longer.

Two developments upset this arrangement. First, the Pinatubo volcano erupted, covering Clark in a blizzard of ash (and devastating much of the surrounding area as well). Washington decided that digging out would not be worth the expense and dropped Clark from the deal. (The Filipino communities were left to dig themselves out.)

And then the Philippine senate rejected the proposed treaty. Nationalists in the senate asserted that the time had come to rid the Philippines of the American incubus once and for all. Skeptics, noting Aquino's support for the treaty, suggested that her opponents wanted to keep the nationalist stick handy for use in the 1992 Philippine elections. Aquino momentarily considered taking her case to the Philippine people, as she had in 1986. Public-opinion polls showed strong popular backing for letting the Americans stay. But the opposition threatened impeachment, and the two sides settled—apparently—on a three-year American phaseout. Not even this deal stuck, however. Talks on the speed of the phaseout broke down in December 1991. Facing continued nationalist pressure, the Aquino administration ordered the Americans out of Subic by the end of 1992. Washington did not contest the decision.

Conclusion

I. The dimensions of power

If one drew a graph measuring effective American power vis-à-vis the Philippines from the 1890s to the 1990s, it would show a sharp increase from the beginning of the Spanish-American War in 1898 through the suppression of the Filipino resistance after the turn of the century, followed by a long, gradual and occasionally interrupted decline. During the first few years of the American period the United States spared no effort enforcing its will on the Filipinos, employing direct military means, sometimes of the most brutal sort, to bring the recalcitrant colonials into line. The termination of the Philippine war placed the use of raw military power against Filipinos largely out of bounds, with the principal exception being intermittent expeditions against the Moros.

With the establishment of civilian government in the islands, American officials shifted from military to principally political methods of achieving American ends. Americans saw themselves as ruling in the interests of the Filipinos as well as of Americans, and this interpretation of the American role constrained what American officials felt able to do. It also led to the cultivation of a class of Filipinos as intermediaries between the American government and the masses of the Filipino people. The American decision to govern indirectly required American officials to temper their reforming tendencies and accommodate the interests of the Filipino elites. In the process, the balance of power between the United States and the Philippines shifted inexorably in the direction of the latter.

The shifting accelerated during the governorship of Francis Burton Harrison when Washington handed essential home rule to the Filipinos. It slowed and momentarily reversed course under Leonard Wood, though Osmeña and Quezon managed to prevent the retrogression from proceeding very far. The general trend resumed with the passage of the Tydings-McDuffie Act and the establishment of the commonwealth. American power in the Philippines temporarily dropped almost to zero after the evacuation of Corregidor and the surrender of Bataan. It rebounded with the Leyte invasion, then began to decline once more with the 1946 transfer of sovereignty to the Republic of the Philippines.

Independence occasioned a second transformation in the predominant mode of American power in the Philippines. If the end of the Philippine war had marked a shift from military to political means in the enforcement of the American will upon the Filipino people, the establishment of a sovereign Philippine nation produced a shift from political to chiefly economic means. In order to secure continuing American interests in the Philippines—the most important being access to military bases, the existence of a stable and friendly government willing to contribute to the fight against communism, and favorable conditions for investment—the United States relied on American aid and on concessions on trade and investment. American officials in the Philippines, from Edward Lansdale to Stephen Bosworth, provided plenty of political, diplomatic and other advice to Philippine leaders, but what gave the American words weight was the value of the grants, loans, military supplies, agricultural commodities, trade agreements and the like the United States could and did furnish to Philippine administrations that accepted the advice.

America's economic leverage with the Philippines, like the political leverage earlier, decreased over time. Where the shift of political power toward Manila had for the most part been deliberate, motivated both by a desire to redeem America's pledge of democracy for the Filipinos and by a wish to be rid of an unprofitable burden, the erosion of economic power was unplanned. It resulted partly from the draining influence of other claims on American resources—aid to Latin America and nonaligned countries like India, for example, and the war in Vietnam. To at least an equal degree it resulted from what might be called the de-Americanization of the Philippine political system. In the 1950s Ramón Magsaysay readily identified with the United States, out of personal conviction as well as out of knowledge that such identification would help him, or at least not hurt him, at the polls. In such circumstances a modest amount of American aid and a few concessions on trade and investment went a long way. By the 1980s Ferdinand Marcos clearly considered the United States primarily a cow to be milked for whatever it was worth, and an increasing number of Filipinos agreed with him. The relationship between the two countries was much more a business proposition than before. Not surprisingly, American dollars did not go as far as previously.

To a certain degree, during the entire period of American relations with the

Philippines the cultural influence of the United States complemented the more direct military, political and economic forms of American power. If cultural influence is defined as the ability to shape systems of values, then cultural influence was what the American experiment in governing the Philippines was supposed to be all about. Whatever strategic and commercial benefits the United States might derive from possession of the islands, America's presence would be justified in the end only by the degree to which Filipinos embraced America's democratic and related values. To some extent the experiment worked, especially in the area of political values, and when it did it facilitated the attainment of other American objectives. Early on the Federalistas and Nacionalistas learned to play the American game, in the process creating the collaborative framework that provided the basis for America's scheme of cooperative government. Manuel Quezon proved a master gamesman, casting himself as just the person Washington needed to lead the Philippines to independence. Magsaysay rallied to the cause of Cold War anticommunism. Marcos, if grudgingly, joined the fight against aggression in Vietnam.

Yet as even this incomplete roster demonstrates, there was at least as much of tactical opportunism about Filipino leaders' embrace of American values as there was of considered conviction. And in this realm as in the others, American influence faded with time. Henry Adams once cited the succession of American presidents from George Washington to Ulysses Grant as refutation of the theory of evolution. The succession of Philippine presidents from Magsaysay to Marcos may or may not have refuted Darwin, but it did demonstrate the declining influence of American values in Philippine politics. (A real cynic might argue that Marcos was simply applying a different set of American values, namely those of the Grant or Harding eras. But Marcos carried his grafting much further than anything Americans had witnessed during the 1870s or the 1920s, and no American president has ever seriously considered nationwide martial law.) By the 1980s Marcos had become downright embarrassing to the United States, and to many observers in American and elsewhere he seemed living evidence of the utter failure of the United States to establish democratic values in the Philippines.

II.   Comparative colonialisms

On the other hand, the Filipino people did eventually throw Marcos out, and in doing so they displayed a commitment to democracy that put even Americans to shame. A person determined to claim success for the American tutelary effort in the Philippines could contend that the People Power movement of 1986, rather than Marcos' misgovernment, was the more representative result of the work of Taft, Forbes, Harrison and the rest.

Maybe so, maybe not. To produce a case one way or the other would require an extensive excursion into counterfactual history. Would the Philippines have spawned a Marcos if not for the American colonial and postcolonial connection? Would the Filipino people have overthrown him? Would democracy in the Philippines have been stronger or weaker in the absence of an American connection? There is no way to know.

All the same, beneath these questions is a more basic question that deserves to be addressed: Did the American presence in the Philippines benefit the Filipinos? Put otherwise, did the United States deliver, at least partly, on its promise of "the Philippines for the Filipinos"?

Answers here run up against some of the same counterfactual difficulties as before. Because the United States *did* annex the Philippines in 1899, there is no way of knowing what the Philippines would have been like in 1991 had the United States refrained from annexing. The issue is not whether the Filipino people were better off in 1991 than in 1899—by most quantifiable measures they were—but whether they were better off than they would have been without the American relationship.

Another way to approach the question is to compare the American performance in the Philippines with the performance of other colonialists elsewhere in the neighborhood. This approach is not entirely satisfactory, since it implicitly assumes that *some* country would have seized the Philippines had the United States not. This is hardly a certainty. Yet, considering the graspingly competitive condition of international politics at the turn of the century and the relatively defenseless state of the Philippines, there is as much reason to believe that the Philippines would have become some great power's Indochina or Korea as to believe it would have remained its own Siam.

How did America's treatment of the Philippines compare with Britain's treatment of India, France's of Indochina, the Netherlands' of Indonesia, or Japan's of Korea?

Rather well, in fact. With the Japanese occupation of Korea and often ferocious repression of the Korean people there is really no comparison. The Japanese considered Korea a conquered territory and made no bones about bleeding its people. The Netherlands behaved better toward the Indonesians, but the Dutch had little concept of seriously developing the Indonesians for self-rule. Two years after the American Congress approved the Tydings Act the Dutch governor of Indonesia declared, "We have worked here in the Indies for three hundred years. We should expect another three hundred years before the Indies will, perhaps, be mature for a form of autonomy." Significantly, Indonesians described the Japanese conquest of their country in 1942 as "liberation" and the arrival of British troops in 1945, preparatory to the return of the Dutch, as the "reoccupation." (Filipinos, by contrast, spoke of the Japanese "occupation" of the Philippines during the war and the American "liberation" at war's end.)[1]

As for the French in Indochina, they were still fighting to hold onto their Southeast Asian colony twenty years after the United States had set a date for Philippine independence and nearly a decade after the United States had handed sovereignty to the Filipinos. The significant fact here was that France had to be driven out of Indochina by military force, while the United States granted Philippine independence voluntarily. (American aid to France in the fight against the Viet Minh indicated not a conversion to colonialism but an aversion to communism. The Eisenhower administration repeatedly pressed France to grant independence to the states of Indochina, both for the sake of self-determination and from fear that if the French hung on too long their heirs would be the communists.) To be sure, a successful nationalist military movement is not conclusive evidence of colonial maladministration. Indeed, in certain respects the Vietnamese and other inhabitants of Indochina appreciated France at least as much as Filipinos appreciated America. Even as committed a nationalist as General Vo Nguyen Giap, the commander who drove out the French (and later the Americans) considered the French language and education in French ways the mark of a cultured person. All the same, despite their professions of a *mission civilisatrice*, the French generally exploited their Southeast Asian colonies far more blatantly than Americans exploited the Philippines. No American governor of the Philippines could have written about the people of Luzon what French governor Paul Doumer wrote about the people of the central portion of Vietnam: "When France arrived in Indochina, the Annamites were ripe for servitude."[2]

Of other colonialisms, the British experience in India most closely paralleled the American experience in the Philippines. The British transferred sovereignty to India (and Pakistan) barely a year after the United States transferred sovereignty to the Philippines. And the British left in relative peace (although India and Pakistan quickly went to war with each other) rather than at the point of a gun. Further, British officials had taken quite seriously their obligation to prepare India for self-rule. India's postcolonial record of democratic practice has at least matched the Philippines'. (Pakistan is another story.) Even so, the British accepted the idea of Indian independence only under great duress and only at the last moment. During the previous quarter-century Britain had sought to stifle the independence movement by violence (at Amritsar in 1919 British troops mowed down nearly four hundred demonstrators) and by massive jailings (Winston Churchill clapped some 100,000 nationalists behind bars in 1942). During World War II millions of Indians hoped the Japanese would beat the British. Thousands helped Subhas Chandra Bose organize the Indian National Army to fight on Japan's side. When Britain left India in 1947, the knowledge that British troops could not keep the independence movement bottled up much longer provided a principal impetus.

If a single trait distinguished American control of the Philippines from the control exercised by the other colonial powers in their colonies, it was the relative diffidence with which a majority of Americans approached the idea of colonialism. Historian Robin Winks once described colonialism as "a state of mind." If so, it was a state Americans as a group never acquired. A few individuals like Taft and Forbes and Wood came close, but they were always offset and eventually superseded by the Wilsons, Harrisons and Murphys. Theodore Roosevelt—himself a half-hearted colonialist once he recognized what colonialism meant for the United States—was right when he predicted that the American people would not long tolerate the burden of governing the Filipinos. Whether because Americans trace their own national existence to an anticolonial rebellion; because they are too attached to the notion of republicanism to deny it indefinitely to others; or because they are too self-centered to persist in efforts to do good for other people—for whatever combination of reasons, Americans never got the hang of colonialism. Lacking the hang, once they initially established American authority in the Philippines they allowed their colonial power to rest relatively lightly on the Filipino people. The Filipinos, at any rate, complained relatively little and then often for form's sake. When Philippine independence arrived, it resulted less from a Filipino desire to have done with America than from an American desire to have done with the Philippines.[3]

III.   Imperialism, old and new

If one accepts that American colonialism in the Philippines was comparatively benign, a question remains whether American treatment of the Philippines *after* independence was what it should have been. Did Americans exploit the enormous disparity in power between the United States and the Philippines to America's advantage and the Philippines' detriment? Did America's economic leverage leave the Philippines, though politically independent, still at America's mercy? Did the United States practice an informal kind of imperialism over the Filipinos?

People can debate endlessly, and have, about what constitutes imperialism. Strict constructionists define imperialism as only that which involves formal empires: where the flag waves, there lies the empire, and nowhere else. Loose constructionists have applied the term to nearly any unequal power relationship. During the last several decades imperialism as a label has acquired a pejorative connotation, rendering matters of terminology the more troublesome. (In the salad days of imperialism in the late nineteenth century many imperialists wore the badge proudly.)

A way around the semantic problem is to adopt the view that imperialism is as imperialism does—or was as did. In the context of the Philippines one might compare the manner and extent of America's application of power before independence to the manner and extent of the application after. By any reasonable definition, American activities in the Philippines before 1946, and especially before 1935, whether onerous or benign, were imperialistic. If the United States exercised comparable influence over the lives of Filipinos after independence, then that influence might fairly be judged imperialistic as well.

By this standard American influence in the Philippines during the first decade or so after independence certainly amounted to informal imperialism. If anything, America exercised greater influence in the aftermath of World War II than it had for decades previous. The war had shattered the Philippine economy, and Washington dangled reconstruction aid before the fledgling Philippine government in order to obtain special treatment for American investment and long-term leases on land for military installations. The parity clause of the Bell Act required the Filipinos to amend their constitution—about as intrusive a non-military exercise of foreign influence as one could imagine.

Through the 1950s American influence diminished somewhat while still remaining strong. Edward Lansdale and the CIA were hardly responsible for the selection of Magsaysay as Philippine president, and Washington did give ground in the Laurel-Langley accord. But on matters ranging from the Manila Pact to the Bandung conference, not to mention the American bases, the Magsaysay administration delivered nearly everything the American government desired.

The 1960s witnessed a further decrease in American influence. American backing for political candidates carried less weight than before, and an ambitious person like Marcos could make a nationalist issue out of Macapagal's desire to send Philippine troops to Vietnam. This said, the prospect of additional American aid caused Marcos, once safely elected, to agree to send the Philippine contingent—a course he almost certainly would not have chosen nor the Philippine legislature accepted without the American bribe. American influence, though declining, still sufficed to override the nationalist scruples of the Philippine government. Not completely: the Philippine legislature after 1966 refused to appropriate funds for the Philippine Vietnam unit, and fear of a Filipino backlash caused the United States to refrain from launching combat sorties against Vietnam from bases in the Philippines. Yet through the end of Marcos' first term Washington got more of what it wanted from him than it had from Osmeña and Quezon during the 1920s.

The termination of the Vietnam War decreased American demands on the Philippines. By the early 1980s the demands had reduced essentially to access to the American bases. Though American influence in the Philippines had continued to decline, it remained strong enough to ensure that access. In other areas the American government had precious little pull with Marcos. His imposition of martial law and his increasingly obvious misrule made him obnoxious to most Americans, government officials included. But with a few exceptions the successive administrations in Washington overlooked his faults and paid his inflating price in order to ensure his cooperation regarding the bases.

By this time America's informal-imperialist powers had dwindled nearly to nothing. A fair argument could be made, and was, although not usually in such loaded language, that what the Philippines needed was *more* American imperialism. Washington had never allowed Marcos-style abuses while the Philippines had been an American colony, and though no one advocated a reoccupation of the country, more than a few thought the United States might take measures to persuade Marcos to shape up or get out. Such advice, though well intended, raised serious philosophical problems. When, if ever, is outside intervention compatible with self-determination? Is good government preferable to self-government? (An affirmative answer to the latter question formed the basis for the Taft-Forbes-Wood approach, as it did for most forms of professedly enlightened imperialism.) The advice also raised tactical problems, in that it would enable Marcos to wrap himself in the Philippine flag.

Yet the imperial bond had not vanished entirely. After the Filipino people routed Marcos from office, Cory Aquino immediately looked to the United States for support. Washington quickly pledged economic aid, and when Aquino decided that bringing the Marcoses back to Manila to try to recover the loot they had stolen was too risky, American prosecutors leveled charges against the couple. During one coup attempt the United States even resorted to military intervention, sending a squadron of American jets from Clark over Manila in a successful show of force designed to intimidate the rebels.

In summary, the American relationship with the independent Philippines did exhibit characteristics of an informal imperialism, with American power at times shaping Filipino behavior in a manner comparable to the manner in which American power had shaped Filipino behavior before independence. America's informal-imperialist influence diminished over time during the postcolonial period, just as America's formal-imperialist influence had diminished during the colonial period. Put differently, in the ninety-year process by which power in the Philippines shifted from Americans to Filipinos, beginning at the turn of the twentieth century and continuing into the century's final decade, the transfer of sovereignty in 1946 signaled no abrupt change. The devolution of power traced a reasonably smooth curve, with formal imperialism shading into informal imperialism, and both losing strength with passing years.

IV. Power and responsibility

One does not have to accept the full imperialist rationale to concede that formal imperialism has one important advantage, for both the imperialists and the imperialized, over informal imperialism: it establishes a clear connection between power and responsibility. Before 1946, and even more so before 1935, if something went wrong in the Philippines there was no doubt where ultimate responsibility lay. The Filipinos who helped American officials govern the country might share the burden of responsibility, as they certainly did in some of the fiascos of the Harrison era, but the buck finally stopped in Washington.

The transition from formal to informal imperialism in 1946 produced a sundering of the connection between power and responsibility. (In fact, one can take this sundering as defining the difference between the two forms of imperialism: formal imperialism equals power with responsibility, while informal imperialism equals power without responsibility.) The disconnection between the two allowed American officials to disclaim responsibility when Philippine presidents like Quirino and Marcos raided the public treasury or otherwise abused their authority, even as Washington retained the power to ensure preferential treatment for American investment and access to military bases.

To gain perspective on the relation between power and responsibility, one might look to the United States' treatment of the countries of Central America and the Caribbean. With the exceptions of Puerto Rico and later the Virgin Islands, the United States never possessed a formal empire in the Caribbean basin. Instead it acted on a strictly informal basis. The region was spared wars of American conquest comparable to the Philippine war, but it did not escape the frequent use of American military force. During the first third of the twentieth century—corresponding to the pre-commonwealth period in the Philippines—American troops invaded and occupied many of the countries of the area, sometimes staying for several years at a time. The invasions and occupations did next to nothing to improve living conditions for the Central Americans and Caribbean islanders. On the contrary, American soldiers, and American political and economic policies in later years, tended to foster autocratic regimes far more violent and oppressive than Marcos'. America's irresponsible exercise of power in the region also generated a deep-seated distrust of the United States and helped create a variety of anti-American revolutionary movements.

By comparison to this situation, America's treatment of the Philippines, at least after the suppression of resistance to annexation, was gentle and well received. Quezon used to complain that the United States did not sufficiently oppress the Philippines. "Damn the Americans!" he said. "Why don't they tyrannize us more?" American rule offered Quezon no hard surface to strike against, no irrepressible nationalist issues to turn to account. Benigno Aquino put the same complaint slightly differently. "The United States really kills you with love," Aquino asserted. "A fire starts and they smother you with foam. They kill you with Hershey bars."[4]

Aquino spoke in 1968. By the time he was really killed, not with Hershey bars but with bullets, for returning to a country controlled by a regime underwritten by American dollars, he might have had a different view. It is significant that the United States enjoyed greater popularity in the Philippines in the early aftermath of the colonial period than it did forty-five years later. Magsaysay counted it a political plus to be identified with the United States, and when Douglas Mac-Arthur returned to the Philippines in 1961 Filipinos filled the streets of Manila in an outpouring of affection and gratitude unmatched in Philippine history. By the beginning of the 1990s the glow had faded dramatically. Cory Aquino's evident dependence on the United States diminished her prestige in many quarters, and Filipino politicians of nearly all stripes felt obliged to speak out against the continuing American presence in the country. On the streets of Manila and in the neighborhoods of Clark and Subic Americans sometimes walked in danger of their lives.

While a variety of factors accounted for the decline in pro-American sentiment, probably none mattered more than the perceived—and actual—irresponsibility of American power in the postcolonial period. Before independence the United States had exercised power in the Philippines, but it had acknowledged its responsibility to use that power for Filipinos' good as well as for Americans'. Often the Americans delivered less than they promised, but most Filipinos conceded that the United States did not egregiously misuse its power. The objective and honest among them would have granted that during the major portion of the colonial period the Americans delivered reasonably good government, perhaps better than Filipinos would have. Eventually Filipino leaders came to value self-government more than good government: Quezon said he would prefer "a government run like hell by Filipinos to one run like heaven by Americans." But Filipinos who knew conditions elsewhere in Asia recognized that in comparison their country was well treated.[5]

After independence the United States no longer recognized any significant responsibility for the welfare of Filipinos. As the hearings and negotiations preceding passage of the Tydings-McDuffie Act demonstrated, that was much of the point of granting independence. To be sure, among some Americans there existed a residual desire to do right by America's former dependency, but the American government found it distressingly easy—distressing to those who had hoped for better—to act as though the Filipinos' problems had nothing to do with the United States. From this attitude came the willingness to tolerate Marcos' hijacking of the Philippine treasury and his subversion of the political and human rights of Filipinos, so long as he let the United States keep Clark and Subic.

Had the United States possessed no influence with Marcos, no one could reasonably have blamed the United States for Marcos' excesses. Doubtless many of Marcos' opponents in the Philippines and elsewhere overestimated Washington's ability to get him to change his ways. Further, as noted above, there were philosophical as well as tactical problems associated with any overt American intervention in Philippine affairs. Yet it was not unreasonable to suggest that after nearly fifty years of colonial rule, and while Washington still paid many of the Philippine government's bills, the United States had certain obligations to the

Filipino people. If the United States could not actively intervene to restore democracy, then at least it should not collaborate in democracy's destruction.

As a group, American officials engaged in foreign policy are neither stupid nor venal—the stupid don't last and the venal quickly learn that other fields pay better. American officials involved in policy toward the Philippines during the Marcos era understood the trade-offs dealing with Marcos entailed. With their eyes open they decided that America's security interests in the Philippines outweighed—for the United States—the interests of the Filipino people in good government and national development. For awhile they did not consider the goals incompatible, but even after the Marcos regime degenerated into unvarnished despotism they chose access to the bases over democracy for Filipinos.

Was the choice justified?

An answer to this question requires answers to two subsidiary questions. First, did the United States in fact have any residual obligations to the Filipino people? Phrased another way: Was American raison d'état sufficient basis for determining American policy? Second, assuming it was sufficient basis, did American raison d'état require winking at Marcos' misdeeds? Alternatively: Were the bases all that important?

Obviously these questions have no easy answers. The first requires a moral judgment about the proper role of government. "Realists" have held that governments act morally only when they pursue the collective self-interest of the individuals they represent. Anything more is vanity and delusion. "Idealists" grant greater scope for action on behalf of other nations and peoples.

Whatever the merits of the opposing arguments in the realist-idealist debate as it applies to international affairs generally, it would appear that the Philippines occupied a special position vis-à-vis the United States. By no choice of their own, Filipinos fell under American rule at the end of the nineteenth century. For almost five decades the United States professed to govern the Philippines in the interests of Filipinos. Had American power in the Philippines disappeared in 1946, perhaps American responsibility could be said to have disappeared too. But power persisted, and so, one would think, did responsibility.

The second question—whether American interests dictated acquiescence in dictatorship—is no easier. American governments from the 1940s to the 1990s valued the bases in the Philippines for the ability the bases provided the United States to project American power into Southeast Asia and adjacent regions. Was this ability crucial? Assuming the wisdom of the containment premises of American Cold War policies, it might have been. On the other hand, in light of the fact that the bases received their heaviest use in support of the tragic American war effort in Vietnam, a case can be made that whatever might have discouraged the United States from making that effort would have been to America's advantage (not to mention the advantage of the Vietnamese and everyone else drawn into the maelstrom). Certainly the fading away of the Cold War in the late 1980s indicated a need for reconsidering premises that for long seemed almost unchallengeable.

The problem of balancing power and responsibility has lain at the heart of American international affairs for a century. During the 1890s Americans had more power than their history had prepared them for. In the ebullience of their power they seized the Philippines. Simultaneously they launched on a career of globalism that within two generations afforded them power unmatched by any nation in world history. Meanwhile Americans' sense of responsibility also increased, though not at the same pace as their power. With respect to the world at large, the sense of responsibility lagged behind the power through two great wars, catching up only during the second. For a time after the second, power and responsibility ran a close race, as the United States committed itself to defending half the planet against communism. Eventually power faltered, leaving Americans with responsibilities, most dramatically in Southeast Asia, they could not fulfill.

In pondering their path down from the summit of world power and responsibility, American leaders might have looked to their country's experience in the Philippines. The issues of power and responsibility between the United States and the Philippines were not identical to the issues of power and responsibility between the United States and the rest of the world, but similarities existed. If Americans had not always succeeded in matching power and responsibility in relations with the Philippines, their failures, as well as their successes, furnished lessons potentially applicable elsewhere.

Manuscript Collections Cited

Dean Acheson papers, Truman Library, Independence, Missouri.
Emilio Aguinaldo papers, Library of Congress, Washington.
American Anti-Imperialist League papers, University of Michigan, Ann Arbor.
American Civil Liberties Union papers, Princeton University, Princeton, New Jersey.
Edward Atkinson papers, Massachusetts Historical Society, Boston.
Henry Hill Bandholtz papers, University of Michigan.
Edward Bell papers, Harvard University, Cambridge, Massachusetts.
Stephen Bonsal papers, Library of Congress.
Bureau of Insular Affairs records, National Archives, Washington.
Myron Cowen papers, Truman Library.
Wayne Coy papers, Franklin Roosevelt Library, Hyde Park, New York.
Miguel Cuaderno papers, University of the Philippines, Quezon City.
Nathaniel Davis papers, Truman Library.
Department of State records, National Archives, Washington.
Jacob Dickinson papers, Harvard University.
John Foster Dulles papers, Eisenhower Library, Abilene, Kansas.
John Foster Dulles papers, Princeton University.
Clarence Edwards papers, Massachusetts Historical Society.
Dwight Eisenhower papers, Eisenhower Library.
Homer Ferguson papers, University of Michigan.
W. Cameron Forbes papers, Harvard University.
Gerald Ford papers, Ford Library, Ann Arbor, Michigan.
Carlos García papers, National Library, Manila.
Lindley Garrison papers, Princeton University.
Francis Burton Harrison papers, Library of Congress.
Joseph Ralston Hayden papers, University of Michigan.
Roger Hilsman papers, Kennedy Library, Boston.
George Hoar papers, Massachusetts Historical Society.
Harry Hopkins papers, Roosevelt Library.

Roy Howard papers, Library of Congress.
Louis Howe papers, Roosevelt Library.
Lyndon Johnson papers, Johnson Library, Austin, Texas.
Joint Chiefs of Staff records, National Archives, Washington.
J. Weldon Jones papers, Truman Library.
Edward Kemmerer papers, Princeton University.
John Kennedy papers, Kennedy Library.
Edward Lansdale papers, Hoover Institution, Stanford, California.
José Laurel papers, Laurel Memorial, Manila.
James LeRoy papers, University of Michigan.
Henry Cabot Lodge papers, Massachusetts Historical Society.
Douglas MacArthur papers, MacArthur Memorial, Norfolk, Virginia.
Frank McCoy papers, Harvard University.
Frank McCoy papers, Library of Congress.
John Van Antwerp MacMurray papers, Princeton University.
Ramón Magsaysay papers, Magsaysay Foundation, Manila.
John Melby papers, Truman Library.
R. Walton Moore papers, Roosevelt Library.
Henry Morgenthau papers, Roosevelt Library.
Frank Murphy papers, University of Michigan.
National Security Council records, National Archives, Washington.
Ron Nessen papers, Ford Library.
Office of Strategic Services records, National Archives, Washington.
Office of Territories records, National Archives, Washington.
Sergio Osmeña papers, National Library, Manila.
Philippine Insurgency records, National Library, Manila.
Philippines collection, National Security Archive, Washington.
Manuel Quezon papers, National Library, Manila.
Elpidio Quirino papers, Ayala Museum, Manila.
Claro Recto papers, University of Michigan.
Carlos Romulo papers, University of the Philippines.
Franklin Roosevelt papers, Roosevelt Library.
Theodore Roosevelt papers, Library of Congress.
Theodore Roosevelt Jr. papers, Harvard University.
Samuel Rosenman papers, Roosevelt Library.
Manuel Roxas papers, National Library, Manila.
Francis Sayre papers, Library of Congress.
Henry Stimson papers, Yale University, New Haven, Connecticut.
Moorfield Storey papers, Library of Congress.
Moorfield Storey papers, Massachusetts Historical Society.
William Howard Taft papers, Library of Congress.
Harry Truman papers, Truman Library.
Frank Waring papers, Truman Library.
G. Mennen Williams papers, University of Michigan.
James Wilson papers, Ford Library.
Leonard Wood papers, Harvard University.
Leonard Wood papers, Library of Congress.
Dean Worcester papers, University of Michigan.

Notes

1. Manic Depression

1. Jacob A. Riis, *How the Other Half Lives* (New York, 1890, 1957), 101.

2. Walter LaFeber, *The New Empire* (Ithaca, N.Y., 1963), 188–194.

3. Thomas J. McCormick, *China Market* (Chicago, 1967), 73, 94.

4. William Appleman Williams, *The Tragedy of American Diplomacy* (New York, 1988 ed.), 48.

5. LaFeber, 181.

6. Williams, 49; McCormick, 94–95.

7. Richard Hofstadter, *Social Darwinism in American Thought* (Boston, 1955 ed.), 13; John Fiske, "Manifest Destiny," *Harpers* 70 (1885), 578–590.

8. Josiah Strong, *Our Country* (New York, 1885, 1891), 15, 45, 58–59, 83–84, 91.

9. Ibid., 208–210, 216, 221–222, 227.

10. Brooks Adams, *The Law of Civilization and Decay* (New York, 1896, 1910), viii–ix, 350, 362–363.

11. A. T. Mahan, *The Influence of Sea Power upon History* (Boston, 1890, 1916), 27, 83.

12. Roosevelt review of Mahan, *Atlantic Monthly*, October 1890, reprinted in *The Works of Theodore Roosevelt* (New York, 1924), 14:306–316.

13. Roosevelt review of Adams, *Forum*, January 1897, reprinted in *Works*, 14:129–150.

14. Howard K. Beale, *Theodore Roosevelt and the Rise of America to World Power* (Baltimore, 1956), 24, 37.

15. Ibid., 31–40.

16. Robert L. Beisner, *From the Old Diplomacy to the New* (New York, 1975), 91.

17. LaFeber, 54; Cleveland message to Congress, *Congressional Record*, 12/18/93, 309–312.

18. Olney to Bayard, 7/20/95, *Foreign Relations of the United States, 1895*, 1:545–562.

19. Salisbury to Pauncefote, 11/26/95, ibid., 563–576.

20. Dexter Perkins, *The Monroe Doctrine, 1867–1907* (Baltimore, 1937), 189–192.

21. Charles S. Campbell, *The Transformation of American Foreign Relations* (New York, 1976), 209–210; Beale, 50–52.

2. Dewey . . . or Don't We?

1. H. Wayne Morgan, *America's Road to Empire* (New York, 1965), 8.

2. Richard E. Welch, Jr., *Response to Imperialism* (Chapel Hill, N.C., 1979), 4.

3. Beale, *Roosevelt*, 63.

4. Diary entry for 2/26/98, in Margaret Long, ed., *The Journal of John D. Long* (Rindge, N.H., 1956), 217; Roosevelt to Dewey, 2/25/98, in Beale, 63.

5. George Dewey, *Autobiography* (New York, 1916), 186.

6. Long to Dewey, 4/25/98, in ibid., 195.

7. Dewey to Long, 5/4/98, in ibid., 297–300.

8. Morgan, 75.

9. McKinley interview, 11/21/99, in Charles S. Olcott, *The Life of William McKinley* (Boston, 1916), 2:110–111.

10. McKinley to Day, 10/25/98, in ibid., 2:107–108.

11. Robert L. Beisner, *Twelve Against Empire* (New York, 1968), 80–82.

12. Ibid., 61, 76–79.

13. Frederic Bancroft, ed., *Speeches, Correspondence and Political Papers of Carl Schurz* (New York, 1913), 6:1–36.

14. Andrew Carnegie, "Americanism versus Imperialism," *North American Review* 168 (January–March 1899), 1–13, 362–372.

15. *Congressional Record*, 1/31/99, 1314.

16. Ibid., 1/31/99, 1317.

17. Ibid., 1/31/99, 1320–1321.

18. Ibid., 2/3/99, 1417–1418.

19. Ibid., 2/3/99, 1422–1430.

20. Beale, 70; *Congressional Record*, 2/4/99, 1533; Lodge to Roosevelt, 7/8/98, Henry Cabot Lodge papers, Massachusetts Historical Society, Boston.

21. Lodge to Chamberlain, 12/2/98, and Lodge to Thayer, 11/28/98, Lodge papers.

22. Atkinson to Carnegie, 6/10/02, Edward Atkinson papers, Massachusetts Historical Society; Lodge to Roosevelt, 5/24/98, and Roosevelt to Lodge, 6/12/98, Lodge papers.

23. Lodge to Roosevelt, 6/15/98, Lodge to Winship, 12/22/98, and Roosevelt to Lodge, 1/26/99 and 3/18/99, Lodge papers.

24. *Congressional Record*, 2/7/99, 1533.

25. Ibid., 1/9/00, 704–711.

26. Paolo E. Coletta, *William Jennings Bryan* (Lincoln, Neb., 1964), 1:233–234.

27. Petitions in George Hoar papers, Massachusetts Historical Society; Beisner, 157–159.

28. Lodge in Albert K. Weinberg, *Manifest Destiny* (Baltimore, 1935), 312–313.

29. Garel A. Grunder and William E. Livezey, *The Philippines and the United States* (Norman, Okla., 1951), 74–77; Thomas A. Bailey, "Was the Election of 1900 a Mandate on Imperialism?," *Mississippi Valley Historical Review* 26 (June 1937), 43–52.

3. The Water Cure

1. Austin Coates, *Rizal* (Hong Kong, 1968), 17, 40.

2. Coates, 110, 144, 153.

3. David Sweet, "The Proto-Political Peasant Movement in the Spanish Philippines: The Cofradia de San Jose and the Tayabas Rebellion of 1841," *Asian Studies* 7 (April

1970), 94–119; Reynaldo Clemeña Ileto, *Pasyon and Revolution* (Quezon City, 1979), 38 ff.

4. Ileto, 80–85.

5. Teodoro A. Agoncillo, *The Revolt of the Masses* (Quezon City, 1956), 48–50.

6. Teodoro M. Kalaw, *The Philippine Revolution* (Quezon City, 1969 ed.), 14–19.

7. Leon Wolff, *Little Brown Brother* (New York, 1970), 24–25.

8. Coates, 300, 321–323.

9. Agoncillo, 213–214, 264.

10. Kalaw, 67–71.

11. Aguinaldo diary, in Emilio Aguinaldo with Vicente Albano Pacis, *A Second Look at America* (New York, 1957), 34.

12. Kalaw, 91–92.

13. Dewey, *Autobiography*, 246–247.

14. W. E. Retana, comp., *Archivo del Bibliófilo Filipino* (Madrid, 1905), 5:330–331, 363.

15. Long to Dewey, 5/26/98, and Dewey to Long, 6/27/98, in Dewey, 311–312.

16. Corbin to Merritt, 8/17/98, *Correspondence Relating to the War with Spain* (Washington, 1902), 754.

17. Retana, 341.

18. Statement by the secretary of war (Malolos), undated, file 151/14, Philippine Insurgency records, National Library, Manila.

19. Kalaw, 161.

20. Aguinaldo proclamation, 1/16/99, Emilio Aguinaldo papers, Library of Congress, Washington.

21. Kalaw, 164–167.

22. Welch, *Response to Imperialism*, 26–27.

23. Wolff, 245–247.

24. Grunder and Livezey, *Philippines and United States*, 54–55.

25. Hay to Alger, 1/31/99, Bureau of Insular Affairs (BIA) records, National Archives, Washington.

26. *Report of the Philippine Commission to the President*, Senate document 138, 56th Congress, 1st session (Washington, 1900), 5.

27. Schurman to Hay, 4/13/99, BIA records.

28. Kalaw, 176–177.

29. John Morton Gates, *Schoolbooks and Krags* (Westport, Conn., 1973), 102.

30. Schurman to Hay, 4/13/99, BIA records.

31. Peter W. Stanley, *A Nation in the Making* (Cambridge, Mass., 1974), 70–71.

32. *Report of the Philippine Commission*, 90.

33. Aguinaldo statement, 7/27/99, Philippine Insurgency records; Wolff, 252.

34. Dean C. Worcester, *The Philippines Past and Present* (New York, 1914), 1:285–286; Welch, 33.

35. Root to Henry Cabot Lodge, 2/17/02, in *Charges of Cruelty, etc., to the Natives of the Philippines*, Senate document 205, 57th Congress, 1st session (Washington, 1902), 1–3.

36. Brian McAllister Linn, *The U.S. Army and Counterinsurgency in the Philippine War, 1899–1902* (Chapel Hill, N.C., 1989), 145–146.

37. *Affairs in the Philippine Islands*, Senate document 331, 57th Congress, 1st session (Washington, 1902), 77.

38. Welch, 137–138; Stuart Creighton Miller, *Benevolent Assimilation* (New Haven, 1982), 208–209.

39. Aguinaldo manifesto, 4/15/00, Philippine Insurgency records.

40. David Howard Bain, *Sitting in Darkness* (Boston, 1984), 87–89.

41. Ibid., 344 ff.; Miller, 167–168.

42. Aguinaldo proclamation, 4/19/01, and Edwards to Hinds, 8/10/01, BIA records.

4. Progressivism from Above

1. Henry F. Pringle, *The Life and Times of William Howard Taft* (New York, 1939), 1:3, 21, 35.

2. Taft to H. W. Taft and Horace Taft, 1/28/00, in Pringle, 1:160.

3. Roosevelt to Lodge, 1/22/00, Lodge papers.

4. Taft to H. W. Taft and Horace Taft, 1/28/00, in Pringle, 1:148 and 160–161.

5. Worcester, *Philippines,* 1:330–331.

6. Edwards to Schmidlapp, 11/29/01, and Taft to Root, 2/6/03, BIA records; Worcester, 340–341.

7. Schurman report, 1:68–69.

8. Michael Cullinane, "Implementing the 'New Order': The Structure and Supervision of Local Government during the Taft Era," in Norman G. Owen, ed., *Compadre Colonialism* (Ann Arbor, Mich., 1971), 13–76.

9. Taft to Root, 4/3/01, William Howard Taft papers, Library of Congress; Stanley, *Nation in the Making,* 68–70.

10. Joseph Ralston Hayden, *The Philippines* (New York, 1942), 317–318.

11. Taft to Root, 1/23/01 and 1/30/01, Taft papers.

12. Taft to Root, 3/3/03, Taft papers.

13. Schurman to Hay, 4/13/99, BIA records; Kemmerer memo, 7/13/04, Edwin Kemmerer papers, Princeton University; Taft speech to New York Chamber of Commerce, 4/21/04, BIA records; Wright to Edwards, 2/20/02, Clarence Edwards papers, Massachusetts Historical Society, Boston; Bandholtz to Carpenter, 5/22/05, Henry Hill Bandholtz papers, University of Michigan, Ann Arbor.

14. Taft speech at Cebu, 8/22/05, and Taft speech at Iloilo, 8/15/05, James LeRoy papers, University of Michigan.

15. Glenn Anthony May, *Social Engineering in the Philippines* (Westport, Conn., 1980), 80–81, 93.

16. Hayden, 465; Forbes, *Philippine Islands,* 1:416; Agoncillo, 250–253.

17. May, 82.

18. *Report of the Philippine Commission,* House document 2, 58th Congress, 2nd session (Washington, 1904), 3:700–701.

19. Taft to Chatauqua Society, 8/11/04, BIA records; LeRoy in May, 43.

20. *Report,* 3:700–701.

21. McKinley to Taft, attached to McKinley to Root, 4/7/00, William McKinley papers, Library of Congress.

22. Olcott, *McKinley,* 2:111.

23. Kenton J. Clymer, "Protestant Missionaries and American Colonialism in the Philippines," in Peter W. Stanley, ed., *Reappraising an Empire* (Cambridge, Mass., 1984), 143–170; Welch, *Response to Imperialism,* 89, 95.

24. Clymer, "Protestant Missionaries," 147–150; Clymer, *Protestant Missionaries in the Philippines* (Urbana, 1986), 156.

25. Miller, *Benevolent Assimilation,* 18.

26. Clymer, *Protestant Missionaries*, 162–164.

27. Clymer, "Protestant Missionaries," 157–159.

28. Schurman report, 1:118.

29. Harry Luton, "American Internal Revenue Policy in the Philippines to 1916," in Owen, 129–156.

30. Pringle, 1:208.

31. Senate Philippines committee hearings, Senate document 331, part 1, 57th Congress, 1st session (Washington, 1902), 156–157.

32. Stanley, 146–147.

33. Akira Iriye, *Pacific Estrangement* (Cambridge, Mass., 1972), 43–44.

34. William Reynolds Braisted, *The United States Navy in the Pacific, 1897–1909* (Austin, Tex., 1958), 143–144.

35. Beale, *Roosevelt*, 268.

36. Roosevelt to Spring-Rice, 3/19/04, Roosevelt papers.

37. Taft to Root, 7/29/05, Taft papers; Roosevelt to Taft, 7/31/05, Roosevelt papers.

38. Bandholtz to Bruce, 7/8/07, Bandholtz papers.

39. Roosevelt to Taft, 8/21/07, Roosevelt papers.

40. Gillespie to Bureau of Insular Affairs, 7/11/04, BIA records.

5. Politics from Below

1. Dapen Liang, *The Development of Philippine Political Parties* (Hongkong, 1939), 70–79.

2. Maximo M. Kalaw, *The Development of Philippine Politics* (Manila, 1926), 304.

3. Liang, 80–83.

4. Bandholtz to Bruce, 7/8/07, Bandholtz papers.

5. Liang, 83; Bonifacio Salamanca, *The Filipino Reaction to American Rule* (Norwich, Conn., 1968), 66.

6. Pringle, *Taft*, 1:204.

7. Stanley, *Nation in the Making*, 117–123.

8. Journal entries, 5/31/09, 9/14/09 and 6/28/09, W. Cameron Forbes papers, Harvard University.

9. Forbes to Taft, 7/14/10, and Forbes journal, 7/20/10, Forbes papers.

10. Forbes to Dickinson, 9/28/09 and 11/27/09, BIA records; Forbes journal, 2/18/09, Forbes papers.

11. Stanley, 145.

12. Journal, 5/20/09, Forbes papers.

13. Frank Jenista, Jr., "Conflict in the Philippine Legislature: The Commission and the Assembly from 1907 to 1913," in Owen, *Compadre Colonialism*, 82.

14. Jenista, 86–88.

15. Journal, 5/3/09, Forbes papers.

16. *La Voz de Mindanao*, 7/23/10, and *El Ideal*, 8/25/10, in Jacob Dickinson papers, Harvard University.

17. Lewis E. Gleeck, Jr., *The Manila Americans* (Manila, 1977), 57–58.

18. Stanley, 164–167.

19. Grunder and Livezey, *Philippines and United States*, 114–116.

20. May, *Social Engineering*, 169–170.

21. Forbes journal, 8/6/09 and 8/7/09, Forbes papers.

22. Ide quoted in *Cablenews-American*, 10/24/05, clip in Kemmerer papers; Forbes speech, 11/24/09, BIA records.

23. Forbes speech, 11/24/09, BIA records.

24. Forbes to Dickinson, 4/5/10, BIA records; Forbes, *Philippine Islands,* 244.

25. Pringle, 1:227–231.

26. Quezon to Dickinson, 9/1/10, copy in Moorfield Storey papers, Library of Congress; Stanley, 157–161.

27. Atkinson to Carnegie, 6/10/02, Atkinson papers, Massachusetts Historical Society; Winslow to Welsh, 5/7/02, American Anti-Imperialist League papers, University of Michigan.

28. Bandholtz to Bruce, 7/8/07, Bandholtz papers.

29. Storey speech, 12/19/09, Moorfield Storey papers, Massachusetts Historical Society.

30. *El Renacimiento,* 8/23/07.

31. Quezon to Kalaw, 6/11/12, Manuel Quezon papers, National Library, Manila.

32. Stanley, 212–213.

33. Quezon to Pardo de Tavera, 5/18/12, Quezon papers.

6. Filipinization

1. Arthur M. Schlesinger, Jr., ed., *History of American Presidential Elections* (New York, 1971), 2176.

2. Roosevelt to McBee, 8/27/07, Theodore Roosevelt papers, Library of Congress.

3. Bandholtz to Wood, 11/2/12, Bandholtz papers.

4. Reynaldo C. Ileto, "Orators and the Crowd: Philippine Independence Politics, 1910–1914," in Stanley, *Reappraising an Empire,* 99–100.

5. Schlesinger, 2184.

6. Forbes to Wilson, 3/5/13, and Forbes journal, 8/26/13, Forbes papers.

7. Gleeck, *Manila Americans,* 109.

8. Manuel Luis Quezon, *The Good Fight* (New York, 1946), 125–126; Francis Burton Harrison, *The Corner-stone of Philippine Independence* (New York, 1922), 3–4.

9. Quezon to Legarda, 9/1/13, Quezon papers.

10. Forbes to Garrison, 8/25/13, BIA records.

11. Harrison statement, 10/6/13, Lindley Garrison papers, Princeton University.

12. Harrison to Garrison, 10/24/13, Francis Burton Harrison papers, Library of Congress; Stanley, *Nation in the Making,* 207–209.

13. *La Vanguardia,* undated, Garrison papers; Stanley, 207–209.

14. Dean C. Worcester, *The Philippines Past and Present* (New York, 1914 and 1930), 696–697.

15. Harrison to McCoy, 1/30/14, Harrison papers; Garrison memo, 7/30/14, Garrison papers.

16. Worcester, 704.

17. Forbes speech, 7/27/11, BIA records.

18. Leonard F. Giesecke, *History of American Economic Policy in the Philippines* (New York, 1987), 113–117; Stanley, 237–247.

19. Harrison to McIntyre, 11/14/20, Harrison papers.

20. *La Democracia,* 10/13/14.

21. Liang, *Philippine Political Parties,* 96–99.

22. Stanley, 212–213.
23. Grunder and Livezey, *Philippines and United States*, 151–152.
24. Forbes, *Philippine Islands*, 2:252.
25. Harrison to McIntyre, 3/31/16, Harrison papers; Harrison to Garrison, 6/17/16, BIA records.
26. Osmeña to Harrison, 3/11/16; Osmeña to acting governor-general, 4/26/16; Osmeña to Quezon, 4/1/16; Quezon to Harrison, 4/26/16; all in Harrison papers.
27. Braisted, *The United States Navy in the Pacific, 1909–1922* (Austin, Tex., 1971), 291.
28. Braisted, *Navy 1897–1909*, 216–223.
29. Braisted, *Navy 1909–1922*, 19, 127.
30. Ibid., 123–140.
31. Memo from commander-in-chief, U.S. Navy, 4/9/17, BIA records.
32. Burton F. Beers, *Vain Endeavor* (Durham, N.C., 1962), 115–116.

7. Republicanization

1. Memorandum of conversation (Forbes and Harding), 1/14/21, and Forbes to Harding, 2/7/21, Forbes papers.
2. Forbes and Wood to Weeks, 9/11/21, and Forbes journal, 8/19/21, Forbes papers.
3. Forbes to Weeks, 8/6/21, Forbes papers.
4. Forbes, *Philippine Islands*, 2:291–292.
5. Forbes to Weeks, 8/6/21, Forbes papers.
6. Forbes to Weeks, 11/12/21, Forbes papers.
7. *Report of the Special Mission to the Philippine Islands to the Secretary of War*, House document 325, 67th Congress, 2nd session (Washington, 1922).
8. Najeeb M. Saleeby, *The Moro Problem* (Manila, 1913); Ralston Hayden, "What Next for the Moro?," *Foreign Affairs* 6 (July 1928), 633–644.
9. Hermann Hagedorn, *Leonard Wood* (New York, 1931), 2:3–4; Ronald K. Edgerton, "Americans, Cowboys, and Cattlemen on the Mindanao Frontier," in Stanley, *Reappraising an Empire*, 179.
10. Hagedorn, 2:20.
11. Ibid., 2:45.
12. Wood to Weeks, 2/8/24, Leonard Wood papers, Library of Congress; Wood to Worcester, 1/20/22, Dean Conant Worcester papers, University of Michigan; Forbes to Dickinson, 4/5/10, BIA records.
13. Harrison to Quezon, 3/11/16, Harrison papers; Teodoro M. Kalaw, *Aide-de-Camp to Freedom*, trans. Maria Kalaw Katigbak (Manila, 1965), 267–270.
14. Carpenter to Quezon, 11/3/16, Quezon papers; Harrison, *Corner-stone*, 214–215.
15. Liang, *Philippine Political Parties*, 135–152.
16. Kalaw, 162–163.
17. Osmeña to Harrison, 3/11/16, Harrison papers; Osmeña to Quezon, 2/13/16 and 2/16/19, Quezon papers.
18. McCoy to Forbes, undated, Frank McCoy papers, Harvard University; Wood to Weeks, 8/22/23 and 9/18/23, Wood papers, Library of Congress (LC).
19. Quezon to Harrison, undated, Harrison papers.
20. McCoy memo, 7/12/23, Frank McCoy papers, Library of Congress.
21. Hagedorn, 2:429.

22. Wood to Weeks, 7/14/23, Wood papers (LC).

23. *Philippines Herald*, 7/15/23 and 7/18/23; Kalaw, 176–179.

24. Wood to Weeks, 9/18/23, Wood to McIntyre, 8/11/23, and Weeks to Wood, 8/15/23, Wood papers (LC).

25. Kalaw, 183.

26. Wood to Weeks, 5/29/23 and 8/25/23, Wood papers (LC).

27. Wood to Weeks, 6/1/23, Wood to McIntyre, 4/13/23, and Wood to Weeks, 8/3/23, Wood papers (LC).

28. *New York Times*, 1/10/24.

29. Hagedorn, 2:446–448.

30. Forbes, 2:548–553.

31. Osmeña address, 6/10/24, Wood papers (LC).

32. Kelly to Quezon, 6/12/25, Quezon papers.

33. McCoy to Forbes, 3/17/24, McCoy papers.

34. Kalaw, 197–201.

8. The Bottom Line

1. Hagedorn, *Wood*, 2:470–481.

2. Read to Quezon, 8/15/27, responding to Quezon to Mrs. Wood, 8/8/27, Quezon papers.

3. Henry L. Stimson and McGeorge Bundy, *On Active Service in Peace and War* (New York, 1948), 9.

4. Stimson, "First-Hand Impressions of the Philippine Problem," *Saturday Evening Post*, 3/19/27, 6 ff.

5. Osmeña to Quezon, 12/21/27, and Stimson to Quezon, 12/16/27, Quezon papers; Quezon to Harrison, 5/25/28, Harrison papers; Kalaw, *Aide*, 220–221.

6. Quezon to Stimson, 6/8/28, Henry Stimson papers, Yale University.

7. Kalaw, 176.

8. Stimson, 136–138; *Annual Report of the Governor General of the Philippine Islands*, House document 133, 71st Congress, 2nd session (Washington, 1930).

9. Quezon to Stimson, 2/2/28, Stimson papers; Quezon, *Good Fight*, 146–147.

10. *Annual Report*.

11. Stimson to Kittelle, 6/30/28, Stimson papers; Consuelo V. Fonacier, comp., *At the Helm of the Nation* (Manila, 1973), 232.

12. *Annual Report*; Stimson, 140–142.

13. Stimson, 227.

14. Ibid., 255.

15. Davis to Hurley, 10/6/31, BIA records.

16. Liang, *Philippine Political Parties*, 192–206.

17. For example: Storey to Quezon, 4/5/19; Harrison to Quezon, 9/18/35; various Quezon to Howard and Howard to Quezon; Quezon to Sokolsky, 7/28/27; Sokolsky to Quezon, 8/5/27; various Quezon to MacArthur and MacArthur to Quezon; all in Quezon papers.

18. Teodoro A. Agoncillo and Oscar M. Alfonso, *History of the Filipino People* (Quezon City, 1967 ed.), 377; Liang, 208–209.

19. Kalaw, 233.

20. Ibid., 248–249.

21. Agoncillo, 380–381; Theodore Friend, *Between Two Empires* (New Haven, Conn., 1965), 82–83.

22. Bruno Lasker, *Filipino Immigration to Continental United States and to Hawaii* (Chicago, 1931), 348–349.

23. Ibid., 36; Friend, 84.

24. Lasker, 13–14, 358–365.

25. United States Senate, Committee on Territories and Insular Affairs, *Hearings on S. 3377*, 2/11/32 and 2/13/32 (Washington, 1932), 7–12, 29–34.

26. *Public Papers of the Presidents: Herbert Hoover, 1932–33* (Washington, 1977), 932–940.

27. Davis to Good, 11/1/29 and 11/13/29, BIA records.

28. Davis to Parker, 1/23/30, BIA records.

29. Roosevelt to Forbes, 9/6/32, Theodore Roosevelt Jr. papers, Harvard University.

30. Roxas to Paredes, 4/7/33, Quezon papers; Murphy to Howe, 7/18/33, and Murphy report for 1933 to War Department, 8/15/34, Frank Murphy papers, University of Michigan.

31. Friend, 138–140; Quezon, 151–152.

32. Grunder and Livezey, *Philippines and United States*, 220–223; Friend, 140; *New York Times*, 1/18/34; Theodore Roosevelt, Jr., *Colonial Policies of the United States*, (Garden City, N.Y., 1937, 180–181.

33. *New York Times*, 3/3/34.

34. Liang, 226–229.

9. The Datu and the Proconsul

1. Roosevelt to Forbes, 7/4/37, Theodore Roosevelt Jr. papers; Carr memo, undated (1933), and Reuchard to Murphy, 7/12/33, Murphy papers.

2. Wood to Forbes, 3/3/24, Wood papers, Harvard University; Davis to Hurley, 3/28/30, BIA records.

3. Milner to Manahan, 5/25/33, Murphy papers.

4. Roxas to Paredes, 4/7/33, Quezon papers; *Herald*, 3/28/34; Van Schaick memo, 7/18/33; *Tribune*, 4/13/34 and 1/22/35; all in Murphy papers.

5. Carr memo, undated (1933), and Murphy to Dern, 8/15/34, Murphy papers; Roosevelt to Murphy, 8/25/33, Franklin Roosevelt papers, Roosevelt Library, Hyde Park, New York.

6. Carr memo, undated (1933), Murphy papers.

7. Hayden, *Philippines*, 37.

8. Friend, *Two Empires*, 154; John Gunther, "Manuel Quezon," *Atlantic Monthly* 163 (1939), 59–70.

9. Friend, 155.

10. Hayden, 442–443.

11. Memo of Roosevelt meeting with House leaders, 5/1/34, in Morgenthau diary, Henry Morgenthau papers, Roosevelt Library.

12. Dern to Murphy, 8/16/35, and Murphy to Dern, 9/23/35, Franklin Roosevelt papers.

13. Murphy to Dern, 2/1/36 and 2/3/36, and Murphy to Philippine Department of

Interior, 2/19/34, Murphy papers; Hayden diary, 1/16/34 and 2/18/34, Joseph Ralston Hayden papers, University of Michigan; Murphy to Roosevelt, 7/9/36, Franklin Roosevelt papers.

14. Douglas MacArthur, *Reminiscences* (New York, 1964), 31–32.

15. Wood to Weeks, 5/9/24, Wood papers, Library of Congress.

16. Carol Morris Petillo, *Douglas MacArthur: The Philippine Years* (Bloomington, Ind., 1981), 147–148.

17. Eisenhower memo, undated (c. 1936), Eisenhower Library, Abilene, Kansas; Quezon, *Good Fight*, 153–154.

18. Louis Morton, *The Fall of the Philippines* (Washington, 1953), 8–10.

19. Stephen E. Ambrose, *Eisenhower* (New York, 1983), 1:105.

20. MacArthur to Quezon, 4/27/36, Douglas MacArthur papers, MacArthur Memorial Archives, Norfolk, Virginia; Morton, *Fall*, 11–12.

21. Quezon to MacArthur, 10/4/38, MacArthur papers; Hayden, 737–739.

22. Eisenhower to Ord, 9/1/37, MacArthur papers; Eisenhower diary, 1/20/36, Eisenhower papers.

23. Ambrose, 1:105–107.

24. Friend, 151.

25. David R. Sturtevant, *Popular Uprisings in the Philippines, 1840–1940* (Ithaca, N.Y., 1976), 215–242.

26. Gunther, "Quezon."

27. Ponce to Quezon, 1/21/29, and Communist party pamphlet, 6/8/35, Quezon papers.

28. Jones to Cox, 12/7/36, J. Weldon Jones papers, Truman Library, Independence, Missouri.

29. Ibid.; Jones to Cox, 10/22/36, Jones papers.

30. Memo of telephone conversation, 6/15/37, Morgenthau papers.

31. Memo of Interdepartmental Committee on Philippine Affairs, 2/19/37, John Van Antwerp MacMurray papers, Princeton University; Friend, 156–159.

32. Veatch memo, undated (1934), Louis Howe papers, Roosevelt Library.

33. Grunder and Livezey, *Philippines and United States*, 228–229.

34. Quezon to Howard, 10/24/37, Roy W. Howard papers, Library of Congress; Quezon to McNutt, undated (early 1938?), MacArthur papers.

35. Bryce Oliver, "Japan Takes Over the Philippines," *American Mercury* 48 (1939), 257–263; Hayden, 717–719.

36. Veatch memo, 3/24/37, *Foreign Relations of the United States 1937* (Washington, 1954), 4:790.

37. Willard Price, "Japan in the Philippines," *Harper's Magazine* 172 (1936), 609–619; Oliver.

38. Oliver.

39. Communist party pamphlet, 6/8/35, Quezon papers; Hayden, 723, 946–947.

40. Wood to Weeks, 7/7/23, Wood papers, Library of Congress.

41. Louis Morton, *Strategy and Command* (Washington, 1962), 37–39.

42. Hayden, 742–745.

43. MacArthur to Fellers, 6/1/39, MacArthur papers.

44. Morton, *Strategy*, 31–33.

45. Robert Dallek, *Franklin D. Roosevelt and American Foreign Policy* (New York, 1979), 148–152.

46. Morton, *Strategy*, 41–43.

47. MacArthur, 106; Quezon, 175–180; Quezon to Howard, 10/24/37, Howard papers.

48. Frederic S. Marquardt, *Before Bataan and After* (Indianapolis, Ind., 1943), 241; Friend, 192–193.

49. Marquardt, 241; MacArthur press release, undated (late 1939), MacArthur papers.

50. Memo of conversation, 12/28/36, R. Walton Moore papers, Roosevelt Library; McNutt to Murphy, 8/27/38, Jones papers.

51. Francis Bowes Sayre, *Glad Adventure* (New York, 1957), 197.

52. Quezon to Sayre, 4/7/41, Francis Sayre papers, Library of Congress.

53. Quezon to Sayre, 4/3/41, Sayre papers.

54. Sayre to Roosevelt, 4/23/41, 6/18/41 and 7/31/41, Sayre papers.

10. Retreat

1. Morton, *Strategy*, 95.

2. Marshall to MacArthur, 6/20/41, MacArthur papers.

3. Laurel to MacArthur, 7/29/41; MacArthur to Quezon, 8/16/41; both in MacArthur papers; Sayre, *Glad Adventure*, 217.

4. Morton, *Strategy*, 71–72.

5. Morton, *Fall*, 31.

6. Ibid., 32–50.

7. Sayre, 219; Quezon speech, 11/28/41, Sayre papers.

8. John Jacob Beck, *MacArthur and Wainwright* (Albuquerque, N.M., 1974), 11–13.

9. Ronald H. Spector, *Eagle Against the Sun* (New York, 1985), 107–108.

10. Ibid.; MacArthur, *Reminiscences*, 120.

11. Morton, *Fall*, 92–97.

12. Ibid., 98–144.

13. MacArthur, 124.

14. Roosevelt speech, 12/29/41, Sayre papers.

15. Sayre to Roosevelt, 12/9/41, Sayre papers; Sayre to Swope, 12/26/41, Office of Territories records, National Archives, Washington; Quezon to Roosevelt, 12/15/41, Morgenthau papers; Quezon to Roosevelt, 10/11/40, MacArthur papers.

16. MacArthur, 122.

17. MacArthur to war department, 1/7/42, Roosevelt papers.

18. Morton, *Fall*, 146; Stimson, *Active Service*, 395.

19. Morton, *Fall*, 151–152.

20. Roosevelt to Knox, 12/30/41, Roosevelt papers.

21. Barbara W. Tuchman, *Stilwell and the American Experience in China* (New York, 1972 ed.), 309.

22. Sayre to Roosevelt, 1/21/42, Sayre papers; Quezon to Roosevelt, 1/13/42, Roosevelt papers.

23. Quezon to Roosevelt, 2/8/42, Roosevelt papers.

24. MacArthur to Roosevelt, 2/8/42, Roosevelt papers.

25. Diary, 2/9/42, Stimson papers.

26. Ambrose, *Eisenhower*, 1:139.

27. Roosevelt to MacArthur and Quezon, 2/9/42, in *Foreign Relations 1942*, 1:897–898.

28. D. Clayton James, *The Years of MacArthur* (Boston, 1975), 2:62; Spector, 111.

29. Spector, 117.

30. Beck, 197.

31. Morton, *Fall*, 357–360.

32. MacArthur to Marshall, 2/16/42, Roosevelt papers; Quezon, *Good Fight*, 298–315.

33. Petillo, *MacArthur*, 205–213.

34. Benedict J. Kerkvliet, *The Huk Rebellion* (Berkeley, Cal., 1977), 66–68.

35. MacArthur to AGWAR: Confesor to Quezon, 2/8/44, Quezon papers.

36. Claro M. Recto, *Three Years of Enemy Occupation* (Manila, 1946), 7.

37. Ickes to Donovan, 12/29/41, Office of Territories records; David Joel Steinberg, *Philippine Collaboration in World War II* (Ann Arbor, Mich., 1967), 49.

38. Friend, *Two Empires*, 211–216; Steinberg, 57.

39. Quezon to MacArthur, 1/28/42, *Foreign Relations 1942*, 1:888–889.

40. Friend, *Two Empires*, 233–234.

41. José P. Laurel, *War Memoirs* (Manila, 1980), 17–18; Friend, *Two Empires*, 238–241; Friend, *The Blue-Eyed Enemy* (Princeton, N.J., 1988), 123–125.

42. Friend, *Two Empires*, 240–244, Steinberg, 97–98.

43. Laurel, 14.

44. Laurel to Monzon, 3/11/43, José Laurel papers, Laurel Memorial Corporation, Manila.

45. Laurel to Horikawa, 3/12/43, Laurel papers.

46. Agoncillo and Alfonso, *History*, 466–467.

47. Ibid., 465–473; Agoncillo, *The Fateful Years* (Quezon City, 1965), 2:586, 754–755.

11. Return

1. William Manchester, *American Caesar* (New York, 1978), 427.

2. William B. Brewer, *Retaking the Philippines* (New York, 1986), 46–50.

3. Douglas MacArthur, *A Soldier Speaks: Public Papers and Speeches* (New York, 1965), 132–133.

4. MacArthur, *Reminiscences*, 216–218.

5. Spector, *Eagle against the Sun*, 417–444.

6. MacArthur, *Reminiscences*, 233.

7. Ibid., 239; Brewer, 121.

8. Robert Ross Smith, *Triumph in the Philippines* (Washington, 1963), 88–103.

9. Ibid., 306–307; Agoncillo, *Fateful Years*, 2:862–863.

10. Carmen Guerrero Nakpil, "Consensus of One," Manila *Sunday Times Magazine*, 4/23/67, quoted in Gleeck, *Manila Americans*, 272–273.

11. MacArthur, *Reminiscences*, 252.

12. Brewer, 14–21; various reports on Philippine intelligence, Office of Strategic Services records, National Archives.

13. Smith, 651–652.

14. Roosevelt to Sayre, 2/12/42, and Sayre to Roosevelt, 3/9/42, Sayre papers; Davis diary, 1/12/42 and 6/2/42, and Davis to Swiss minister, 4/16/43 and 10/14/43, Nathaniel Davis papers, Truman Library.

15. Morgenthau to Roosevelt, 12/19/41, Morgenthau papers; Sayre to Roosevelt, 1/28/42, Sayre papers; Sayre, *Glad Adventure*, 235–236.

16. Hoover to Watson, 6/15/42, Sayre papers; Quezon to Hull, 12/22/42, and Hull to

Quezon, 1/2/43, Quezon papers; Hopkins to Roosevelt, 6/9/42, Hopkins memo, 6/9/42, and Quezon to Hopkins, 6/19/42, Harry Hopkins papers, Roosevelt Library.

17. Roosevelt to Sayre, 6/30/42, Sayre papers; Quezon to Ickes, 6/20/42, and Hull to Roosevelt, 7/24/42, Roosevelt papers; Roosevelt to Ickes, 9/16/42, Office of Territories records.

18. Confesor to Quezon, 6/19/43, and Roosevelt to Quezon, 2/1/43, Roosevelt papers.

19. Roosevelt to Quezon, 10/15/43, Quezon to Roosevelt, 10/17/43, and Coy memo, undated (October 1943), Wayne Coy papers, Roosevelt Library.

20. Fortas to Roosevelt, 10/2/43, Samuel Rosenman papers, Roosevelt Library; Hester to Coy, 10/22/43, Coy papers.

21. Hester to Coy, 10/22/43, Coy papers.

22. Quezon to MacArthur, 6/12/43, Quezon papers.

23. Ickes to Morgenthau, 5/25/42, Morgenthau papers.

24. *New York Times*, 7/1/44.

25. Valdes to Osmeña, 9/8/44, Sergio Osmeña papers, National Library, Manila; Baja to Osmeña, 11/17/43, Quezon papers; Osmeña to Stimson, 10/4/44, Osmeña papers.

26. Osmeña to MacArthur, 10/20/44, Osmeña papers; Steinberg, *Philippine Collaboration*, 111–112.

27. Laurel to Yamashita, 12/21/44, Laurel papers.

28. Laurel to MacArthur, 9/14/45, Laurel papers.

29. Quezon to MacArthur, 6/12/43, Quezon papers.

30. Ickes introduction to Hernando J. Abaya, *Betrayal in the Philippines* (New York, 1946), 9.

31. Osmeña to Ingeniero, 12/16/44, Quezon papers; Confesor to Osmeña, 3/21/45, Osmeña papers.

32. Ickes to Osmeña, 9/11/45, Osmeña papers.

33. Steinberg, 132–133.

34. Roxas to Howard, 11/1/45, Manuel Roxas papers, National Library, Manila; Steinberg, 165.

35. Hester memo, undated, Coy papers.

36. Tydings to Rosenman, 10/14/43, Rosenman papers.

37. McCloy to Fortas, 9/14/44, Rosenman papers.

38. Forrestal to Stettinius, 4/30/45, and Stimson to Truman, 5/11/45, *Foreign Relations 1945*, 6:1205–1207.

39. Osmeña to Truman, 11/8/45, Osmeña papers; statement of principles, 11/14/45, *Foreign Relations 1945*, 6:1208–1209.

40. Osmeña to Quezon, 12/23/44, Quezon papers; report of meeting of Philippine Rehabilitation Commission, 7/24/44, Coy papers.

41. Grunder and Livezey, *Philippines and United States*, 260–261.

42. Osmeña to Truman, 11/8/45, Osmeña papers.

12. Cold War in Asia

1. Abaya, *Betrayal*, 252, 266–267.

2. Agoncillo, *History*, 505.

3. Abaya, 258.

4. Stephen Rosskamm Shalom, *The United States and the Philippines* (Philadelphia, 1981), 52.

5. Agoncillo, 508.

6. Roxas to Elizalde, 10/30/46, Roxas papers.

7. Patterson to Byrnes, 11/29/46, *Foreign Relations 1946*, 8:934; Patterson to Byrnes, 12/27/46, ibid., 940.

8. Roxas to McNutt, 7/29/46, Roxas papers; McNutt to Byrnes, 1/27/47, *Foreign Relations 1947*, 6:1103.

9. CIA report (ORE 11-48), 4/28/48, Harry Truman papers, Truman Library, Independence, Missouri.

10. CIA report (ORE 78-48), 3/30/49, Truman papers; Recto speech, 9/4/49, Claro Recto papers, University of Michigan; Shalom, 69.

11. Memo of conversation, 8/9/49, Dean Acheson papers, Truman Library.

12. Romulo to Quirino, 11/14/48, 3/16/50, 3/20/50, 9/26/50 and 9/27/50, Elpidio Quirino papers, Ayala Museum Library, Manila.

13. Melby to Jessup, 8/31/49, John Melby papers, Truman Library.

14. CIA report (ORE 78-48), 3/30/49, Truman papers; Shalom, 70.

15. Report of economic survey mission, 10/9/50, Frank Waring papers, Truman Library.

16. Melby to Merchant, 9/6/49, Melby papers.

17. CIA report (ORE 33-50), 8/10/50, Truman papers.

18. Laurel memo, 5/31/41, Quezon papers.

19. Luis Taruc, *He Who Rides the Tiger* (New York, 1967), 19.

20. Eduardo Lachica, *The Huks* (New York, 1971), 113–114; Kerkvliet, *Huk Rebellion*, 111–114.

21. Lachica, 114.

22. Kerkvliet, 111–114.

23. Luis Taruc, *Born of the People* (Westport, Conn., 1973 rpt. of 1953 ed.), 214.

24. Kerkvliet, 153.

25. Taruc, *Born*, 238–240.

26. Kerkvliet, 159.

27. Madamba in minutes of negotiations, 7/2/48–8/24/48, and Quirino to Abello, 8/7/48, Quirino papers.

28. CIA report (ORE 78-48), 3/30/49, Truman papers; Edward Geary Lansdale, *In the Midst of Wars* (New York, 1972), 2.

29. Quirino to Truman, 8/24/49, Quirino papers.

30. Romulo to Quirino, 3/30/50, Quirino papers.

31. Romulo to Quirino, 9/18/50, Quirino papers.

32. Romulo to Quirino, 12/19/50 and 12/21/50, Quirino papers.

33. Doty to Anderson, 3/31/50, Quirino papers.

34. Hobbs to Quirino, 9/7/50, Quirino papers.

35. José V. Abueva, *Ramón Magsaysay* (Manila, 1971), 145–146.

36. Lansdale to Abueva, 11/5/62, Edward Lansdale papers, Hoover Institution, Stanford, California; Lansdale, 24–25.

37. Abueva, 163.

38. Alvin H. Scaff, *The Philippine Answer to Communism* (Stanford, Calif., 1955), 45.

39. Lansdale, 72–75.

40. Terry to Cowen, 5/3/51, *Foreign Relations 1951*, 6:1540; ibid., 1535 n.3; Cowen to Bradley, 6/21/51, ibid., 1549; Cowen memo, 7/9/51, ibid., 1550; Shalom, 82.

41. Acheson to Cowen, 4/25/51, *Foreign Relations 1951*, 6:1536.

42. Carlos P. Romulo and Marvin M. Gray, *The Magsaysay Story* (New York, 1956), 151–152.

43. Truman to Quirino, 12/8/51, Quirino papers.

44. NSC 84/2, 11/9/50, National Security Council Records, National Archives, Washington.

45. Memos of conversation, 4/19/49 and 4/25/49, Acheson papers.

46. Edelstein to Roxas, 7/10/47, Roxas papers.

47. Benitez to Romulo, 7/17/51, Carlos Romulo papers, University of the Philippines, Quezon City.

48. Romulo statement, 7/13/49, Myron Cowen papers, Truman Library.

49. Progress report on NSC 84/2, 2/11/52, NSC records.

13. A Special Relationship

1. Romulo to Quirino, 9/27/50, Quirino papers.

2. Cauderno to Quirino, undated (late 1952), Quirino papers.

3. José Lava, *Analysis of the Developing Situation and Our Tasks,* cited in Lachica, *The Huks,* 125–126.

4. "The New People's Army," document issued by the Meeting of Red Commanders and Red Soldiers, 3/29/69, captured by the Philippine army, 6/9/69, reproduced in Lachica, 302–316.

5. Taruc, *Rides the Tiger,* 160.

6. Magsaysay to Quirino, 2/28/53, Ramón Magsaysay papers, Magsaysay Foundation, Manila.

7. Spruance to Dulles, 3/6/53, Department of State central files, National Archives, Washington.

8. Spruance statement in Spruance to Dulles, 3/30/53, Department of State central files.

9. Allen Dulles to Lansdale, 11/21/63, Allen Dulles papers, Princeton University; Joseph Burkholder Smith, *Portrait of a Cold Warrior* (New York, 1976), 109; Thomas B. Buell, *The Quiet Warrior: A Biography of Admiral Raymond A. Spruance* (Boston, 1974), 414.

10. Lansdale to Abueva, 11/5/62, Lansdale papers; Shalom, *United States and Philippines,* 91; Cecil B. Currey, *Edward Lansdale* (Boston, 1988), 126.

11. CIA Current Intelligence Weekly, 6/5/53, CIA records, reproduced in *Declassified Documents,* 85:2396.

12. Smith, 112–113.

13. Spruance to Dulles, 3/31/53, Department of State central files; Ferguson to Dulles, 7/13/55, in Dulles to Eisenhower, 7/26/55, Dwight Eisenhower papers, Eisenhower Library, Abilene, Kansas; Currey, 131, 371–372; Lansdale to Shaplen, 5/30/65, Lansdale papers.

14. Laurel to Azana, 6/10/54, Laurel papers.

15. Eisenhower to Cowen, 11/6/53; memos of discussion at 166th NSC meeting, 8/13/53, and 170th NSC meeting, 11/12/53; all in Eisenhower papers; CIA Current Intelligence Weekly, 11/20/53, CIA records, *Declassified Documents,* 85:2398.

16. Chief of military advisory group to army chief of staff, 2/3/54, Joint Chiefs of Staff records, American National Archives; Recto speech, 4/10/54, Recto papers; García address, 3/22/57, Carlos García papers, Philippine National Library.

17. Menon to Romulo, 4/28/55; Magsaysay statement, 2/3/55; Romulo statement in Romulo to Serrano, 10/7/58; all in Romulo papers.

18. Quirino statement in Quirino to Romulo, 8/3/49; Romulo to Quirino, 7/14/49; both in Quirino papers.

19. Romulo to Quirino, 7/11/49, 7/12/49 and 7/14/49, Quirino papers.

20. Romulo to Quirino, 2/5/51 and 8/19/52, Quirino papers.

21. Romulo to Quirino, 8/28/52, Quirino papers.

22. Romulo to Quirino, 1/14/53; Romulo to Eisenhower, 1/30/53; both in Quirino papers.

23. Magsaysay to Romulo, 8/6/54 and 8/16/54; Romulo to Dulles, 8/16/54; all in Romulo papers.

24. Ogburn to Drumright, 7/23/54, *Foreign Relations 1952–1954*, 12:664.

25. Proceedings of third plenary session of Manila conference, 9/7/54, ibid., 876.

26. Dulles to Romulo, 9/7/54, Romulo papers; memo of telephone conversation with Judd, 9/14/24, John Foster Dulles papers, Eisenhower Library.

27. Dulles statement at Manila, 2/21/55, John Foster Dulles papers, Princeton University; progress report on NSC 5413/1, 8/12/54, NSC records.

28. CIA report, "Philippine Elections," 10/28/65, Lyndon Johnson papers, Johnson Library, Austin, Texas; NSC progress report, 8/12/54, NSC records; press analysis by Wesley Edward (army attaché, Manila), 11/12–18/56, Joint Chiefs of Staff records; Ferguson to Dulles, 7/13/55, and Dulles to Eisenhower, 7/26/55, Eisenhower papers.

29. Waring to Quirino, 6/9/48 and various subsequent; Pedrosa to Quirino, 6/9/49; all in Quirino papes; Frank H. Golay, *The Philippines: Public Policy and National Economic Development* (Ithaca, N.Y., 1961), 68–69.

30. *Report to the President of the United States by the Economic Survey Mission to the Philippines* (Washington, 1950), 1.

31. Carpio to Montinola, 12/13/52; Montinola to Quirino, 12/27/52; Quirino to Eisenhower, 3/7/53; all in Quirino papers.

32. Laurel to Knowland, 11/10/54; Laurel to Johnson, 11/10/54; Laurel to Gillette, 11/10/54; Laurel to Langer, 11/10/54; Laurel to Goldwater, 11/13/54; Laurel to Gore, 11/13/54; Goldwater to Laurel, 2/8/55; Hayden to Laurel, 2/8/55; Laurel to Eisenhower, 10/15/54; Robertson to Laurel, 9/23/54; Humphrey to Laurel, 10/25/54; Laurel to Dulles, 12/3/54; all in Laurel papers.

33. Laurel to Magsaysay, 6/21/54, Laurel papers.

34. Laurel to Dulles, 10/15/54 and 10/23/54; Ohno memo, 9/18/54; Sycip to Laurel, 7/22/54; Elizalde to Laurel, 1/18/55; all in Laurel papers.

35. Memo of conversation, 11/9/54, Miguel Cuaderno papers, University of the Philippines, Quezon City; memo of conversation, 9/27/54, Laurel papers; Laurel to Magsaysay, 10/1/54, Laurel papers; Spruance to Laurel, 10/28/54, Laurel papers.

36. Elizalde to Laurel, 1/18/55, Laurel papers.

37. Magsaysay to Laurel, 11/15/54, Cuaderno papers; Golay, 47–48, 173–174, 320–321; Shalom, 95–98; Robert Aura Smith, *Philippine Freedom, 1946–1958* (New York, 1958), 185–191.

14. The Ground Softens

1. Lansdale to Magsaysay, 8/10/54, Magsaysay papers.

2. Robertson to Magsaysay, 1/18/54, Magsaysay papers; *New York Times*, 3/18/57.

3. Abueva, *Magsaysay*, 240.

4. Manila to Department of State (DOS), 3/18/57, Department of State central files; progress report on NSC 5413/1, 8/21/57, NSC records.

5. Smith, *Philippine Freedom*, 240–243; Garcia speech, 12/5/57, García papers.

6. Smith, *Portait*, 290.

7. García addresses, 6/19/57, 3/19/58, 6/18/58 and 6/14/60, García papers; García to Dulles, 12/2/57, John Foster Dulles papers, Princeton.

8. Romulo to García, 5/5/58, 3/18/59, 5/6/59, 9/3/59, 5/4/61 and 9/18/61; García speech, 12/5/57; all in García papers. García to Romulo, 5/12/60; Romulo to García, 4/29/60, 6/24/60 and 10/7/60; all in Romulo papers.

9. Romulo to Serrano, 9/25/59, Romulo papers.

10. CNO to JCS, 11/4/58 (JCS 1519/120), JCS records.

11. Magsaysay quoted in *Manila Bulletin*, 3/10/56, clip in Homer Ferguson papers, University of Michigan.

12. Eisenhower telephone conversation with Dulles, 12/24/53, Eisenhower papers; memoranda for the record, 8/23/53 and 10/24/55, JCS records.

13. Robertson memo, 8/21/56, Eisenhower papers.

14. JCS memo, 10/24/55; memo for the record, 11/18/55; Twining to Wilson, 2/27/57; Edward press analysis for JCS, 11/12-18/56; all in JCS records.

15. Memo of conversation, 10/24/55, JCS records.

16. Edward press analysis, 11/12-18/56, JCS records.

17. Dulles to Magsaysay, 4/24/56; memo of conversation at 280th NSC meeting, 3/12/56; both in Eisenhower papers.

18. Memo of conversation with García, 6/18/58, Eisenhower papers.

19. Charles Bohlen, *Witness to History* (New York, 1973), 452; Bonisteel to Ferguson, 1/17/56, Ferguson papers.

20. Smith, *Portrait*, 315.

21. Dillon to Eisenhower, 10/11/60; memo of conversation, 10/13/60; both in Eisenhower papers. Romulo to García, 10/17/60, Romulo papers.

22. García to Romulo, 11/17/60; Romulo to García, 11/17/60; both in Romulo papers.

23. García to World Affairs Council, 6/26/58, García papers.

24. García to Kennedy, 5/24/61, John Kennedy papers, Kennedy Library, Boston.

25. Romulo to García, 12/17/60, and Romulo to Rusk, 12/17/60, Romulo papers.

26. David Wurfel, *Filipino Politics* (Ithaca, N.Y., 1988), 98–100; Smith, *Portrait*, 315.

27. Memo of conversation, undated (1/10/62), Kennedy papers.

28. Kennedy to Macapagal, 5/10/62; Macapagal to Kennedy, 5/14/62; and Abello to Rusk, 6/11/62; all in Kennedy papers.

29. Macapagal to Kennedy, 6/17/63; and memo of conversation, undated (1/10/62); both in Kennedy papers. Romulo to García, 3/5/61, 3/13/61 and 5/4/61, García papers.

15. What Allies Are For

1. Romulo to García, 12/20/60, Romulo papers.

2. MacArthur quoted in Walter LaFeber, *The American Age* (New York, 1989), 561.

3. García toast, 5/13/61, García papers.

4. Memo of conversation, 11/26/63, Roger Hilsman papers, Kennedy Library.

5. Gleason to Brubeck, 1/22/63, Kennedy papers; Ball to Manila, 12/13/64, Johnson papers; Johnson to Macapagal, 12/13/64, Johnson papers.

6. Department of State (DOS) to Manila, 7/19/65, Johnson papers.

7. Manila to DOS, 8/10/65, Johnson papers.

8. Raymond Bonner, *Waltzing with a Dictator: The Marcoses and the Making of American Policy* (New York, 1987), 13.

9. Manila to DOS, 6/22/56, DOS central file.

10. CIA memo: "Philippine Elections," 10/28/65, Johnson papers.

11. Blair to Rusk, 6/10/65, Johnson papers.

12. Blair to Rusk, 7/5/65, Johnson papers.

13. Blair to Rusk, 11/27/65, Johnson papers; Rusk to Johnson, 7/6/66, Johnson papers.

14. Wurfel, *Filipino Politics*, 86–87.

15. Ibid., 52–53.

16. CIA report: National Intelligence Estimate 56–66, 2/17/66, Johnson papers.

17. Thomson to Rostow, 5/4/66, Johnson papers.

18. CIA intelligence memo: "Philippine President Marcos' Problems at Midterm," 12/7/67, Johnson papers.

19. Captured NPA documents reproduced in Lachica, *Huks*, 167–168, 283–301.

20. Wurfel, 154–156.

21. CIA intelligence memo, 4/18/67, Johnson papers.

22. Blair to Rusk, 5/19/67, Johnson papers.

23. Lachica, 222.

24. Underhill memo in Manila to DOS, 1/27/71, National Security Archive, Washington.

25. Johnson to Marcos, 4/9/68, Johnson papers.

26. CIA intelligence information cable, 7/27/68, Johnson papers.

27. *Manila Chronicle*, 4/18/68; *Evening News*, 6/17/68; *Cebu Advocate*, 4/19/68; *Manila Times*, 4/18/68; all clips in G. Mennen Williams papers, University of Michigan.

28. Talking paper for meeting with Williams, 5/1/68, Johnson papers.

29. Wurfel, 103–104.

30. Gregg R. Jones, *Red Revolution: Inside the Philippine Guerrilla Movement* (Boulder, Colo., 1989), 59–69.

16. Democracy Undone

1. Stanley Karnow, *In Our Image: America's Empire in the Philippines* (New York, 1989), 380–381.

2. Wilson to Williams, 1/13/70, James Wilson papers, Gerald Ford Library, Ann Arbor, Michigan; Karnow, 357.

3. NSSM 155, "Philippine Policy—Annex on Martial Law," 10/17/72, National Security Archive.

4. Department of State (DOS) Intelligence Note, "The Philippines Tries One-Man Democracy," 11/1/72, Nat. Sec. Arch.

5. Wurfel, *Filipino Politics*, 140–141.

6. Ibid., 168–170.

7. Unidentified AID official quoted in David A. Rosenberg, ed., *Marcos and Martial Law in the Philippines* (Ithaca, N.Y., 1979), 119.

8. Wurfel, 226–229.

9. Manila to DOS, 11/5/74, Nat. Sec. Arch.

10. Manila to DOS, 7/7/75, Nat. Sec. Arch.

11. Manila to DOS, 10/1/75, Nat. Sec. Arch.

12. Underhill to DOS, 2/9/77, Nat. Sec. Arch.

13. "Foreign Assistance: 1976 Budget—Issue 7e: Military Assistance to the Philippines," undated, Gerald Ford papers, Ford Library.

14. Salinger notes of Marcos interview, 12/7/75, Ron Nessen papers, Ford Library.

15. Scowcroft to Ford, 4/13/76, Ford papers.

16. Kissinger to Ford, 10/27/75, with Ford note, Ford papers.

17. Manila to DOS, 4/20/77, Nat. Sec. Arch.

18. Bonner, *Waltzing*, 224–231, 240–246.

19. Murphy to DOS, 11/2/78, repeated in DOS to Bangkok, 11/2/78, Nat. Sec. Arch.

20. Newsom in Manila to DOS, 11/15/77, Nat. Sec. Arch.

21. Bennet to Guyer, 3/14/79, Nat. Sec. Arch.

22. Newsom in Manila to DOS, 2/8/78 and 11/15/77, Nat. Sec. Arch.

23. Manila to DOS, 4/6/83, Nat. Sec. Arch.

24. "The Day of the Generals: Corruption in the Military," in Manila to DOS, 4/11/75, Nat. Sec. Arch.

25. Wurfel, 158–164.

26. Manila to DOS, 8/21/81, Nat. Sec. Arch.

27. Manila to DOS, 4/14/82, Nat. Sec. Arch.

28. Manila to DOS, 4/25/83, Nat. Sec. Arch.

29. Manila to DOS, 6/9/84, Nat. Sec. Arch.

17. Vox Populi

1. Stoessel to Bush with attachment, 6/18/81, Nat. Sec. Arch.

2. *Far Eastern Economic Review*, 6/26/81.

3. Wolfowitz to Shultz, 6/16/83, Nat. Sec. Arch.

4. Ibid.

5. *Far Eastern Economic Review*, 4/18/85.

6. *Far Eastern Economic Review*, 4/24/81.

7. Newsom in Manila to DOS, 11/7/77, Nat. Sec. Arch.

8. *Far Eastern Economic Review*, 4/24/81.

9. Karnow, *In Our Image*, 401–402; Laurel interview with Theodore Friend, December 1983, related to author, 4/23/90.

10. Armacost in Manila to DOS, 9/2/83, Nat. Sec. Arch.

11. Armacost in Manila to DOS, 9/6/83, Nat. Sec. Arch.

12. Bureau of Intelligence and Research report, "Causes of the Philippine Communist Insurgency," 9/18/84, Nat. Sec. Arch.

13. Manila to DOS, 6/7/84, Nat. Sec. Arch.

14. Bureau of Intelligence and Research report, "Causes of the Philippine Communist Insurgency," 9/18/84, Nat. Sec. Arch.

15. Bonner, *Waltzing*, 352.

16. *New York Times*, 10/22/84.

17. Sandra Burton, *Impossible Dream: The Marcoses, the Aquinos, and the Unfinished Revolution* (New York, 1989), 249.

18. Wurfel, *Filipino Politics*, 283–292.

19. Bonner, 403.

20. Kirkpatrick, "Our Interests in the Philippines," *Chicago Tribune*, 12/15/85.

21. Wurfel, 298–300.

22. Bosworth in Manila to DOS, 2/11/86 (two cables) and 2/11/86, Nat. Sec. Arch.

23. Bosworth in Manila to DOS, 2/12/86, Nat. Sec. Arch.

24. *Asia 1990 Yearbook* (Hong Kong, 1991), 212.

25. *New York Times*, 9/11/86.

26. *Manila Daily Globe*, 1/11/89; *Manila Bulletin*, 12/7/89.

27. *New York Times*, 5/26/88.

28. *Manila Bulletin*, 12/7/89.

29. *Far Eastern Economic Review*, 4/7/88.

30. Wurfel, *Filipino Politics*, 321–323.

31. *New York Times*, 12/28/87; *Far Eastern Economic Review*, 4/21/88.

32. *Department of State Bulletin*, June 1986; *New York Times*, 9/1/86.

33. *Time*, 9/29/86.

34. Wurfel, 316.

35. *Far Eastern Economic Review*, 3/17/88.

36. *Department of State Bulletin*, June 1986.

37. *Manila Bulletin*, 12/7/89.

Conclusion

1. Friend, *Blue-Eyed Enemy*, 7, 33.

2. Stanley Karnow, "Giap Remembers," *New York Times Magazine*, 6/24/90; *Vietnam* (New York, 1983), 116.

3. Robin W. Winks, "Imperialism," in C. Vann Woodward, ed., *The Comparative Approach to American History* (New York, 1968), 255.

4. Friend, *Between Two Empires*, 4; *Blue-Eyed Enemy*, 271.

5. Kalaw, *Aide-de-Camp*, 209.

Index

Philippine politics, as well as the ambivalence of American rule, in which liberal principles of self-determination clashed with the desire for empire and a preoccupation first with Japan and later with communism. The book comes right up to the present day, with an incisive account of the rise and fall of Ferdinand Marcos, the accession (and subsequent troubles) of Corazon Aquino, the Communist guerrilla insurgency, and the debate over the American military bases.

"Damn the Americans!" Manuel Quezon once said. "Why don't they tyrannize us more?" Indeed, as Brands writes, American rule in the Philippines was more benign than that of any other colonial power in the Pacific region. Yet it failed to foster a genuine democracy. This fascinating book explains why, in a perceptive account of a century of empire and its aftermath.

ABOUT THE AUTHOR

H.W. Brands is Professor of History at Texas A & M University. He is the author of *Inside the Cold War* as well as *Cold Warriors, The Specter of Neutralism,* and other books.